"A book that has the courage to look inside the excellence of our country, telling its treasures, its know-how and its talent. The future of the Made in Italy luxury lies in the ability of our companies to be ambassadors in the world of the model of uniqueness and excellence that defines the Italian style. By reading this book, the new generations will be able to learn from our heritage to build a future that combines our DNA with the opportunities of technology and sustainability."

Renzo Rosso, *OTB Chairman and Founder*

Made in Italy and the Luxury Market

Made in Italy holds a highly significant position in the global luxury market, as an economic, cultural, and social phenomenon, and the textbook example of the country-of-origin effect. Whilst in the past luxury was conceptualized as an exclusive benefit of the few, it is now a highly diversified ecosystem with disruptive challenges to its identity and authenticity, led by new customer segments. This book – through an analysis of diverse cases – answers the key issues in the industry of the new Made in Italy luxury, with a particular focus on sustainability.

The book provides an in-depth view into luxury Made in Italy, from historical roots, heritage, and tradition to major forces of change and innovative, entrepreneurial adaptations in the 21st century. It situates Made in Italy in the broader global context of change, with regards to the call for sustainable manufacturing and consumption. Written by an international pool of academics and experts in luxury brand management, the book presents a series of case studies to explore how the industry is responding to new consumer expectations and demand to maintain competitive advantage.

This unique collection will be of interest for academics, scholars, and upper-level students across the fields of luxury management and marketing, brand management, consumer behavior as well as sustainability.

Serena Rovai, PhD, is Senior Professor in Luxury Brand Management and Chair of the Luxury BRaND Lab at Excelia Business School, where she created and directs the luxury and fashion specializations. She is Visiting Professor at Stanford University in Luxury and Fashion Management among others – IULM, ISCTE, Bocconi, Polimoda, Curtin University, Università degli Studi di Firenze.

She has more than 25 years of international experience in higher education in academic and executive roles, business consulting, and directing programs in Luxury and Fashion Brand Management – Italian Ministry of Foreign Affairs, Chinese Ministry of Education, and World Bank. She conducts research on fashion and sustainability in Made in Italy and her work has been published widely in scientific journals.

Manuela De Carlo, PhD, is Full Professor at IULM University in Milano, where she founded and directs the M.Sc. in Hospitality and Tourism Management (dual degree with the University of Central Florida). She has a Master's degree in International Tourism and Hospitality and graduated with specialization in Luxury Hospitality and Client Experience.

Manuela has published widely in the areas of collective capabilities development; technology adoption in luxury hospitality; service personalization and customer centricity; and place image formation and evaluation. She has conducted numerous consulting and applied research projects and provided advice for OECD, Italian Ministry of Tourism, and Italian Ministry of University and Research.

Routledge Studies in Luxury Management

This series explores the luxury industry through an interdisciplinary lens, bringing together cutting-edge research to define and advance this growing field. Contributions to the series present original research from established and emerging scholars across the globe, offering a diverse range of empirical and critical perspectives on the luxury industry. Topics include, but are not limited to, marketing, brand management, sustainability, and supply chain management.

The Rise of Positive Luxury
Transformative Research Agenda for Well-being, Social Impact, and Sustainable Growth
Edited by Wided Batat

Made in Italy and the Luxury Market
Heritage, Sustainability and Innovation
Edited by Serena Rovai and Manuela De Carlo

For more information about this series, please visit: www.routledge.com/Routledge-Studies-in-Luxury-Management/book-series/RSLM

Made in Italy and the Luxury Market

Heritage, Sustainability and Innovation

Edited by Serena Rovai and Manuela De Carlo

Routledge
Taylor & Francis Group
LONDON AND NEW YORK

First published 2023
by Routledge
4 Park Square, Milton Park, Abingdon, Oxon OX14 4RN

and by Routledge
605 Third Avenue, New York, NY 10158

Routledge is an imprint of the Taylor & Francis Group, an informa business

British Library Cataloguing-in-Publication Data
A catalogue record for this book is available from the British Library

ISBN: 978-1-032-30438-0 (hbk)
ISBN: 978-1-032-30439-7 (pbk)
ISBN: 978-1-003-30509-5 (ebk)

DOI: 10.4324/9781003305095

Typeset in Bembo
by KnowledgeWorks Global Ltd.

Contents

Preface

The Italian luxury industry represents a very significant part of our country's economy, worth 126 billion euros, roughly 7.4% of GDP. And Italy is a leading player in luxury manufacturing, thanks to its unique, invaluable ecosystem of supply chains, and because our companies operate and excel in a variety of highly diversified sectors: automotive, design, fashion, food, hospitality, jewelry, and yachting.

Luxury goods are intrinsically "sustainable" as they are manufactured using the highest quality materials, by highly skilled people, and they are first and foremost made to last, and – when needed – can be repaired instead of being replaced. In addition, Italy's high-end brands have a close connection to the area where they are based and often contribute to the economy and development of their local communities.

Now, however, sustainability has become a necessity, as well as a major challenge for all our companies. Today's consumers are less interested in status and more focused on brands that resonate with their identity and values. When a new, younger generation of consumers, more concerned about environmental and social issues, demanded a stronger engagement on ESG issues, luxury brands were ready to fulfill those needs. They integrated sustainability into their business models and invested in it: as market leaders they were perfectly aware that they were expected to act as true ESG role models. They embraced this new global challenge because historically they have always been closer to their local areas and their people. Not to mention their distinctive ability to envision and embody the values of society and the zeitgeist, the spirit of the times, expressing this through their work, products, and experiences.

The new luxury we explore and attempt to define in this work has a completely new set of values, shifting its focus from exclusivity to inclusion, from aesthetics to ethics, from product-driven strategies to more experience-based approaches that put people at the center. People are the priority: consumers and their new values, employees and their new needs, and external stakeholders and their social issues. This is reinforcing the impact and raising the profile of luxury companies, which are also ambassadors of our lifestyle, advocates for our highest aspirations, and Italy's most significant soft power.

Fondazione Altagamma, which represents 113 Italian high-end brands, has identified sustainability as a key pillar. The three dimensions of sustainability – environment, social, and governance – have now become the cornerstone of Italian-made quality. As we will see in the pages that follow, Italian luxury brands have a lot to say about ESG and our ability to innovate, adapt, and interpret the changes taking place around us and, above all, within us.

Matteo Lunelli
Chairman of Fondazione Altagamma

Author Biographies

Gaetano Aiello is Full Professor of Marketing at the University of Florence, Florence, Italy. His research interests include retail internationalization, fashion and luxury management, and digital marketing. His work has been published in several international journals, such as *Journal of Retailing*, *Journal of Business Research*, and *Psychology & Marketing*.

Jacopo Cammeo is Research Assistant at the Department of Business and Law, University of Siena, Siena, Italy. He graduated from the University of Florence (MSc cum laude in Economics) and from the University of St Andrews (MSc in Sustainable Development and Environmental Economics). His research areas lie with sustainability, clusters and innovation eco-systems, transition management, and digitalization.

Elena Casprini is Senior Researcher at the Department of Business and Law, University of Siena, Siena, Italy. During her Ph.D. in Management at Scuola Superiore Sant'Anna, she was a Visiting Ph.D. Student at Cass Business School, London, UK. Her research interests focus on business models innovation, open innovation, and family firms. She is an expert in qualitative research methodologies, in particular case studies. She has published in international as well as national journals and she is involved in national and international research projects.

Michele Coletti is Associate Professor of Innovation at the Grenoble Ecole de Management, where he manages the MBA Specialization of Smart and Sustainable Business. He is regularly consulting for EU projects and brands in the field. He holds a Ph.D. degree from Politecnico di Milano, where in he is also Visiting professor. He is regularly publishing in international and national scientific journals.

Costanza Dasmi is a PhD student in Business Administration and Management, a joint program of the University of Pisa, Florence, Italy, and Siena, Italy. Her research interests include CSR, sustainability, sustainable communication, and retail.

Dr.oec. HSG Fabio Duma, is Head Competence Team Luxury & Creative Industries, Center for Culture & Creativity in International Business at the International Management Institute of the School of Management and Law, Zurich University of Applied Sciences. He is Qualitative Researcher, Consultant & Coach for Entrepreneurs. Co-Founder of the The New Luxury Alliance, Duma is Member of the Academic Board at the Luxury Venture Group. Member of the Swiss Center for Luxury Research he is internationally recognized in his expertise.

Mark Esposito is recognized internationally as a top global thought leader in matters relating to The Fourth Industrial Revolution. He is Co-Founder and Chief Learning Officer, Nexus FrontierTech, an AI scale up venture. He also holds academic appointments as Harvard University, University of Cambridge, Arizona State University's Thunderbird School of Global Management, Hult International Business School, and IE Business School. He is a global expert of the World Economic Forum and advisor to national governments as to the Prime Minister Office of the UAE for the National Program on Artificial Intelligence. He is Distinguished Fellow at UNESCO. He has published 13 books, over 150 publications, and more than 40 case studies.

Mauro Ferraresi is Associate Professor at the IULM University, Milan, Italy. He is also the Director of the first-level Master's in Management of Made in Italy, Director of the first-level Master's in Management and Communication of Beauty and Wellness, and Director of the Specialist Master's in Management and Communication of Events. He teaches in Consumer Sociology and Business Culture, among others.

Martha Friel is Assistant Professor of Economics and Business Management in the Faculty of Arts and Tourism, IULM University, Milan, where she teaches culture and tourism management and marketing. Her research areas cover the economy and management of culture, of the creative industries and tourism on which she collaborates with national and international institutions. She is senior fellow of the Santagata Foundation for the Economy of Culture.

Francesca Goi graduated from Bocconi University, and she is DBA candidate. Expert in yachting industry, consultant and adjunct professor, specialized in luxury marketing management, she's also correspondent for several yachting magazines.

Laura Grazzini is Assistant Professor in Marketing at the University of Florence, Florence, Italy. Her research interests lie in the areas of consumer behavior, sustainable consumption, and experimental research. Her work has been published in several international journals, such as *Journal of Retailing*, *Journal of Business Research*, and *Psychology & Marketing*.

Jinju Hu is a doctoral candidate at the Ecole des Ponts ParisTech, and a researcher in the interlinkage among innovation, sustainability, and luxury. She serves as Innovation Advisor for Chanel and holds visiting professorships with Burgundy School of Business and Excelia Group.

Fabio Iraldo is Full Professor at the Istituto di Management, Scuola Superiore Sant'Anna in Pisa, and Research Director at IEFE – "Institute for Environment and Energy Economics", Bocconi University, Milan, Italy. He is also Advisor and Consultant for Sustainability certifications and processes.

Stefania Lazzaroni has been the Executive Director of Fondazione Altagamma since 2013. She is a member of the executive team and coordinates the Foundation's activities. Altagamma is the Italian Association of Luxury brands.

Jessica Antonios is currently the chairperson of Marketing at AUST-Lebanon, and in 2007, she received a B.A. degree in Psychology from the Lebanese American University, Beirut, Lebanon. She then traveled to Grenoble, France, and earned her M.Sc. degree in Marketing from Grenoble Graduate School of Business, Grenoble, France, in 2009, and then went on to complete her Doctorate in Business Administration with a concentration in Marketing–Consumer Behavior from Grenoble Ecole de Management, Grenoble, France, in 2016.

Amedeo Migali, Ph.D. in Naval Architecture, Adjunct Professor of "high speed craft" at Trieste University, Trieste, Italy, Expert of the European Climate Infrastructure Environment Executive Agency, he manages Micad, company active in yacht design.

Olga Nachaeva is a PhD student in the Business Administration and Management joint program of the University of Pisa, Florence and Siena, Italy. Her research interests are brand management, consumer culture, and consumer psychology.

Cecilia Pasquinelli is Associate Professor of Management in the Department of Management and Quantitative Studies, University of Naples Parthenope, Naples, Italy. She previously worked in the *GSSI Cities* at Gran Sasso Science Institute in L'Aquila, Italy, and in the Department of Social and Economic Geography, Uppsala University, Uppsala, Sweden. She is an Associate Editor of the *Journal of Place Management and Development*.

Ian Phau is Distinguished Senior Professor of Consumer Behavior and Brand Management at Curtin University, Bentley, WA, and the Editor-in-Chief of *Asia Pacific Journal of Marketing and Logistics*. In the past, he has been the Founder and Director of the Marketing School, Curtin University. His current research specializes in country of origin, advertising appeals, and branding specifically in luxury brands. He has also published extensively in *Social Behavior and Personality*, *Psychology & Marketing*, *Journal of Business Ethics*, and *Journal of Consumer Marketing*, among others. His business experience includes management consulting and market research in the luxury fashion industry in Europe, Australasia, and Asia.

Silvia Ranfagni is Associate Professor of Marketing at the University of Florence, Florence, Italy, is an expert in Luxury Brand Management, and she is consulting in the field. She gained teaching experience at various University Masters – Bocconi University, EXCELIA Business School University of Macerata. She received the "Marketing Trends Awards" at the 2012 edition for his contributions to the study of the consumer in the fashion sector. She is extensively publishing and researching in the field of Luxury brand and authenticity and published in top journals as Journal of Business Research, Psychology and Marketing, and Journal of Brand Management, among others.

Susanne Rank is Professor at Mainz University of Applied Sciences. Since 2015, she has been the Head of the Academic Section Human Resource Management at the School of Business. Her teaching experience is mainly in Business Administration, HRM, and Change Management at the School of Business. She has been the Course Director of M.Sc. International Business Management in cooperation with the LSBU, UK, and Change Management Senior Business Consultant and HRD consultant at SAP AG, Walldorf, Germany. She is actively researching and publishing in the field and was invited as guest speaker and Visiting Professor.

Matilde Rovai is currently specializing in International Business at the Grenoble Ecole de Management with a passion in international business relations and sustainability. She was research assistant for the Kartell case at the Kartell Museum. She has developed an international experience in Asia, US, and Europe. She served at the Robert Kennedy Foundation within the frame of her studies.

Giada Salvietti is resercher at the Università degli Studi di Parma, specialising in Business and Management with a specific focus on fashion and luxury. She has published and consulted extensively in academia in the field.

Elena Tinacci has dual Master's degrees in Hospitality & Tourism Management obtained from IULM University in Milan and University of Central Florida – Rosen College in Orlando. While completing her final thesis, she started developing an academic interest toward the vast topics of CSR, sustainability, and employee behavior in the context of the latest trends affecting the hospitality industry. She has recently started a career in the luxury hotel field.

Daniela Toccafondi is currently President of PIN, the Prato-based Executive branch of the Università degli Sudi di Firenze in the heart of Made in Italy clusters. After serving in the municipal government as Adjunct Major and being Director of Pratofutura, a nonprofit association composed of the Italian city of Prato's leading entrepreneurs whose aim is to investigate the area's future development. Daniela is also a university Professor in Applied Economics at the Prato Campus of Florence University.

Giulia Tonucci is PhD in Fashion and Performing Arts with an interdisciplinary project on the relationships between theatre, technology, and fashion, developed at the University of Bologna and Paris 8. She was also a member of the Design and Performance Lab, based in London, focusing on multimedia integration in theatre garments. Today, as an independent researcher and a professional, she continues to investigate the implications of digital technologies in fashion and their aesthetic and sustainable repercussions in the work of a new generation of designers. Currently, she collaborates in the Degree Course in Fashion and Creative Industries at the IULM University of Milan.

Dennis Valle, Chief Brand Officer at Corneliani, is one of the main experts in digital marketing for luxury brands in Italy, thanks to his extensive expertise in the field. After a long-term experience at Diesel Groups as main Digital Specialist, he has been appointed Vice President for Digital Marketing at Dolce & Gabbana and Chief Marketing Officer for Versace.

Lorenzo Zanni is Full Professor of Management and Marketing in the Department of Business and Law (University of Siena). A cum laude graduate of the University of Florence since 2001, he has been a full professor at the University of Siena. His main research interests are in SMEs and Entrepreneurship, International Marketing and Management, and Marketing of Made in Italy products. He is a member of the Editorial Board of the journal "World Review of Entrepreneurship, Management and Sustainable Development" and of the Scientific Committee of the journal "Micro & Macro Marketing". He has served as Pro-Rector (Vice-Chancellor) for Technology Transfer and Business Relationships of the University of Siena; President of the Academic Spin-off Commission of the University of Siena; and Member of the Board of Directors of the Toscana Life Science Foundation.

Introduction

Luxury “Made in Italy”

Serena Rovai and Manuela de Carlo

This book – through an analysis of diverse cases – answers the key issues in the industry of the new “Made in Italy” luxury. We assume that market trends are radically changing and that the industry is attempting to reposition itself in order to respond to new consumers’ orientations and to maintain its competitive advantage. This takes place in a differentiated way, according to the diversity of specific sectors. The text has been written by an international pool of academic authors and experts in luxury brand management and “Made in Italy”.

In the past, luxury had been conceptualized as an exclusive benefit of the few. Its unique mode of consumption concerned only a privileged segment of customers. In contrast, luxury is nowadays a highly diversified ecosystem with disruptive challenges to its identity and authenticity brought by the emerging consumer segments and in particular the young. “Made in Italy” holds a highly significant position in the global luxury market. An economic, but also cultural and social phenomenon, Made in Italy is a powerful example and a textbook case of the so-called “country-of-origin” effect, emphasizing the unique characteristics derived from the “savoir faire” and expertise located in the Italian manufacturing areas. Although historically Made in Italy does not refer only to luxury products, its association with luxury has been increasingly relevant and the related brands have acquired a significant competitive position globally.

Thanks to its characteristics of high-quality craftsmanship, style, authenticity, and heritage, Made in Italy has been able to play a specific role in the development of the luxury industry, with special reference to some sectors such as clothing, leather and jewelry. Later on, Made in Italy brands extended their operations from the original core products to accessories, perfumes and cosmetics, tourism and hospitality, yachts and supercars, household, and design.

This success story needs to be reassessed in the light of the present changes in luxury markets. The recent demographics of the millennial segments and the so-called “democratization of luxury” lead to a reappraisal of the conventional characteristics of heritage and authenticity associated to a Made in Italy product as “*Bello and Ben Fatto*” (“Beautiful and Well Made”). New values and

DOI: 10.4324/9781003305095-1

expectations emerge in luxury consumers, emphasizing ethical and sustainable orientations – that can also compensate for the negative perceptions traditionally attached to luxury spending. Excellence in production must increasingly include a sustainability dimension and while this does not necessarily coincide with the manufacturing expertise of the historic clusters, it may find a more credible answer coming from alternative locations worldwide.

The iconic Italian Style and the "*Bello e Ben Fatto*" features are no longer sufficient to ensure global competitiveness. The call for "Responsible Luxury" has imposed an acceleration in the implementation of individual and collective strategies focused on sustainability in its social, economic, and ecological dimensions but also in its innovative one. The 2015 introduction of the "Made Green in Italy" scheme, that is promoting sustainable patterns in manufacturing and consumption as well as guaranteeing transparency in environmental performance, is just one example of the push to foster the eco-competitiveness of Italian brands at national and international levels, developing a new conceptualization of the Italian Made in Italy excellency.

Luxury shoppers are expecting luxury brands to increase their sustainable engagement and behave more responsibly through a tangible involvement in the social, economic, and environmental aspects. The COVID-19 pandemic has also extensively disrupted the luxury industry and in particular the Made in Italy which is a key component of the entire luxury industry besides being its cradle. "Beauty will save the world" wrote Dostoevskij and beauty is an integral part of the Made in Italy, the so defined "Bello e Ben Fatto" derived from the Italian "Sprezzatura" that has developed a reputation globally to the country. However, until a few years ago, beauty was not necessarily associated to a responsible engagement neither in the Made in Italy nor in the luxury industry that in the name of beauty was justifying non-sustainable choices and operations.

Luxury customers have become increasingly engaged in sustainability and expecting luxury brands to strengthen their commitment to sustainability and develop into new concrete improvements. Most of the luxury shoppers, especially younger adults, have already altered their experience consequently. Luxury shoppers have modified their luxury lifestyle and tried to reduce the environmental impact through their brands choices by preferring those that adopt eco-friendly operations. In the post-pandemic age, the new luxury shopper is mindful, environmentally engaged and socially involved, aiming at avoiding traditional models of consumer behavior. Contemporary luxury customers need to designate their own shopping criteria, give a sustainability-related connotation to the luxury experience, and to make their purchase decisions accordingly. In a post-COVID perspective, Luxury Made in Italy brands have started to plan a responsible future and consequently embrace and uphold the call for sustainability so as to increase trust from customers, in particular from new millennials.

There are increasingly responsible "Made in Italy" brands in the luxury sector that have started to integrate sustainability to their brand value and identity and that are demonstrating that a conscious luxury approach does not necessarily mean to sacrifice ethics for esthetics. Nowadays, the new Luxury paradigm has shifted from being about the product to being about the experience. The New Luxury, that saw its birthplace in Italy, initially within Made in Italy and the fashion sector nowadays is experiencing a different identity embodying the concept of inventive design, manufactured in a zero-waste environment, experienced in an energy-efficient innovative retailing environment. Luxury has been transformed from a "Gold Iconic Product" into a "Responsible Brand Experience" appreciated for its luxury products characteristics of exclusivity, rarity, high-quality but also for its responsible commitment to improve the people's lives, the planet's environment, and the way profit is made and invested. Luxury brands from the diverse business sectors have realized the increasing importance of the new Luxury role and created often philanthropic brand narratives that can highlight the brand value and market differentiation and in so doing safeguarding the customer loyalty. Even though some Made in Italy brands consider the sustainable orientation a new challenge, it is nowadays considered a must-do to ensure a competitive positioning in the more recent global luxury scenario. Those Italian Made in Italy brands from the luxury sector that have already understood the value of sustainability for the brand and the luxury industry, have been able to innovate and reposition themselves in the global game. However, it is not a choice that requires a completely different perspective; creating single sustainable initiatives does not require the same commitment and effort as becoming a sustainable innovator. Those luxury champions of the Made in Italy, who can engage in an innovative sustainable commitment, are worth being analyzed in their practices and operations in an applied knowledge perspective. Within an industry that is inherently conservative and takes pride in its heritage, this repositioning is likely to occur only to the extent that creative entrepreneurs (and possibly a new generation of creative entrepreneurs) take the lead in a new wave of innovations, redefining and re-establishing a long-term competitive position. This book will contribute to answer two main research questions:

1 Have "Made in Italy" luxury brands been able to integrate sustainability into the product features and attributes that are relevant to their customers? Is this a sincere, real engagement or it is only done instrumentally for marketing purposes ("green washing")?
2 Is there some "uniqueness" or at least some specificity in the way this is happening for Italian companies?
3 Local roots (industrial districts), tradition, craftsmanship: are these references consistent with the perception of a productive system that inherently pays more attention to issues like bio, natural materials, sustainable production processes, etc.?
4 Is the prevailing role of SMEs and niche producers (rather than large multinationals) also perceived as a factor leading to more responsible behavior?

5 What is the role of innovation and creativity? What is the potential of new "creative" companies (start-ups) that are "born sustainable" (i.e., integrate sustainability in their business idea since the beginning)?

The book answers these two main research questions through an analysis of exemplary case studies of companies that have addressed – and in some cases hastened – the major transformations in the luxury sectors by capitalizing on a new conceptualization of Made in Italy excellence.

The volume is organized into three sections, introduced by an academic assessment of the specific issue concerned and comprises a series of innovative, sustainability-oriented case studies that cover a wide range of Made in Italy sectors.

In the introduction to the first section, Cecilia Pasquinelli, delves into why and under what conditions Made in Italy today, as a unique and non-imitable asset, is able to address current trends of change and competition in luxury markets. First, by reviewing the academic debate on country of origin and Made in Italy, Pasquinelli identifies the key dimensions and assets of Made in Italy related to tradition, authenticity, and creativity. Second, she discusses in depth how these assets can be transformed into distinctive and credible value propositions in response to the key challenges of sustainability and digitization. Finally, the author outlines three areas of inquiry that enable us to understand how companies in the sector can overcome repetitive patterns of exploitation of Made in Italy in favor of innovative – and risky – modalities to fully exploit its potential. The first area of inquiry deals with the relationship and synergies between heritage and innovation. Protecting and preserving Made in Italy's value and making it understandable to young global luxury consumers requires a constant search for innovative ways to communicate and experience tradition. A second area of investigation concerns the relationship between the country's national image and the evolution of a "living" Made in Italy in order to express authentic narratives that accurately reflect contemporary lifestyles and values as well as tangible issues of local communities and Italian territories. The third is about the possibilities that digital technologies offer luxury companies to help tackle the challenges of sustainability. The five chapters in this first section provide an exploration of these industry trends through four flagship case studies for luxury Made in Italy.

Second-hand and vintage have taken the luxury and fashion retailing by storm, particularly for the millennial customer segment. However, until now no luxury and fashion brand in the market has directly included second-hand retailing in their strategy. Serena Rovai and Ian Phau analyze this innovative strategy undertaken by Diesel. Diesel has decided to integrate specific second-hand retailing actions in their brand strategy, recognizing the added value that it can give to the brand reputation.

The luxury industry has been challenged by the responsible call for people, planet and profit and to proactively engaging to meet the challenges of sustainability. This reorientation implies a profound cultural shift, as well as the need for innovative ways of communicating this rising change and new mindset to consumers. This includes pointing out sustainable innovations that may not be immediately visible in products or rectifying a perceived image that does not align with the new brand identity. The chapter by Jessica Antonios describes how Vogue Talents, part of Vogue Italia, has played a major role in addressing these needs of the luxury industry through the dissemination of knowledge, the exploration of up-to-date communication codes, and the development of a new generation of young designers with a sustainability mindset.

The DNA of luxury and sustainability is defined by quality, durability, rarity, and support for local economies through the promotion of craftsmanship and Made in Italy. 10 Corso Como, the conceptual brand and multifunctional space founded in Milan in 1990 by Carla Sozzani, offers an intriguing example of how a luxury retail brand can integrate these elements of sustainability into its concept and communicate it effectively across different channels. The uniqueness of 10 Corso Como's strategy, described by Gaetano Aiello and Laura Grazzini, is based on a multiplicity of synergistic elements: the choice of products and collections, the selection of designers to partner with, the ability to communicate through their spaces and displays, and in more recent years, the endeavor to renew communication through digital technologies. In its varied path of development, 10 Corso Como has acted as a key stimulus for the luxury retail sector to integrate sustainability into its offerings and the image of its brands.

Luxury business models are being transformed toward sustainability because company owners firmly believe this change is necessary to ensure a company's continued growth. The pandemic has been a timely period to invest in innovative projects that will produce beneficial effects on the luxury sectors in the years ahead. This is the experience of the Italian family company Yamamay as told by Fabio Iraldo in his chapter of this book. In 2021, as part of the process of rethinking operations and products according to new sustainability values strongly desired by the family, the company launched a new swimsuit line called EDIT (eco-designed innovative textile) that has already achieved impressive results in terms of reducing the impact of products and packaging on the environment.

The second section examines the processes of transformation of Made in Italy in response to the challenge of sustainability with reference to specific luxury sectors. In her introduction, Stefania Lazzaroni, from the privileged perspective of the Altagamma network, extensively documents how sustainability is a top priority for luxury brands today, and how companies are implementing sustainability in their core business strategy and the results thereof. The author develops two highly interesting analytical perspectives. The first is that the drive for sustainability appears to be hard-wired into Italy's high-end companies as an essential feature of their mission and philosophy. Several reasons can be cited for this: (i) to preserve the high-quality natural resources used in their production processes; (ii) to create products made to last, to be resold, as opposed to disposable; (iii) to ensure high levels of employee wellbeing in order to attract and retain people whose expertise (handcrafting, customer interaction …) are unique assets difficult to replace; (iv) to have direct control over the entire supply chain thus ensuring the most stringent sustainability standards; and (v) to remain faithful to the values of the "Made in Italy" meta-brand to which consumers around the world attribute intrinsically sustainable qualities: attention to detail, artisanal production, natural materials, and authenticity. Luxury Made in Italy companies need to recognize this inherent attitude to sustainability as a potential competitive driver.

The second key argument of this chapter holds that the concept of luxury is undergoing a radical transformation and that "the shareholders and stakeholders now expect companies to have a purpose, something that goes beyond just being responsible". Nowadays, with their strong commitment to sustainability, luxury companies are redefining their relationship with consumers, shareholders, and local communities based on shared values and beliefs, thereby becoming important social and cultural actors. Italy's high-end brands have always represented authentically sustainable development and therefore enjoy a potential advantage. They have gone from being primarily manufacturers in the 1980s, to retailers with international development in the 1990s, to true media companies that communicate digitally with their customers. Nowadays, they find themselves in a new phase of development where they can act as trailblazers and innovators by implementing unique and virtuous models of sustainability.

We explore this changing scenario with reference to diverse sectors of Made in Italy luxury through an in-depth analysis of several paradigmatic cases: Ferretti in yachting & sailing; Brunello Cuccinelli in knitwear and personal goods; Gucci in fashion and apparel; Principe di Savoia – Dorchester in hospitality; Kartell in household and design; Ferragamo in leather and accessories; and Cantine Ferrari in food and wine.

Flexibility and careful monitoring of the entire supply chain have always been key factors for luxury brands to ensure the excellence of their products. For the yachting & sailing sector, which typically features custom-made and highly elaborate products, this need becomes even more complex to manage, given the requirements of an increasingly sustainability-conscious clientele. The chapter by Francesca Goi and Amedeo Migali analyze how the 360-degree commitment to sustainability of the Ferretti Group, a leading leisure boating company with excellent brands and international distribution, has stimulated other players in the entire production chain to undertake sustainable paths of development.

Within the very fabric of the strategic choices for sustainability that Made in Italy luxury brands are implementing, there is always an underlying vision of the company and its future, its goals, and its management style that is, however, rarely made explicit. This vision is mostly left implicit yet expresses itself throughout all operations of the company. The chapter by Susanne

Rank illustrates, through the experience of Brunello Cuccinelli – the Italian leading manufacturer of luxury fashion apparel – what is termed "humanistic capitalism". This is a rather unique human resource and cultural model that strives for business growth and profit-seeking by putting the well-being of people, employees, and the local environment at the center. This approach, profoundly innovative from the short-term shareholder-driven business perspective, has proven its value and may inspire successful sustainable business models of luxury start-ups in the future.

Giulia Tonucci and Mauro Ferraresi's chapter addresses the luxury phenomenon in Italian fashion from a sociological viewpoint. First, the authors explore the concept of luxury and the evolving role of storytelling in luxury through the centuries, starting from the concept of *megaloprépeia* or magnificence in Greek philosophical thought up to core aspects that define contemporary luxury. The second part focuses on Italian luxury and fashion, which has always been narrated and portrayed through craftsmanship and manual labor, and how it is currently reinterpreted within the context of sustainability. The Gucci case illustrates this process of brand repositioning, starting from the traditional values of exclusivity, preciousness, and product refinement, and then reinterpreting them with the new values of sustainability while leveraging the opportunities offered by digital technologies.

The chapter by Elena Tinacci, Manuela de Carlo, and Martha Friel investigate the "Italian way" toward sustainable luxury hospitality. Following a review of the literature on CSR in the hospitality sector, they discuss the case of the Hotel Principe di Savoia. The authors examine the sustainable commitment of this five-star property owned by the Dorchester Collection from an environmental, but more importantly, social point of view, observing how attention to sustainability strengthens the relationship between the hotel and its guests, thus creating a competitive advantage.

In the following chapter, Michele Coletti and Matilde Rovai tackle a key issue that luxury Made in Italy needs to address in response to current demands for sustainability. The traditional concept of Italian design products as "Belli e ben fatti" (Beautiful and well-made) must evolve into "Belli, buoni e ben fatti" (Beautiful, good, and well-made), with unpredicted implications on rethinking business models.

The authors address this topic through a thought-provoking analysis of the case of Kartell, a design-driven company that has produced timeless objects such as the "Bookworm", "La Marie" chair, and the "Bourgie" table lamp, by aiming for the innovative use of plastic materials. In the last few years, attention to sustainability issues has led Kartell to introduce novel materials such as recycled plastics and biopolymers, thereby embarking on a path of brand repositioning that could soon lead the company to a radical shift from its classic design-driven innovation approach. The drive to redefine its business model according to emerging sustainability trends has also shaped two other iconic cases of Made in Italy luxury: Ferragamo brand in the leather and accessories sector and Cantine Ferrari in the wine industry. The chapter by

Cecilia Pasquinelli and Serena Rovai identify the three pillars of the sustainability architecture that has guided the redefinition of the Ferragamo brand's strategy: (i) integration – the ability to turn sustainability into an integral approach to business management; (ii) experimentation – the readiness to innovate products and production processes; and (iii) engagement – the striving to pursue sustainability by involving internal and external stakeholders. In particular, the author explains the essential role of corporate heritage and place heritage in the sustainability architecture of luxury firms.

Delving into the case of Cantine Ferrari, a leading Italian winery that has positioned its sparkling wine internationally as a sustainable luxury product, Jacopo Cammeo, Elena Casprini, and Lorenzo Zanni identify the core features of successful strategies in the luxury wine sector: (i) excellence – a high quality of production processes, choice of raw materials, and packaging; (ii) scarcity – the availability of unique natural and knowledge-based resources; and (iii) relationships with internal and external stakeholders. These three key elements along with sustainability and technological innovation have firmly established the quality of the product and its uniqueness.

Italy has always stood out as a place where great business-model innovations take place in a range of luxury industries including fashion, food & wine, and culture & arts. The last section of the book features several emblematic cases of start-ups that, in recent years, have achieved extraordinary gains in terms of internal and external innovation, both incremental and disruptive, either in keeping with traditional values or even redefining the rules of the game in their respective sectors. These case studies, each in a different way, suggest interesting avenues for future generations of innovators – or for anyone interested in responding to new needs and addressing emerging trends in the luxury industries – by drawing inspiration from Italian ingenuity.

Dennis Valle's introduction to this section examines the factors and dynamics that define these innovative business models. Subsequent chapters discuss a number of interesting cases of innovation, with three attributes in common: a keen awareness of one's heritage, a strong connection to the environment, and the ability to create regenerative business models. Such models strive for their own development by responding to the needs of new luxury customers, thereby resulting in positive social, environmental, and economic spillover effects.

The chapter by Daniela Toccafondi describes the development path of Rifò, the innovative start-up launched in the city of Prato by young Tuscan entrepreneur Nicolò Cipriani. In 2017, he began to make and sell products recovering 100% of the raw materials from used clothing and knitwear, limiting the use of new fibers. The concept of re-use is deeply ingrained in the culture of the Prato district, where specialization in textile began in the 12th century. The area was already known in the 1950s for its production of wool from recycled rags, packaging scraps, and production leftovers. Rifò's intuition stems from the tradition of this environment where the principles of circular economy were put in place long before they were theorized and sought after by fashion companies to answer new demands for sustainability. The company's innovative development path contributes to renewing and projecting this tradition into the future.

The chapter by Silvia Ranfagni and Giada Salvetti presents the case of La Milanesa, an Italian start-up established in Milan during the pandemic to create luxury handcrafted bags and accessories by combining the recovery of materials and craftsmanship from the past with ethical initiatives aimed at supporting women in distress. The relationship between sustainability and authenticity lies behind the success of this young luxury brand and its remarkable development in Italy and abroad.

The fourth innovation case, analyzed by Jinju Hu and Mark Esposito, tells the extraordinary story of ACBC, the start-up founded by Venetian entrepreneur Giorgio Giacobbe that has radically innovated the footwear industry with a revolutionary business model. The company rapidly established itself as a prime brand with prime international positioning. Its unique value proposition grew out of a radical rethinking of product design as well as the entire production value chain, from raw materials and supplier relations to engagement with responsible consumers.

In the last chapter, Fabio Duma draws an interesting picture of bespoke tailoring in Italy, documenting the role of craftsmanship as a distinguishing feature of Made in Italy. In addition, the author highlights this sector's ongoing contribution to economic, ecological, and social sustainability and to individual well-being. The study focused on an in-depth analysis of five bespoke tailors established between the late 1940s and early 1950s in five different Italian regions (Campania, Lombardy, Puglia, Umbria, Tuscany) and each one still owned by the founder family. The results offer an interpretative framework useful for appreciating the value of many other Made in Italy sectors characterized by a high number of very small businesses deeply connected to the territories where they operate.

Section I

1 The Luxury Industry and "Made in Italy"

New Perspectives and Challenges

Cecilia Pasquinelli
Università degli Studi di Napoli
Parthenope – Scuola Superiore Sant'Anna

Introduction

The search for novel value creation paradigms is inherent to luxury, which means the sector is constantly changing and improving. The pandemic has undoubtedly triggered awareness of the need to accelerate ongoing innovation trajectories in the luxury industry, boosted by the long-term temporariness of COVID-19. The pandemic scenario draws particular attention to sustainable and digital transformations that, firmly rooted in the pre-pandemic context, found fertile ground during COVID times before becoming priorities.

Sustainability implies a reinterpretation of the essence of luxury, focusing on some aspects of the luxury experience such as its value and meaning for consumers, marking a necessary transition encompassing and going beyond the single luxury brand and firm. In recent years, sustainability has become a trending topic in the fashion industry. Indeed, according to Google Trends, informed by the search interests of Google users, the annual average worldwide interest rate for "sustainable fashion" evidently increased, shifting from 26.5 in 2017 to 84.3 in 2020 and 76.4 in 2021, compared to the relatively decreasing interest in "fashion" (64.3 in 2017 vs. 53.7 in 2020 and 51.2 in 2021).

Although a raw indicator of interest for sustainability, this trend mirrors the debate on luxury in transition. After neglecting the potential synergies between luxury and sustainability (Hu, Henninger, Boardman, & Ryding, 2019), scholars and practitioners have been rapidly catching up with the discussion and the adoption of sustainability practices and models (Kapferer & Michaut-Denizeau, 2020). A surprising delay remains, rare for an industrial domain like luxury that usually anticipates trends and standards. Although theory and practice are far from consolidated, green manufacturing and supply chains, raw materials selection, product lifecycles, and sustainability marketing have entered the luxury industry. Environmental, social, ethical, and more inherently territorial and cultural aspects of sustainability deserve further attention.

DOI: 10.4324/9781003305095-3

An intertwined force pushing change in the luxury industries is digitalization. Luxury sales growth and change in distribution and retailing strategies (Pentina, Guilloux, & Micu, 2018; Zhang & Kim, 2013) are the tip of the iceberg under which digitalization impacts brand positioning, influencing the brand image, identity, and experience (Guercini, Bernal, & Prentice, 2018; Ko & Megehee, 2012; Naeem & Ozuem, 2021; Rovai, 2016). It is the other side of the sustainability coin as we can see that digitalization processes influence modalities, motivations, qualities and quantities of luxury consumption, and production. Digitalization and social media marketing helped newcomer consumers freely and easily "experiment" luxury brands online, closing the gap with many consumers who historically had remained marginal in luxury markets. Young generations approaching luxury for the first time and in an early phase of their life will represent 40% of the market by 2035 (Bain & Company, 2019). Studies revealed distinct traits of Gen Z consumers concerning luxury engagement and purchasing behaviors (McKinsey, 2018; Sun, Wang, Cao, & Lee, 2021), which align with this segment's relationship with digitalization.

With this background in mind, it is crucial for luxury brand to understand the assets and drivers of value creation that may support them through the transition in addressing contemporary and future market challenges. How and to what extent can consolidated and traditional levers of value creation potentially support luxury firms through their path of change? How may the country of origin and the country image provide valuable support in these scenarios?

Luxury and fashion sectors have been significantly exploiting country image and culture to create brand value (Kapferer, 2009; Lee, Ko, Lee, & Kim, 2015). The country-of-origin effect is consolidated in literature, understood as the market value of stereotypical country images (Bilkey & Nes, 1982), as the market value of & reputation and representation of a country becomes associated with product quality (Kotler & Gertner, 2002). It is an established yet controversial concept (Aiello et al., 2009; Godey et al., 2012; Ko & Megehee, 2012). In practice, creative industries rely on area identities, and national and local cultural heritage (Power & Scott, 2004) to impose a premium price in the market (Carcano & Lojacono, 2018).

The concept of the origin of a product itself has been transitioning. At least two forces influenced its sophistication. First, place-images and brand-place associations have increasingly included not only the manufacturing phase (and place) of value creation (the proper "made in") but also phases and spaces "behind the factory gates" (Jansson & Power, 2010), such as the place where the company is headquartered and historically established (Thakor & Lavack, 2003), the place where the product was designed (Insch & McBride, 2004), the "usage context" (Pike, 2015), the place experience embodied by a brand (Tokatli, 2013), and the place where a brand is physically experienced, being in luxury capitals (Rovai, 2016) or cultural tourism destinations (Bellini & Pasquinelli, 2016). The image of all of the aforementioned places does contribute to the formation of the perceived origin. Second, not only the country's origin but also "smaller sub-national places" of origin (Papadopoulos, Cleveland, Bartikowski, & Yaprak, 2018) are considered potential sources of value, such as cities and regions. However, this research route remains significantly unexplored.

This book, and mainly this book section, contribute to exploring critical areas of inquiry on the "Made in Italy" country of origin in an attempt to address the following questions: how and to what extent is "Made in Italy" a distinctive and competitive asset for luxury brands in transition? How does "Made in Italy" contribute to luxury firms' operationalization of distinctive and credible value propositions in terms of sustainability? How do luxury firms capitalize on the "Made in Italy" experience in the frame of the pervasive digital transformation? What role and meaning of "Made in Italy" will characterize the next generations' relationship with luxury?

The following section describes the distinctive dimensions and assets of "Made in Italy" as a form of country heritage, based on the review of the available literature. The first section discusses traits specific to "Made in Italy" concerning the emerging global challenges for luxury. The next section outlines the critical areas of inquiry emerging from the proposed analysis of "Made in Italy".

"Made in Italy": Key dimensions and assets

"Made in Italy" is not a label for any product manufactured in Italy. Instead, it is an architecture of values to which product and corporate brands belong (Carcano & Lojacono, 2018) and demonstrate involvement. It summarizes the industrial profile of the country but goes beyond its industrial essence. It became a central component of the country's *cultural heritage*, framing "qualities, traditions or features of life that have continued over many years and have been passed on from one generation to another", borrowing the Collins dictionary's definition of heritage.

A process of heritagization (Harrison, 2013) turned objects, practices, and places inherent to "Made in Italy" into cultural heritage. "Made in Italy" is an "assemblage" (Harrison, 2013) of assets, rooted in the display of how products are manufactured, which have become heritage through social mechanisms of sense-making and value construction. Through the heritagization process, an "epic richly imaginative background" (Segre-Reinach, 2010) consolidates around "Made in Italy". Fashion history studies highlight its narratively constructed meaning, combining facts and tailored imaginaries.

Based on the review of the available literature, two key dimensions, i.e., *history* and *authenticity*, frame Made in Italy. These two slippery concepts generally apply to the notion of country of origin, contributing to the difficulty of harnessing the concept theoretically and empirically. Therefore, the challenge is to frame these two key dimensions as repositories of relevant assets configuring a distinctive luxury brand-building model (Kapferer & Bastien,

2009) inherent to "Made in Italy". Identifying these "assets" implies framing facts and tailored imaginaries, leaving room to scratch the surface of the most consolidated (and powerful) stereotypical images, and unveiling the untapped potential of hidden, overlooked, or silent aspects of "Made in Italy".

History is a source of value in global markets, providing brands with legitimacy, stability, and reliability (Merlo & Perugini, 2015). And the "Made in Italy" concept significantly contributes to these mechanisms by narrating the historical birth of the iconic national style, the history of Italian entrepreneurship, and the corporate heritage (Figure 1.1).

The narration of the *birth of the Italian style* often refers to the 12th of February 1951, the date of the first high fashion show organized in Florence, going back to a post-war context to the symbolic birth of Italian high fashion and the contemporary notion of "Made in Italy". Beneath highly symbolic imagery related to the national rebirth and post-war reconstruction, fashion studies identified a more recent birth of the iconic Italian style. In the 1970s–1980s, the high fashion system moved from Florence to Milan's industrial "magic circle" (Tokatli, 2014). In this context with agglomerating fashion stakeholders, media, advertising, design, publishing companies, and urban bourgeoisie consumers, it became a fertile milieu for cross-fertilizations and an original concept of Italian style (Ferrero-Regis, 2008; Segre-Reinach, 2010) took place. Probably less symbolically powerful than the first high fashion show in the 1950s, the early 1980s witnessed a decisive shift of the

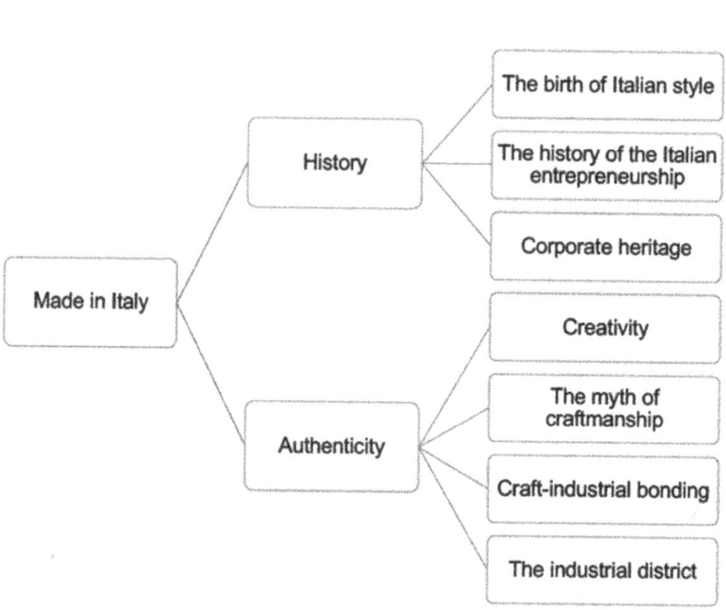

Figure 1.1 "Made in Italy": Key dimensions and assets.

Italian high fashion from French-like "products of art and culture" to the Italian fashion as "practice of modernity" (Segre-Reinach, 2015).

History as a key dimension of "Made in Italy" includes the *history of Italian entrepreneurship*. This concept relates to the legendary small-sized manufacturing firms that often coincide with the family businesses of the Italian luxury and fashion industry. Eighty-three percent of Italian fashion companies are, in fact, family-owned or controlled companies (Carcano & Lojacono, 2018). If family businesses generally characterize the Italian industrial sector, in the fashion and luxury domains this is an even more substantial characteristic (Corbetta, Quarato, & Minichilli, 2018). Continuity, long-term connections with clients, employees, territorial communities, and suppliers are considered the drivers of family businesses' success (Carcano & Lojacono, 2018). These traits are part of the corporate brand, with the family representing the *fil rouge* of creativity and success over time. An example is Salvatore Ferragamo, positioning the history of the family and the family members at the core of the brand identity. Some of the iconic stories that make up the brand's culture include the wife of the founder leading the company after the husband's death and the daughter who created the iconic women's shoe "Vara" and the *gancino* lock, becoming the distinctive graphic element of the brand identity.

Corporate heritage, including the family business background, is another "Made in Italy" asset. An interesting study provided insights into the understanding of "Made in Italy" from corporate executives' points of view (Kohler & Perrino, 2017). The authors highlighted that firms' engagement with "Made in Italy" is framed as a mission inherited from history, a "moral discourse" on the responsibility to safeguard and respect "Made in Italy" values as a collective identity. Another interesting aspect of this study was the emphasis on "the Italian cultural DNA". For the interviewed executives, "the Italian cultural DNA" is the wealth of art and history the Italian entrepreneurs are immersed in, which nurtures their "taste of beauty". Corporate heritage, deeply intertwined with the national cultural heritage, is celebrated for instance through corporate museums, which, proliferating globally, became an important brand-building lever for "Made in Italy" brands.

Authenticity is the other key dimension of "Made in Italy". It is a somewhat controversial concept, but beyond the theoretical challenges, the appropriation of the "authentic aura" of "Made in Italy" productions is sought after by many foreign luxury companies, integrating "Made in Italy" ingredients in their final products. This is the case of "Made in Italy" shirt couture lines by Ralph Lauren or "Made in Italy" leather bags by Louis Vuitton (Kapferer & Bastien, 2009). Data confirmed Italy is the leading country for luxury manufacturing, producing about 9 billion euros a year, one-third of that figure fueling foreign companies' supply chains (Pambianco/Accademia del Lusso, 2018).

It is crucial to explain what authenticity means for "Made in Italy". Using Thompson, Rindfleisch, and Arsel's (2006) words, "Made in Italy" can be understood as providing an "authenticating narrative" whose components are the "model of the original" and a "sincere contact" with the local community (Taylor, 2001). The model of the original refers to the "prototype product" and so to the creativity characterizing "Made in Italy" products. Studies aimed to isolate the "Made by Italian creativity" component perceived by consumers, finding it plays a significant role, prevailing over the "Made in Italy" component, especially in younger generation (Paciolla & Mai, 2011). Creativity is a critical success factor for "Made in Italy" brands, not only when creating a unique style and design, but also in relation to creating a lifestyle.

The model of the original, then, resides not only in the conceptual creation of the product but also in the original manufacturing modality following the traditions inherited from the past. This refers, for instance, to the authenticity of Italian artisan skills that were proved to be driving positive consumer luxury product judgment (Cheah, Zainol, & Phau, 2016). "Made in Italy" is especially grounded in the association of the country image with craftsmanship.

The "myth of craftsmanship" (Dallabona, 2014) is a core asset of "Made in Italy" and waves of branding in mid-2010s showed its marketing appeal. Two examples are the Gucci Artisan Corner (2010) developed in several stores worldwide and Fendi's *Fatto a Mano* [Handmade] campaign (2012), recreating the artisan workshop atmosphere where Florentine artisans performed the crafting process for the clients.

"Made in Italy" authenticating narratives often push the origins of craftsmanship far into the past, not without creating "historical falsehood" (Segre-Reinach, 2010). Continuity with the Renaissance as the origin of craftsmanship and artisans' creativity emerged in empirical studies (Kohler & Perrino, 2017). The current narrative is that, historically, "Made in Italy" was born from the bonding of craftsmanship with industrial manufacturing, rather than being the result of "innate talent [...] [it is] the outcome of a precise industrial history" (Segre-Reinach, 2010, 2015). In other words, "Made in Italy" configures "a marriage of traditional craftsmanship, innovative design and modern industrial technology .... The artisanal production of industrial goods" (Dallabona, 2014). This footprint is present in luxury brands like Prada, which has always adopted a straightforward approach to narrating automated production, industrial know-how, and technological innovations (Dallabona, 2014). The recent brand narrative of nylon production is an example, with a web series (i.e., Prada Nylon Farm) centered on a futuristic ultra-technological factory immersed and in harmony with uncontaminated nature.

Industrial production is an essential source of authenticity for "Made in Italy". In this regard, the industrial sector broadly represents the Italian industrial structure and history, often narrated as the cradle of small-sized, flexible, and highly competitive "Made in Italy" firms. Constructed of a dense territorial network of contractors and subcontractors, designers, specialized services, machinery, and equipment providers, the sector has shown an increase in jobs, income, exports, and social mobility (Dei Ottati, 2009). Despite its failures (Dei Ottati, 2009), the industrial sector has remained the predominant model in several luxury and fashion sectors, such as leather and tanneries, shoes, jewelry, eyewear, knitwear, clothing, and textile, where companies keep benefiting from this specific industrial organization (Iraldo & Trenti, 2018).

The industrial model was romanticized (Hadjimichalis, 2006), and the following text from the book titled *Italian Fashion since 1945. A cultural history* explained well how:

> *A fascinating model [...] the Italian way to achieve development. In this case, it would be worth mentioning the advantages of economic backwardness [...] the persistence in Italy of many small artisan enterprises, "backward" in the sense that they were linked to old know-how, to flexible productive models, family labour or little more, to relations with kin or friends, with territorial physical proximity – businesses not yet swept away by the economies of scale of the large companies, as was the case in other countries – was a competitive advantage.*
>
> (Scarpellini, 2019)

The industrial sector, we can argue, contributes to establishing what we can call the "sincere contact" component of the "Made in Italy" authenticating narrative. It provides a concrete point of contact between brands and territorial communities, which may play as a form of guarantee for genuineness and trustful relationships, decreasing the perceived commercial content (Holt, 2002) of the manufactured products originated in a tangible territorial and social context.

"Made in Italy": Key challenges

If these are the key dimensions and assets of "Made in Italy" emerging from the literature, what potential successes and pitfalls characterize it in both current and future scenarios? What contribution will Made in Italy keep giving luxury brands, boosting their relevance and differentiation? As highlighted in the Introduction, sustainability and digitalization are the areas where discussing and testing the potential and pitfalls of "Made in Italy" is most relevant, opening routes of inquiry on the (necessary) evolutions of "Made in Italy" in the luxury industry.

"Made in Italy" and sustainability: The social beside the environment

According to market analysts, "Made in" has a greater market potential than in the past, since places and place-based manufacturing modalities are firmly associated with quality, safety, and ecological standards (Goffee, 2019). Until recently, sustainability was not a variable taken into account when defining the localization of production sites and the configuration of supply chains (Macchion et al., 2015), but the recognition of sustainability has been rapidly growing, including geographical implications for firms' strategies.

In the post-pandemic context, market analysts also agreed on the shift in luxury consumer behavior and desire for more responsible consumption, and therefore the consequent need for firms to be more transparent and willing to inform consumers on products and processes (McKinsey, 2020). Another trend concerns the post-crisis "silent luxury", with consumers paying more attention to the core content of luxury products, such as craftsmanship and heritage, rather than simply esthetic and *status quo* elements of conspicuous luxury consumption (McKinsey, 2020).

In this context, it is worth focusing on how "Made in Italy" is an effective lever to build distinctive and innovative models of sustainability. Evidence of increasing environmental concern in the Italian fashion system was provided regarding reducing textile waste, decreasing use of polluting chemicals, and adopting environmental certifications (Iraldo & Trenti, 2018). In 2012, the *Manifesto for Sustainability in Italian Fashion*, promoted by the National Chamber of Fashion, introduced eco-design among the pillars of sustainable Italian fashion, the production process, and the raw materials introduced in the process. Eco-design drew attention to the design of products and their whole lifecycle, including product durability, packaging, and modalities for final disposal, all fundamental aspects of sustainability.

Iconic "Made in Italy" firms have been on the forefront of sustainability, integrating it at the core of their industrial innovation strategies. For example, in 2019, Prada signed a sustainability bank loan (50 million euros with Credit Agricole), the first luxury group to do so globally. The loan conditions were linked to a set of sustainability targets, such as the number of stores with LEED (Leadership in Energy and Environmental Design) Gold or Platinum certification, the number of training hours for employees, and the use of Prada Re-Nylon (regenerated nylon from plastic waste and fishing nets). This was followed by other loans in 2020 with the Japanese bank Mizuho (75 million euros), and in 2021 with Unicredit bank (90 million euros), with targets of regeneration and reconversion of production waste and energy self-sufficient production plants (Prada Official website).

Besides the environmental concern, the social dimension of sustainability is a field in which some "Made in Italy" brands have also been at the forefront. The "unique manufacturing proposition" by Brunello Cucinelli (Deserti, 2014), an iconic luxury cashmere garments brand, is a relevant example. Respect for the dignity and wellbeing of the workers and artisans curating the whole production process, from raw materials selection and treatment to the finished product, is a central value for the "humanistic company". The small village of Solomeo, in the Umbria region (central Italy), where the company is headquartered and hosts the production, physically materializes the combination of ethics and esthetics laying at the core of the company's value proposition.

The social dimension has generally remained ancillary in the practice of sustainability and the academic debate on luxury, compared to the centrality of the environmental dimension. S*low fashion*, which emerged in antithesis to fast fashion, is rooted in the social dimension of sustainable manufacturing.

It highlights the adoption of production methods and techniques for which workers' skills and creativity are central, implying longer fabrication time and high cultural (and human) content of products (Cimatti, Campana, & Carluccio, 2017).

Alongside the best practices of sustainability, from a social and environmental perspective, we also must consider systemic failures threatening the credibility of important "Made in Italy" sectors. An example is the recent scandal regarding the toxic wastes produced by the tannery manufacturers in the Santa Croce district (Tuscany). This is Italy's most prevalent leather district, with companies like Chanel and Lvhm invested in the district. The scandal cast light on the fragility of "two decades of projects and proclaims on the environment and circular economy" (Pieraccini, 2021) in the area and the sector.

Another prominent example is the so-called "luxury slavery" phenomenon. Revealed by a national TV show named "Report" in 2007, it resonated nationally and internationally, demonstrating how controversial "Made in Italy" can be. As the Los Angeles Times explained, "there are products made completely in Italy but by Chinese immigrants without proper documents and [for whom] labor conditions are especially nasty". As an alternative to offshoring, maintaining the production in Italy has not been a guarantee for acceptable labor and human conditions. Over ten years later, in 2018, the New Yorker focused on the luxury leather district in Tuscany (central Italy), describing how Chinese-immigrant labor represented an inexpensive labor force for luxury fashion houses producing expensive "Made in Italy" handbags and accessories.

Industrial districts are dense networks of contractors and subcontractors, giving luxury firms only indirect control over the whole process and the involved organizations. For this reason, "Made in Italy" companies started implementing actions to improve the network of subcontractors and create mechanisms promoting subcontractors' sustainable practices. Gucci promoted the *Gucci Equilibrium* action to develop a sustainable supply chain in the Florentine leather district. Accordingly, suppliers and sub-contractors must stick to the *Gucci Sustainability Principles,* such as sustainable sourcing, legal compliance, environmental preservation, human rights, workers' rights protection, and adherence to the *Modern Slaver Act.* Audits, random checks, and blacklisting are used to enforce this approach. Gucci also invested in promoting know-how formation in the Florentine area, facilitated business networks, and provided small and micro-businesses with guarantees and certifications, based on their quality and reliability, to have access to bank loans and, thus, invest in innovation.

Counterfeiting and the adequate protection by national and European laws of what is significantly manufactured *in* Italy are well-known challenges. However, another crucial challenge is to push the manufacturing ecosystem physically based in Italy to be transparent, reliable, and capable of effectively contributing to the hosting communities' wellbeing from a social, environmental, and cultural perspective. This sustainability challenge is at the core of any projection of a competitive "Made in Italy" in the future.

"Made in Italy" and the digital transformation: Reshaping the essence of luxury

Connected to the sustainability challenge, the digitalization challenge represents "a hard new reality" (Barton et al., 2016) for many luxury firms, creating visible tensions between the notion of luxury exclusivity and the hardly controllable digital access to luxury brands. Digital transformation is said necessary in luxury (Mastropetrou & Bithas, 2021 to enable transparency, storytelling, and innovative experiences, going well beyond the definition of engaging social media strategies.

Diverse technologies and their synergies can make a difference in the luxury industry. For instance, blockchain technologies were investigated, fostering traceability and transparency in the supply chains. However, organizational and cultural constraints emerged (de Boissieu, Kondrateva, Baudier, & Ammi, 2021). Luxury brand and retail management were digitally contaminated (Pentina et al., 2018), not only through developing online retailing but also integrating on-site and online retailing toward innovative brand experiences (Rovai, 2016). The challenge of creating a personalized digital experience comparable to the in-store quality standards is nowadays evident and recognized in the luxury industry (McKinsey, 2020).

"Made in Italy" luxury companies moved toward digitalization well before non-luxury firms by developing their online channels for e-commerce (Pambianco and Accademia del Lusso, 2018). There is a critical need for significant financial investments to fully exploit the digitalization potential and define innovative and cutting-edge ways to integrate digitalization in luxury management and marketing (Iannilli, 2014). The financial aspect is especially relevant within the Italian industrial network of small-sized companies (Carcano & Lojacono, 2018) in need of functional upgrades (Dei Ottati, 2009).

According to some, the "Made in Italy" brands have generally lagged in terms of deploying multichannel and omnichannel strategies to personalize product, service, and experience. It is not only a matter of adopting digital tools but also a matter of developing new forms of storytelling through digitally orientated languages (Scarpellini, 2019) and the combination of diverse available technologies. Historically, the distinctive trait of Italian luxury retailing has been envisioning the retail as a "creative filter … an act of styling" (Iannilli, 2014) and it is worth asking how and to what extent this "Made in Italy" trait can be valuably enhanced and re-envisioned through digitalization.

Luxury and "Made in Italy": Emerging paths of inquiry

The "Made in Italy" concept's dimensions and assets mobilize powerful imaginaries about places and the modalities to conceive and manufacture a product, to use and make such a product part of a distinctive and appealing lifestyle. This represents the basis for the concept's contribution to distinctive luxury brand building. In a transitioning industry, where luxury firms need to address key challenges, including sustainability and digitalization, the potential of "Made in Italy" is untapped and must be framed. Previous sections explored the rich, versatile, and even controversial nature of "Made in Italy", drawing attention to tensions that may represent potential entry points for reinterpreting "Made in Italy" and its role in luxury.

Such tensions emerge from the juxtaposition of stories and facts in "Made in Italy" management and marketing. The epic and mythological narratives of "Made in Italy" crystallized in fragments that, rooted in customers' minds as stereotypes, represent partial (constructed) versions of "Made in Italy". These instrumentally hide factual sides that can be particularly valuable in current and future markets if rediscovered and recombined with the consolidated traits of "Made in Italy".

Experimental approaches to leveraging "Made in Italy" are necessary. Repetitive patterns of exploitation, coinciding with the adoption of a pre-given "Made in Italy" script, is certainly the easiest and most immediate way to extract value from it. On the other hand, however, innovative – and risky – modalities to fully exploit this lever are necessary to develop the full potential of "Made in Italy".

At least three areas of inquiry on the "Made in Italy" in the transitioning luxury industry provide some starting points to understand the emerging business practices and sustainability models, revealing the potential trajectories of the evolution of "Made in Italy".

The first broad area of inquiry concerns the *relationship and synergies between heritage and innovation*. "Made in Italy" was framed as heritage, more specifically the country's cultural heritage, nurtured by history and authenticity as repositories of assets for luxury brand building. There is more than an impulse to protect "Made in Italy" heritage according to the cultural heritage protection mission. This is necessary as the normative protection and entrepreneurial mission to preserve "Made in Italy" as a collective identity are essential mechanisms for maintaining the concept "alive". In this frame, however, it is important to stress how innovation represents a way to protect and preserve the "Made in Italy" heritage, avoiding its crystallization as a close set of pre-given narratives which may struggle to assist luxury in its transition. This aligns with Miuccia Prada's warning: "In Europe we have to retain values – there is so much history. But how can it survive, unless there is a contemporary way to show our history in a way that young people get it?" (Miuccia Prada, 2010, quoted in Pike, 2015). The heritage-innovation relationship is at the core of all the contemporary challenges "Made in Italy" faces, including the sustainability challenge, for it to be a "living heritage".

"Made in Italy" imaginaries and facts offer contrasts to build on, such as craftsmanship and technology, history, and "the practice of modernity" (Segre-Reinach, 2015), romanticized industrial forms and critical societal challenges in the contemporary world (i.e., human wellbeing), the digital and the physical content of productions, or finally "innate talent" (Segre-Reinach, 2010) and built know-how and constant research. Firms working on original combinations of these extremes can evolve from a mere exploitative appropriation of "Made in Italy" to a co-creative approach constantly rejuvenating "Made in Italy" values.

The second area of inquiry concerns *the relationship between the country image and the evolution of a "living" "Made in Italy"*. The country image nurtures "Made in Italy", and its updating, thickening, and sophistication are the engine of the country-of-origin concept's evolution. The consolidated images of the *Bel Paese*, combined with the "bello e ben fatto" and the "dolce vita", do need to be irrigated by the values that are lived in the country and engage the national community (Pasquinelli, 2021). Contemporary lifestyles, values, and the concrete issues encountered and faced when living and working in Italian cities and territories are vital sources of imaginaries and facts, potentially expanding and reinterpreting the "Made in Italy" authenticating narratives. Even the darker sides or the less symbolically appealing sides (at least conventionally) of "Made in Italy" can fruitfully coexist with the romanticized aspects of "Made in Italy" in the frame of distinctive sustainability routes that, while contributing to local communities, can be understood and valued by global luxury consumers.

The third area of inquiry concerns *the relationship between sustainability and digitalization*, investigating how and to what extent digitalization may enhance a sustainable "Made in Italy". There is growing interest in digital technologies boosting traceability, transparency, and the luxury consumer experience. In this frame, there is room to focus on the key sustainability challenges characterizing Made in Italy, including social and environmental challenges. How and to what extent do technologies enable luxury firms to innovatively address sustainability challenges? How and under what (organizational, financial, cultural…) conditions may digital technologies boost social and environmental sustainability? Technologies can make customers experience (and learn about) the manufacturing process, giving a thorough and first-hand insight into luxury productions, their cycles, meanings, and implications of producing for companies, their workers, and the local communities. Digitalization and a sustainability culture in the luxury industry should be investigated, creating awareness and expectations of the impacts of luxury as well as a fertile ground for novel products and solutions.

References

Aiello, G., Donvito, R., Godey, B., Pederzoli, D., Wiedmann, K. P., Hennigs, N., … Singh, R. (2009). An international perspective on luxury brand and country-of-origin effect. *Journal of Brand Management, 16*(5–6), 323–337. https://doi.org/10.1057/bm.2008.52.

Bain & Company. (2019). *Bain & company luxury study* (18th ed.). Bain & Company, Fondazione Altagamma.

Barton, C., Bonelli, F., Gurzki, H., Pianon, N., Tsusaka, M., & Mei-Pchtler, A. (2016). *Digital or die: The choice for luxury brands*. Boston, MA: Boston Consulting Group. https://www.bcg.com/it-it/publications/2016/digital-or-die-choice-luxury-brands

Bellini, N., & Pasquinelli, C. (2016). Urban brandscape as value ecosystem: The cultural destination strategy of fashion brands. *Journal of Place Branding and Public Diplomacy*, 12(5–6), 5–16.

Bilkey, W. J., & Nes, E. (1982). Country-of-origin effects on product evaluations. *Journal of International Business Studies*, *13*(1), 89–112.

Carcano, L., & Lojacono, G. (2018). *Made in Italy industries: Managerial issues and best practices*. Milano, Italy: Egea.

Cheah, I., Zainol, Z., & Phau, I. (2016). Conceptualising country-of-ingredient authenticity of luxury brands. *Journal of Business Research*, *69*(12), 5819–5826.

Cimatti, B., Campana, G., & Carluccio, L. (2017). Eco design and sustainable manufacturing in fashion: A case study in the luxury personal accessories industry. *Procedia Manufacturing*, *8*, 393–400.

Corbetta, G., Quarato, F., & Minichilli, A. (2018). Dieci anni di capitalismo familiare. X Osservatorio AUB. AIDAF Italian Family Business, Bocconi, University.

Dallabona, A. (2014). Narratives of Italian craftsmanship and the luxury fashion industry: Representations of Italianicity in discourses of production. *Global Fashion Brands: Style, Luxury & History*, *1*(1), 215–228.

de Boissieu, E., Kondrateva, G., Baudier, P., & Ammi, C. (2021). The use of blockchain in the luxury industry: Supply chains and the traceability of goods. *Journal of Enterprise Information Management*, *34*(5), 1318–1338.

Dei Ottati, G. (2009). An industrial district facing the challenges of globalisation: Prato Today. *European Planning Studies*, *17*(12), 1817–1835.

Deserti, A. (2014). Shaping the identity of Italian fashion brands: The role of design between tangible and intangible. *Journal of Design, Creative Process & Fashion Industry*, *6*(2), 243–261.

Ferrero-Regis, T. (2008). Fatto in Italia: Refashioning Italy. *Journal of Multidisciplinary International Studies*, *5*(2), 1–17.

Goffee, T. (2019). The importance of 'Made in'. *FutureBrand*. Retrieved from https://www.futurebrand.com/news/2019/the-importance-of-made-in.

Godey, B., Pederzoli, D., Aiello, G., Donvito, R., Chan, P., Oh, H., … Weitz, B. (2012). Brand and country-of-origin effect on consumers' decision to purchase luxury products. *Journal of Business Research*, *65*(10), 1461–1470.

Guercini, S., Bernal, P. M., & Prentice, C. (2018). New marketing in fashion e-commerce. *Journal of Global Fashion Marketing*, *9*(1), 1–8.

Harrison, R. (2013). *Heritage: Critical approaches*. New York, NY: Routledge.

Hadjimichalis, C. (2006). The end of the third Italy as we knew it? *Antipode*, *38*(1), 82–106.

Insch, G. S., & McBride, B. (2004). The impact of country-of-origin cues on consumer perceptions of product quality: A binational test of the decomposed country-of-origin construct. *Journal of Business Research*, *57*(3), 256–265.

Holt, D. B. (2002). Why do brands cause trouble? A dialectical theory of consumer culture and branding. *Journal of Consumer Research*, *29*, 70–90.

Hu, S., Henninger, C. E., Boardman, R., & Ryding, D. (2019). Challenging current fashion business models: Entrepreneurship through access-based consumption in the second-hand luxury garment sector within a circular economy. In: M. Gardetti, & S. Muthu (Eds.), *Sustainable luxury. Environmental footprints and eco-design of products and processes*. Springer, Singapore. https://doi.org/10.1007/978-981-13-0623-5_3

Iannilli, V. M. (2014). Retailing Made in Italy: An evolutionary reading towards emerging paradigms. *Journal of Design, Creative Process & the Fashion Industry*, *6*(2), 201–220.

Iraldo, F., & Trenti, S. (2018). Segnali di economia circolare nel settore della moda. The Green Economy Observatory, Università Commerciale Luigi Bocconi-Intesa San Paolo.

Kapferer, J. N. (2009). The specificity of luxury management: Turning marketing upside down. *Journal of Brand Management, 16*(5–6), 11–22.

Kapferer, J. N., & Bastien, V. (2009). *The luxury strategy: Break the rules of marketing to build luxury brands.* London: Kogan Page.

Kapferer, J. N., & Michaut-Denizeau, A. (2020). Are millennials really more sensitive to sustainable luxury? A cross-generational international comparison of sustainability consciousness when buying luxury. *Journal of Brand Management, 27*(1), 35–47.

Ko, E., & Megehee, C. M. (2012). Fashion marketing of luxury brands: Recent research issues and contributions. *Journal of Business Research, 65*(10), 1395–1398.

Kotler, P., & Gertner, D. (2002). Country as brand, product, and beyond: A place marketing and brand management perspective. *Journal of Brand Management, 9*, 249–261.

Jansson, J., & Power, D. (2010). Fashioning a global city: Global city brand channels in the fashion and design industries. *Regional Studies, 44*(7), 889–904.

Kohler, G., & Perrino, S. (2017). Narrating "Made in Italy". Brand and responsibility in Italian corporations. *Narrative Inquiry, 27*(1), 187–207.

Lee, M., Ko, E., Lee, S., & Kim, K. (2015). Understanding luxury disposition. *Psychology and Marketing, 32*(4), 467–480.

Macchion, L., Moretto, A., Caniato, F., Caridi, M., Danese, P., & Vinelli, A. (2015). Production and supply network strategies within the fashion industry. *International Journal of Production Economics, 163*(May), 173–188.

McKinsey (2018). The influence of Gen Z – the first generation of true digital natives – is expanding. *McKinsey & Company.* Retrieved from https://www.mckinsey.com/industries/consumer-packaged-goods/our-insights/true-gen-generation-z-and-its-implications-for-companies.

McKinsey (2020). A perspective for the luxury-goods industry during – and after – coronavirus. Retrieved from https://www.mckinsey.com/industries/retail/our-insights/a-perspective-for-the-luxury-goods-industry-during-and-after-coronavirus.

Merlo, E., & Perugini, M. (2015). The revival of fashion brands between marketing and history: The case of the Italian fashion company Pucci. *Journal of Historical Research in Marketing,* 7(1), 91–112.

Naeem, M., & Ozuem, W. (2021). The role of social media in internet banking transition during COVID-19 pandemic: Using multiple methods and sources in qualitative research. *Journal of Retailing and Consumer Services, 60*(May), 1–15.

Paciolla, R., & Mai, L.-W. (2011). The impact of Italianate on consumers' brand perceptions of luxury brands. In A. Bradshaw, E. Hackley, C. Maclaran, & P. Duluth (Eds.), *European advances in consumer research* (Vol. 9, pp. 360–366). Duluth, MN: Association for Consumer Research.

Papadopoulos, N., Cleveland, M., Bartikowski, B., & Yaprak, A. (2018). Of countries, places and product/brand place associations: An inventory of dispositions and issues relating to place image and its effects. *Journal of Product and Brand Management, 27*(7), 735–753.

Pasquinelli, C. (2021). Italy. In J. Freore (Ed.), *Nation branding in Europe.* London: Routledge.

Pentina, I., Guilloux, V., & Micu, A. C. (2018). Exploring social media engagement behaviours in the context of luxury brands. *Journal of Advertising, 47*(1), 55–69.

Pieraccini, S. (2021). 'Ndrangheta in Toscana, rifiuti tossici nelle concerie per il fondo stradale. Sole 24 Ore. Retrieved from https://www.ilsole24ore.com/art/-ndrangheta-toscana-rifiuti-tossici-concerie-il-fondo-stradale-AEvDqWB.

Pike, A. (2015). *Origination: The geographies of brands and branding*. New York, NY: Wiley.

Power, D., & Scott, A. (2004). *Cultural industries and the production of culture*. London: Routledge.

Rovai, S. (2016). *Luxury the Chinese way. New competitive scenarios*. London: Palgrave Macmillan.

Scarpellini, E. (2019). *Italian Fashion since 1945*. Singapore: Springer.

Segre-Reinach, S. (2010). If you speak fashion you speak Italian: Notes on present day Italian fashion identity. *Critical Studies in Fashion & Beauty, 1*(2), 203–215.

Segre-Reinach, S. (2015). The meaning of 'Made in Italy' in fashion. *Craft + Design Enquiry, 7*, 1–17.

Sun, Y., Wang, R., Cao, D., & Lee, R. (2021). Who are social media influencers for luxury fashion consumption of the Chinese Gen Z? Categorisation and empirical examination. *Journal of Fashion Marketing and Management, 26*(4), 603–621.

Taylor, J. (2001). Authenticity and sincerity in tourism. *Annals of Tourism Research, 28*(1), 7–26.

Thakor, M. V., & Lavack, A. M. (2003). Effect of perceived brand origin associations on consumer perceptions of quality. *Journal of Product and Brand Management, 12*, 394–407.

Thompson, C., Rindfleisch, A., & Arsel, Z. (2006). Emotional branding and the strategic value of the doppelganger brand image. *Journal of Marketing, 70*, 50–64.

Tokatli, N. (2013). Doing a Gucci: The transformation of an Italian fashion firm into a global powerhouse in a 'Los Angeles-izing' world. *Journal of Economic Geography, 13*(2), 239–255.

Tokatli, N. (2014). 'Made in Italy? Who cares!' Prada's new economic geography. *Geoforum, 54*(July), 1–9.

Zhang, B., & Kim, J. H. (2013). Luxury fashion consumption in China: Factors affecting attitude and purchase intent. *Journal of Retailing and Consumer Services, 20*(1), 68–79.

2 Consumers' Committment to Brand Recognition

Diesel Sustainability Strategy for "Responsible Living" & the Second-Hand

Serena Rovai[1] *and Ian Phau*[2]
[1]Excelia Business School
[2]Curtin University

Background

Diesel was founded by Renzo Rosso in 1978 and, together with Maison Margiela, Marni, Jil Sander, Viktor & Rolf and the companies Staff International S.p.A. and Brave Kid S.r.l., is currently part of Only the Brave (OTB) Group. In 2021, Diesel achieved an important milestone by launching its Second-Hand project, proposing a carefully curated selection of Diesel pre-owned denim, meticulously restored, renewed, and available in Italian selected stores and online throughout Europe. Through this buyback and resale model, entirely and directly managed by the brand, Diesel extends its denim lifecycle and increase Diesel products' use.

Second Hand represents a step toward the circularity of the fashion system and through this initiative Diesel gives customers the opportunity to actively participate in its sustainability strategy "For Responsible Living" that was launched in January 2020, a commitment to take actions for the benefit of current and future generations. Indeed Diesel's initiative starts from an assumption that in a world of 7.9 billion inhabitants, each person owns an average of six pairs of jeans. Buying and selling used denim, therefore, becomes a creative and stimulating way to take a step toward new and more circular business models. The refurbished Diesel Second-Hand garments become an iconic garment for some customers that reinforces the brand identity and increases the bonding between the brand and the customer.

The Second-Hand market has been on the incline for years, with no signs of slowing down. Fashion and luxury brands in the denim sector have followed the trend, each recently launching its own take on a resale program. Diesel Second Hand is becoming increasingly concrete as a major achievement of the brand sustainability strategy and fully aligned with the broader "Be Responsible. Be Brave" launched by OTB Group in the second half of 2021. On top of remarking a strong commitment toward circularity, OTB Group set specific objectives by 2030 in terms of environmental protection,

DOI: 10.4324/9781003305095-4

attention to the product, and social commitment. As an example, in August 2021, OTB announced to have joined Zero Discharge of Hazardous Chemicals' (ZDHC) Roadmap to Zero Program: an international initiative, which promotes sustainable chemical management along the value chains of the textile, leather, and footwear sectors.

In addition to Second Hand and in line with its sustainability journey and goals, Diesel launched the Diesel Library within its Spring/Summer 2022 collections: an evergreen line of genderless garments which embodies a 360 degrees approach to sustainability since all fabrics, treatments, and trims applied to Diesel Library items have lower environmental impact compared to more traditional alternatives. This project led Diesel to include a much higher percentage of recycled, organic, and lower impact material, together with more responsible cotton within the Denim collection. Furthermore, the brand implemented innovative treatments that allowed for conspicuous water and chemical reductions as well as less impactful alternatives to traditional washing and finishing procedures (e.g., alternative pumice stone, abrasive drum, nebulization, ozone, laser, etc.).

In this context, Andrea Rosso, son of Renzo Rosso, has been appointed as Diesel Sustainability Ambassador and has led and supervised the initiative "Diesel Upcycling For", which was fully aligned with his values and the idea of Diesel's contribution to a more sustainable future. Son of art, born and raised in the Diesel family, he has always had a natural inclination for the fashion business and how everyday life and fashion can contribute to a better environment. In this perspective, in 2014 he also launched his fashion line MYAR: a collection of used military garments that he personally searches on the stalls of vintage markets and in old warehouses, in search of details, fabrics, and accessories no longer in production. After being sartorially remodeled, each MYAR garment acquires a contemporary fit, preserving the history of its past. Andrea's commitment and vision to a more sustainable lifestyle and attitude fueled Diesel "For Responsible Living" strategy and the relevance of Second Hand.

Second-hand luxury

Many studies have specified that the "green fashion" can enhance brand image, improve fashion companies' competitiveness, and retain higher volumes of customers Luxury product manufacturers have started to consider not only the quality and uniqueness of their products but also the ethical factors to meet their consumers' expectations with environmental protection. If past research highlighted how sustainability was irrelevant for fashion and appeared to be incompatible with luxury (Dean, 2018), at present the situation has substantially been modified. The pandemic scenario has accelerated the sustainable call and luxury and fashion brands are responding with a specific and diversified engagement. And, in the sustainable call, the Second-Hand fashion market is gaining incredible momentum.

Since the early 1990s, the industry has rapidly expanded due to heightened interest from consumers, investors, and retailers, and, at the moment, Second-Hand luxury fashion is estimated at over 20 billion euros with an annual growth of 12%, especially in Europe (Hansen, 2010). In addition, the fast growth of digital platforms increased the global image of preowned fashion garments. The number of Second-Hand, vintage, and thrift stores opening, particularly those offering online resale, is growing fast. To add to this, EBay and Facebook flea market groups also reach tens of thousands of consumers who are actively buying and selling used goods (Sihvonen & Turunen, 2016). The full size of the resale market is challenging to estimate, because actors in the market may also be private consumers. However, the evidence shows that high-quality resale is a multi-billion-dollar industry and is among the fastest-growing segments in retail.

Second-Hand garments and consumption have thus been investigated in different empirical contexts (Edbring, Lehner, & Mont, 2016; Ferraro, Sands, & Brace-Govan, 2016) and by different disciplines, including marketing, consumer research, textile and clothing studies, design management, and social science studies (Cassidy & Bennett, 2012; Cervellon, Carey, & Harms, 2012; Veenstra & Kuipers, 2013). Prior investigations have explored the topic of Second-Hand fashion from different perspectives and levels of analysis, such as consumption, business, society, and culture (Isla, 2013; Edbring et al., 2016; Xu, Chen, Burman, & Zhao, 2014). The growth of the Second-Hand luxury market is motivated by new consuming approaches in choosing to wear pre-used garments (e.g., Ferraro et al., 2016); in particular in having a new responsible attitude, in looking for unique goods (Cervellon et al., 2012; Turunen & Leipämaa-Leskinen, 2015), but also in affording normally unreachable luxury products (Amatulli, Pino, De Angelis, & Cascio, 2018). As a result, an increasing interest in understanding consumers' Second-Hand and vintage luxury shopping has appeared in academia (Amatulli et al., 2018; Cervellon et al., 2012) as well as the meaning associated with pre-used luxury (Turunen & Leipämaa-Leskinen, 2015). Second-Hand luxury shoppers appear to be motivated by diverse goals such as functional, psychological, and emotional as well as symbolic.

Second-Hand luxury goods, in equal measure to brand-new luxury, might be used as a basis for self-extension and self-representation. This far, research has focused on consumers as purchasers of preowned luxury and has neglected an important actor on the market: the sellers. Yet, the particularity of the Second-Hand market is that it operates out with the locus of control of luxury brands (in most cases) and is driven by the disposal of preowned goods. Sourcing is a key factor of success for Second-Hand luxury intermediaries. The Second-Hand market involves transactions between purchasers and sellers, hence the word "Second-Hand consumers" which covers multiple realities. To contribute to the existing luxury literature, we aim to understand luxury sellers' behavior.

Second-Hand luxury is defined through the characteristics of the products transacted: Second-Hand luxury products are previously owned, generally used, luxury branded items (Turunen & Leipämaa-Leskinen, 2015) that are sold on alternative "secondary" channels. Thus, the transactions often lack the experiential facets offered through conventional luxury channels (Cervellon & Vigreux, 2018). The price of those goods is usually lower than when purchased First Hand in the designated luxury boutiques (to the exception of certain limited editions and rare iconic models). As an example, on the platform "Vestiaire Collective", in 2019 prices of Second-Hand luxury are between 30% and 70% lower than the price of the goods purchased First Hand. The principal distinction between Second-Hand luxury and First-Hand luxury remains the price accessibility of the goods and the extension it affords the product lifecycle (Cervellon et al., 2012).

The concept of vintage overlaps with Second-Hand luxury, but the terms are not interchangeable. Vintage refers to age, to history, to periods, or specific past eras (Cervellon et al., 2012; Gerval, 2008). Vintage products are testimonies of the past. Most Second-Hand platforms label "vintage" goods that are at least older than ten years. These goods derive their value from their rarity on the Second-Hand market. They might be branded, or not, by luxury brands. Often, sellers of vintage goods are professionals and specialists of certain eras (60s and 70s). Second-Hand and vintage items do not necessarily attract the same profile of consumers: Cervellon et al. (2012) conclude that Second-Hand purchases relate to price-consciousness and frugality, and Kessous and Valette-Florence (2019) added that eco-friendliness, status-driven bargain-hunting, and even social-climbing, might also be determinants of Second-Hand luxury purchases. Vintage consumption, conversely, is driven by nostalgia, need for uniqueness, and timelessness (Amatulli et al., 2018; Cervellon et al., 2012).

Second-Hand luxury goods, including vintage, have symbolic properties that can help buyers express and enhance their personal and social identities. Luxury acquisition and usage might be justified by the expression and enhancement of the social self, projecting status to others, for instance, but also of the private self, related to hedonic and experiential motivations. Berthon, Pitt, Parent, and Berthon (2009) put forward this personal and experiential dimension of luxury, which is often overshadowed by the symbolic and social dimensions. According to Vigneron and Johnson (1999), luxury consumers derive self-directed benefits when acquiring and using luxury products: intrinsic, sensory, and esthetic, pleasure (perceived emotional value), and the feeling of attaining perfection (perceived quality value). Hagtvedt and Patrick (2009: 609) go further in defining a luxury brand as "one that has premium products, provides pleasure as a central benefit, and connects with consumers on an emotional level".

In addition, with Second-Hand consumption, the acquisition of luxury goods may also drive emotional benefits related to treasure hunting (Amatulli et al., 2018; Turunen & Leipämaa-Leskinen, 2015), and the intrinsic pleasure of possessing a high-quality product, purchased at a lower price (Cervellon et al., 2012). From the sellers' perspective, the experiential and personal drivers of Second-Hand consumption are theorized mainly through disposal behavior, where selling represents one aspect of disposal. Lee, Ko, Lee, and Kim (2015, p. 467) point out that selling is often chosen as a method to dispose of luxury goods as "luxury goods encounter a greater amount of perceived financial and psychological costs due to their high price and strong symbolic values". More precisely, Lee et al. (2015) suggest that cognitive (quality and economic) and emotional (symbolic and experiential) values engendered by luxury possessions create a perceived switching cost upon disposition. This suggests that disposing of luxury goods through selling is a meaningful process that has a personal resonance with the seller. If the product carries a negatively charged meaning from the past, the disposition might bring relief, when the product carries positive memories, owners might enter into divestment rituals to wash the personal meanings out of the good. We contribute to the luxury literature by investigating the meaning and the personal value of selling preowned luxury goods.

Most of the studies and research works in the field focus on consumers' motivations to purchase and own a Second Hand but also some analyze consumer motivational factors, or consumer experiences (Guiot & Roux, 2010; Xu Chen, Burman, & Zhao, 2014). The findings related to product-related motivations are mainly associated with economic motivations and critical motivations even though sustainability is emphasized as one of the most important critical motivations, However, a link between environmental awareness and the desire to purchase Second-Hand goods is still to be explored (Cervellon et al., 2012; McNeill & Moore, 2015; Yan, Bae, & Xu, 2015). Aaker (1996) defined brand awareness as the outstanding feature of the brand in the mind of the consumer, categorizing six different types of brand awareness whose brand recognition is part of. Alongside, Keller (2003) recognized brand awareness as customers' capability to recognize the brand as identified by their capability to distinguish the brand in several situations and related it to specific associations in their memory. However, Second-Hand phenomenon had never been analyzed and included in customer brand recognition until now and thus the relevance of this study.

Case study – Diesel

Diesel S.p.A., better known as Diesel, is an Italian manufacturer of men's, women's, and children's clothing. The company also offers accessories, eyewear and jewelry, fragrances, interior design collections, and automotive items. The company was founded in 1978 by Renzo Rosso and his former boss Adriano Goldschmied (founder of the famous AG Jeans company) and Renzo launched its international marketing policy in 1991. The company is now headquartered in Breganze, in the province of Vicenza, Veneto, in northeastern Italy, and counts many subsidiaries throughout Europe, Asia, and North America. Diesel's goal is to create the most forward-thinking and innovative denim on the market. As the oil crisis broke out around the world and Diesel became an alternative fuel, Renzo envisioned his brand as an alternative denim company, as opposed to the already famous casual fashion giants of the time. Since its launch, Diesel has grown from an early denim pioneer to a casual fashion staple, establishing itself as a true alternative to the already established luxury market. Despite its growth, Diesel's philosophy has remained the same: a brand that supports passion, individuality, and freedom of expression.

In January 2020, Diesel launched its holistic sustainability strategy called "Diesel for Responsible Living", which demonstrates its comprehensive commitment to act for the benefit of current and future generations, ensuring Diesel's continued success in a changing world, based on four pillars: Be Alternative; Stand for the Planet; Celebrate Individuality and Promote Integrity. Diesel is an open and inclusive work environment with more than 3,000 employees worldwide, enriched by the diversity expressed by its community. Among these employees, belonging to 67 different nationalities, a percentage of 58% are women. The company is based on values of respect and responsibility, and one of the most important tasks is to constantly instill and strengthen the culture of sustainability throughout the organization. In order to support young generations and creative talents, Diesel collaborates with more than 33 universities and academies around the world, including the Polytechnic di Milano, the European Institute of Design, the University "Ca' Foscari" in Venice, the Central Saint Martins University and the Royal College of Art in London, Bunka Fashion College. In line with its commitment toward people and promoting the implementation of higher social and environmental standards throughout its supply chain, Diesel's suppliers are invited to sign the OTB Group Code of Ethics and Code of Conduct, which set forth the principles and guidelines that should inspire and guide the behavior and actions not only of Diesel but also of all those with whom Diesel does business and has relationships. Within their OTB holding, created by Renzo Rosso, a foundation was created to finance projects that fight against social inequalities in the world. Among these projects, there is Pink Shuttle, a free transportation service exclusively for women in Kabul. OTB also helps the victims of the COVID crisis, the victims of the war in Ukraine and other wars in the world for example.

Along with other brands such as Maison Margiela, Viktor & Rolf, Marni, and Amiri, Diesel is part of the international fashion group OTB, which launched the Group sustainability strategy in July 2021 "Be Responsible. Be Brave" focusing on three main areas: caring for the environment, focusing on products and social engagement. In addition, OTB Group, together with all its brands, joined the ZDHC Foundation's Roadmap to Zero Program, an international initiative, which promotes sustainable chemical management along the value chains of the textile, leather, and footwear sectors and, most recently, the Group adhered to Leather Working Group. OTB Group has set ambitious targets such as having its own operations by 2030 climate neutral. To achieve this, as a goal, Diesel has proposed several circular economy initiatives, including Diesel Second Hand (recollection in all Italian Diesel monobrand stores and resale in Milan, Florence, and Rome stores in addition to online resale throughout Europe on its e-commerce website).

The Diesel develops specific guidelines for creative and sourcing teams to guide their practices, promote a policy of sustainability, encourage the implementation of the most responsible options currently available, and seek alternative solutions consistent with Diesel's environmental and social values. Part of this commitment is illustrated by joining, in February 2020, The Fashion Pact, a global alliance of fashion brands committed to environmental goals. In order to reduce the environmental impact of clothing production, Diesel is working to transition its main production materials to more sustainable alternatives, while maintaining its Diesel DNA. In fact, the first capsule collection launched on Earth Day 2020, a "Respectful Denim with a Diesel DNA" illustrates these ambitions. All pieces have retained the characteristics of DIESEL's iconic line of premium vintage denim but have been created using innovative techniques that significantly reduce the use of water and chemicals during the production process. Each pair of jeans is treated with a minimal amount of GreenScreen-certified chemicals, and the water used is reduced by up to 40% compared to our conventional washing methods. Andrea Rosso, Sustainability Ambassador – recalls the internal process toward sustainability of the Diesel brand. From an in-depth internal scanning to implement a comprehensive approach to sustainability not only planet but also people related to the continuous focus on training to let company employees be aware of the importance of sustainability and to better understand what sustainability means. In relation to Diesel's specific engagement to "providing high-quality clothing and accessories around the world and being committed to ensuring that products are manufactured in an ethical way, Diesel has implemented company-wide actions to reduce the environmental impact of the clothing manufacturing process, which is recognized as one of the most polluting industrial activities in the world. It is important to emphasize that these measures also aim to change the habits of employees by encouraging them to modify their personal lifestyles. Diesel seeks to have an impact on a larger scale and not only on the environmental aspect. For this purpose, the founder of the company has created the OTB Foundation. By participating in projects that help minorities in difficulty such as women in the Middle East and communities' victims of war in their own countries, Diesel proves that it can be an important factor in social change.

In February 2020, Diesel also launched a full line of recycled products, which will be marketed as Diesel Upcycling For. For Diesel, upcycling, or smart recycling, is about transforming products, waste, and unsold goods into new, higher value products. The upcycled collection was branded with an abstract representation of the universally recognized recycling icon and the logo of the brand or designer invited by DIESEL, to show how creative minds can repurpose what we already have. The first version of the Upcycling line was created from unsold items, old collections, and Diesel prototypes, which the company gave new life and style with a 55DSL twist. The result is a limited-edition collection of 5,055 pieces made from limited resources. Andrea Rosso evidenced – in his role as brand Sustainability Ambassador – that "the fact that we are talking about Second Hand is already a positive recognition for the brand, it means that the company has a longevity, it makes products that have durability and a story to tell, a heritage to share by providing an extensive life to the products and consequently to the brand".

With the first 900 jeans collected and re-conditioned, Diesel announced the launch of their innovative Diesel Second Hand. "For the brand, buying Second Hand is something to be celebrated and Diesel invites customers to join the resale revolution, making Second Hand as good as new", Diesel stated. The preowned jeans recollecting phase was following a specific process to ensure a small footprint; those were shipped to a facility only 200 miles away from Diesel's headquarters in Breganze, Italy. In the facility, the jeans garments were washed and sanitized, fixed if necessary with small repairs and a customized "Second Hand" logo is printed on each garment. In the first phase of its Second-Hand pilot Diesel used an innovative textile technology – Polygiene's Viral Off® and OdorCrunch® a combined treatment featuring anti-microbial and odor-resistant properties to win the potential stereotypes and – biases of some consumers' segments.

During a recent interview, Andrea Rosso has stressed how an emotional attachment to a product that shoppers remember, and is part of their life, is extremely important for the brand as the fact that brand's products gave to the customer something is a fact that it gives the right credits for the durability, manufacturing to the brand as well as an extensive life with the second hand". The buyback program will continue to remain active in Italy, with plans to expand to other countries, while the reselling is available in Europe through Diesel e-commerce website. Fitting into the brand's sustainability strategy dubbed, "For Responsible Living", Diesel hopes to keep products in use for years to come. Andrea Rosso and his team also enhanced the relevance for Diesel "as second-hand or vintage attitude from younger customers and their passion to even collect the vintage pieces" can be seen as a further commitment to the brand in the long term "and a recognition of the longevity of a product" that represent a positive aspect for brand recognition.

Conclusion

As previously evidenced, Second Hand has thus been investigated in numerous experimental contexts (Edbring et al., 2016; Ferraro et al., 2016) and by diverse disciplines with various perspectives of analysis. However, as the expansion of the Second-Hand luxury market was mainly driven by the new consuming segments and attitudes (e.g., Ferraro et al., 2016), most of the research was focusing on the importance to understand the consumers' profiling and behavior (Amatulli et al., 2018) and thus neglecting the brand perspective.

The Second-Hand market growth – reaching 33 billion euros in the last year – is not only a phenomenon led by specific segments of the consuming market. The increasing demand for "pre-loved or pre-owned fashion goods" appears to be one of the core trends emerging from the luxury fashion market in relation to a different perspective from the main players in the sector. In fact, the Second-Hand phenomenon can also be an effective way, for luxury and fashion brands, to show their engagement with the new sustainable call. As highlighted by research by McKinsey (2022), luxury Second Hand has also been considered an effective channel to better understand its main consumer segment. In addition, Second-Hand sales also represent a supplementary supply network in the expanding luxury market.

However, the luxury and fashion ecosystem are showing how their brands are still hesitating to directly integrate a Second Hand into their core business, probably doubtful of the impact on their main lines and on their brand identity and recognition. The case of Diesel shows us how a successful Italian fashion brand is effectively answering the new sustainable call through a specific choice to adhere to the Second-Hand trend while enhancing its brand recognition. In so doing, evidencing how in the Keller's brand awareness and recognition perspective (2003), Second Hand can be defined as one of those situations that are enhancing customers' ability not only to distinguish the brand but to associate specifically in their memory.

What is clear is while other luxury brands seem to be jumping into the bandwagon of Second Hand, Diesel comes across as one that embraced the whole concept and integrated every element across other functions of the business. Diesel is probably the first and only luxury brand that introduced a Second-Hand arm to the core business. It also means their initiative of actively collecting old denims and selling reconditioned products with pride and conviction could be a lesson for others to learn.

Acknowledgment

The authors wish to thank you Diesel brand and in particular Andrea Rosso, Sustainability Ambassador at Diesel, and the Sustainability Team for their availability and involvement in the development of the case and information sharing.

References

Aaker, D. (1996). Measuring brand equity across products and markets. *California Management Review, 38*(3), 102–120. https://doi.org/10.2307/41165845

Amatulli, C., Pino, G., De Angelis, M., & Cascio, R. (2018). Understanding purchase determinants of luxury vintage products. *Psychology & Marketing, 35*(8), 616–624.

Berthon, P., Pitt, L., Parent, M., & Berthon, J. P. (2009). Aesthetics and ephemerality: Observing and preserving the luxury brand. *California management review, 52*(1), 45–66.

Cassidy, T. D., & Bennett, H. R. (2012). The rise of vintage fashion and the vintage consumer. *Fashion Practice, 4*(2), 239–261.

Cervellon, M. C., Carey, L., & Harms, T. (2012). Something old, something used: Determinants of women's purchase of vintage fashion vs second-hand fashion. *International Journal of Retail and Distribution Management, 40*(12), 956–974.

Cervellon, M. C., & Vigreux, E. (2018). Narrative and emotional accounts of second-hand luxury purchases along the customer journey. In *Vintage luxury fashion* (pp. 79–95). Palgrave Macmillan, Cham.

Dean, A. (2018). Everything is wrong: a search for order in the ethnometaphysical chaos of sustainable luxury fashion. *The Fashion Studies Journal*, 1–18.

Edbring, E. G., Lehner, M., & Mont, O. (2016). Exploring consumer attitudes to alternative models of consumption: Motivations and barriers. *Journal of Cleaner Production*, 123, 5–15.

Ferraro, C., Sands, S., & Brace-Govan, J. (2016). The role of fashionability in second-hand shopping motivations. *Journal of Retailing and Consumer Services, 32*, 262–268.

Gerval, O. (2008). *Fashion: Concept to catwalk*. London, UK: Bloomsbury.

Guiot, D., & Roux, D. (2010). A second-hand shoppers' motivation scale: Antecedents, consequences, and implications for retailers. *Journal of Retailing, 86*(4), 355–371.

Hansen, K. T. (2010). Secondhand clothing. In Eicher, J. (Ed.), *Berg encyclopedia of world dress and fashion* (Vol. 10, pp. 232–237), Oxford, UK: Oxford University Press.

Hagtvedt, H., & Patrick, V. M. (2009). The broad embrace of luxury: Hedonic potential as a driver of brand extendibility. *Journal of Consumer Psychology, 19*(4), 608–618.

Isla, V. (2013). Investigating second-hand fashion trade and consumption in the Philippines: Expanding existing discourses. *Journal of Consumer Culture, 13*(3), 221240.

Keller, K. L. (2003). *Strategic brand management: Building, measuring, and managing brand equity*. Upper Saddle River, NJ: Prentice-Hall.

Kessous, A., & Valette-Florence, P. (2019). "From Prada to Nada": Consumers and their luxury products: A contrast between second-hand and first-hand luxury products. *Journal of Business Research, 102*, 313–327.

Lee, M., Ko, E., Lee, S., & Kim, K. (2015). Understanding luxury disposition. *Psychology & Marketing, 32*(4), 467–480.

McKinsey, (2020). "Is Luxury Resale the Future of Fashion?" Retrived from: https://www.mckinsey.com/industries/retail/our-insights/is-luxury-resale-the-future-of-fashion

McNeill, L., & Moore, R. (2015). Sustainable fashion consumption and the fast fashion conundrum: fashionable consumers and attitudes to sustainability in clothing choice. *International Journal of Consumer Studies, 39*(3), 212–222.

Rybas, N., & Gajjala, R. (2007). Developing cyberethnographic research methods for understanding digitally mediated identities. *Forum Qualitative Sozialforschung/Forum: Qualitative Social Research, 8*(3), Article 35.

Sihvonen, J., & Turunen, L. L. M. (2016). As good as new-valuing fashion brands in the online second-hand markets. *Journal of Product and Brand Management, 25*(3), 285–295.

Turunen, L. L. M. & Leipämaa-Leskinen, H. (2015). Pre-loved luxury: Identifying the meanings of second-hand luxury possessions. *Journal of Product & Brand Management, 24*(1), 57–65.

Veenstra, A., & Kuipers, G. (2013). It is not old fashioned, it is vintage, vintage fashion and the complexities of 21st century consumption practices. *Sociology Compass*, 7(5), 355–365.

Vigneron, F., & Johnson, L. W. (1999). A review and a conceptual framework of prestige-seeking consumer behavior. *Academy of marketing science review, 1*(1), 1–15.

Xu, Y., Chen, Y., Burman, R., & Zhao, H. (2014). Second-hand clothing consumption: A cross-cultural comparison between American and Chinese young consumers. *International Journal of Consumer Studies, 38*(6), 670–677.

3 Luxury and Sustainability in Shopping Experiences

Vogue Talents and the New Awareness for Sustainable Social Fashion

Jessica Antonios
American University of Beirut

Introduction

Talk of sustainability, natural preservation, and ecology has been around for decades. The uprise and uproar of consumers becoming more concerned with how businesses conduct their work, the materials they are using and so on and so forth, as well as the products they are buying, have set in motion a huge move into sustainable business processes and created the so-called Ethical Era of consumerism and sustainable consumer behavior requiring action to be taken by corporations to integrate sustainability into their business models (Carrigan et al., 2004). This so-called uproar on the consumer end touched every industry, wherein the fashion and luxury industry was no exception to the rule. Specifically, luxury consumers, who have been known to be exigent, hedonistic, elite, lavish, and extravagant in their spending, have moved away from conspicuous consumption to conscious, conscientious, and ethical consumption. Just looking back at the transitional year of 2021, post-pandemic, it brings in full throttle, a new era of conscientious luxury and moves out of a 50-year period of conspicuous luxury consumption that has been driving the industry for decades (Danziger, 2021). True as it may be that something about luxury brands has always had a mystic aura around them, but this is no longer true (Jain, 2020). Nowadays, consumers expect transparency in information about the products they are buying and the brands they're buying from. They need information about every detail: the process of creating the luxury product, the materials used, the backhand laborers, and the rest. They want to make sure that their purchase decisions reflect their ethics (Jain, 2020). The demand, henceforth, for luxury brands to combine socially and environmentally sustainable strategies is becoming critically important in solving urgent issues such as resource insufficiency, climate change, environmental pollution, and growing social concerns among others.

However, shifting one of the most polluting industries on the planet to a sustainable one is not an easy task, nor a task that can be achieved overnight. So how is the luxury industry going about this transformation, how is it communicating it to the consumers, and what do consumers actually perceive as an end result? Those are the questions asked and tackled by the author in this

DOI: 10.4324/9781003305095-5

chapter. Yet in order to attempt answering those questions, a brief background on the so-called paradox of sustainable luxury needs to be ensued. Then a closer look is taken at how individual companies, groups, and the industry as a whole is moving toward sustainability. However, the main focus will be Vogue Talents, part of Vogue Italia, as a flagship case study for that industry shift. This is not to say that the efforts of others in the industry are less important, far from it; however, Vogue Talents has proven to be a leader by example and most importantly a teacher of upcoming generations of designers on how to be sustainable from the get-go. Hence, the importance of educating the public as well as new fashion designers on how to design sustainably and ethically from the start and developing public awareness on the subject.

Literature review

Sustainable luxury: An oxymoron or perhaps a paradox?

Luxury and sustainability are two words that no one would have expected to see in the same sentence a couple of years back. According to Hashmi (2017), "… to many people, 'sustainable luxury' is a term that might best be found in the dictionary under the entry for oxymoron" (2017). Luxus, the Latin origin of the word luxury in the 17th century meaning "excess" used to mean excess in everything from excessive price to high quality, high performance, indulgence, social empowerment, and the elite. It is also closely associated with fashion, an industry inclined toward fads that change quickly. Conventionally, luxury is defined as being an expensive, hedonistic, and a superfluous, desired purchase that is rare or difficult to acquire. Therefore, when looking at luxury goods on the surface, they are perceived to be accessible only to the rich and wealthy, when taken as one part of the complex nature of luxury, making it at odds with the essence of sustainability (Hashmi, 2017), since according to the Brundtland Report, sustainable development is, by definition: "meeting the needs of the current generation without compromising the ability of future generations to meet theirs" (WCED 1987). Therefore, indeed, the two concepts appear entirely contradictory and paradoxical when looked at from the shallow surface. Hence, luxury is argued to be the polar opposite of sustainability since it is superfluous, conspicuous, and excessive; devoid of any utilitarian use, making it solely and purely a hedonic purchase most of the time (Ranfagni & Guercini, 2016). These facts make the term extremely difficult to define, especially in light of sustainability efforts of the past couple of decades and the pressure that is being put on all industries alike.

From excess and waste to sustainability

It's true that the luxury industry has been condemned, critiqued, and scrutinized by sustainability activists for things like the impervious traceability of precious metals and precious gemstones coming from under-developed countries; for exploitation of poor labor conditions in developing countries where many luxury brands manufacture their products; for water use in cotton production; or for resort maintenance of luxury hotels (Kapferer & Michaut-Denizeau, 2014). Discussions around the waste emitted by some of the biggest luxury brand names (e.g., Burberry, Chanel, Luis Vuitton) and the excessive lack of sustainability efforts had taken over the media for a while (e.g., Forbes, Newsweek, OsornClark, ADEME, …, etc.). With horrifying numbers and statistics, for example, 80,690 metric tons of waste was collected from LVMH group alone in 2020 (Statista Department Group, 2021) among other big players in the industry. The role of some luxury clothing brands and retail giants cannot be ignored, as they have admitted to burning unsold stock, thus becoming bad examples of wasteful and non-sustainable actors. Moreover, the fashion industry is one of the most polluting industries on the planet (Woodside & Fine, 2019). It generates 1.2 billion tons of greenhouse gases per year, i.e., 2% of global greenhouse gas emissions according to the French Agency for Ecological Transition. All these unsold and destroyed goods represent a waste of natural resources such as water, leading to sudden rise in number of consumers that are now concerned about environmental protection and find what has transpired over the years absolutely shocking.

Despite all of those staggering and horrific numbers pertaining to the excess, extravagance, and lack of sustainable and environmental considerations of the luxury industry in the past, there is a paradigm shift that is currently taking place where there have recently been positive efforts within the sustainability movement to redefine luxury as something that embodies social and environmental credentials of a product or service. Those giants of the industry that have had tons of bad press are the ones that are changing the game for everyone else. Efforts to become more sustainable in actual effect, teaching consumers how to value what they buy and know what they are buying, to build a new generation of ethical and sustainable designers is on the rise, slow as it may be, but still the effort and the work is being done to shift into the era of actual sustainable luxury. But how could it be if the concept is perceived as paradoxical?

Demystifying the paradox

If we move beyond the obvious and the superficial and return to the very essence of the definition of luxury, it can easily be said that sustainability is part of the luxury DNA (Hashmi, 2017). Sustainable products also share the same "essential" qualities as luxury goods. Those products and services demand extreme ingenuity, creativity, and design; they require the use of rare, expensive, and high-quality materials. This understanding has led to the birth of the concept of "sustainable luxury – a return to the essence of luxury with its ancestral meaning, to the thoughtful purchase, to the artisan manufacturing, to the beauty of materials in the broadest sense, and to the respect for social and environmental issues" (Girón, 2009).

Therefore, now luxury is in the spotlight of sustainable development and making huge strides. As a general trendsetter and strong value creator, the fashion and luxury industry, compared to other industries, holds the unique position to create a larger impact on educating other industries and well as consumers to be less wasteful.

In this context of education, according to Gardetti, "luxury brands offer opportunities for artisans of the world to regain their dignity; contribute to creating awareness for responsible products through sharing know-how and help develop respect for traditional knowledge. This in turn would mean contribution to culture, art, and innovation of different nationalities, to build upon the legacy of local craftsmanship" (2011).

Talk of sustainable luxury has ultimately gone from solely creating "feel-good" products and services by the luxury industry to acknowledging the potential for creating business value, consumer value, and highlighting the need for sustainable management of luxury. One such example is the Sustainable Luxury Working Group made up of giants in the industry such as Gucci Group, Tiffany&Co, Mulberry Group, Cartier and Burberry Ltd, and LVMH Moët Hennessy – Louis Vuitton that are all founding members committed to advancing and implementing proper social, environmental, and animal-welfare practices in their business operations, including but not limited to sustainable sourcing practices. This is definitely the tip of the iceberg in terms of the endeavors being undertaken by the luxury industry, but it is surely a huge move toward a better sustainable future while not forgoing the pleasures that luxury has to offer.

So how is luxury doing it?

All of this talk of a shift in the paradigm from waste to sustainability, in theory, sounds great and comparatively easy to implement. Nevertheless, despite the growth and high profit margins, the global fashion and luxury market is affected by macroeconomic and socio-political events. Supply network complexity, fragmentation of production, geographical dispersion, demand unpredictability, economic crisis, rising labor costs in emerging countries, social sustainability issues, time-based competition, and the mounting sensibility to environmental issues challenge the overall value proposition within the industry. In this competitive environment, fashion companies must change their institutional logics to re-build aspiration, credibility, and trust and properly communicate their efforts and vision of the future of the industry to the public.

> *The question still remains: how are they going about it internally and how and what are they communicating to their stakeholder?*

Behind the scenes: SLOW and circular

The literature seems to reveal that an integral part of actually becoming sustainable is focusing on the multiplayers and the stakeholders involved in the process of production, management, marketing, and overall communication. Specifically, the plethora of literature points to two major ways, among others, of doing that: one being the implementation of the Sustainable Luxury for Overall Well-being (SLOW) model and integrating circular economy processes.

Wherein the first model, SLOW, in short, is a conceptualized model of value creation that can permit the healthy and proper implementation of sustainability in the luxury industry; this model is called SLOW. This model implemented is essential in this context because the luxury industry seems to be very promising in terms of the creation of social value for overall well-being. What this means is that, through this endeavor, the luxury industry has the upper hand in removing the guilt that consumers have in terms of purchasing luxury and replacing it with a sense of pleasure and feeling of happiness, by offering the fulfillment of desires and removing the guilt by guiding better consumer choices without compromising the essence of what makes luxury what it is. According to Hashmi (2017) among other authors (Gardetti, 2011; Li & Leonas, 2019), "Luxury brands have the ability to make sustainable behavior an aspirational mainstream lifestyle choice, which is a much more effective way for creating social value in the form of social change than simply using guilt to make people feel bad about the environment".

Luxury companies and mainly the giants of the industry that have taken on strategic sustainability as part of their way forward and wanting to be the new voice of change do so by establishing innumerable collaborations with NGOs, government bodies, and other private companies to change the rules of the game in solving specific sustainability challenges around the world. Wherein, the SLOW value creation model serves this ultimate purpose. For clarification, SLOW refers to "slow value creation", not only because the actual process of value creation is slow moving since the rules are changing and it takes time to build new collaborations and make an impact, but also because it is connected to what started out as the "slow food" movement that originated in Italy in 1986 created by Carlo Petrini. This type of sustainability engagement accentuates the creation of value fundamentally for society's overall well-being, which entails at its core that each component of the value creation process is made regionally with value created to develop and enhance local craftsmanship, preserve, and protect local resources, and cultivate local clusters through collaborations for capacity-building of the luxury industry, industry-related infrastructure improvements, etc.

The second way that the luxury industry is adopting and implementing sustainability within its fabric is the concept of Circular Economy as a business model. The concept has progressively grown in prominence for both firms and governments alike (Brennan, Tennant, & Blomsma, 2015). It has been defined as "an industrial economy that is restorative or regenerative by intention and design" (MacArthur, 2013). Consequently, Circular Economy represents a business model, advantageous to accomplishing sustainable development (Murray, Skene, & Haynes, 2017), as well as a fair society, based on child labor interventions and laws, increasing workplace equality, preventive health care, and an improved and fair distribution of income as a result (Eyal, Hurst, Norheim, & Wikler, 2013). This, in simple terms, is a model that replaces the "end-of-life" concept with that of decreasing alternative reuse, recycling, and recovery of materials in production and consumption processes as a whole.

This business model in and of itself, if implemented properly, can lead to a decrease in dependency on and waste of natural resources, which in turn leads to a decrease in submission to the negative impact of resource price shocks with an increase in company competitiveness (MacArthur, 2013; Preston, 2012). More so, the Circular Economy business model is also based on a global not just local and regional perspective, emphasizing an undeniable need for better integration between economic, social, and environmental aspects, in order to achieve different expectancies by companies and countries alike. In other words, Circular Economies can be understood, according to Rashid, Asif, Krajnik, and Nicolescu (2013), as a different way of interpreting and implementing the traditional economic paradigm all-the-while keeping sustainability principles in mind from the start of the process (Rashid et al., 2013).

However, adopting and implementing Circular Economy principles in the luxury industry doesn't come without its hardships and obstacles from both business and consumer ends. On the one hand, from a business perspective, as contested by Kapferer and Michaut-Denizeaut, luxury firms in their essence are customarily immersed in the high quality they provide to their consumers and most often than not they are family-owned or established businesses. Keeping that in mind, therefore, they usually have control over most of the supply chain links if not all of them; from raw materials used to the end merchandizing, and they are, therefore, not in the habit of giving much importance to the dissemination of how they carry out their business functions but rather apply themselves heavily on the storytelling and the fantasy in the hopes of safeguarding "the dream image they are selling" (Kapferer & Michaut-Denizeaut, 2014).

On the other hand, luxury consumer purchases are extravagant, sporadic, and motivated by different intrinsic and extrinsic needs. Although the rise in consumer ethics and them wanting to buy products that are sustainable and that represent their new values, their attentiveness regarding sustainable behaviors of companies is very limited and superficial. It seems like they want to know that the products they are buying are ethical and stand for a cause, but they don't really care for the details as much as was initially indicated, at least for luxury consumers, excluding of course social and environmental activists.

In summary, therefore, the adoption of Circular Economy principles by luxury companies is easier said than done as was mentioned earlier, and made harder even by the reduced communicative and structural characteristics of the industry as well as the lack of seeming consumer awareness of such efforts and practices (De Barnier et al., 2012).

With all the above mentioned, how are then luxury giants moving forward, but more specifically, why has Vogue Talents gained the interest of the author in terms of sustainability efforts as a whole as opposed to other players in the fashion and luxury arena?

Case – Vogue Talents

There are many examples of companies that are fully taking on the issue of sustainability and weaving it into their mission, vision, and organizational objectives, which brings us to why the author has chosen Vogue Talents as a flagship case study when there are so many other examples out there.

Communicating this rising change and this so-called new mindset; it is necessary to reach the consumer and affirm a new consumption paradigm. Committed to facing the challenges of sustainability, the world of luxury is looking for a new language to communicate to consumers and to young designers (for pedagogical reasons) about products that have sustainable innovations that are not visible but are intrinsic in the product. The consumer should be taught to value both material and immaterial aspects of the products they purchase. In this transition, the role of communication is fundamental. Hence, the birth of Vogue Talents as an enhancement project for emerging designers who struggle to make themselves is known. But it has since then become a space for the growth and communication of responsible fashion: a brand that is born today cannot help but be responsible.

A brief history

When the first issue of the special Vogue Talents came out in 2009 as part of Vogue Italia, Franca Sozzani, the former Editor-in-Chief of Vogue Italia, and her niece Sara Sozzani Maino, the current Deputy Director of Vogue Italia, both had a clear idea of what they wanted Vogue Talents to achieve and become. In a particular moment for the fashion world, when it seemed that everything had already been seen, there was great difficulty in managing the generational change in fashion and the speed at which it was evolving. From this came the initial aim and birth of Vogue Talents, with a mission to highlight the talent of unknown and upcoming designers giving them the chance and proper opportunity to put their work forth. To them, for such young designers to have the chance to make themselves known on a Vogue special issue can be a huge boost that kick-starts their career as it has done for many others before them. Today Vogue Talents is a brand through which Condé Nast Italia supports the new generation of rising designers, a solid multimedia platform that has established itself as a reference point for creatives and talent scouts from all over the world. In February 2010, the Vogue Italia digital platform was born with a section of the website dedicated to new talent. However, the main aim of Vogue Talents, which was discovering and highlighting new designers didn't stop there. The brand decided that not only did they want their focus to be on novelty but more importantly on designers that understood the importance of emerging topics of sustainability and ethical design within the frame of fashion and luxury. Hence, from that moment forward, it was decided that the February print edition of Vogue Talents has and always will be dedicated to designers who can be defined as future talents of sustainability.

The success of Vogue Talents is the result of relentless research that has led to the discovery of a new generation of creatives in unexplored territories. As it has evolved, Vogue Talents has attested to its capability for epitomizing the aesthetic and social inclinations that have defined the past 13 years of international fashion and fashion sustainability in all its forms.

From the birth of Vogue Talents, Sara Maino and her staff have discovered talented people on the Internet and social media, in the world's most advanced fashion schools and in fashion week events. They have traveled tirelessly in search of the purest and most genuine creatives in the four corners of the globe. "Vogue Talents was created to support the new generation of creatives at a time when few people believed in talent", says Sara. "It's borderless and barrier-free, and it searches the world, because there's talent everywhere! Our mission going forward is to act responsibly and set an example that the world needs to change". Thirteen years running, Vogue Talents is an established international reference point for emergent fashion in all its facets; an authentic platform that enables the joining of talent and sustainable business under one roof so to speak.

Over the course of the years since its establishment, Vogue Talents has become an important communication and educational tool when it comes to dissemination of information on the changes taking place in the fashion world. It has helped the creation of platforms and arenas where sustainable fashion has found its space, investigating new luxury models. The concept of exclusivity has profoundly changed in recent years: today luxury is exclusive when it produces something special and personalized, with handcrafted details. The new generations of creatives who have been discovered by Vogue Talents now have this concept of exclusivity in their DNA, which needs to be shared, in order to be understood. Storytelling and the representation of new aesthetic are two fundamental ingredients that have contributed to educating luxury consumers on new values linked to sustainability. The designers selected by Vogue Talents pay great attention to materials and production methods, each focusing on different aspects of integrated sustainability. For example, some of those designers are focused on circularity, while others on the origin of materials. There are creative projects that try to reduce waste and make room for new consumption models, such as modularity projects. There are designers who, thanks to the application of artisanal techniques, are specialized in upcycling. All these projects are based on different aesthetics from that normally offered to luxury consumers, which can safely be defined as breaking innovative models and approaches to fashion and luxury. To this end, concepts like innovation in aesthetics, in materials, as well as in production models as part of sustainable luxury, have been heavily promoted in recent years by Vogue Talents. Thanks to their efforts, consumers were thus able to face new issues, and learn how to make their own purchase evaluations all-the-while considering different factors that help in buying the right products that reflect their ethics. Vogue Talents, therefore, over time has assumed a more pedagogical role in informing consumers on best practices as well as building new generations of sustainable designers through their variety of yearly challenges pushing the sustainable luxury envelope.

Over the years, the platform's continuing discourse between "traditional and digital publishing, print and social media, events and competitions, and creative and entrepreneurial vision" as was written by the Bulletin magazine, has amounted to a myriad of partnerships between designers and brands, "a Talents Lab that's the natural consequence of constant research and scouting".

The list, discovered by Vogue Talents, of creatives who have now become established brands and who have found success, as a result, is immensely long and the number incalculable. However, some of the most prominent names just to include a few are brands such as J.W. Anderson, Aquazzura, Giannico, Paula Cademartori, Arthur Arbesser, Simone Rocha, Bethany Williams, and Sara Battaglia. Those once veiled and anonymous names have turned into professionals and internationally recognized brands in the fashion arena that can inspire the generations of the future through their enthusing work that all began once upon a time with Vogue Talents.

Raising a new generation

Vogue Talents over the course of the past 13 years running, as was mentioned earlier, has selected and highlighted hundreds of designers that are now known in the market. Not only do they search for established designers in their own right and make them known, but more interestingly they hand-pick students from fashion schools giving them headway in the business, guiding them, and accompanying them on their mission to becoming the future of sustainable fashion and luxury. In an interview conducted for the tenth anniversary of the magazine with Sara Maino, who is not only the Deputy Director of Vogue Italia but is now the Head of Vogue Talents, she said "For a designer born today it is essential to be responsible". Specifically so, and since 2017, the issue and focus on sustainability has become increasingly accentuated in Vogue Talents solely focus on building responsible designers for the future and simultaneously educating the public, a decision made final in 2020.

As a result of this decision, in September 2020, a new platform "The World of Vogue Talents: The New Frontiers of Awareness" was published, totally interactive, with the inclusion of 3D experiences and a new way of proposing the use of fashion through the platform. In this interactive space, creatives and designers committed to the theme of sustainability are able to make their work known. Therefore, reiterating Vogue Talents' belief that the time had come to focus the effort on promoting the new generations of designers but only those who were able to demonstrate all-inclusive, holistic design encompassing ethics and aesthetics. To this effect, and after the release of the first edition, Emanuele Farneti, Editor-in-Chief of Vogue Italia, commented in an article saying "After the success of the first digital edition, Vogue Talents is proud to be returning, now with an even richer and more comprehensive lineup. An essential tool for professionals, the platform in this edition – which features new creative solutions – also provides news and ideas to the general public to wholeheartedly embrace the issue of sustainability, with a view to encouraging people to make more conscious, informed choices in everyday life" showcasing Vogue Talents' efforts not only in raising a new generation of sustainable minded designers, but in building the awareness of its importance.

With this endeavor, Vogue Talents has thus become a trend laboratory and an unofficial academic incubator capable of representing the great creative ferment that has taken place in recent years in the fashion world. They have been on the leading frontier of aesthetic and social changes that have actually changed the face of international fashion, in not only scouting such talent, but also building it from the ground up. In this context, sustainability has been represented in all its forms in Vogue Talents' projects, from the use of innovative materials, rediscovery of craftsmanship, enhancement of new ethnic perspectives, and inclusions in fashion to modular constructions and circular fashion chains. Their research on the matter also lies heavily on social and ethical issues such as inclusive beauty, gender fluidity, openness to all ages and generations, and new social feministic trends.

Although the topic of sustainability is neither new to businesses nor to the world of fashion and luxury, it has been interpreted and dealt with differently as was mentioned earlier on in this chapter. However, Vogue Talents' take on things has gained the interest of the author for many reasons, but primarily for their knowledge dissemination and educational efforts to inform the public and build a new generation of ethical designers that have a sustainability mindset alongside their creative sparks.

Particularly in the past two years, Vogue Talents has focused on topics such as *inclusion* (where fashion becomes inclusive: designers are looking for stylistic solutions that free the body from a stereotyped image and where beauty has no measure); *cultural and ethnic diversity* (discovery of designers from countries that have a strong cultural tradition to enhance their aesthetics and authenticity and eliminate cultural appropriation); *slow fashion modeling* (shedding light on exclusive designs made to order, rather than giving into the bulimia of compulsive buying and over production that goes to waste); and *Circular Economy models* for the fashion and luxury arena among others (considered to be the new fashion paradigm in the making, where the attempted aim is to start the production a garment while already thinking about its end of life and trying to make it usable for as long as possible; therefore, considering eco-design in every phase and aspect of the creation and production process).

Discussion

In the context of education and as was discussed thoroughly in the literature review of this chapter, luxury brands offer opportunities for artisans of the world to regain their poise, contribute to creating awareness of responsible products through sharing of know-how and craftsmanship, and help develop respect for traditional and artisanal knowledge. This would mean contribution to culture, art, and innovation of different cultures and ethnicities, and build upon the legacy of local craftsmanship and authenticity of origin (Gardetti, 2011). To this end, the case above briefly sheds light on why Vogue Talents is a leading voice in the education and building of the new generation of creatives that have awareness and respect for the art of fashion and luxury but that also have sustainability mindsets to catapult the world of design into the future. Therefore, it is noteworthy to delve further into the limitless efforts put forth by Vogue Talents in making this sustainable future happen in the world of fashion and luxury to support the authors' focus on them versus others.

In particular, other than the topics focused on by Vogue Talents over the years, four major challenges have been taken on by Vogue Talents in collaboration with different designers and organizations, which have truly set them apart from other players in the industry, and as such given them the leading role in the education of the public as well as the building of a new generation of sustainable designers fit for a brighter future. Those endeavors among many others of course, elaborated on, further below are: the Vogue YOOX challenge, the focus on changing how sustainable luxury is perceived, and every subsequent volume of Vogue Talents that has been released with a particular issue since 2020, the Upcycling Challenge that commenced in 2021, Tackling the issue of "Sustainability vs. Awareness: The Blending of Ethics & Aesthetics" while educating both the public and future designers, and releasing cause-related issues completely dedicated to concepts of sustainable luxury, which was an endeavor that started with the "Strength of Purpose" issue in 2020.

Vogue YOOX challenge

One of the major ways Vogue Talents has managed to force the discussion and rise of sustainable designers is by collaborating on the "Vogue YOOX Challenge – The Future of Responsible Fashion" by scouting for the appropriate talents and the discovery of the appropriate designers that fit the bill proposed. The project is run by Vogue Italia and YOOX in support of designers, creatives, and start-ups that have innovatively approached their creations from a responsible and sustainable method of design. For Vogue Italia and YOOX, their efforts to support the latest generation of designers remain to be a challenge that must be faced head-on in order to create a new path and raise awareness for a brighter more sustainable future ahead in terms of textile, design, and clothing systems within the fashion and luxury industry. This challenge allows for the non-discriminate selection of creatives, whether they are individual designers or groups, start-up businesses, social enterprises, or tech start-up companies, provided they meet the criteria set forth, which are primarily the following as stated by the entry requirements listed on Vogue Italia's website (Vogue.it, 2021):

- "Innovation of materials: creating new, more sustainable materials or with a lower impact on the environment than traditional ones"
- "Innovation of design & manufacturing, to find new sustainable ways to produce and develop fashion and furniture products"
- "Innovation in retail, for a more conscious distribution: reuse, recirculation, sharing of the collections and design pieces"
- "Cultural innovation, capable of highlighting the value of transparency and focusing the attention on sustainability-related themes"

Keeping all of this in mind, Vogue Talents tackles different sustainability issues, which need to be highlighted and delineated in terms of implementation, in order to further showcase their tremendous effort in creating holistic sustainability mindsets without nitpicking at the concept.

The upcycling challenge

Vogue Talents have recently launched *the Upcycling Challenge*, a new scouting project together with *CONAI* (Italian National Packaging Consortium). This project was created and dedicated to creatives who with their design vision are capable of capturing and understanding the boundless possibilities of recycled materials and the ability to transform them into inventive and stylish clothes and accessories. The initiative allows young creative talents the opportunity to create a "capsule collection" of sustainable clothing. Among the recycled materials, and hence upcycled materials that can be used for the collection or as accessories that complete it are steel, aluminum, paper and cardboard, wood, plastic, biodegradable and compostable plastic and glass, to be transformed into yarns, fibers, buttons, hangers, labels, or other items. At the end of this challenge, three winners are chosen by a jury made up of Condé Nast and CONAI representatives, where the first-place winner will have the opportunity to create a sustainable capsule collection. The outcome of this challenge will be spread to everyone in the Partnership for Community Actions (PCA) community as well as future creatives and the public in order to once again push the sustainable luxury envelope and embark on a bright and responsible future for the world of luxury.

Tackling sustainability vs. awareness: The blending of ethics and aesthetics

For many years, sustainable fashion has been talked about at length and was unfortunately perceived by the consumer as something unattractive, "sad". At first, sustainable materials were underperforming; they had a "weird fit" as consumers described it. This made their use particularly difficult in garments of a certain level. Consumers were biased toward this type of offer, just as they were very biased toward recycled products. However, the research carried out by emerging designers and the awareness efforts carried out by Vogue Talents, among others, have highlighted the specialty of a responsible product. Wearing your values is now possible, even if you need to inform yourself and ask yourself the right questions. Vogue Talents tries to provide help to consumers by always dedicating an in-depth section to illustrating some particular theme to provide the consumer with adequate knowledge to make informed choices.

In addition to that, from the consumers' perception and Vogue Talents' observation, it was realized that the issue of sustainable fashion is at the center of the conversation of the new generation of consumers more than ever before, although more often than not approached in an imprecise or superficial way. The use of incorrect or vague terms creates confusion among consumers and risks leading to greenwashing. In this light, and to help professionals use words properly, Condé Nast launched the glossary of sustainable fashion in 2020.The Sustainable Fashion Glossary is a long-standing commitment to drive change in the world of fashion, design, and style, bringing together academic rigor. It has been created by Condé Nast, in partnership with the Centre for Sustainable Fashion, London College of Fashion, University of Arts London. The team working with Vogue Talent has been involved in setting up this tool, as they are pioneers in the world of educating designers and the public on sustainable fashion.

From this came the new linguistic and operational mission and vision of Sara Maino in 2021, in an article discussing the New Frontiers platform, where she commented saying: "Vogue Talents continues to push its boundaries and commitments. We have a duty to continue to support the new generation in all its creative forms. This edition is dedicated to social responsibility, featuring a selection of international designers along with plenty of initiatives and suggestions on how we can all live more consciously". From this point forward, it was decided after consumer and designer feedback and research as well as collaboration with Condé Nast, to put less weight on the term sustainability and instead embrace that of awareness, as it was realized, that not only has the term been overused, abused, and sometimes even misused, but consumers have the need to buy ethical products that are sustainable but don't want to lose the magic and mystery that fashion and luxury provide. Hence, this is when and why The World of Vogue Talents – The New Frontiers of Awareness platform was born.

Strength of purpose

In the works at the time, there was also the publication of the September 2020 issue "Strength of Purpose", released by Vogue Talents as part of Vogue Italia. The issue was totally dedicated to the vitality and importance of an ethical and conscious approach to fashion and luxury. *"In this challenging moment"* – explains Sara Maino – "*it is essential to give a voice to creatives who believe and invest for a better future not only through their being responsible but also by helping social communities. 'Strength of purpose' is dedicated to the whole new generation who want to participate and make a real change*". Another powerful voice that emerged in that issue of Vogue Talents was that of Matteo Ward, a young designer discovered by Vogue Talents who ended up eventually joining the team soon after they discovered him, and who is one of three founding members of WRÅD. He wrote an article in the issue focusing on the consumer perspective of how they see sustainable luxury. He shed light on the fact that the world of luxury is looking for new paradigms, and that luxury consumers are confused by the messages that come from the media on the environmental impact of what we wear. The world of luxury understands that it is no longer enough to be exclusive and elegant, today fashion must go to the discovery of "purpose". For some years, the luxury giants have been trying to communicate their vision by making their values and mission public on their sites. Being transparent has become the new imperative: consumers want to know more about what they are wearing. The strength of the brand alone is no longer enough. Moreover, interestingly but not surprisingly, the collaboration between Vogue Talents and Matteo Ward continued further and farther than the September 2020 issue, with the aim of educating the public and the private sector on the importance of being sustainable in the world of fashion. To this end, they even created a course in collaboration with Timothy Parent, President of Harvard Alumni for fashion, luxury, and retail at Harvard called "Better Design". Timothy explains that "*Better Design may seem ambiguous and relative, but the philosophy and practices that Matteo Ward and Sara Sozzani Maino have advocated for will certainly create a better world for both people and planet. We all know that we need to change how we design and create, so come learn how to execute better design through better materials, better processes, and better making. We will discuss philosophies, principles, practices, and physical manifestations of this crucial movement, so register now so you won't miss out on this unique opportunity to hear from two of the leading voices on the future of design*".

Conclusion

The case that the author has examined is one that revolves around the concept of sustainable luxury and how, on the one hand, it is being pursued by players in the fashion and luxury world, and on the other hand, how it was perceived at the start of it all by consumers vs. how they see it today. Not only that, but the case also discusses the efforts of one entity, in particular, that being Vogue Talents, and how they have been playing a major role in bridging the gap between luxury consumer perspectives on sustainable luxury and the industry itself. However, more importantly, the focus on Vogue Talents primarily comes from their knowledge dissemination and educational efforts to inform consumers and rectify their image of what sustainable luxury actually means and build a new generation of ethical designers that have a sustainability mindset tied to their creative designs.

After examining the literature on sustainability and sustainable luxury and how they are both academically talked about and perceived by consumers, the author has come to the validation that her focus on Vogue Talents was worth the investment. As it has been shown in the case presentation and the discussion, Vogue Talents is indeed an exemplary fashion and luxury industry player and participant in the race to integrate and educate on sustainable luxury, and it has proven its importance and vitality in educating for a better and more responsible and conscious future of designers, creatives, and consumers. Research and interviews with prominent figures in the world of Vogue Talents, such as Sara Maino (Director of Vogue Italia and the Head of Vogue Talents), Emanuele Farneti (Editor-in-Chief of Vogue Italia), and Elisa Pervinca Bellini (Sustainability Editor of Vogue Italia and Executive Editor of Vogue Talents), have shed more light on the efforts being made to push for a better tomorrow in the world of sustainable and conscious fashion and luxury. It is evident that for the past 13 years since the conception of Vogue Talents, and more so in the last two years than ever before, the team has worked tirelessly to show that sustainable luxury is possible without risking the allure, intrigue, mystery, and seductive nature that surrounds luxury's aura so to speak. One of the ways they have done that is by disseminating the proper knowledge of what it is for fashion and luxury to be sustainable, showing luxury consumers that the magic is still there but that now they can "wear their values" instead of just bulimically buying with no purpose or positive conscious outlook on the future. This is continuously being done through their digital platform in collaboration with Condé Nast (The World of Vogue Talents – The New Frontiers of Awareness), social media accounts (Instagram, Facebook, Twitter, …, etc.), and the individual podcasts, classes, and workshops, and talks being held all over the world. Another way they have managed to push for sustainability is through their collaboration with Vogue Italia and YOOX to create the yearly challenge to encourage new and upcoming designers to think sustainably in the creation of their designs hence building a new generation of conscious creatives. In addition, with the recent "Upcycling Challenge", helping designers envision sustainable collections made solely of recycled materials to help with circularity and repurposing of material toward the main objective of sustainable luxury. In addition, of course, to all the scouting efforts to discover new creatives who believe in inclusion, diversity, circularity, slow and eco-designed fashion, and sustainability in general and who holistically share Vogue Talents' vision for the future of fashion and luxury. And not forgetting their continued efforts to create academic courses in collaboration with universities and designers on sustainable luxury such as the one they created in collaboration with Timothy Parent, President of Harvard Alumni for fashion, luxury, and retail at Harvard called "Better Design".

Therefore, it is clear that Vogue Talents is truly an educational institution building a new generation of conscious consumers and sustainable designers around the world, not just a simple media platform for fashion. They are pedagogical pioneers as well as major players in making the two main theoretical concepts of SLOW and Circular Economy models more plausible and implementable in reality through their challenges, platforms, and academic courses. Their efforts continue to spread far and wide, year after year giving the future of luxury a brighter, more sustainable light.

References

Brennan, G., Tennant, M., & Blomsma, F. (2015). Business and production solutions: Closing loops and the circular economy. In H. Kopnina & E. Shoreman-Ouimet (Eds.), *Sustainability: Key issues*. London, UK: Taylor and Francis.

Brundtland, G. H. (1987). *Report of the World Commission on environment and development: Our common future*. United Nations World Commission on Environment and Development.

Carrigan, M., Szmigin, I., & Wright, J. (2004). Shopping for a better world? An interpretive study of the potential for ethical consumption within the older market. *Journal of Consumer Marketing, 21*(6), 401–417. https://doi.org/10.1108/07363760410558672

Danziger, P. N. (2021). Luxury turns from conspicuous to conscientious in 2021: Challenges and opportunities ahead. (Taken from *(16) (PDF) Key Determinants of Luxury Marketing Accordant with Sustainability-Oriented Value Perspectives*.)

De Barnier, V., Falcy, S. & Valette-Florence, P. (2012). Do consumers perceive three levels of luxury? A comparison of accessible, intermediate and inaccessible luxury brands. *Journal of Brand Management, 19*, 623–636. https://doi.org/10.1057/bm.2012.11

Eyal, N., Hurst, S. A., Norheim, O. F., & Wikler, D. (Eds.). (2013). *Inequalities in health: Concepts, measures, and ethics*. Oxford, UK: Oxford University Press.

Gardetti, M. A. (2011). Sustainable luxury in Latin America. In Conference delivered at the Seminar Sustainable Luxury & Design within the framework of IE—Instituto de Empresa—Business School MBA, Madrid, Spain.

Girón, M. E. (2009). *Inside Luxury*. Madrid: Editorial LID. (Taken from *Handbook of Sustainable Luxury Textiles and Fashion*, Volume 2. (2015). Singapore: Springer Nature Singapore.)

Hashmi, G. (2017). Redefining the essence of sustainable luxury management: The slow value creation model. In Gardetti, M. (Ed.), *Sustainable management of luxury. Environmental footprints and eco-design of products and processes*. Singapore: Springer. https://doi.org/10.1007/978-981-10-2917-2_1

Hashmi, G. (2017). Redefining the essence of sustainable luxury management: The slow value creation model. In *Sustainable management of luxury* (pp. 3–27). Singapore: Springer.

Jain, H. (2020). What is Sustainable Luxury, *Luxury Abode*, 12 May. Retrieved from https://www.luxuryabode.com/blog/what-is-sustainable-luxury/artid61

Jain, S. (2021). Role of conspicuous value in luxury purchase intention. *Marketing Intelligence & Planning, 39*(2), 169–185. https://doi.org/10.1108/MIP-03-2020-0102

Kapferer, J., & Michaut-Denizeaut, A. (2014). Is luxury compatible with sustainability? Luxury consumers' viewpoint. *Journal of Brand Management, 21*(1), 1–22.

Li, J., & Leonas, K. K. (2019). Trends of sustainable development among luxury industry. M. A. Gardetti and S. S. Muthu (Eds.) In *Sustainable luxury* (pp. 107–126). Singapore: Springer.

MacArthur, E. (2013). *Towards the circular economy, economic and business rationale for an accelerated transition* (pp. 21–34). Cowes, UK: Ellen MacArthur Foundation.

Murray, A., Skene, K., & Haynes, K. (2017). The circular economy: An interdisciplinary exploration of the concept and application in a global context. *Journal of Business Ethics, 140*(3), 369–380.

Preston, F. (2012). A global redesign? Shaping the circular economy. Briefing Paper, Chatham House, London.

Ranfagni, S., & Guercini, S. (2016). Beyond appearances: The hidden meanings of sustainable luxury. In *Handbook of sustainable luxury textiles and fashion* (pp. 51–72). Singapore: Springer.

Rashid, A., Asif, F. M., Krajnik, P., & Nicolescu, C. M. (2013). Resource Conservative manufacturing: An essential change in business and technology paradigm for sustainable manufacturing. *Journal of Cleaner Production, 57*, 166–177.

WCED (World Commission on Environment and Development). (1987). *Food 2000: A global strategy for sustainable agriculture*. London and New Jersey: Zed Books. (Taken from Brian R. Keeble. (1988). The Brundtland report: 'Our common future'. *Medicine and War, 4*(1), 17–25. https://doi.org/10.1080/07488008808408783)

Woodside, A. G., & Fine, M. B. (2019). Sustainable fashion themes in luxury brand storytelling: The sustainability fashion research grid. *Journal of Global Fashion Marketing, 10*(2), 111–128.

Zhijun, F., & Nailing, Y. (2007). Putting a circular economy into practice in China. *Sustainability Science, 2*, 95–101. https://doi.org/10.1007/s11625-006-0018-1

4 Facing the Global Customer

10 Corso Como Innovative Path

Gaetano Aiello, Laura Grazzini, Olga Nachaeva, and Costanza Dasmi
Università degli Studi di Firenze

Introduction

In recent years, the topic of sustainability has become increasingly popular, taking a special role in our society and becoming one of the most important management elements for both governments and companies. Moreover, governments, private organizations, and consumers are pushing for the adoption of new consumption and business models that are more ecologically sustainable (Franco, Hussain, & McColl, 2020). Because society has paid greater attention to issues related to environmental sustainability, firms have become more interested in implementing sustainability initiatives (Bartels, Reinders, & Van Haaster-De Winter, 2015). Specifically, it has become a key for retailers who pursue the financial benefits of a business but within the bounds of sustainable development (European Commission's, 2008). The retail sector occupies a strategic position within markets, thus many resources can be directed toward sustainability issues (Naidoo & Gasparatos, 2018).

Sustainability issues are especially important in the luxury retail sector, given its widespread reach, which is reflected in the international components of its goods, services, and experiences: e.g., fashion, automobiles, travel, gastronomy, alcohol, and fine art (D'Arpizio, Levato, Kamel, & de Montgolfier, 2017; D'Arpizio, Levato, Zito, Kamel, & de Montgolfier, 2016; Hennigs, Wiedmann, Klarmann, & Behrens, 2013). Luxury, more than others, is a sector marked by the growth of sustainable production and, thus, by the development of business models based on sustainable supply chains. More specifically, environmental conservation drives luxury companies to redefine their sourcing, manufacturing, and distribution processes, and in the process gaining efficiency, promoting innovation, and increasing brand value (Guercini & Ranfagni, 2013). There is an increasing tendency to support the idea that sustainability can create value. François-Henri Pinault, CEO of Kering, the world's N°2 luxury group, recently reaffirmed his conviction that an approach based on sustainability would generate new revenue and long-term competitive advantage for the group (Kapferer & Michaut-Denizeau, 2013).

DOI: 10.4324/9781003305095-6

Sustainable luxury includes the scope of design, production, and consumption that is environmentally or ethically conscious (or both) and is oriented toward correcting various perceived wrongs within the luxury industry, including animal cruelty, environmental damage, and human exploitation (Lundblad & Davies, 2015). For example, Tiffany started to certify its diamonds as "conflict-free", Chanel incorporated "earthy materials" in its 2016 collection, and Bulgari recently funded the restoration of the famous Spanish Steps in Rome (Donato, De Angelis, & Amatulli, 2020). However, there are conflicting views on the concept of sustainable luxury, and thus the relationship between sustainability and luxury. Some scholars suggest that luxury and sustainability are antagonistic concepts, showing that consumers' propensity to consider sustainable aspects in luxury products is very low (Achabou & Dekhili, 2013; Streit & Davies, 2013), while others perceive sustainable luxury products positively (e.g., De Angelis, Adıgüzel, & Amatulli, 2017), and think that sustainability and luxury have many common traits and converge on certain elements such as durability, rarity, authenticity, rigor, collective sharing, quality, and the preservation of handmade traditions (Grazzini, Acuti, & Aiello, 2021; Guercini & Ranfagni, 2013).

Furthermore, high quality, preservation of handmade traditions, and durability are essential characteristics of the concept of "Made in Italy". Although the "Made in Italy" concept does not refer to luxury goods only, big representatives of the luxury segment such as Prada, Dolce&Gabbana, Gucci, etc., base themselves on some "Made in Italy" attributes. With the emergence of a new generation of consumers, the demand for sustainability is high (Amatulli, De Angelis, Korschun, & Romani, 2018). Thus, the "Made in Italy" concept needs to implement sustainable strategies to remain competitive in the global market. Paying attention to the current market trends, the present chapter aims to shed light on the way sustainability can be integrated into the characteristics of luxury "Made in Italy" brands, and how this integration can be communicated to the consumer in a visible and clear manner. With this research, we hope to offer valuable insights to luxury managers seeking to integrate sustainable strategies and luxury brand concepts.

To fulfill this aim, this research focuses on the case of 10 Corso Como. 10 Corso Como is an Italian brand that was founded in Milan in 1990 by Carla Sozzani. It is a luxury retailer that offers not only apparel, but also a variety of other products such as art, books, and hospitality services. This brand was chosen due to its sustainable approach, its unique concept that stands out from other Italian luxury retailers, its craftsmanship, and the valorization of the "Made in Italy" tradition. It is a wonderful micro-world immersed in the art within a city that is always on the move.

The chapter is structured as follows. We first present the conceptual background of our research. After that, we describe our process of collecting data, methodological tools, and techniques used. In the fourth part, we illustrate the findings of the study. Finally, in the last section, we make conclusions and present the limitations of our work.

Conceptual background

Sustainability in retailing

In recent years, the topic of sustainability has gained prominence in many sectors, including retail. Tackling sustainability is undeniably one of the increasingly important operations management issues faced by retailers today and a viable way for firms to differentiate their offerings and achieve a competitive advantage (Tang, Lai, & Cheng, 2016). Indeed, a longitudinal survey by Retail Systems Research (2009) found that 48% of retailers viewed sustainability as a strategic choice in their business operations, up from 44% 12 months earlier. Moreover, the retail sector is a global economic power that has an average annual growth rate of 3.8% since 2008 and a turnover of around 28 trillion dollars (BusinessWire, 2016). The sector represents 31% of the global gross domestic product (GDP). Hence, it is evident the significant economic influence that characterizes this sector and the huge resources that can be directed toward sustainability issues (Naidoo & Gasparatos, 2018). Furthermore, the importance of sustainable consumption in retailing is widely evidenced by literature (Naidoo & Gasparatos, 2018). Retailers are very important figures within the market: they can be considered active intermediaries between producers and consumers. Thanks to their position, they can encourage the use of sustainable production methods and influence consumers in the adoption and purchase of ecological products (Naidoo & Gasparatos, 2018). Due to their gatekeeping position between producers and customers, retailers are in a unique position to promote sustainability in society (Durieu, 2003) and are key actors in the promotion of healthier and more sustainable patterns of consumption (Lehner, 2015).

Luxury and sustainability

The issue of sustainability is also relevant to the luxury retail sector and the notion of "responsible luxury" has received considerable attention in recent years (Janssen, Vanhamme, Lindgreen, & Lefebvre, 2014). However, there are conflicting views on the relationship between sustainability and luxury. On one hand, luxury and sustainability may be seen as two separate things and seem counterintuitive. By comparing the components of sustainable development with those of luxury, it becomes possible to identify potential elements of contradiction. For example, all elements related to ostentation will oppose the fairness or social harmony facets of sustainable development. Similarly, pleasure and superficiality are opposed to altruism, moderation, and ethics. Furthermore, luxury reflects excess, hedonism, and ostentation while the latter elicits sobriety, restraints, and morality (Carrier & Luetchford, 2012). For this reason, many authors consider luxury and sustainability as separate if not opposite concepts (Achabou & Dekhili, 2013; Streit & Davies, 2013). On the other hand, unlike fast fashion, the word luxury is also associated with high quality, know-how, slow processes, the preservation of handmade traditions, and the transmission from generation to generation of timeless products: these elements are compatible with sustainability (Kapferer & Michaut, 2015). Additionally, one of the fundamental principles of a true luxury strategy is to produce locally by talented artisans and respect the sources of raw materials (Kapferer & Michaut, 2015).

Moreover, luxury and sustainability, especially in its environmental dimension, converge in the features of *durability* and *rarity*, which bridges potential differences between them. Durability is the heart of luxury as well as of environmental sustainability, whose fundamental purpose is to pursue the protection over time of natural resources. Luxury's durability impacts environmental sustainability: luxury's long life reduces waste in the use of natural resources, favoring their preservation (Grazzini et al., 2021). Luxury is also about rarity (Florence, 2012), which may be due to the use of rare materials (skins, leathers, pearls, etc.) and rare craftsmanship. Its value, then, depends on the uniqueness of its constitutive resources and thus on environmental sustainability (Guercini & Ranfagni, 2013). Research demonstrates that "luxury products are perceived by consumers as rare products; when over-diffused, they gradually lose their luxury character" (Janssen et al., 2014). Sustainability and luxury converge also in *authenticity* which is linked to the manifestation of territorial identity where natural resources come from. It converges in *collective sharing* just as sustainability preserves open collectively shared spaces, luxury based on shared values joining its producers and consumers. It converges on *quality* just as sustainability pursues environmental quality, luxury is based on the quality of the specialized skills and technical abilities. Finally, the gap is bridged on *rigor*, as sustainable luxury presupposes lasting common principles in the supply chain to maintain a convergent mindset for generating positive levels of performance (Grazzini et al., 2021; Guercini & Ranfagni, 2013).

"Made in Italy" and sustainability

"Made in Italy" refers to Italian handicraft and industrial products that have often excelled in international business competitions due to the equilibrium between specific technical economic components (involving characteristic clusters of skills and knowledge) and specific territorial-cultural components (based on socio-historical consolidation). Indeed, many Italian products have been recognized as having a significant quality of workmanship, attention to detail, and design form (Conti & Vacca, 2008; Fallan & Lees-Maffei, 2014; Iannilli, 2014). "Made in Italy" products present both tangible (raw materials, production techniques, and so on) and intangible (social methods of working, the territory of origin, and so on) characteristic elements (Qureshi, 2017). This excellence is evidenced by successful "Made in Italy" brands in various segments and industries, from mass-market to luxury. For example, Ferrero, Barilla, and Lavazza in the food industry (Brand Finance, 2018), Pantofola d'Oro in the footwear industry, especially in the USA, or MGM Mondo del Vino in the wine industry, especially in Russia (Sacc-Simest, 2018). Luxury brands actively utilize the power of the "Made in Italy" branding as well. For example, Gucci, Prada, and Armani in fashion; Ferrari, Maserati, and Alfa Romeo in the automotive industry; and MooRER in the personal luxury goods, especially in Japan (Festa, Rossi, Kolte, & Situm, 2020).

Young consumers are changing the definition of luxury, including "Made in Italy" luxury. Research by GlobalWebIndex shows that 67% of regular luxury goods purchasers are between 25 and 44 years old and they account for 30% of global luxury sales (Buckle, 2019). Millennials (born between 1981 and 1996) and Gen Z (adults born after 1997) are willing to support brands that align with their personal values (Bain, 2018), in line with how Corporate Social Responsibility had a significant positive impact on the purchase of luxury goods for both Gen Z and millennials. Among the former, an increase in sustainable consumer habits was positively correlated with an increase in luxury product consumption (Youn & Cho, 2021). Thus, sustainability is one of the strongest values among young people who consume luxury products (Atkinson & Kang, 2021).

According to the current market demand, it is no longer enough to only be "Made in Italy": brands must also implement sustainability into the existing label. "Made *green* in Italy" is a new Italian initiative aimed to support and promote environmentally sustainable products on the national level. Currently, it is essential to see how the three elements (segment of luxury, the unique effect of "Made in Italy", and sustainability) can successfully co-exist. This chapter thrives to analyze the relevant case of a sustainable luxury retailer from Italy "10 Corso Como".

Methodology

Research design

This paper draws on qualitative data based on the method of the case study. The case study method provides a structured approach to data collection and facilitates the triangulation of data collected from multiple sources to improve the reliability of the study (Gunarathne & Sankalpani, 2021; Yin, 2017). The method was chosen because it provides detailed anecdotal evidence about the Italian sustainable luxury retailer engaged in Corporate Social Responsibility (CSR) initiatives.

As a primary source of data, our study employs an in-depth interview with the brand communication manager. In particular, to analyze the sustainable communication strategy of the luxury retailer, the interview protocol was structured considering the variables of the marketing mix model, which are product, promotion, price, people, and place. First, questions regarding brand creation, brand history, and brand values were asked to create an overall picture of who 10 Corso Como is. Next, we focused on the topic of sustainability and sustainable communication. In order to do this, we conducted a four-part analysis. First, we examined how 10 Corso Como products and designers' collections reflect sustainable ideas and how those are communicated to consumers, how the luxury retailer selects the designers for future collaborations, and if sustainability is an important criterion for this choice. Second, we investigated how 10 Corso Como venues display the concept of sustainability and how these ideas are included in the interiors. Third, we studied the social sustainability of the brand where we specifically focused on aspects such as gender equality and diversity. Fourth, we analyzed the in-store and online sustainable communication of 10 Corso Como. Particularly, we paid attention to the brand's official website, social media accounts, and other online fashion magazines such as Vogue Italia.it. Finally, we asked the brand manager if the prices of products justify the high quality, craftsmanship, and natural materials used in the productions. Table 4.1 presents the interview protocol.

Sampling

10 Corso Como is a conceptual brand and a multifunctional space that was founded in Milan in 1990 by Carla Sozzani, sister of Franca Sozzani, the former director of Vogue Italia. Currently, the retailer has stores in Milan,

Table 4.1 In-depth interview protocol

Marketing mix	*Questions*	*Objective*
Product	How is the concept of sustainability included in the products of 10 Corso Como? How do you select the products to sell in-store and online? What are the selection criteria for potential collaboration with brands?	To understand the sustainability of 10 Corso Como products
Place	How do 10 Corso Como's spaces reflect the concept of sustainability? How does 10 Corso Como include sustainability inside the store?	To understand the sustainable communication of 10 Corso Como spaces (store, café, restaurant, hotel …)
Promotion	Does 10 Corso Como communicate sustainability to consumers? Which channels are used?	To understand sustainable communication strategies of the brand (in-store, social media, website, magazines …)
People	How does 10 Corso Como guarantee gender equality and diversity?	To understand sustainable gender and cultural policies
Price	How does 10 Corso Como justify the prices of their products based on sustainable ideas?	To understand if price formation is based on a sustainable approach

Seoul, and Shanghai. The brand includes several branches: fashion designer stores, restaurants and bars, hotels, galleries, and bookshops, all of which are located within the store. The multi-brand store sells its own branded products as well as products made by other designers (clothes, accessories, house decorations, and goods for free time activities). The brand of 10 Corso Como is intended to continue the cultural and aesthetic path that has made it a symbol of the city, of "Made in Italy" and of international creativity.

Data collection

To achieve a deep understanding of case-study research, multiple sources of data were used, including an interview and content analysis of 10 Corso Como's social media accounts on Instagram, Facebook, and Twitter, as well as their website. Yin (2017) suggests that to make research as strong as possible, the researcher should gather data from as many sources of evidence as possible. Our primary data collection method involved a semi-structured interview with the communication manager of 10 Corso Como. During this interview, we had a list of semi-structured questions developed based on prior literature (Park & Kim, 2016; Salem & Alanadoly, 2020; Vătămănescu, Dabija, Gazzola, Cegarro-Navarro, & Buzzi, 2021). The interview lasted for 1 hour.

Data analysis

In the data analysis stage, the interview was fully transcribed from audio recordings. The transcribed interview and notes were thematically analyzed. Thematic analysis was used because it interrogates the data, analyzes the data, and identifies patterns or themes within the data (Braun & Clarke, 2006). The data collected from other sources were compared for data triangulation and supplementing the interview findings (Gunarathne & Sankalpani, 2021). In particular, the analysis of 10 Corso Como's social media accounts, the website, and mentions in online media helped to see if the sustainable strategy of the luxury retailer is reflected in its communication and messages online.

Research findings

This study aims to analyze how sustainable elements can be included in the concept of a luxury "Made in Italy" brand and communicated to consumers. To investigate the sustainable communication strategies of the brand and structure the findings, we employed the Marketing Mix 5P model. The model consists of five elements (product, price, place, promotion, and people) which are used to position a business strategically (Lin, Lee, & Lin, 2012; McCarthy, 1981). In our work, we divided the findings according to the 5P elements. In the "product" category, we investigate how sustainable elements are integrated into the products of 10 Corso Como; "price" is devoted to the connection between the premium price of 10 Corso Como luxury products and their sustainability; "place" is dedicated to how sustainability is reflected in the location of 10 Corso Como stores; "promotion" describes the way how sustainable messages of 10 Corso Como are delivered to consumers via various communication channels; "people" involves the social policy of 10 Corso Como.

Brand history

10 Corso Como was created at the beginning of the '90s by Carla Sozzani, former fashion editor and publisher. The original headquarters consisted of a large railing house, previously a garage, at number 10 Corso Como. In the beginning, the place functioned as an art gallery, but one year later it became a store. Unexpected for a luxury brand, the store was founded in a suburban area of Milan rather than in the famous fashion district of the city (Via Spiga, Via Manzoni, etc.). According to the brand manager of 10 Corso Como, although the context cannot be considered very luxurious, it is very lively. Moreover, the store was different from other luxury boutiques of that time due to its eclectic atmosphere: a large variety of products was presented and made available to consumers, from shoes to perfumes. Carla Sozzani was inspired by examples of concept stores from abroad such as Biba in London. Differently from Biba, 10 Corso Come had an art gallery that made it unique. In 1998, the restaurant and the cafeteria were opened because consumers loved to spend time in the store. Last to be integrated in 2003, the 3 Rooms Hotel is an exclusive boutique hotel with only three available suites. This boutique hotel is unique due to its décor and design, because Kris Ruhs, the architect who developed the concept of the hotel, has a distinctive style and utilized exceptional and uncommon materials that reflect the concept of 10 Corso Como. Over the years, 10 Corso Como participated in several cross-cultural collaborations and opened stores abroad in Tokyo (2002), Seoul (2008), Shanghai (2013), Beijing (2014), New York (2018), and Taipei (2019).

Product

10 Corso Como (10CC) is described by the communication manager of the brand as a "*bazaar, and a concept store*" where multiple products can be purchased: clothes, shoes, beauty, perfumes, design, books, small accessories, and a photo gallery. This is how Carla Sozzani succeeded in connecting fashion with culture. 10 Corso Como carefully picks the products that are sold in-store as well as the designers with whom to collaborate. The designers with whom 10 Corso Como works enhance the craftsmanship and sustainability of their products, including Salvatore Ferragamo "*which has substantially almost handcrafted productions*", Stella McCartney, and "*young emerging designers who have the sustainable part as their own founding element*". For instance, 10 Corso Como collaborated with the Bulgarian designer Chopova

Lowena to combine cultural folklore with sportswear while emphasizing sustainability and craftsmanship (10CorsoComo.it). Another collaboration with Giorgio Armani supports the idea of durability and gender equality "capi senza tempo" (timeless garments), where masculine and feminine codes merge for an urban, elegant, exclusive style (Vogue.it). The importance of craftsmanship is highlighted in the official Instagram account of the brand.

This guarantees a high level of quality and differentiation from competitors. The products sold inside the stores are defined as "*little capsule collections and selections*" by the communication director, "*the proposals presented by 10 Corso Como are different from what the brand offers in a department store, creations of emerging designers, always exclusive proposals for 10 Corso Como or collaborations and small choices of great collections within the space of 10 Corso Como*". This limited production generates significantly less waste and less dispersion, as reported by the communication director of 10CC.

Moreover, the style of the brand and of the designers with whom 10 Corso Como collaborates is unique. As reported by the brand's communication manager, Carla Sozzani was among the first to bring designers such as Martin Margiela, Comme des Garcons, and the Japanese Junya Watanabe to Milan, these brands not yet known in Italy. As the head of communication of 10CC states, it is about: "*very particular fashion constructions that are different from what was available around at that time, minimal, essential and not ostentatious fashion, completely understatement but extremely interesting*". It is because of this uncharacteristic style that the target clientele is very experienced and has expertise in the field and can be defined as "*fashion professionals*".

Given the care the brand takes in selecting a designer collaborator, in the style that characterizes it, and in the support that the brand gives to emerging designers, we can say that 10 Corso Como integrates sustainability into its products, creating a new genre of sustainable luxury.

Place

Sustainable characteristics are reflected in the location of 10 Corso Como and the store's architecture. According to the brand's communication manager, the main idea of the venue is to communicate the concept of accessible luxury: "*You have to go inside, it's a bit of a maze, you don't see things [luxury products] right away, you don't understand where to go... but you see these plants, these flowers... It's not a 'stiff' place. It's not a place that communicates coldness or distance, it's another idea of luxury*". The geographical location of 10 Corso Como is different from other luxury retailers. While the concentration of premium-level products is in the Monte Napoleone Street, the so-called fashion district of Milan, 10 Corso Como is located away from the main streets, in a private house with a greengrocer on the ground floor, more lively than luxurious. When 10 Corso Como was founded, it resembled a bazaar with various categories of products on sale: clothes, perfumes, books, household goods, and accessories. Nowadays, the place still holds the atmosphere of a bazaar.

The choice of products for sale is another way to communicate sustainability on the spot. As previously mentioned, 10 Corso Como collaborates with environmentally friendly brands such as Stella McCartney and Ferragamo as well as a range of young designers of sustainable fashion. The way their products are presented in-store is a significant part of the brand's sustainable communication strategy, paired with posters, signs, and labels displaying eco-friendly messages. The green environment of 10 Corso Como's stores is also illustrated through the social media posts of the brand. Special attention is paid to the garden and the restaurant decorated with plants and flowers.

As stated earlier, 10 Corso Como is not just a shop, rather it is a concept store and a creative space. The location is used not only for the retail function but also for artistic purposes, this duality aligning with sustainability values. Art exhibitions take place in the 10 Corso Como Sozzani Gallery. For example, the Prix Pictet exhibition is one of the most important exhibitions of contemporary photography in the field of sustainability: every year, the Pictet bank awards 12 photographers chosen from around the world for projects that meet very precise selection criteria. This year's theme was Hope. Another exhibition is the historical exhibition of WordPress Photo, which has taken place in the Sozzani Gallery for 27 years. This exhibition of photojournalism awards the title of the photo of the year, the most significant photo among all the photographers who take part in the competition. Professional photographers submit photos related to the previous year. They are often strong images of war or conflicts, photos of real-world issues. According to the communication manager of 10 Corso Como, it is one of the "*blockbuster exhibitions that always has a very wide and transversal meaning because reportage photography, current affairs photography is something that concerns everyone regardless of age and cultural competence*". The audience at the WordPress exhibition in Sozzani Gallery is always diverse, not reserved to luxury consumers.

Promotion

We will now focus on the ways 10 Corso Como communicates their sustainability to their consumers and stakeholders. As mentioned before, the venture of 10 Corso Como, its design, its location in the city, and its role as a host for activities, have always been the main channel for the brand to share the sustainable strategy and approach. Until now, we have focused predominantly on "in-presence" communication, so little attention has been paid to communicating sustainability on social media. Content analysis of the brand's accounts on Instagram, Facebook, and Twitter identified several main thematic clusters: "branded products", "location facilities" (restaurant, bookstore, coffee bar, garden), "announcement of forthcoming events", and "new collections/collaborations with designers". According to the communication manager of 10 Corso Como, the challenge the brand is facing now is how to transfer the intrinsic, implied sustainability of the physical store to its social media and website. What distinguishes 10CC for the director of communication is the "*visual identity that is very recognizable, the Heritage that has been built in 30 years and that makes it different from other realities*". However, this aspect is difficult to transfer to the digital environment. As the director of communications says: "*The big challenge we are facing is the possibility of transferring the Heritage of 10 Corso Como in the digital environment*". Nevertheless, given the importance of digital communication that increasingly characterizes everyday life, in part due to the physical isolation caused by the pandemic, 10 Corso Como is slowly entering the digital world. With the acquisition of 10CC in 2020 by Tiziana Fausti, the e-commerce site has become live and the presence of the brand on social media increased.

Events are one of the promotional tools that communicate the sustainable characteristics of the brand, such as the launch of Prom-Peru project, an exclusive collection of clothes created by Peruvian designers for 10 Corso Como. The focus of the project was on the local traditions of making clothes, hand-made production, and having a window into another culture. The project highlighted the importance of cultural diversity and preserving unique craftsmanship traditions. As the brand's communication manager stated, some of the pieces from the collection were sold, which shows diversity is a commercially successful direction for luxury brands. Among the designers of the project is Ana Maria Guiulfo who proposed creations inspired by ceramics and hand-painted art. Another collaborator was Annaiss Yucra, who presented the Pachamama collection which means "Mother Earth" in Quechua and is an allegory for what has been sown during the year and integrates the expectations for the future with the values of sustainability, inclusion, and biodiversity. Ayni, by Adriana Cachay and Laerke Skyum, presented the Munay collection, a Quechua word that means beauty, freedom, desire, and willpower, that speaks of the intertwining of different heritages. Andar De Paso Peruano is the title of Claudia Bertolero's collection that wanted to highlight the importance of the traditions and customs of her country. Meche Correa was also inspired by the millenary tradition of Peru for her capsule collection, and finally the brand Kuna selected the best alpaca, vicuña, llama, and guanaco yarns, protecting at the same time both the farms and the communities that take care of them (VogueItalia).

Among other significant events were the cocktail party dedicated to the launch of the Armani x 10 Corso Como collection where the topic of sustainability was reflected in the collection items themselves; the world premiere of the new "Green Capsule 2022" of Ports 1961 that was conceived by Artistic Director Karl Templer in collaboration with Tonne Goodman, Sustainability Editor of Vogue America; and collaborations with SAPIO, a refined and production-conscious Italian sartorial designer, and Federico Cina, an emerging Italian award-winning designer with a focus on the essence of culture and history of Romagna region, where his roots come from. According to the communication manager of 10 Corso Como, the events stimulate positive word-of-mouth from consumers and stakeholders, and they attract the attention of the media. For example, the article about the Prom-Peru project was published in Vogue Italia, and the launch of the Armani collection in Women's Wear Daily, MFfashion, Reppublica, D.it, Ansa.it, and Vogue Italia.

People

According to the Triple Bottom Line model, which refers to initiatives that are undertaken for managing strategic sustainability, people, profit, and planet are the key dimensions to be addressed on the way to sustainable development (Hacking & Guthrie, 2008; Hubbard, 2009). People refer to employees' safety, security, educational measures, and quality of life. 10 Corso Como pays attention to the issues of gender equality. As the brand's communication manager shared: "*The characteristic of 10 Corso Como has always been that of inclusions right from the beginning. In fact, at one point there was not even a distinction between the male and female parts. Then, for a question of functional logistics, it was restored. But in this, fashion has always been very open*". This aspect is evident also from the selection of the designers who create gender-neutral collections for 10 Corso Como, such as Giorgio Armani.

Alongside gender equality, the brand supports cultural diversity through collaborations with foreign designers, integrating traditions of other cultures into new collections, as evidenced from the Prom-Peru project described above.

Price

The prices of the products sold by 10 Corso Como are very high. As aforementioned, this is dictated by the high quality and exclusivity of products, the sophistication, the collaboration with well-known and prestigious brands, the limited and exclusive collections, and the painstaking selection of products. Many authors highlight the link between luxury and high prices to show the brand's prestige (Parguel, Delécolle, & Valette-Florence, 2016) as a means to express the social status and public self-consciousness (Balabanis & Stathopoulou, 2021) as well as to underline the high quality (Mundel, Huddleston, & Vodermeier, 2017).

Due to the high prices, 10 Corso Como is orientated toward a particular type of customer defined as "*fashion professionals*" by the director of communication. These fashion professionals are expert customers in the field of fashion "*who are very familiar with the collections and are looking for something different and new*". Thus, due to its uncommon and unique products, 10 Corso Como satisfies these customers' niche.

Conclusion

Practical implications

The present chapter examined the sustainable initiatives undertaken by luxury fashion retailer 10 Corso Como. The study included an interview with the brand communication manager and content analysis of the company website and social media accounts.

The most significant conclusion to be drawn from the case study is that luxury and sustainability can successfully coexist. Indeed, integrating sustainable values into the luxury brand's concept does not jeopardize its prestigiousness and premium quality, but only serves to illuminate its willingness to make social and environmental contributions. Sustainability and luxury have some common traits such as quality, durability, rarity, the valorization of craftsmanship, and the importance of "Made in Italy" that are relevant for the stimulation of local markets and local economies.

10 Corso Como gives an example of how a luxury brand can implement sustainable efforts into its concept and communicate it through various channels. Firstly, through the premium product itself, its high-quality production, and sustainability-focused presentation. This, in return, leads to a justified increase in price and, consequently, fewer items in stock and less production waste. Thirdly, the location of the brand communicates its sustainable orientation through interior design, its rather private geographical positioning in the city, the presence of sustainability-focused art exhibition inside the venue, and its indoor print posters promoting sustainable ideas. Next, the brand's sustainable approach is communicated to consumers and stakeholders through private and public events, triggering a word-of-mouth effect and drawing media attention. Last but not least is expressing sustainable values through posts on the brand's social media accounts.

As previously stated, what grounds 10 Corso Como is the culture it has built over time. However, this aspect is difficult to transfer online. Nevertheless, 10 Corso Como is integrating the digital world with the opening of the e-commerce site and its presence on the main social media platforms. Moreover, 10 Corso Como must thrive to use these new channels to convey the values that characterize it such as sophistication, refinement, high quality, exclusivity, sustainability, and craftsmanship. This is especially important in the current context because of the pandemic and because of the heavy use of social media by consumers. Indeed, social media has become a powerful tool to create online communities, understand consumer reactions and perceptions, convey values, and increase brand image and consumer perceptions (Dang, Nguyen, & Wang, 2020; Dunn & Harness, 2019; Testa, Bakhshian, & Eike, 2021).

In terms of practical implications, this data can be a useful tool for luxury brand managers to structure their communication properly and stress their sustainability efforts. Moreover, the case of 10 Corso Como is a rare example of luxury that can encourage and motivate other retailers to integrate sustainable strategy in their offerings and their brand image.

Limitations

The research acknowledges some limitations. Firstly, the research is based on a single case study analysis which limits the generalization of results. Consequently, future research can expand the number of cases to make a more profound analysis and see if other luxury brands can communicate their sustainability effectively. Secondly, the research focuses on an Italian luxury retailer and there may be cultural differences in the way how foreign brands communicate sustainability.

For future research, it would be interesting to focus on consumers' perception of sustainable messages delivered by luxury retailers and to analyze behavioral consequences. Particularly, it would be fruitful to analyze the importance that consumers attribute to sustainability and its connection to the world of luxury.

References

Amatulli, C., De Angelis, M., Korschun, D., & Romani, S. (2018). Consumers' perceptions of luxury brands' CSR initiatives: An investigation of the role of status and conspicuous consumption. *Journal of Cleaner Production, 194*, 277–287.

Achabou, M. A., & Dekhili, S. (2013). Luxury and sustainable development: Is there a match? *Journal of Business Research, 66*(10), 1896–1903.

Atkinson, S. D., & Kang, J. (2021). New luxury: Defining and evaluating emerging luxury trends through the lenses of consumption and personal values. *Journal of Product & Brand Management, 31*(3), 377–393.

Bain, M. (2018). *Nobody knows what luxury is anymore*. The Quartzy Newsletter. What is luxury? Instagram, millennials, and the sharing economy are changing it (qz.com)

Balabanis, G., & Stathopoulou, A. (2021). The price of social status desire and public self-consciousness in luxury consumption. *Journal of Business Research, 123*, 463–475.

Bartels, J., Reinders, M. J., & Van Haaster-De Winter, M. (2015). Perceived sustainability initiatives: Retail managers' intrinsic and extrinsic motives. *British Food Journal, 117*(6), 1720–1736.

Brand Finance. (2018). *Italy 50 2018*. Retrieved from http://brandfinance.com/images/upload/ brand_finance_italy_50_report_2018_website_version.pdf

Braun, V., & Clarke, V. (2006). Using thematic analysis in psychology. *Qualitative Research in Psychology, 3*(2), 77–101.

Buckle, C. (2019). *The luxury market in 2019: What brands should know*. Retrieved from https://blog.globalwebindex.com/chart-of-the-week/luxury-market-2019/

BusinessWire. (2016). *Global retail industry worth USD 28 trillion by 2019-analysis, technologies & forecasts report 2016-2019-research and markets*. Retrieved from http://www.businesswire.com/news/home/20160630005551/en/GlobalRetail-Industry-Worth-USD-28-Trillion

Carrier, J. G., & Luetchford, P. (2012). *Ethical consumption: Social value and economic practice*. New York, NY: Berghahn Books.

Conti, G. M., & Vacca, F. (2008). Textile traditions and fashion design. New experiential paths. In *Changing the change. Design, visions proposals and tools: Torino 2008* (pp. 1–14). Turin, Italy: Umberto Allemandi & C.

Dang, V. T., Nguyen, N., & Wang, J. (2020). Consumers' perceptions and responses towards online retailers' CSR. *International Journal of Retail & Distribution Management, 48*(12), 1277–1299.

D'Arpizio, C., Levato, F., Zito, D., Kamel, M.-A., & de Montgolfier, J. (2016). *Luxury goods worldwide market study, fall-winter 2016*. Bain Report. Retrieved from http://www.bain.com/publications/articles/luxury-goodsworldwide-market-study-fall-winter-2016.aspx

D'Arpizio, C., Levato, F., Kamel, M.-A., & de Montgolfier, J. (2017). *Luxury goods worldwide market study, fall-winter 2017*. Bain Report. Retrieved from http://www.bain.de/Images/BAIN_REPORT_Global_Luxury_Report_2017.pdf

De Angelis, M., Adıgüzel, F., & Amatulli, C. (2017). "The role of design similarity in consumers' evaluation of new green products: An investigation of luxury fashion brands". *Journal of Cleaner Production, 141*, 1515–1527.

Donato, C., De Angelis, M., & Amatulli, C. (2020). Sustainable luxury: The effect of corporate social responsibility strategy on luxury consumption motivations. In I. Cantista, & T. Sabada (Eds.), *Understanding luxury fashion* (pp. 221–241). Cham, Switzerland: Palgrave Macmillan.

Dunn, K., & Harness, D. (2019). Whose voice is heard? The influence of user-generated versus company-generated content on consumer scepticism towards CSR. *Journal of Marketing Management, 35*(9–10), 886–915.

Durieu, X. (2003). How Europe's retail sector helps to promote sustainable production'. *Industry and Environment, 26*(1), 7–9.

European Commission's. (2008). *Sustainable consumption and production and sustainable industrial policy action plan*. Retrieved from https://www.eea.europa.eu/policy-documents/com-2008-397

Fallan, K., & Lees-Maffei, G. (2014). *Introduction: The history of Italian design*. In G. Lees-Maffei, & K. Fallan (Eds.), *Made in Italy: Rethinking a century of Italian design*. London, UK: Bloomsbury.

Festa, G., Rossi, M., Kolte, A., & Situm, M. (2020). Territory-based knowledge management in international marketing processes – The case of "Made in Italy" SMEs. *European Business Review, 32*(3), 425–442.

Franco, J. C., Hussain, D., & McColl, R. (2020). Luxury fashion and sustainability: Looking good together'. *Journal of Business Strategy, 41*(4), 55–61.

Grazzini, L., Acuti, D., & Aiello, G. (2021). Solving the puzzle of sustainable fashion consumption: The role of consumers' implicit attitudes and perceived warmth. *Journal of Cleaner Production, 287*, 125579.

Guercini, S., & Ranfagni, S. (2013). Sustainability and luxury: The Italian case of a supply chain based on native wools. *Journal of Corporate Citizenship, 2013*(52), 76–89.

Gunarathne, N., & Sankalpani, U. (2021). Diffusion of cleaner production in a developing country: The case of Sri Lanka. *Journal of Cleaner Production, 311*, 127626.

Hacking, T., & Guthrie, P. (2008). A framework for clarifying the meaning of triple Bottom-line, integrated, and sustainability assessment. *Environmental Impact Assessment Review, 28*(2–3), 73–89.

Hennigs, N., Wiedmann, K. P., Klarmann, C., & Behrens, S. (2013). Sustainability as part of the luxury essence: Delivering value through social and environmental excellence. *Journal of Corporate Citizenship, 2013*(52), 25–35.

Hubbard, G. (2009). Measuring organizational performance: Beyond the triple bottom line. *Business Strategy and the Environment, 18*(3), 177–191. doi: https://doi.org/10.1002/bse.564

Iannilli, V. M. (2014). Retailing made in Italy: An evolutionary reading towards emerging paradigms. *Fashion Practice, 6*(2), 201–220.

Janssen, C., Vanhamme, J., Lindgreen, A., & Lefebvre, C. (2013). The Catch-22 of responsible luxury: Effects of luxury product characteristics on Consumers' perception of fit with corporate social responsibility. *Journal of Business Ethics, 119*(1), 45–57.

Kapferer, J. N., & Michaut-Denizeau, A. (2013). Is luxury compatible with sustainability? Luxury consumers' viewpoint. *Journal of Brand Management, 21*(1), 1–22.

Kapferer, J. N., & Michaut, A. (2015). Luxury and sustainability: A common future? The match depends on how consumers define luxury. *Luxury Research Journal, 1*(1), 3–17.

Lehner, M. (2015). Retail store influence on sustainable consumption behaviour. *International Journal of Quality and Service Sciences, 7*(4), 404–423.

Lin, T. T., Lee, C. C., & Lin, H. C. (2012). Analysis of customer profit contribution for banks with the concept of marketing mix strategy between 4Cs and 5Ps. *Service Business*, 7(1), 37–59.

Lundblad, L., & Davies, I. A. (2015). The values and motivations behind sustainable fashion consumption. *Journal of Consumer Behaviour, 15*(2), 149–162.

Florence, P. V. (2012). Meta-luxury: Brands and the culture of excellence/Luxury strategy in action. *Journal of Brand Management, 19*(7), 637–640.

McCarthy, J. E. (1981). *Basic marketing: A managerial approach* (7th ed.). Homewood, IL: R.D. Irwin.

Mundel, J., Huddleston, P., & Vodermeier, M. (2017). An exploratory study of consumers' perceptions: What are affordable luxuries? *Journal of Retailing and Consumer Services, 35*, 68–75.

Naidoo, M., & Gasparatos, A. (2018). Corporate environmental sustainability in the retail sector: Drivers, strategies and performance measurement. *Journal of Cleaner Production, 203*, 125–142.

Parguel, B., Delécolle, T., & Valette-Florence, P. (2016). How price display influences consumer luxury perceptions. *Journal of Business Research, 69*(1), 341–348.

Park, H., & Kim, Y. K. (2016). An empirical test of the triple bottom line of customer-centric sustainability: The case of fast fashion. *Fashion and Textiles, 3*(1).

Qureshi, M. I. (2017). The value relevance of intangibles: Some evidence on industry sector, firm performance and size effects. *International Journal of Accounting, Auditing and Performance Evaluation, 13*(3), 293.

Salem, S. F., & Alanadoly, A. B. (2020). Personality traits and social media as drivers of word-of-mouth towards sustainable fashion. *Journal of Fashion Marketing and Management: An International Journal, 25*(1), 24–44.

Streit, C-M., & Davies, I. A. (2013). Sustainability isn't sexy: an exploratory study into luxury fashion. In M. A. Gardetti, & A. L. Torres (Eds.), *Sustainability in fashion and textiles: values, design, production and consumption*. Sheffield, UK.: Greenleaf Publishing.

Tang, A. K., Lai, K. H., & Cheng, T. (2016). A multi-research-method approach to studying environmental sustainability in retail operations. *International Journal of Production Economics, 171*, 394–404.

Temperini, V., Gregori, G. L., & Palanga, P. (2016). The brand made in Italy: A critical analysis. *Management Studies, 4*(3).

Testa, D. S., Bakhshian, S., & Eike, R. (2021). Engaging consumers with sustainable fashion on Instagram. *Journal of Fashion Marketing and Management: An International Journal*, 25(4), 569–584.

Tortora, L. (2021, November 18). *Giorgio Armani e 10 Corso Como lanciano una collezione senza tempo*. Milan, Italy: Vogue Italia. Retrieved from https://www.vogue.it/moda/article/giorgio-armani-10-corso-como-collaborazione-collezione.

Vătămănescu, E. M., Dabija, D. C., Gazzola, P., Cegarro-Navarro, J. G., & Buzzi, T. (2021). Before and after the outbreak of Covid-19: Linking fashion companies' corporate social responsibility approach to consumers' demand for sustainable products. *Journal of Cleaner Production, 321*, 128945.

Yin, R. K. (2017). *Case study research and applications: Design and methods* (6th ed.). SAGE Publications, Inc.

Youn, S. Y., & Cho, E. (2021). CSR ads matter to luxury fashion brands: A construal level approach to understand Gen Z consumers' eWOM on social media. *Journal of Fashion Marketing and Management: An International Journal, 26*(3), 1316–2026.

5 The New Road to Certified Sustainability in Luxury

Beachwear and Lingerie

The Yamamay Case

Fabio Iraldo
Scuola Superiore Sant'Anna

Case study: Yamamay – The EDIT line

The fashion industry represents an important sector in the global economy, providing jobs for lots of people around the world. However, today the textile system operates in an almost completely linear way: large quantities of non-renewable resources are extracted to produce clothes that are often used only for a short time, and then the materials are mostly sent to landfills or incinerated. It is estimated that globally less than 1% of textile materials are recycled into new garments, managing to close the cycle of the supply chain (Ellen MacArthur Foundation, 2017). Fast fashion – the rapid changing of clothing lines and fashion trends – promotes increased consumption and reduces the life span of clothing, consequently fostering an increase in the textile waste generated.

The textile-clothing sector is therefore characterized by a high ecological footprint: it is the fourth worst pressure category for use of primary raw materials and water (after food, construction, and transport) and the fifth worst for greenhouse-gas emissions (responsible for 10% of emissions worldwide) (European Commission, 2020). Moreover, the European Environment Agency (EEA) estimates that textile production is responsible for about 20% of the global pollution of drinking water due to processes such as dyeing and finishing and that washing synthetic garments is responsible for 35% of the primary microplastics released into the environment.

Due to the high use of resources and the high impact on the environment, the textile sector has been identified in the EU 2020 Circular Economy Action Plan as one of the priority sectors on which to act for the application of new business models that promote the transition to the circular economy. In the same Action Plan, the Commission announced that it would adopt an EU Textile Strategy with the aim to lay out "conditions and incentives to boost the competitiveness, sustainability and resilience of the EU textile sector" and address both the environmental and social impact of the textile industry.

The Strategy for Sustainable and Circular Textiles was presented on 30 March 2022 by the European Commission. This document highlights the

DOI: 10.4324/9781003305095-7

Commission's willingness to develop a series of key actions for sustainable and circular textiles, including: introducing mandatory eco-design requirements; stopping the destruction of unsold or returned textiles; tackling microplastics pollution; introducing information requirements and a Digital Product Passport; green claims for truly sustainable textiles; extended producer responsibility and boosting reuse and recycling of textile waste; launching the transition pathway for the textiles ecosystem of the future; reversing the overproduction and overconsumption of clothing; ensuring fair competition and compliance in a well-functioning internal market; supporting research, innovation and investments; developing the skills needed for the green and digital transitions; due diligence for environmental and social fairness; and addressing the challenges from the export of textile waste.

The textile-fashion industry is one of the most important part of Italian manufacturing covering 45,000 companies, 398,000 employees, and having turnover of about 55 billion euros (equal to 31% of the entire European textile-fashion industry). For this reason, many companies have begun to embrace the strategic directions in the field of the circular economy for textiles indicated at the European level, seeing opportunities rather than threats. One of these proactive companies is Yamamay.

Yamamay, a brand owned by Inticom S.p.A., was born in Italy in 2001 and is among the Italian leaders of single-brand retailers of underwear, swimwear, and sea clothing, with over 600 stores in 42 countries. Since 2011, Yamamay has been working with the Carpisa brand, creating the Pianoforte Group. Each year, Yamamay stores sell about 12 million products designed entirely in Italy, and in 2020 sales generated retail proceeds of 172 million euros, despite the COVID-19 pandemic and related lockdowns.

Yamamay's path toward a more sustainable business model starts with a strong belief of the Cimmino family: the only way to guarantee a future for the company is to rethink processes and products by integrating a new system of values into the corporate culture. The work on sustainability involved the company and all its stakeholders, through a series of projects.

Since 2014, the company has invested in the eco-design of its products. This choice makes it possible to seize the competitive opportunities linked to sustainability and circularity, at the same time giving a strong message of commitment along the entire supply chain and aiming at involving the consumer in key choices to encourage the development of innovative materials.

Yamamay affirms that:

We create and design in compliance with the principles of eco design thinking about how important it is for people to use beautiful, functional products with reduced impact on the environment and people. To open ourselves up in transparency to all stakeholders, we have decided to voluntarily publish the Sustainability Report starting from the one for the year 2019. We take care to give the best possible service to ensure an engaging customer experience, destined to establish a relationship over time between people, our world and our products.

Yamamay says it wants to contribute to the construction of a development model that generates shared value among people and communities around the world. The company aims to implement this by assiduously participating in the objectives identified by the United Nations with the 2030 Agenda. In doing so, Yamamay seeks to operate responsibly in order to protect the environment, safeguard biodiversity, reduce waste and emissions. In that approach, the company includes raising awareness among employees and other stakeholders about sustainable development and decarbonization. Moreover, sustainability in a period of change implies for Yamamay a focus on people as an essential value. *Inclusiveness and the enhancement of people are the fundamental elements on which we base our relationship with human capital, local communities, suppliers and all our collaborators.*

Following its path in the field of sustainability and the development of a circular economy, in spring 2021 Yamamay launched a new swimwear line called EDIT (eco-designed innovative textile), with the aim of reducing the environmental impact of products both downstream and upstream of its life cycle. EDIT is a capsule collection of swimwear entirely made with mono-polymer fabric, 100% recycled and 100% recyclable so that it can be completely "circular". The collection consists of two one-piece swimsuits (fantasy and purple), two two-piece swimsuits (fantasy, blue, and purple), and a patterned beach robe.

The polymers used for the production of the fabric and accessories applied to the swimsuits were produced by Tide Ocean SA and are made of plastic recovered from the oceans. Yamamay has been a partner of the One Ocean Foundation for years and is committed to the creation and dissemination of product models that concretely demonstrate the commitment to reducing the impact of the fashion industry on the oceans, also supporting the "Save the Ocean" campaign promoted by the foundation. The choice to support this type of non-profit organization also derives from the strong connection between Yamamay's swimwear business and the topic of plastic pollution of the seas.

The recycled polyester fabric was manufactured in Italy by partner Tiba Tricot and is elastane-free, to further guarantee total recyclability at the end of the swimsuit's life cycle.

The print of the patterned swimsuits is made thanks to a collaboration between Yamamay and young students from the "Aldo Galli"-led network of Como School of Fine Arts, who reworked some maritime-themed designs by fabric designer Beppe Spadacini, taken from the homonymous historical archive. The print selected for EDIT was reproduced on the mono-polymer fabric with the ecological transfer system.

The level of circularity of the entire EDIT swimwear line was measured using the Check-up Tool applied by Ergo Srl, a spinoff of the Scuola Superiore Sant'Anna of Pisa. The tool, taking into consideration the different phases of the value chain (procurement, design, production, distribution, consumption, management, and recovery of waste), allowed to evaluate the overall performance of the product in terms of circularity, highlighting excellent results, in particular, for the design phase and the use phase, thanks to the use of 100% recycled and recyclable polymers.

The EDIT capsule collection was an integral part of the Yamamay beachwear collection for summer 2021 and was sold in a limited edition in selected Yamamay flagship stores and on the brand's website.

The product packaging as well as the showcase dedicated to the EDIT collection have been made with sustainable materials:

- Packaging: tag in FSC (Forest Stewardship Council) certified paper, thread in polypropylene with at least 70% post-consumer recycled plastic, care-label in 100% recycled polyester, and polybag in 100% recyclable polypropylene with 50% recycled material.
- Showcases: FSC-certified paper digitally printed, water-based inks, and glue.

An important investment was also made in terms of communication and consumer involvement: the information relating to the measurement of the circularity of the swimwear has been disclosed to the public through the website and through a QR code placed on the tag of each product.

EDIT is currently the only example of a mono-component swimsuit in the beachwear market, which manages to combine the maintenance of the functional and aesthetic properties of the product with respect for the principles of eco-design in the development and production phases.

The characteristics of the product were also well appreciated by consumers, who welcomed the launch of the capsule collection on the market and the information relating to the circularity of EDIT, as also testified by the comments received on Yamamay's social channels.

In 2022, EDIT was developed in collaboration with two new Italian partners: Radici Group (supplier of polymers) and Carvico (weaving of swimwear).

The same innovative fabric applied for the EDIT capsule collection was used in 2022 to make swimwear and uniforms for a team of biologists who took part in M.A.R.E. (Marine Adventure for Research & Education), a study and dissemination project on the state of health of the Mediterranean Sea. The project was developed by the Centro Velico Caprera in collaboration with One Ocean Foundation and involves a number of partners, including Yamamay.

The EDIT initiative also represents the first step by Yamamay for the development of a take-back system that aims to effectively close the life cycle of the products, further involving the consumer in the realization of a completely circular process, which allows the recovery of post-consumer products. This step is a new challenge for the company that is always eager to implement new circular economy projects in the textile-clothing sector. With regard to this initiative, it should be noted that from 1 January 2022 in Italy the obligation of separate collection of textile waste was introduced.

Italy has brought forward the deadline (scheduled for 1 January 2025) to comply with the requirement introduced by the Circular Economy Package of the European Union.

References

Ellen MacArthur Foundation. (2017). *A new textiles economy: redesigning fashion's future.* Retrieved from https://ellenmacarthurfoundation.org/a-new-textiles-economy

European Commission. (2020). *Circular economy action plan for a cleaner and more competitive Europe.* Retrieved from https://docs.wbcsd.org/2020/11/WBCSD_Circular_Economy_Action_Plan_2020%E2%80%93Summary_for_business.pdf

Section II

6 Luxury Made in Italy in Transition and the Sustainable Engagement

Cases from Different Sectors

Stefania Lazzaroni
Altagamma

Introduction

Sustainability is a key issue for Italy's high-end brands, just as it is for European brands in all industries: the EU Green Deal, launched in 2019, positions sustainability as one of the two pillars of an innovative European strategy that can enhance our reputation worldwide granting our continent a modern, competitive economy with net zero emissions of greenhouse gases by 2050 (55% down on 1990 levels by 2030). Italy's high-end brands are necessarily at the forefront of this collective movement, which is changing the world as we know it, and strongly resonates with our culture and heritage. Also in 2020 Ursula Von Der Leyen, the President of the EU Commission, launched the "New European Bauhaus Project", which brings a cultural and creative dimension to the European Green Deal, aimed at rethinking our ways of living and showcasing how sustainable innovation can create tangible, positive experiences in our daily life.

Within this framework, Europe's high-end brands have shown they are ready to spearhead and model change in the field of sustainability, and – although it is a responsibility shared between companies, governments, and consumers – these industries have committed to very specific action plans to change their business models. Moreover, they have pledged to leverage their influence with consumers and suppliers to drive positive change. **On average, these companies spend 0.8–1.5% of their annual revenue on sustainability innovation** and Italian brands in particular have been investing more and more in environmental, social, and governance (ESG) projects, inspired by significant changes in consumer behavior, and by the Italian government's support for companies changing their business models to meet sustainability goals through the PNRR (the Italian National Recovery and Resilience Plan), with the general awareness that climate change is a global issue that cannot be ignored, especially by companies held up as thought leaders.

According to the latest report by ECCIA (the European Cultural and Creative Industries Association that Altagamma is a founding member of) and Bain & Company, Europe's high-end brands are at the forefront of ESG

DOI: 10.4324/9781003305095-9

with corporate strategies designed to ensure the sustainability of products and processes, and with initiatives dedicated to workers and consumers. This applies to many areas, and many companies have deployed:

- a climate change strategy that reduces their environmental footprint
- blockchain-based supply chain traceability program
- circular business models that include recycling raw materials
- initiatives to protect natural ecosystems and preserve biodiversity
- R&D investments to identify new sustainable raw materials/packaging
- awareness-raising campaigns on various social issues (gender equality/ racism)
- career development program to foster inclusion.

It is also important to note that by increasing their engagement in ESG issues and integrating sustainability into their core business strategy, 63% of companies have also seen very positive returns.

If properly carried out, investments in sustainability can:

- boost company reputation
- foster innovation
- retain existing customers and attract new ones
- enhance return on investments
- reduce costs
- attract talents
- protect resources
- energize and motivate employees
- improve productivity
- attract investors who uphold environmental, social and governance (ESG) values, and prevent companies being excluded by traditional investors due to these criteria.

As we write this introduction, **the Russia-Ukraine war** exploded in February 2022 is inevitably changing the focus for most Italian companies: the shortage of traditional energy sources (gas and oil) is boosting the demand for fossil fuels. Will this be a step back on the path toward a solid circular economy? Some believe it might have the effect of delaying the significant changes that were being implemented and that, due to a concrete lack of alternative resources, many green commitments may have to be put on hold temporarily. We really hope this does not have a major effect on current EU strategies and that, on the contrary, the situation will accentuate the need for alternative, clean energy sources.

Italy's high-end companies currently represent 126 billion euros for the Italian economy, 7.4% of the country's GDP and about 10% of the Global Luxury market, which pre-COVID was worth 1.3 billion euros. In 2021, after the first-ever double-digit decrease for the sector, it dialed back to 1.14 billion worldwide. The **Altagamma Foundation** gathers the top 113 Italian luxury brands in a variety of sectors, from **fashion to jewelry, design, yachts, food & wine, hospitality, automotive, and wellness**. Though diverse, all devote the same level of attention to their discerning, extremely sophisticated consumers. Altagamma has analyzed the action being taken on ESG issues (environment, social, and governance) by these companies and mapped their efforts and needs: the challenge is enormous, and the path has just begun, but from 2012 to 2022 significant progress has been made and currently 70% of our companies have their ESG report published; most of them have board members with specific ESG competences and all of them are aware that both consumers and the financial community are expecting a robust paradigm shift. In 2022, Altagamma published its Charter of Values, developed in collaboration with all our members, which details the key parameters that our companies, albeit in their different sectors, acknowledge as minimum common requirements. The Charter of Values lists six ESG pillars that all our members are encouraged to adopt:

1 Preserve the environment and biodiversity
2 Favor a circular, low-impact economy
3 Create a sustainable ecosystem
4 Promote a culture of Corporate Social Responsibility
5 Valorize human capital
6 Support the local area and "Made in Italy" and promote cooperation between companies.

Aligned with the United Nations' 17 sustainable development goals, these six key areas not only cover environmental issues (including all the due technical parameters of decarbonization and circular consumption) but also address the social impact of our businesses. They highlight the pressing need for a more inclusive approach, respectful of diversity, and sensitive to the gender gap, and the ongoing demand for corporate skills development to respond to our fluid, ever-changing society.

According to a recent survey, **luxury consumers are less and less willing to compromise**, with 70% saying they are prepared to pay more for a product they deem sustainable. In the last year and a half, online searches on this topic have risen by five times. The effects of this are being felt further up the line too: buyers are ready to drop brands whose image does not meet their demand for a consistent, solid commitment to sustainability. It has been estimated that four years from now, an average of 40% of orders from major buyers will be for sustainable products. Once an aspirational factor, sustainability has now become an essential prerequisite that drives the purchasing behavior of around 80% of the youngest luxury customers.

Investors and shareholders are increasingly interested in sustainable projects/brands, with about one-third of global assets managed according to responsible investment practices. In a recent survey by BNP Paribas,

81% of the investors interviewed already take account of ESG factors when managing their portfolios, while 16% plan to start doing so within the year. Blackrock, for example, is incorporating sustainability into risk management, portfolio construction, the creation of new products, and interactions with companies. The largest investor in the world believes that sustainability has to be the new investment standard.

Italy's luxury firms **differ greatly in size**, and this explains their different attitudes and approaches to sustainability. Some are part of international groups (LVMH, Kering, Haworth, Nestlé), which enables them to coordinate with centralized strategic teams, making it easier to formulate consistent, long-term objectives; some are independent businesses with solid financial capabilities which means they can invest significant amounts, and rapidly, in adapting their business models (Brunello Cucinelli, illycaffè, Zegna, Salvatore Ferragamo, Moncler); others are smaller, family-owned businesses, currently engaged in curating their ESG goals and storytelling, and sometimes discovering that many of the strategies they have implemented organically for years (i.e., attention to employee welfare, involvement in the local community, use of high-quality, durable materials, support for local cultural heritage) were actually intrinsically sustainable.

The key point here is that **sustainability appears to be hard-wired into Italy's high-end companies**, an integral element of their mission and philosophy. First of all, these firms have always been strongly connected to their local areas, making them keenly aware that the natural resources they use in their production processes need to be safeguarded. Secondly, all of these companies are committed to producing superlative quality products that are made to last, produced in limited quantities using the finest natural materials. These are products that become an investment for the consumer, that can be re-sold, and are "the contrary of disposable", i.e., the opposite of the planned obsolescence that characterizes fast fashion. Thirdly, they are committed to ensuring employee welfare, given that the expertise that goes into making their products, often including hand-crafting, represents a unique asset that is not easy to replace. Just think that on average it takes our companies 5–7 years to train people in the specific skills they require. To highlight this aspect and explore it in greater detail, Altagamma has recently published a book entitled "I Talenti del Fare 2", in which authoritative figures stress the importance of this manufacturing know-how for our brands and testify to the inestimable value of this knowledge for cultural and creative companies. Italian luxury brands are strongly committed to engaging with the younger generations, given that many young people appear to be unaware of the employment opportunities offered by the country's luxury brands and their supply chains. In the Altagamma-Unioncamere study presented in the book (Figure 6.1), we have highlighted that by 2026 the various sectors of the luxury industry will need 346,000 new resources (70% of this figure is due to retirement). It is estimated that only 50% of this number will be found, generating a major gap between brands' needs and the number of new, skilled workers available.

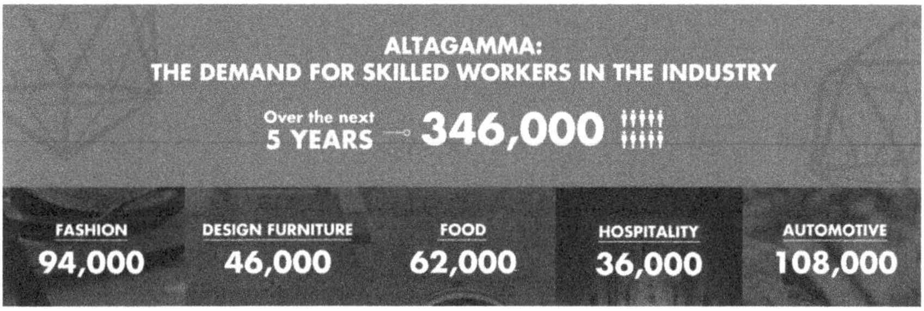

Figure 6.1 Altagamma: The demand for skilled workers in the industry.

The fourth key element is the fact that many of our companies have direct control over their supply chains. Italy is the only country that boasts almost 100% vertical integration in so many different sectors, thanks to the invaluable ecosystems represented by its specialized production districts. We have estimated that in the luxury industry more than 90% of production takes place in Italy. This enables almost total control over compliance with environmental and social sustainability parameters, and we have recently seen many Italian brands investing in upskilling the ESG capabilities of their suppliers and partners. Each Altagamma company has an average of 150–200 external suppliers, many of which are small companies whose business depends almost entirely on their relationship with the major brand. Nowadays, to be effectively sustainable, external suppliers have to meet the same standards as the brands themselves, and brands need to support suppliers in implementing new paradigms. Some brands have gone as far as acquiring their own supply chains in order to be able to fulfil the most stringent sustainability standards and ensure maximum alignment with company strategies (i.e., Zegna acquired Tessitura Ubertina, Brunello Cucinelli acquired Lanificio Cariaggi, Prada and Zegna acquired Filati Biagioli Modesto).

Lastly, Italian brands benefit from the **Made in Italy concept**, a crucial element that contributes to positioning Italian products as intrinsically sustainable. The "Made in Italy" concept is a metabrand that consumers all around the world appreciate and identify with high-quality, impeccably crafted products. "Made in Italy" is an intrinsic soft power that conveys both technical and cultural aspects: on one hand it is a symbolic guarantee that the product is well-made and of excellent quality; on the other hand, it evokes the beauty of our country, the "dolce vita" life, and the natural style and spontaneous warmth Italians are renowned for. Italian style is a unique selling point that attracts luxury consumers all over the world who are looking for superlative quality based on craftsmanship, sustainable production, natural materials or ingredients, and innate authenticity. These include 435 million high-net-worth individuals who together spend more than 1.1 billion euros.

It is interesting to note that the organic "sense of responsibility" displayed by Italy's high-end brands is not a recent phenomenon; it is not something taken from international standards and added on as a marketing tag. Italian luxury belongs to the so-called Economy of Beauty, which revolves around the concepts of "il bello, il buono e il ben fatto", i.e., beautiful, good, and well-made. Sustainability and social responsibility are an intrinsic part of these values. In the culture of Ancient Greece, which so richly informs our country's heritage, the expression ***kalòs kai agathòs*** or ***kalokagathos*** indicates the direct link between aesthetics and ethics. For Plato, **beauty** equates to **truth** and **goodness** (Phaedrus). Beauty, therefore, represents the ideal, the unique, a vision of God, and an expression of the global harmony we are all striving to achieve. Now more than ever, this sense of beauty can inspire us to "do good" and drive change on crucial issues. When it comes to luxury brands, customers no longer want just superlative quality products: they want ethical products, outstanding corporate behavior, and brands that pay attention not only to shareholders but also to all their stakeholders and the communities that host them. Our companies have to acknowledge this and become fully aware that responding effectively to cultural and social changes is a roadmap for enduring success.

Italy's high-end brands have evolved significantly: from being solely manufacturers, over 40 years ago, to being retailers when they started their global expansion in the 90s, to being media companies when they began communicating digitally with their consumers. Nowadays, with their strong commitment to sustainability, they have become "social and cultural actors". They are increasingly committed to improving people's lives, helping to clean the planet, and showcasing better ways of making and investing profit (B Corporation goes in this direction). This is a very different approach to the marketing strategies of the '80s, which were entirely centered on aesthetic elements. These brands have also learned to use their soft power to engage with the world and advocate on both environmental questions and key social issues (respect for human rights, gender equality, Black Lives Matter, etc.). They have reinvented their relationship with consumers and are intent on building global communities united by common values and beliefs.

A new concept of luxury

It is therefore clear that **the concept of luxury is evolving**. On one hand, as many studies have described, we are witnessing a world of luxury where products do not stand alone and experiences hold increasing appeal. Having a unique sensorial experience – be it a travel or food experience – has become pivotal for consumers, and retail concepts are adapting to this new concept too. Stores not only sell specific items – often researched online – but are first and foremost a stage for brand values. In stores, customers not only want products, but an entirely new sensorial, immersive dimension where they feel they belong, where they are entertained and engaged in a 121 personal relationship.

Then there are the **shareholders and stakeholders, who now expect companies to have a "purpose"**, something that goes beyond just being responsible. Companies are required to invest in the welfare of their employees and society at large: giving back has become a priority, especially for luxury brands.

In this new vision of luxury, Italian companies can play a leading role. They are part of a highly diversified luxury community that boasts world-leading brands in many sectors – fashion, food, design, automotive, yachting, jewelery, and hospitality. This makes it easier for them to offer synergistic experiences spanning different sectors, and their deep-rooted connection to their local areas links them to the landscape and respect for the natural world. Now, in addition to creating value for shareholders, Italy's high-end brands are also being called on to ensure well-being, safety, equity, and justice for their employees, their external stakeholders, and their communities. They are expected to have a higher purpose organically integrated into their business models.

The **impact of COVID – from 2020 to 2022 – has inevitably thrown the focus on human health** as inextricably linked to the question of climate change. Sustainability is an extremely topical issue, and since the pandemic, the link between environmental problems and their global impact has become more evident than ever before. Companies are therefore required to embrace the mission of taking care of people, their employees, and their communities, considering both physical and mental health. **Wellbeing** is now and will probably continue to be the cornerstone of new luxury business practices: companies will have to comply with both imperatives: save the planet and protect human health. We are therefore witnessing a transition to a new, more conscious, and more sustainable kind of luxury. As the Dutch trend forecaster Li Edelkoort said: "The virus has taught us to slow down and change our ways". We believe that a slower pace of life will make people appreciate more value-conscious products whose aura endures over time. Let's not forget, for example, that luxury brands have always been at the forefront in **emergency situations and have never failed to step up for their communities**. During the pandemic, for instance, Altagamma brands donated more than 43 million euros to help fight the virus and acted immediately to convert their production to manufacture face masks, hand sanitizer gel, and medical devices. Currently, only four weeks after the Russia-Ukraine war broke out, they have pledged 10 million euros in various ways. These initiatives, inspired by a sense of connection and active citizenship, are a badge of honor for Italy's enlightened luxury brands.

Not only do these brands step up in bad times to support their people and their customers, **but they are also the first to invest in Italy's cultural heritage**, with renowned examples including Tod's, which contributed to the restoration of the Colosseum, Zegna, with the Oasi Zegna nature reserve, Brunello Cucinelli's project in the village of Solomeo, and Fendi's restoration of the Trevi Fountain. They invest in culture, protect the past, and keep investing in the future, as the creation of corporate museums demonstrates (there are around 25 within Altagamma alone), such as the Prada Foundation and the Bisazza Foundation. Then there are the various educational initiatives that 60% of our brands promote and support: 41 corporate academies, the "Adopt a School" project where 17 brands have adopted a class in a public school and a large number of diverse contributions to master's degrees and university programs.

In short, it can be said that Italy's high-end companies, and luxury brands in general, never stop changing: 30 years ago they were about exclusivity, today they are prioritizing inclusivity; status symbols have made way for social messages. Aesthetics and craftsmanship will always be the cornerstone of luxury brands, but they are now deepening their engagement with social issues and broadening the scope of their action. They are embracing **a more conscious, authentic vision of luxury**, grounded in being true to their ideals, honest with their customers, and fully transparent. Customers want to know what brands stand for and expect them to walk the talk.

However, there are differences between the **western market**, a more mature market characterized by older, more traditional consumers, and the **Asian market**, which has younger consumers energized by a fast-growing economy. The more fluid, vibrant spirit of the Asian market calls for a bolder, more entertainment-based approach from brands. Europe and North America still seem to be pursuing a more understated approach to luxury. This two-pronged global reality is a challenge for Italian high-end brands – especially family-owned companies – which are required to design and create new aesthetics to meet two different standards (eye-catching in the East/discreet in the West); to communicate on completely different social media ecosystems (Wechat and Weibo in the East/Facebook/Instagram in the West) and to distribute through multiple digital touchpoints (brand e-commerce, e-retailers, stores, wholesalers).

The scenario has seen profound, rapid changes in a number of different areas: only ten years ago digital was not viewed as relevant to luxury brands, and sustainability was not an issue at all. Of course, **luxury has always been evolving**, coming to mean slightly different things from decade to decade. High-end brands and their iconic communications have always tapped into our aspirations, and these can be profoundly modified by the changes taking place in society. Factors driving these changes include **technology and the new breed of global luxury consumers, who are now getting younger and younger**, are **more likely to be Asian** (about 40% of luxury purchases are made by Asian millennials), are **more dynamic** (digital distribution parallel to the brick & mortar) and **have a completely new set of values**, much more conscious of contemporary new social issues. **Digitalization** has also made it easier to communicate visions and trends globally and has created a new media ecosystem, with social media enabling direct B2C communication, as opposed to B2B in the past, mediated by print media and ADV. Up to the year 2000, communications were top-down and easier to control. Nowadays interaction is a bottom-up, 121 process, based on authentic, real-time contact. And as in all live interactions, the ability to listen is sometimes more important. By listening more, and becoming more transparent and more authentic, high-end companies have realized that their consumers have changed and are expecting to see some form of brand activism. This has changed everything. Given the continuous scrutiny of social media – with brands being judged and criticized in a direct, public way – combined with growing consumer activism, high-end brands are under increasing pressure to be seen as companies that care. Consumers are demanding a transition to an inclusive society, and a unique window has opened for luxury brands to become better agents of social change by aligning their missions, values, and strategies with a social purpose. They can accomplish this by effectively leveraging their cultural standing and their communications tools, and recognizing the influence they can have on millions of people, something which offers vast potential but also bears great responsibility.

As mentioned above, digital transformation is also a key driver for future growth, as it not only impacts on communications models but also on product manufacturing and distribution. This vital, complex transformation requires a review of established organizational models and legislative frameworks. Just as Italian high-end industries are investing heavily in technology to integrate AI into their business models, they must invest as much in human capital through employee reskilling and upskilling. The online channel has almost doubled over the past two years: after a 50% jump from 2019 to 2020, it continues to power on, growing by 27% from 2020 to 2021 to reach an estimated 62 billion euros in market value this year, thanks to accelerated adoption during COVID, with newly acquired customers. Brand-controlled websites now make up 40% of the online segment, up from 30% in 2019. Online and monobrand stores combined were the key channels for recovery in 2021 and will lead to growth in the midterm.

Ten years ago, it was believed that digital could jeopardize the aura of luxury brands and the sense of exclusiveness that is traditionally part of brands' identity. Now the overarching development of new technologies has actually strengthened the customer-brand relationship, which has become more direct. Just like sustainability, technological innovation is such a radical phenomenon that it impacts all business processes. The ultimate frontier in the digital realm seems to be social gaming, and the Metaverse experience, which has created a parallel digital universe where digital high-end brands are not only represented but also virtually created in the shape of NFTs (non-fungible tokens) on the blockchain. The metaverse market is expected to be worth $800 billion globally, and this could result in $50 billion of additional sales for luxury brands (Morgan Stanley, November 2021): definitely a realm worth exploring.

All in all, digital is therefore a second huge challenge – a real game changer – which also involves setting up omnichannel, "seamless" distribution ecosystems. In short, we might say luxury brands are taking on the challenge of sustainability, but the latter is directly linked to brands' ability to digitally upgrade their entire organizations.

While the main ESG factors apply across all sectors, **each sector has its own specific challenges**. **Fashion** is dealing with key issues regarding the management of unsold products and the industry's carbon footprint. In 2019, the "Fashion Pact" created by Macron involved many Italian and European brands, drawing up very precise new protocols to change the scene. Of course, substantial investments are needed for these to really be effective and luxury brands are clearly in a better position to take on the extra investments. The **yachting and automotive** industries are facing the challenge of zero-emission vehicles, which will mean a shift to electric motors or, for yachting, a reduction in fuel consumption, reengineering boat design, and eliminating plastic. The **jewelery sector** is working on responsible sourcing practices that safeguard human rights. Luxury branded jewelery is better placed to guarantee this and work only with selected and certified partners. The **food industry** has always been very careful about safety and health, and a lot has been done to reduce additives and chemicals used to increase production. **Hospitality** is also working on very different areas, from food donations to solar panels, from sustainable architecture to 100% renewable energy (green certified), to reducing waste and water usage.

In Altagamma we try to support all our members by offering an unbiased perspective, with the aim of fostering the sharing of best practices, outlining the priorities on the global agenda for our industries, supporting member companies in identifying gaps, and setting up common standards that are updated twice-yearly. We offer specific training on the most important international ESG standards and monitor the constantly evolving legislative panorama so as to foster efficient peer-to-peer communications and information exchange. That said, each company selects and works specifically on its own personal ESG strategy: completely tailor-made, aligned with the investment potential of the company and its specific business area. Each Italian high-end brand can represent a unique, virtuous model of sustainability, given that this is embedded in our heritage and traditions, and an integral part of a lifestyle that gravitates around a love of beauty and an appreciation for quality and the finer things in life.

To date, Europe has always been the biggest producer of luxury, the biggest exporter of luxury items, and the biggest market for luxury. Cultural and creative brands are a European asset to be protected and enhanced. It is time to stand up for our craftsmanship, our communities, our skills; to celebrate our traditions and our creativity. Italy boasts an incredibly rich, multi-layered cultural heritage, shaped by different civilizations over the centuries, from the Ancient Greeks to the Renaissance to the religious influence on art and craftsmanship. This is embedded in the DNA of Altagamma brands, which represent a true national asset. And Italy's luxury industry involves not just a hundred or so high-profile players, but also thousands of smaller, locally-based companies: a very precious, fragile eco-system that needs to be preserved, recognized, and robustly supported. Our industry can lead the way, and it can also exert its "soft power" globally, promoting and advocating western values based on respect for others and the unique planet we inhabit.

Bibliography

Altagamma. (2021). *Altagamma Internal Survey and Desk Analysis.*

Altagamma. (2022). I Talenti del Fare 2. Skira.

Bain & Altagamma. (11 November 2021). *Luxury is back... to the future.* Retrieved from https://altagamma.it/media/source/Altagamma%20-%20Bain%20Luxury%20Market%20Monitor%202021.pdf

BCG-Altagamma. (2021, June). *True-luxury global consumer insight.* Retrieved from https://web-assets.bcg.com/f2/f1/002816bc4aca91276243c72ee57d/bcgxaltagamma-true-luxury-global-consumer-insight-2021.pdf

Bianca Ifis. (2021). *The economy of beauty.* Retrieved fromhttps://www.bancaifis.it/en/fattorei/economy-of-beauty/

Bloomberg Intelligence. (2021). *Metaverse may be 800 billion market next tech platform.* Retrieved from https://www.bloomberg.com/professional/blog/metaverse-may-be-800-billion-market-next-tech-platform/

Chevalier, M. (2012, July 20). *Luxury brand management.* New York, NY: Wiley and Sons.

ECCIA & Bain&Company. (2020, January). *The contribution of the high-end cultural and creative sector to the European economy.* Retrieved from https://altagamma.it/media/source/REPORT_ECCIA_Bain%26Co_V11.pdf

European Commission. (2022). *Delivering the European Green Deal.* Retrieved from https://ec.europa.eu/info/strategy/priorities-2019-2024/european-green-deal/delivering-european-green-deal_en

McKinsey&Company. (2019, November 14). *Five ways that ESG creates value.* Retrieved from https://www.mckinsey.com/business-functions/strategy-and-corporate-finance/our-insights/five-ways-that-esg-creates-value

McKinsey&Company. (2019). *Sustainability matters, but does it sell?*

Morgan Stanley (2021). "Metaverse: a $50 Billion Revenue Opportunity for Luxury?", Retrieved from: https://www.businessoffashion.com/news/technology/metaverse-a-50-billion-revenue-opportunity-for-luxury/

7 Luxury Yachting and Sailing – Opportunities and Challenges of Sustainable Development for Italian Boating Industry

The Ferretti Group Case

Francesca Goi[1] *and Amedeo Migali*[2]
[1]EXCELIA Business School
[2]Università degli Studi di Trieste. MICAD

Yachting industry background

The boating industry is one of undisputed Italian excellence and a sector with some peculiarities. Despite being a relatively small industry, with only a few productive countries, distribution of products is global. Industry's dimensions and the lack of official figures means that academic studies on its detailed operations are lacking. For this reason, we found it necessary to briefly introduce the sector before dealing with the topic of sustainability. The choice of a chapter dedicated to the Yachting Industry is appropriate for a book on Luxury Made in Italy. After all, Italy is one of the leading countries of leisure boating worldwide and the absolute leader in superyacht production (Boat International, 2021).

Production within the boating industry can be divided into three major axes: shipbuilding, engines, and accessories. A fourth but rapidly growing axis is service provision. Regarding value creation, shipbuilding is the most important sector in terms of turnover and the number of employees in our country (La Nautica in Cifre, 2021). At a global level, the engine sector generates important turnover, but only a few manufacturers are actually based in Italy. A brief note on accessories is necessary here as it is a fragmented sector, of which the figures could be misleading. In fact, this category includes both products exclusively designed for nautical use, which are included in official industry figures, and a range of products from a variety of other fields. These product ranges are constantly growing, with the example of electronics, home automation, and interior design to name a few. Finally, within shipbuilding itself, a distinction is made between boats measuring up to 80 feet (24 meters) and those of greater length which are commonly called Superyachts.

For an industry overview, we relied on the report released annually by Confindustria Nautica, the Italian Trade Association of the boating industry. The following figures have come from the last edition of the document

DOI: 10.4324/9781003305095-10

(La Nautica in Cifre, 2021), which was presented at the 61st Genova Boat Show in September 2021. Due to the COVID-19 pandemic, global turnover for 2020 was 4.66 billion euros, showing a limited decrease of 2.6%, compared to 2019. This figure is in countertrend to the +61% increase registered over the last five years (La Nautica in Cifre, 2021). Despite the decrease of the industry as a whole, the shipbuilding sector registered an increase of +1.36%.

Thanks to negotiations with the government during lockdown, shipyards obtained permission to reopen early, allowing them to catch up with orders. As such, the following figures are unexpectedly positive, with a growth of shipbuilding exports for the rolling year Q3 2020–Q2 2021, reaching a record of 2.8 billion euros. The forecast for 2021 shows a +23.8% growth (with +/−5% range of variation), meaning a global turnover between 5.5 and 6.0 billion euros. Positive figures are confirmed by a 2.4% increase in employees, which totaled more than 24,000 in 2020, and the increased weight of the GDP's contribution, registered at 2.37% (2.22% in 2019).

Export represents 66% of total turnover for the industry, referring to the turnover generated by national production and import, further validating the positive trade balance. When the export rate is considered in relation to national production only, the figure increases to 76%, and 86% for shipbuilding specifically. This performance jumps to 95% when taking into consideration the superyacht sector, where Italian shipyards are the outright leaders.

According to Stefano Pagani Isnardi, head of the research department at Confindustria Nautica (Pagani Isnardi, 2022),[1] "With the exception of a few big groups, companies [of the Italian boating industry] are small to medium-sized. They are often family-run businesses. The average turnover is between 1 million and 70 million euros for smaller businesses and up to 500 million–1 billion euros for the few big industrial groups. The landscape is not much different abroad, with only few big industrial groups". Despite their size, Italian organizations represent a *savoir faire* closely linked to the territory. As often happens with *Made in Italy* products, various districts of production can be identified. These consist of local clusters, where neighboring businesses have reached a high level of specialization. However, they usually remain independent, rather than being acquired by larger manufacturers. In addition to small-to-medium-sized companies, there are a few industrial groups, but not many. Most notable are the Ferretti Group and Sanlorenzo in central Italy and the Azimut-Benetti Group in the north.

A yacht is an elaborate product, so a wide variety of skills and technologies are required for its production, therefore the number of units sold globally is relatively small. As a result, clusters of highly specialized small-to-medium-sized companies are more common than vertically integrated industrial groups. The result is a network of interdependent companies, representing world-class excellence and strongly linked to the *Made in Italy* concept.

Luxury and yachting

Unlike with other industries, where mass-market, premium, and luxury offers can exist for the same category of products, a yacht is, by definition, a luxury product. Although it is true that entry-level options are now more accessible, actually owning a yacht still remains a symbol of exclusivity, not just a show of financial means. Even if scholars haven't yet agreed on a universal definition of luxury, the characteristics of luxury goods, in general, are shared.

Exclusivity and rarity are intrinsic to the product. When speaking about superyachts, the financial impact, high level of customization, and long production time means they are only made to order. For this reason, market performances are considered when examining order books rather than the number of products sold and delivered. Every year, the UK-based magazine Boat International publishes the Global Order Book, a snapshot of the superyacht sector compiled in collaboration with shipyards from all over the world. According to the last report, published in December 2021, there were 821 superyachts on order or under construction in 179 yards around the globe, keeping in mind that it can take several years to build a superyacht. Of those projects, 407 are being assembled by Italian shipyards (Boat International, 2021).

Uniqueness, another characteristic of luxury products, is central to the yachting industry. In general, there is a direct proportionality between boat dimensions and the level of customization, even if the dimensions themselves are not the sole criteria. Superyachts are generally unique pieces, but smaller boats also can have a great level of customization. One-offs are not unusual.

Quality is not an option, because boats are a synthesis of craftsmanship and technology. According to an owner's desires, yachts can be made of various materials (steel, aluminum, wood, and various composites), and equipped to different levels of comfort. A fiberglass hull has a different production process than an aluminum one; a day cruiser won't have the same needs in electronic equipment such as radar and sonar that a transoceanic sailing boat will have. Expertise and specific skills are required to produce a luxury boat. The owner's desires must be made compatible with technical constraints, as much as the hydrodynamic and safety requirements of the vessel itself.

By walking around a marina, it is evident that boats are **durable**, both in terms of material and in design, including not only classic wooden boats but also fiberglass yachts, with intriguing histories and several renowned owners. This characteristic is similar to the durability of classic cars and timeless fashion garments.

In summary, the luxury and exclusivity comes at a price: yachts are **expensive** objects.

Sustainability

Scholars continue to debate about luxury and sustainability as a common vision of their interlinking still hasn't been found. For some, due to its elitist and superfluous character, luxury cannot be sustainable. To others, because high quality and timelessness are inherent attributes of luxury, sustainability is intrinsically embedded (Janssen, 2014; Kapferer, 2014; Kunz, 2020; Wells, 2021).

For the purpose of this research and reflection, it is vital to circumscribe the concept of sustainability to understand its compatibility with the yachting industry. Leaving aside the evolution of the concept, it is worth recalling the most shared definition of sustainable development. As established by The United Nations in 1987 in the renowned document *Our Common Future*, the definition states: "Sustainable development is development that meets the needs of the present without compromising the ability of future generations to meet their own needs" (Our Common Future, 1987). The principle of the statement is not difficult to understand, but in order to embed the model within a business strategy, companies often employ *the Triple Bottom Line* (Elkington, 2013).

The Triple Bottom Line

Conceived by John Elkington in 1994, the Triple Bottom Line (Elkington, 2013) is a business model that measures sustainable performances. The concept is multipolar, as performances are evaluated on three axes: economic, social, and environmental. These are also called the 3Ps, standing for "Profit, People and Planet".

The Triple Bottom Line is tightly linked to stakeholder's needs, urging businesses to shift their focus from the shareholder's interest to the stakeholder's one. Developed in 1984 by the American philosopher and professor R. Edward Freeman (1984), stakeholder theory advocates that businesses should aim at creating value for all entities impacted by their activity. According to the theory, examples of stakeholders include shareholders employees, customers, local communities, governments, and financial institutions.

As this research will use the Triple Bottom Line framework to analyze sustainable performances of both the yachting industry and the Ferretti Group, here is an overview of the three pillars:

- **Profit** refers to financial performances. Business strategies are generally conceived to maximize profit for shareholders. If considered from a stakeholder's perspective, a profitable company is a company more willing to persist operationally in the long term, with evident advantages for all stakeholders, including the shareholders.
- **People** takes into consideration the societal impact of business activities. Relations between businesses and employees, local communities, or suppliers are considered in this social dimension.
- **Planet** refers to the ecological dimension of the model and takes into consideration all aspects impacting the environment, including but not limited to waste disposal, energy use, and the management of scarce resources.

Yachting and sustainability

Scholars disagree on the compatibility of luxury with the concept of sustainability. Two different systematic literature reviews highlight this limitation and the lack of academic literature on the matter (Athwal, 2019; Kunz, 2020). Some academic studies on sustainability explore luxury sectors but, except for a case on one specific shipyard (Amatulli, 2017), we did not find any contributions exploring the boating industry and its role within the overarching theme. We have therefore investigated the matter using the Triple Bottom Line concept. The analysis will first highlight boating industry performances according to the three pillars of the model (profit, people, and planet). Next, we will present the Ferretti Group case.

The choice of the Ferretti Group is justified by a set of reasons. The Group is a renowned player of the Italian boating industry with worldwide distribution. The shipbuilding company is specialized in the design, production, and commercialization of boats from 8 to 95 meters, with several distinct brands, and it is today one of the very few Italian shipbuilding companies to publish a sustainability report.

The symbolic relevance of luxury goods is particularly evident when speaking about boats. A yacht is not only a means to spend time on the sea but also a clear status symbol. This aspect is emphasized by the product's physical attributes, particularly its size. Furthermore, in some cases, a yacht can be so unique that it is immediately recognizable from a distance, such as the legendary *Nabila,* commissioned in 1978 by billionaire Adnan Khashoggi. Thereafter the 86-meter motor yacht was used in a James Bond movie and it became the property of the Sultan of Brunei, who then sold it to Donald Trump. After Trump's ownership, it was sold to Prince Al-Waleed bin Talal. More recent examples would be *Seven*, owned by David Beckham, *Great White* owned by Rafa Nadal or the *Amphitrite*, formerly owned consecutively by J.K Rowling and Johnny Depp (Boat International). The above examples go to show that a boat is a powerful means to express consumer identity and ethical values.

Celebrities and trendsetters, for whom public image is a sensitive matter, are becoming increasingly concerned about sustainability. To a certain extent, this is also the case for the buyers of luxury goods. Even when sustainability is not a priority, guilt-free consumption remains an issue. According to Stefano Pagani Isnardi of Confindustria Nautica (Pagani Isnardi, 2022)[1]: "If a few decades ago a boat was mainly a status symbol, today's customers are looking for more sustainable products. Yacht owners are, in general, concerned about sea protection as they are lovers and beneficiaries of the sea".

Planet

Sustainable development in recreational boating goes through three main axes: cleaner construction, more sustainable use, and environmentally friendly "end-of-life" disposal. For this reason, manufacturers are not the only players involved. Consumers' awareness is crucial and two-fold. On one hand is the responsible use of the boat, which is fundamental for oceans' preservation. On the other is their demand for a more sustainable product as an incentive toward cleaner production.

As it has been said earlier in the chapter, a yacht does not go unnoticed. Its signaling power is greater than other more discreet luxury goods and is no longer only a symbol of wealth. It has also become a medium to communicate an owner's consciousness and adherence to the environmental cause. If it is propitious that customers replace their boats with a more sustainable one, it also becomes necessary for manufacturers, international organizations, and authorities to work together to manage the end-of-life of the boats themselves. As we will discuss later, disposal and recycling is a weak link. However, the industry's players are hard at work to find appropriate solutions.

Several aspects need to be considered when investigating the boating industry's environmental impact.

Boat production

In terms of **land use,** shipyards and boatbuilders need large facilities. Manufacturers, particularly superyacht builders, are often based in industrial areas, often with easy access to the sea. The efficient and respectful use of these valuable areas is crucial for the sustainable development of the industry. There is an urgent need for investments, as sustainability is not yet a priority for production processes. Composite production requires large molds, which are bulky objects, usually made of composite, wood, and metal, and may only be used to make a handful of units. They are then stored near the facility.

Water and energy consumption

Fresh water use is not particularly relevant for production process but is used in considerable volume for maintenance and refit activities.

In general, yacht assembly is not particularly energy intensive. In aggregate form (electricity, gas, diesel for sea trials, etc.), a value between 0.05 and 0.1 kWh/€ is needed. A big contribution to this low-energy activity comes from human resources. Workers, for example, generally use portable electric tools. On top of this, at the end of the product's life, the metal can be recycled, using only 5% of the energy used in the standard production process. Solar panels are also increasingly present, although they are still not sufficient to balance consumption.

On the other hand, some processes of composite construction require climate control and/or use of a curing oven, resulting in higher energy demand in both hot and cold weather conditions. When it comes to large metal construction, energy is needed to produce steel and aluminum plates. Depending on the process, between 380 and 750 kWh/t are necessary for steel production. Even though bauxite (aluminum ore) is available in large quantities, it cannot be considered a renewable resource. Aluminum production from bauxite ore is energy intensive: to produce 1 ton of aluminum, 4–5 tons of bauxite are needed, plus a large amount of water. The energy required for the electrolytic manufacturing process also involves carbon dioxide emissions (CO_2).

Structural materials

Wood was the first material used in naval constructions. Up to the middle of the 19th century, it was the only material available for shipbuilding, and there are a lot of different processes to build boats and yachts with wood. Whereas timber construction is considered green and sustainable in itself, a few considerations are necessary. Boats are used in aggressive environments and are exposed to a variety of potentially harmful agents, including excessive humidity, salt, ultraviolet radiation, wind abrasion, and temperature changes. Not all quality of woods can perform and endure in such conditions. This is why the industry often makes use of exotic "hard" wood types, coming from far-away growing sites, which naturally have an environmental impact due to transportation and the uncontrolled exploitation of natural resources. However, optimism is emerging due to the development of sustainable wood.

New processes, designed to increase the mechanical characteristics of wood construction, require glues and resins with unavoidable environmental impacts of their own. In this regard, new materials are being introduced using increased bio-content with better recycling abilities. For large yachts, typically those over 40 meters long, hulls are often made of metal. For smaller and production boats, metallic materials are not as convenient. When the thickness of a structure is reduced, typically for smaller boats, it becomes more difficult to achieve the complex geometric design due to the limitations of welding technology. The solution is the use of more epoxy fillers, resulting in supplementary weight and recycling issues.

Most yachts measuring from 5 to 40 meters long are composite-built. The use of composite materials for yacht building started in the 1960s for many reasons, including the low cost of materials and processes, good performance-to-weight ratios, freedom to develop complex geometries, and the ability to build in series. These all resulted in a durable and low-maintenance product for the consumer. From a production point of view, the possibility to blend two or more materials to make a completely new composite one has great advantages as manufacturers can select components according to the physical and mechanical properties they need. On the other hand, the use of multiple materials in a single composite has an important drawback when considering dismantling and recycling. From this point of view, for certain materials such as reinforced thermoplastics, recycling is theoretically simple, but to raise the value of mechanical properties, higher transition temperatures are required. This means additional energy is required for both production and for recycling, as the fibers and matrices are more difficult to separate. For the same mechanical properties, thermosets are less expensive, which is why they are broadly used for yacht production. However, their low rate of recyclability also has a high environmental cost.

Installation materials

Many materials are necessary when fitting out a yacht, including glass, aluminum, a wide variety of metals, plastics, marbles, composites, wood, and electronical components. At present, it is not possible to evaluate the suitable quantity of these materials to be used on a boat since yachts are complex artifacts with a high level of customization. A generalization of materials needed is therefore not appropriate. At present, few examples of scientifically comparable sustainability data have been presented using the Life Cycle Assessment approach (Cucinotta, 2016; Favi, 2018; IVL Swedish Environmental Research Institute, 2021; Moreau, 2009). To measure improvements and enhance sustainability, reference parameters are mandatory for future generations of boats.

Boats use

ENERGY CONSUMPTION

On board, energy is needed for two reasons: propulsion and life aboard. The power efficiency for cruising is linked to hull geometry. Hull design is not only a matter of aesthetics as hydrodynamic performance, correct displacement, and longitudinal center of gravity all have a great impact on fuel consumption. Cleanliness of the hull and distribution of weight on board must also be considered. Air-conditioning is probably the most energy-intensive feature onboard. Natural ventilation is often overlooked. Thermal insulation is not only a matter of the quality of life onboard, but also a tool for lower fuel consumption and, by consequence, lower atmospheric pollution. Sustainable practices aboard could also help prevent energy losses. For instance, the use of exhaust gas to warm water could replace electric boilers.

AIR POLLUTION

Exhaust gas is the primary cause of a boat's air pollution. In the last couple of years, this issue has been tackled by a variety of different actors, one of these being the International Maritime Organization (IMO). "IMO is a specialized agency of the United Nations with responsibility for the safety and security of shipping and the prevention of marine and atmospheric pollution by ships. IMO's work support the UN sustainable developments goals" (IMO, 2022). The agency introduced a set of standards for safety and security of international shipping (IMO-Tier 2/3/4) with specific requirements for engine producers. Perhaps most notable is the use of Selective Catalytic Reduction and/or equivalent systems, reducing air pollution for yachts over 24 meters.

NOISE EMISSION

Noise emissions impact the lives of all kinds of sea-dwelling species. Most of these emissions are made by engines and generators, which is why electric boats are relevant to this issue.

WASTE DISPOSAL

Garbage collection on board is an issue and a potential matter for bad practices. This is particularly true for cruising boats, and research is ongoing. Private service providers are becoming more and more common, particularly in the areas where yachting is popular. During the last edition of the Vendée Globe, the solo non-stop round-the-world yacht race, weight-critical waste management was a highly debated topic. Extreme sailing and other marine sports events are a good opportunity for research and awareness.

Wastewater from onboard facilities is another potential source of pollution. Whilst newer boats are increasingly equipped with holding tanks and systems for water treatment, this is not always the case for smaller or older boats. Wastewater management has to deal with two distinct types – black water (toilet discharge) and grey water (drainage from washing, laundering, and showering).

Even if the use of black water tanks is mandatory, at the time of this research, only a few marinas have systems to collect and send organic wastes to purification plants. The consequence is that the waste is often discharged at sea. Although national and international authorities regulate wastewater evacuation, compliance with regulations is not always met. Improvement on this aspect strongly depends on users' awareness of sustainability issues. Manufacturers, in turn, must continue to innovate to propose user-friendly solutions.

Maintenance

As with cars, regular maintenance is not only a way to extend boat life, but it is also a sustainable practice. As an example, entering the engine room of a used boat, it is not uncommon to see oil or fuel leakages in the bilge of the hull. Those liquids are sometimes pumped out with the bilge discharge, having a great impact on water pollution. The quality and appropriate maintenance of a yacht will help avoid these kinds of issues. For their part, manufacturers should have maintenance accessibility in mind when designing their boats. A clean, fouling-free hull reduces resistance whilst cruising, resulting in lower fuel consumption. Antifouling paints prevent organic materials (algae and marine fauna) from sticking to the underwater hull. However, those paints contain metals, which are released into the water. Producers are working on new formulations of coatings that are free from copper and other metals, and they are also exploring alternative methods. A good example is the Aircoat foil (Aircoat, 2022), a Horizon 2020 EU-funded project for the development of an innovative, sustainable ship-coating system.

Profit

As with other luxury sectors, the boating industry is quite an artisanal field. With the exception of a few industrial groups, the Italian boating industry is characterized by small and medium companies, often family-run, usually set in highly skilled geographical clusters. The boating industry has a high-income elasticity of demand (La Nautica in Cifre, 2021), also similar to other luxury sectors, meaning the industry's GDP fluctuations are amplified by the national GDP's fluctuations. Effects of high elasticity were evident during the economic downturn in the early 2000s, when the industry turnover went from 6.2 billion euros in 2007 to 2.43 billion in 2013, experiencing a bigger decrease compared to the national economy. Layoffs and business shutdowns followed. The pre-crisis industry results haven't been fully restored today.

Solid financial foundations and a business model able to absorb business fluctuation are necessary elements for a sustainable profit dimension. Some of the smaller yards follow a fragile business model. A yacht's time to market can be very long, sometimes several years, which has consequences on cash flows. Relying on one or two orders a year could mean excessive financial exposure and business risk. Today, some superyachts yards offer refit services in addition to yacht building. This is a good way to exploit the existing skill base, diversify the activity, and lower the financial risk. Larger and more structured businesses opt for business diversification. The Ferretti Group has a wide brand portfolio, and Azimut-Benetti, besides two boat brands, is active in services and marinas. In terms of product, expanding the offer by introducing more standardized product lines could lead to economies of scale. The industrialization of some production phases can result in better cost management and reduction, more reliable forecasting, continuity of production, and better cash flows.

People

According to the Triple Bottom Line, a company aiming for a sustainable social dimension is one that has shifted its focus toward stakeholder value creation rather than just the shareholder's. From an employment point of view in small-to-medium companies, the distance between the employees and owners is reduced, and HR are often managed directly by the latter. This is the case for several businesses in this industry. Employees are multi-skilled, and the working relationships are often durable. On the other hand, industrial groups have procedures for HR management. Their expansion is recent and welcomed by local communities, who benefit from local taxes and employment.

The geographic cluster locations, in addition to the need (in some cases) to be close to the sea, can be due to the ability to repurpose the land. This is the case with *Il Miglio Blu,* a mile-long area on the Liguria region coastline (La Spezia Municipality, 2020). Conceived in 2020 by the La Spezia Municipality and the Liguria Region, the project involves some renowned players of Italian

Boating Industry such as the Ferretti Group, Baglietto, Sanlorenzo Fincantieri Cantieri Navali La Spezia, and Navale Michelini e Gruppo Antonini (Città de La Spezia, 2021). Apart from urban redevelopment, the project aims to respond to training, residential, and research needs for both residents and businesses. Of particular note is the collaboration between the university, organizations, and the Ligurian Marine Technology District (Barche, 2021).

Scholars agree that a robust supply chain is critical to luxury brands (Athwal, 2019), as the quality of products depends also on timely supplies and raw materials. One element key to the success of the Italian boating industry is the network of interconnected, small-and-medium, skilled, and flexible organizations. Yacht owners are extremely demanding, and requests can sometimes be unusual. Flexibility and mastery of the entire supply chain are crucial to offer a high-level product.

Innovation

It is clear that sustainability passes through innovation (Adams, 2012), not only from a technological point of view, but every aspect of the value chain is affected by innovation (Evans, 2017). New and sophisticated tools for design and engineering, digitalization, and measurement automation are precious allies of resources management, productive processes, and a product's performance. Good practices must be sought both on the production and the consumer's side. The latter must be encouraged and accompanied with product design as sustainable practice shouldn't be a constraint for users. The following is a non-exhaustive roundup of recently introduced or soon-expected innovations for the boating industry that will affect environmental impact.

Materials

Regarding materials, weight is a critical aspect. There is constant research for lighter materials that can grant the same – or even better – performances as heavier ones. New composites are expected in the short term. They will be made of bio-based resins (current rate is close to 50% of resins made using bio resources) and completely new materials. A new class of polymer known as vitrimers offer a cross-linked, but reversible and remoldable, connection between monomers, and Elium™ is a liquid thermoplastic resin that could offer equivalent properties of current thermoset materials while adding post-thermoformability and recyclability. The most common reinforcements, such as glass, carbon, and aramid fibers, could be recycled in a limited way and at a significant cost, giving the second-life material poorer mechanical properties. However, natural alternatives, like basalt and linen fibers, are also gaining popularity.

Hydrodynamic improvement to reduce resistance

The work of naval architects and engineers has always focused on minimizing resistance to motion. A significant proportion of a boat's impact on the planet derives from cruising, so even small reductions in resistance will help lower environmental impact. Efficient design requires lower propulsion power, meaning lower consumption and, by consequence, lower pollution. Weight distribution enhancement would also lower environmental impact. The question designers (and users) should bear in mind during a boat's life should be: "Is it possible to have lighter solutions?"

Several interesting hydrodynamic devices have recently come to light, significantly improving resistance to motion. Appendages such as Interceptors divert water flow and easily correct the running trim of the hull, others such as foils provide hydrodynamic thrust to reduce the resistance to motion and the effects of impacts.

Digitalization

Digitization of production enables a significant reduction in errors and rework in production due to outdated or incorrect information, which normally corresponds to more scrappage, increased energy use, and frustration for the team.

Simulator software can optimize development time and produce better-performing products, avoiding or reducing the expensive trial and error phase. Thanks to artificial intelligence, modern simulators can reproduce navigation conditions specific to a certain geographical area or period of the year, and study boat's reactions under different conditions.

For users, predictive maintenance techniques make it possible to optimize interventions, while the use of home automation, with sensors and remote controls with integrated apps, result in savings on air conditioning and lighting, with consequent lower environmental impact.

Propulsion

A yacht's energy demand is significant, with most of the energy produced onboard used for propulsion. Although electric and hybrid solutions exist, the main concern is power storage and/or production. For smaller boats, hybrid or electric propulsion could be sustainable alternatives, while for bigger yachts, at present, several constraints prevent them from being the preferred choice:

- Energy used onboard is essentially stored in chemically based batteries. The environmental impact of those batteries is considerable, either during the extraction of the minerals used in production (lithium, cobalt, manganese, etc.) and the issue of end-of-life disposal.
- Most of the time, the batteries are recharged with non-sustainable energy.
- Full electric yachts would require the storage of large and heavy batteries on board, to the detriment of performance and energy savings.
- Recharging batteries onboard is difficult, and solar panels cannot fulfill all energy needs.

- Hybrid yachts are obliged to add an electric engine to the drive line, adding weight and costs as well as reducing accommodation space onboard. Furthermore, a diesel engine is required to produce the power to recharge the electric one.

The use of hydrogen is very promising. There are now several experimental applications, including one led by Energy Observer (2022), a real sailing laboratory. The main concerns of hydrogen are linked to refueling challenges, the safety of pressure vessels, and producing the gas in a sustainable way. It is also possible to use batteries to offer a power booster, when and where necessary, with fuel cells of lower power than the propulsion engines.

Country of origin

The Italian boating industry is a global leader, not only in terms of its turnover, but also due to the recognized *Made in Italy* concept. As previously outlined, a boat is a blend of design, elegance, technology, and innovation. An intangible element is included in the mix – the emotional promise.

In addition to the product and the brand, the promise is linked to the notion of country of origin (CO). As for other Italian excellences, "*Made in Italy*" is not only a matter of production, but linked to the broader *Italian lifestyle* concept (Kapferer, 2011). Quality, style, but also heritage, and durability contribute to the country-of-origin effect, which is able of adding value to the product.

According to Amatulli (2017), *Made in Italy* encompasses quality, excellence, traceability, and durability amongst other things. As all those values are intrinsic to sustainability, the CO can become a symbol of sustainability. The indicator function of CO is of particular interest when it is difficult for a customer to appreciate the quality and value of a product, as is the case for a boat, given its complexity. The informative potential of "*Made in Italy*" contributes to the customers' perceived value. It is what Han (Han, 1989) describe as the *Halo effect,* which allows, in the case of unknown or difficult-to-evaluate products, to confer a certain value to an object. The tradition of excellence of the Italian boating industry, linked to iconic brands that contributed to its success, embed "*Made in Italy*" with a strong signaling value, not only through aesthetics but also quality, excellence, and durability, which are all assets contributing to the sustainable image of the Italian boating industry.

Communicating sustainability: Reporting

What has been written so far aims to demonstrate that sustainability impacts the very functioning of organizations and affects all those who are impacted by its activity. Consequently, it is a multifaceted matter and one difficult to measure.

In general, the luxury industry has always been marked by an aura of secrecy. The mystery is not to be understood as a lack of reliability and transparency, but rather linked to the secret of traditional *savoir faire*. It amounts to a heritage that has been handed down for years and which is part of brand's DNA. Although this secrecy remains part of the exclusiveness and rarity of luxury brands, there is today an increasing demand for transparency and dialogue.

Digitalization played a crucial role in altering the relationship between brands and consumers. The latter today is more informed, and keen to engage in conversation with brands. Top-down communication is not relevant anymore. In this framework, sustainability is no longer a choice. Nevertheless, it's up to organizations to decide how to communicate on the matter. The question is crucial for an industry so related to image and emotions. The risk of been accused of greenwashing cannot be underestimated.

Reporting is one of the most popular ways to communicate on sustainable conducts. The most utilized reporting standards are the Global Reporting Initiative (GRI) guidelines. The GRI is described as "*The independent, international organization that helps businesses and other organizations take responsibility for their impact, by providing them with the global common language to communicate those impacts*" (Global Reporting Initiative, 2022). GRI guidelines provide organizations a common frame and a common language to explain engagement with sustainability.

Reporting is still not common within the boating industry. We examined one of the very few companies that are regularly reporting, namely the Ferretti Group. As one of the most celebrated players in the yachting industry, the Ferretti Group presented its first Sustainability Report, according to GRIs guidelines, in 2020 (referred to year 2019) (Ferretti Group, 2022b). At the time of this research they are on their second edition (Ferretti Group, 2022c), confirming the commitment of the Group to sustainable development. To deepen the Ferretti Group's engagement with sustainable development, we discussed the matter with company representatives. The Group's answers to our questions are reported below.

Ferretti Group

The Ferretti Group is one of the worldwide leaders of the boating industry. With its seven brands, namely Ferretti Yachts, Riva, Pershing, Itama, CRN, Custom Line, and Wally, the group designs, builds, and sells boats from 8 meters to over 95 meters. Although its history started in 1968, when the Ferretti brothers started selling boats, some of the brands are even older. Riva, for example, was founded right back in 1842, whilst CRN was established in 1963. As stated on the corporate website, the group's values are: "*luxury, growth, innovation, people and sustainability*" (Ferretti Group, 2022a).

Production can be divided into three main categories: serial models (from 30 to 99ft LOA), semi-custom model (from 100 to 160ft LOA), and custom models (over 140ft LOA) (Ferretti Group, 2022c). Two statistics within the Ferretti Group Sustainable Report are vital to appreciate its exclusivity and rarity within the boating industry: annual production and build time. Every year, the Group produces over 150 boats, confirming the exclusivity of the boating industry. Build time varies according to boat category, but average values are from 2 to 7 months for a serial model, 6 to 13 for a semi-custom design, and over 24 months for a custom model. As with other prestigious brands, patience is required to enjoy luxury.

2020 Sustainability report

COVID-19 affected lives and businesses over the last two years, and it comes as no surprise that the topic is quite present in the 2020 report. After the first lockdown, the company (and the entire industry as we previously saw in Confindustria Nautica figures) demonstrated reactivity and flexibility, achieving unexpected performances. The pandemic confirmed the importance of stable and solid relations with local communities and authorities.

Planet

> *On the environmental front, we are continuing to tackle the challenges of using materials that are increasingly durable and sustainable, of lessening the environmental impact of our production and transportation, and of reducing energy consumption and GHG (greenhouse gas) emissions at both product and process levels. In this area, we are researching and proposing solutions to mitigate both the environmental impact of our products - in particular with research into hybrid engines and new technologies to reduce the weight of hulls - and those related to processes, implementing measures to increase efficiency and optimize work at our shipyards. This is the motivation for extending ISO 14001 certification to the environmental management systems at every one of the Group's shipyards.*
>
> (Ferretti Group, 2022c)

The introductory statement (above) of the group's CEO summarizes in a few essential words the Ferretti Group's commitment to environmental sustainability, and the main means to achieve them. They were among the first to take action in boating industry to increase the emblematic value and durability of luxury products, engage with hybridization, and reduce the weight of their boats, all of which have an impact on both production and general usage (Figure 7.1).

It shows results from interviews about sustainability with a group of customers (Ferretti Group, 2022c). Outcomes give a clear vision of the growing sensitivity to issues concerning environmental protection. Customers' awareness is essential for manufacturers to feel confident in pursuing the "sustainable way".

> *In the interests of product sustainability and to respond to the changing context and growing awareness of the issue, design choices are gradually moving towards 'life cycle design thinking', including in the maritime sector. This approach involves integrating information on the environmental footprint of products at every stage*

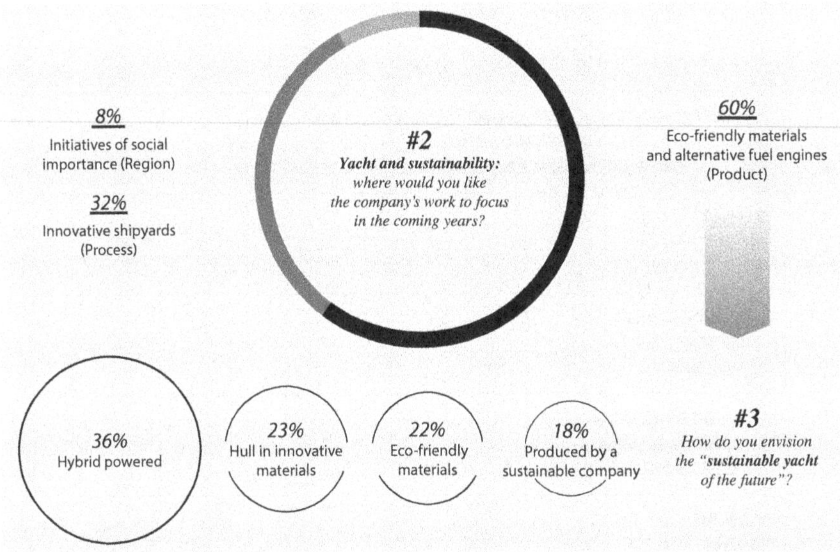

Figure 7.1 Results of customer sustainability questionnaire.

Ferretti Group Sustainability Report (2020)

> *of yacht development, directing research and innovation towards improving and optimizing the consumption of natural resources.*
>
> (Ferretti Group, 2022c)

The approach to Life Cycle Thinking is new and positive. From the perspective of the initiatives taken (*Chapter 4.2 of the report*), including weight reduction, efficiency improvement, product's life extension, and end-of-life management, it remains difficult to identify measurable and monitorable data over time (Figure 7.2).

One of the most valuable aspects of regular reporting is the possibility to document environmental improvement. Thereby, we expect that in future reports we will be able to visualize environmental enhancements of the Ancona shipyard. Since 2019, the superyacht yard has undergone important investments to become a "trigeneration" plant.

People

> *Building some of the world's most beautiful yachts requires a special crew, one that is able to bestow on our products the distinctiveness, innovation and quality that set Ferretti Group apart. Our employees are the ultimate embodiment of these values and as such are the source of our success. Our crew adds expertise, experience, and a strong sense of belonging to the pride of building unique masterpieces (Chapter 6.1).*
>
> (Ferretti Group, 2022c)

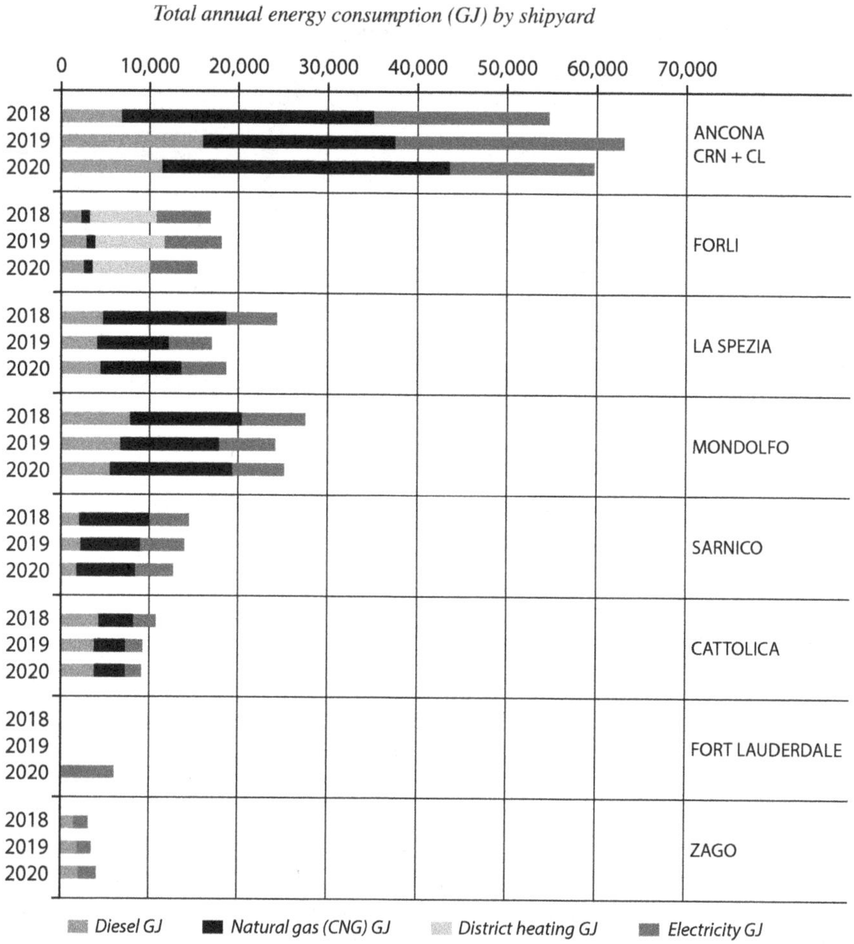

Figure 7.2 Ferretti Group (2020).

Chapter 6 is the one dedicated to "People". Meanwhile, "Structure" simply updates the 2019 report.

No major changes are to be reported as far as composition of employee demographics, which reflects the predominance of men in the global boating.

An interesting figure regards the rate of seniority:

> *The Group also features particularly high levels of seniority. Around a third of employees have between 11 and 15 years of continuous experience in the company. This is certainly the result of a stimulating, ever-changing working environment, which has helped create a stable, long-lasting team. At the same time, however, it may represent a risk, if new recruitment policies aimed at encouraging the entry of young people and the renewal of skills are not implemented. The Group is aware of this risk and has in recent years strengthened its relations with schools and*

> *universities in the area where it operates, encouraging the addition of young people under the age of 30.*
>
> (Ferretti Group, 2022c)

Major changes compared to previous reports are mainly due to the impact of COVID-19. In particular, the pandemic heavily impacted training: "*In 2019 more than 15,000 hours of training were provided to our 1,483 employees. This is a significant increase on previous years, up to 60% compared to 2017*" (Ferretti Group, 2022b). However, at the height of the pandemic, this figure changes dramatically. "*As a result of the restrictions in place following the Covid-19 pandemic, in 2020 only 8,756 hours of training could be provided to our 1,537 employees*" (Ferretti Group, 2022c). Due to national lockdown, the largest impact of COVID-19 was on production. In this regard, it is worth mentioning that on April 14, 2020, the Ferretti Group, major unions representatives, and local authorities signed an agreement to safely re-open production sites, thereby minimizing production downtime.

In the report we find mentions of actions related to local communities, as the participation to *Il Miglio Blu (The Blue Mile)* that we previously introduced. During the COVID-19 health crisis, the Ferretti Group made donations to hospitals and launched the digital campaign "A wave of Caring", intended to help raise money for hospital and intensive care centers.

With regard to the supply chain, the Report says: "In selecting its suppliers Ferretti Group maintains the highest quality standards and takes into account the individual characteristics of each brand" (Ferretti Group, 2022c). Made in Italy is intended for the entire value chain as "*It should also be noted that the vast majority (93%) of Ferretti S.p.A., CRN S.p.A. and Zago S.p.A.'s suppliers are located within the national territory, and that the non-Italian exceptions are well-structured, reliable multinationals, such as suppliers of engine parts or electronic components*" (Ferretti Group, 2022c).

Profit

As previously explained, financial strength is an important indicator of economic sustainability.

> *Financially, the Group's end-of-year results reflect the solidity and flexibility that define it. The latter part of 2020 saw an increase in new customer orders as measures restricting movement between countries were eased and travel once again became a possibility.*
>
> (Ferretti Group, 2022c)

Economic solidity is crucial to overcome unpredictable and/or uncontrolled events (e.g., economic downturns) as was the case with COVID-19:

> *In 2020, the Ferretti Group generated approximately 640 million euros in total economic value, down 8.6% on 2019 and 4.6% on 2018. This decline reflects*

> *the ongoing difficulties related to the Covid-19 health crisis. Of the economic value generated, that distributed to the various stakeholders, including suppliers (operating costs), employees, capital providers, the Public Administration, shareholders, and the local community, represents approx. 90%.*
>
> (Ferretti Group, 2022c)

The "Sustainability from Profit" point of view is a precious resource for local communities.

> *Confirming the Group's strong local presence, there is a concentration of turnover in the regions where its shipyards are located. In 2020, 30% of Italian purchases were made in the Marche region (22% in 2019), home of the Ancona and Mondolfo shipyards, 22% in Emilia-Romagna (18% in 2019), where Ferretti S.p.A. is present at the Forlì and Cattolica facilities, 15% in Lombardy, location of the Sarnico shipyard and offices in Milan (17% in 2019), and 6% in Liguria, home to the La Spezia shipyard.*
>
> (Ferretti Group, 2022c)

> *For years, more than 75% of the total economic value generated has been distributed along the Group's supply chain. This has led to the creation of a real and ever-expanding ecosystem, predominantly made up of small-and-medium-sized Italian companies, with whom Ferretti Group has a long history of productive collaboration. The SMEs working with the Group are emblematic of the flexibility, excellence, and sustainability of local production systems, and often boast decades of collaboration with Ferretti Group brands and a relationship that is more than simply professional.*
>
> (Ferretti Group, 2022c)

Interview

The Ferretti Group kindly requested that we publish their answers as a "Corporate Voice". For this reason, we will not publish the name of our interviewees, but will still take the opportunity here to thank them for their valuable collaboration.

Ferretti Group is one of very few companies in the sector to produce a sustainability report. What inspired you to embark on this journey toward sustainable development?

Ferretti Group: *Ferretti Group is active in over 70 countries around the world, and we are conscious of how important it is to consider all stakeholders. The company is especially attentive to the interests and sensitivities of everyone impacted by our activities. Not only clients and suppliers, then, but also the media, competitors, and people living near where we operate. The 2019 and 2022 IPO processes confirmed how important sustainability data and initiatives are to financial stakeholders. This inspired us to act even faster.*

So, we decided to be absolutely transparent – with an annual report about our governance, our remuneration structure, and our impact on the environment and residents near production sites. This approach has afforded us an even clearer understanding of the state of the art in business ESG, providing new objectives to further reduce our impact on the world around us. The feedback we have received from key stakeholders is strongly positive, endorsing our commitment and allowing us to kick on with greater ambition.

Besides the desire to help leave a better world to future generations, what are the strategic and economic implications of sustainable development?

Ferretti Group: *It is no longer conceivable to run a business without taking into account how it affects the surrounding world.*

Clients and other stakeholders are now sensitive to sustainability issues, especially the environmental impact. They are calling for governance to report on and improve these aspects. Clients are increasingly demanding sustainably made products, be that propulsion systems or construction materials, underlining that business and sustainability are closely linked.

The Group's main departments therefore need to be involved: R&D, production, sales, and finance. Ferretti Group is committed to being a proponent of cutting-edge sustainable solutions to cut atmospheric emissions.

Financial sustainability is also important for us. Lending banks regularly send out surveys requesting information on ESG, and in the future sustainable finance will become the gold standard, by increasingly spurring organizations to report on ESG. Once again, Ferretti Group is in the vanguard.

You recently ran a customer survey, and you are in constant touch with your dealer network. In light of this ongoing exchange, how aware would you say luxury customers are of sustainability matters?

Ferretti Group: *More and more boat owners are placing emphasis on sustainable solutions like hybrid propulsion, and sustainable and traceable materials. Their sensitivity to these themes focuses more on the end products than on the environmental impact of the manufacturing and production processes.*

To what extent is this sensitivity a real quest for sustainable development and how much is it a question of image?

Ferretti Group: *A bit of both. On one hand, boats must be built to sustainable criteria: quality and traceability with the assurance that it does not harm the environment. On the other, self-image is important to our clients, especially those with a public profile to maintain. By associating themselves with ethical and responsible* *lifestyles, they can further their image and demonstrate their positive contemporary values.*

Does sustainability awareness somehow correlate to geographical areas or product ranges?

Ferretti Group: *The EMEA market is now the most responsive to these themes. Younger owners in particular, perhaps because their generation is more sustainability aware.*

Craftsmanship and customization are fundamental aspects of luxury products, as human skills become central to the value chain. How can these aspects be reconciled with the need for traceability, which is so crucial for sustainability?

Ferretti Group: *As leaders in a luxury sector, we insist on traceability; it is implicit in the quality our customers expect and deserve. Ferretti Group designs and manufactures its boats in Italy. Our 6 production sites are within some of the boating industry's most renowned clusters – in the Liguria region and on the Adriatic. We have developed a dense network of goods and service suppliers there, selected organizations capable of meeting the highest quality standards on the market. The Group can thus guarantee full control of the supply chain, ensuring the same compliance and close observance of working practices for all internal and external workers. A strong commitment to these issues is no less than clients expect from a leading organization like Ferretti Group.*

Broadly speaking, what approach are you planning to implement for the future, to map and improve sustainability aspects of your supply chain? What kind of engagement do you aim to achieve?

Ferretti Group: *Supplier assessment and selection is key to the planning of the supply process. We shall continue to choose our suppliers with care using stringent selection, prequalification, and qualification criteria. Besides appraising their products and services, our constant monitoring also covers quality, financial solidity, and sustainability. Many companies in the boating industry are small- to medium-sized and not yet as well-versed in ESG compared to other arenas. Which is why we need to be even more vigilant and help them comply with our requirements. So, to have greater control over end-product quality, we are taking concrete steps to internalize critical phases of the production process. This is a strategic decision for greater compliance with ESG principles in the value chain.*

Life cycle "from cave to grave". Boats generally have a very long life. Only a few sub-systems tend to become obsolete, including from an environmental standpoint (internal-combustion machines can be superseded when more stringent regulations come in). To what extent can you take these aspects into account when developing new products? How can we engineer refitting and repowering processes to meet sustainability needs in the future?

What is the state of play about boat end-of-life management, and how sensitive are users to these issues?

Ferretti Group: *If built to excellent quality standards and regularly maintained, boats can give long service. They often change hands and undergo refits, modifications, and technology upgrades, which can all extend their life. This is vital because it also makes the product more sustainable.*

Often, old boat refits involve upgrading the technology and replacing the engine with a more efficient, less polluting unit. As with the car industry, legislation has a pivotal role: legal compliance is a major driver for owner investment.

Another important issue for Ferretti Group is the choice of materials for fitting out. Replacing composite materials with more recyclable ones like linen fiber or alloy (for alloy yachts) can certainly contribute to a yacht's overall sustainability.

Finally, our brand portfolio should not be underestimated. To add to Riva, Ferretti Yachts, Pershing, Itama, CRN and Custom Line – historic, iconic names with a focus on innovation fostered by constant R&D investment – Wally has been a recent acquisition. Wally sailing yachts have given the Group a way into the sustainable boat segment par excellence.

Metrics and future goals: you have identified some of the objectives to work on for the 2030 Agenda. You may well pursue others in the future (quality, education, gender quality, etc.), but what key metrics do you envisage to objectively measure your sustainability progress? What would you like to be able to report in a few years' time?

Ferretti Group: *Ferretti Group is right behind the 2030 Agenda for sustainable development. In particular, we have set out 5 objectives linked to our value and the commitment in which we believe. We are convinced that our efforts can contribute toward those goals. The 5 SDGs reflect the material issues identified and are linked to both the production process and the products themselves while enhancing the impact on the supply chain and local communities (Figure 7.3).*

For the environment, we are seeking to reduce our carbon footprint through a series of continual improvements, for example:

- a *We shall invest increasingly heavily in the production sites to install solar panels and other technologies to cut energy consumption, especially of fossil fuels.*
- b *We are constantly developing innovative and alternative materials for a twofold aim:*
    - a *to reduce the boats' weight and slash fuel consumption*
    - b *to design boats with the entire life cycle in mind (end of life included), leveraging re-usable materials.*
- c *We were the first in the luxury yachting sector to invest in implementing hybrid propulsion, with solutions deployed on several of our models since 2008.*

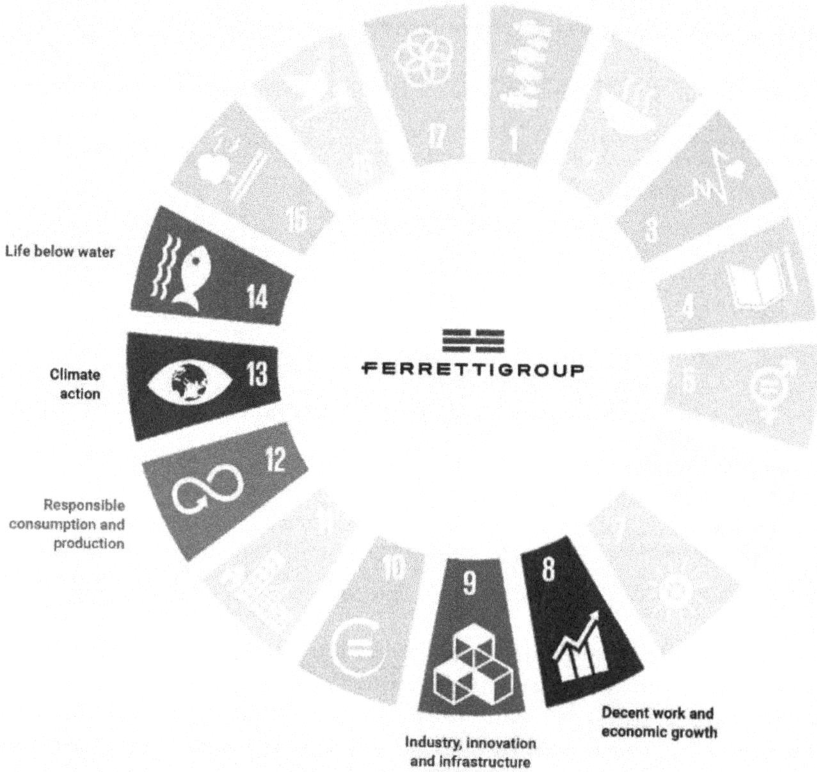

Figure 7.3

While sustainability goes hand in hand with inclusion, innovation and equality, the Group is sensitive to gender equality and takes care to provide employees with the right opportunities for personal and professional growth. Sustainability is a continual journey of research, commitment, and improvement. One that Ferretti Group is determined to pursue.

Conclusion

Being one of the leading countries of the global yachting industry is not only a matter of style and elegance, as a good yacht is much more than just a beautiful object. It is rather a concentrate of technology, craftsmanship, and innovation, and the latter is inevitably linked to sustainability.

By their very nature, yachts cannot prescind from environmental protection, as the environment itself, is an integral part of boating experience. Even on board of the most luxurious yacht ever built, sailing in a polluted ocean would lower the perceived value of the experience and, consequently, its product value.

As regards environment's relevance on customer experience, yachting industry is sometimes associated with luxury hospitality. Success and, somehow, survival of luxury resorts in pristine locations cannot prescind from environmental protection.

Nevertheless, in the case of hospitality, property's owner has the interest, and the opportunity to preserve the environment, as the user experience occurs within the property. In the case of yachting, sustainable conduct while using the boat, is owner's responsibility.

For their part, shipyards can make sure that a sustainable use of the boat is possible and enjoyable, and above all, ensure that sustainable conduct does not detract from luxury experience and perceived value of the yacht.

It hasn't been long since sustainability was perceived as antithetical to elegance, luxury, and design. The evolution of luxury industry in this respect is evident.

Regarding nautical industry, we showed the complexity of boats. A yacht is a product requiring continuous innovation, from an engineering, design, and technological point of view. But it is also an artifact demanding artisanal savoir faire.

The peculiar composition of Italian nautical industry was also shown, mostly consisting of medium-small companies, production clusters, and limited vertical integration, except for few industrial groups. Companies' size and sector's fragmentation explain, on the one hand, the difficulty for certain operators to invest in more sustainable production, and on the other, the complexity of tracing processes and measuring environmental impact.

Nevertheless, not only a yacht is a very complex product, but also a product made to last, and proof is the age of the boats still sailing around the world. This is synonymous with great aesthetic value, and manufacturing excellence: highlights of Italian yachting industry.

Sustainable development is now a topical issue, notably for larger groups. Reporting is one of the tools enabling to appreciate efforts, progress, as well as to chart the way and, hopefully, help smaller companies to undertake their journey to sustainability.

Ferretti Group, an emblematic player of Italian luxury yachting, was among the first to choose to report on sustainability, emphasizing engagement's transparency towards sustainable development. As we were able to appreciate during the case's analysis, sustainable development not only affects products, but concerns all stakeholders.

Country of origin, and, more specifically Made in Italy, take on particular significance and value in the luxury industry. The case we analyzed confirms the strong link with the territory, both nationally and locally. Ferretti Group's brands maintain their strong bond with the territory and represent the excellence of Italian yachting industry in the world.

The commitment of Ferretti Group toward sustainability and reporting, is a great opportunity for the industry to motivate other players to engage with sustainable development.

The commitment of the Ferretti Group toward sustainability and reporting is a great opportunity for the industry to motivate other players to engage with sustainable development.

Acknowledgment

We would like to thank The Ferretti Group and in particular: Federico Peruccio, Head of Corporate Communications and Margherita Sacerdoti, Investor Relations, Compliance & Sustainability Manager.

Note

1 Interview translated by the author from Italian to English.

References

Adams, R. J. (2012). Innovating for sustainability. A systematic review of the body of knowledge. *Network for Business Sustainability.*

Aircoat. (2022). *Home page.* Retrieved from https://aircoat.eu

Amatulli, C. D. (2017). *Sustainable luxury brands.* London, UK: Palgrave.

Athwal, N. W. (2019). Sustainable luxury marketing: A synthesis and research agenda. *International Journal of Management Reviews, 21*(4), 405–426.

Barche. (September 2021). *La Spezia: the Miglio Blu (Blue Mile), a district of excellence in boating, kicks off.* Retrieved from https://www.barchemagazine.com/en/la-spezia-the-miglio-blu/

Boat International. (n.d.). *The yachts owned by celebrities.* Retrieved from https://www.boatinternational.com/luxury-yacht-life/owners-experiences/yachts-owned-by-celebrities–28323

Boat International. (2021, December 13). *2022 Global order book.* Retrieved from https://www.boatinternational.com/yacht-market-intelligence/luxury-yachts-on-order/2021-global-order-book

Città de La Spezia (2021, September 20). *Miglio blu presentato al Salone: "Infrastrutture, innovazione e formazione".* Retrieved from https://www.cittadellaspezia.com/2021/09/20/miglio-blu-presentato-al-salone-infrastrutture-innovazione-e-formazione-408822/

Cucinotta, F. G. (2016). Life cycle assessment in yacht industry: A case study of comparison between hand lay-up and vacuum infusion. *Journal of Cleaner Production, 142*(4), 3822–3833.

Elkington, J. (2013). *The triple bottom line.* London, UK: Routledge.

Energy Observer. (2022). *Homepage.* Retrieved from https://www.energy-observer.org

Evans, S. V. (2017). Business model innovation for sustainability: Towards a unified perspective for creation of sustainable business models. *Business Strategy and the Environment, 26*(5), 597–608.

Favi, C. G. (2018). Life cycle model and metrics in shipbuilding: How to use them in the preliminary design phases. 25th CIRP life cycle engineering (LCE) conference. Copenhagen, Denmark.

Ferretti Group. (2022a). *Our Values.* Retrieved from https://www.ferrettigroup.com/en-us/Corporate#our_values

Ferretti Group. (2022b). *Report 2019.* Retrieved from https://www.ferrettigroup.com/en-us/Sustainability/sust-archive

Ferretti Group. (2022c). *Report 2020.* Retrieved from https://www.ferrettigroup.com/Portals/4/skins/FG_2017/_assets/_assets/FG-Sustainability%20Report-2020-EN-web.pdf

Freeman, R. (1984). *Strategic management: A stakeholder approach.* London, UK: Pitman.

Global Reporting Initiative. (2022). *About GRI.* Retrieved from https://www.globalreporting.org/about-gri/

Han, C. (1989). Country image: Halo or summary construct? *Journal of Marketing Research, 26*(2), 222–229.

International Maritime Organization (IMO). (2022). Homepage. Retrieved from: https://www.imo.org/en

IVL Swedish Environmental Research Institute. (2021). *Investigating the potential circularity of a motorboat using Life Cycle Assessment.*

Janssen, C. V. (2014). The Catch-22 of responsible luxury: Effects of luxury product characteristics on consumers' perception of fit with corporate social responsibility. *Journal of Business Ethics, 119,* 45–57.

Kapferer, J.-N. (2011). France: Pourquoi penser marque? *Revue Francaise De Gestion 37*(12–28), 13–23.

Kapferer, J.-N. (2014). Is luxury compatible with sustainability? Luxury consumers' viewpoint. *Journal of Brand Management, 1*(21), 1–22.

Kunz, J. M. (2020). Sustainable luxury: Current status and perspectives for future research. *Business Research, 13,* 541–601.

La Nautica in Cifre. (2021). Confindustria Nautica.

La Spezia Municipality. (5 June 2020). Il Miglio Blu – La Spezia per la Nautica. Città Della Spezia. Retrieved from http://www.comune.laspezia.it/Comunichiamo/UfficioStampa/news/Il-Miglio-Blu-La-Spezia-per-la-Nautica/

Moreau, R. (2009). *Nautical activities: What impact on the environment? A life cycle approach for "clear blue" boating.* Brussels, Belgium: European Confederation of Nautical Industries.

Our Common Future. (1987). *Report of the World Commission on Environment and Development: Our Common Future.* Retrieved from: https://sustainabledevelopment.un.org/content/documents/5987our-common-future.pdf

Pagani Isnardi, S. (2022, 2 February). Head of Research Department at Confindustria Nautica.

Wells, V. A. (2021). How legitimate are the environmental sustainability claims of luxury conglomerates? *Journal of Fashion Marketing & Management, 25*(4), 697–722.

8 Case Study Cucinelli

Servant and Ethical Leadership for Social Responsibility and Humanism

Susanne Rank[1] *and Serena Rovai*[2]
[1]University of Applied Sciences Mainz
[2]EXCELIA Business School

Introduction

The humanistic capitalism created by Brunello Cucinelli places people, employees, and territory at the core of his entrepreneurial values. Employees benefit from a positive work-life balance, they can have lunch in the canteen and the working day ends categorically at 5:30 pm: business emails outside office hours are forbidden, a human philosophy caring about company organization and human dignity.

The humanistic enterprise exemplifies the recognition of humanistic capitalism, even if the two terms have always been regarded as opposites. Consequently, a humanistic-centered capitalism is highly innovative compared to Taylor's classic management (1911) where the importance of people within organizations is underestimated, focusing on the enormous potential of machinery. Certainly, it was a successful management model in terms of productivity for companies and remuneration for workers. Humanistic capitalism – the humanistic enterprise – places man at the center of attention without losing sight of the economic focus: profit is a way to strengthen the company and allow employees to live with dignity.

An exemplary and realistic example of a humanistic enterprise in Italy is represented by Brunello Cucinelli brand that seeks to create gain by acknowledging ethical policies by respecting the social community inside and outside the company. His belief – from which develops the humanistic enterprise model – is summarized in his own words:

"I would not want to live in a world where everything is sterile led back to profit alone. Money has real value only when it is spent to improve human existence and growth, and this is my goal".

Cucinelli's group turns out to be a transparent example of the degree to which humanistic capitalism is certainly not an oxymoron. In this regard, Golinelli asserted that post-bureaucratic organizations, on the other hand, strongly depend on the human qualities of their managers in terms of trust, moral conscience, ability to learn, initiative, discernment as well as of direction. To train managers capable of meeting these needs, not only technical training and know-how are required, but also instilling a new leadership orientation

DOI: 10.4324/9781003305095-11

built on ethical skills can be part of a new organizational and leadership model mirrored in its business model for present and future generations.

As evidenced during a recent presentation the Cucinelli brand CEO, Francesco Bottigliero, gave at Stanford University Breyer Centre in Florence, Cucinelli draws this new corporate philosophy from his family. His father was a farmer and factory worker who was exhausted by shift work but also mortified in front of others because of his farmer's clothes. Humanistic capitalism was derived from the foundation of these recollections. He wanted to create space for individuals but also for the territory and the communication of knowledge to future generations.

This case explores one company's attempt to experiment with different underlying business models for a capitalist enterprise. Brunello Cucinelli is a leading manufacturer of luxury fashion apparel. Despite being a publicly traded enterprise with annual revenues exceeding 500 million, the company follows a somewhat unique human resources and cultural model. The company's founder, Brunello Cucinelli, has striven to create an enterprise that follows principles of what he calls "humanistic capitalism". Human capitalism, according to Cucinelli, means pursuing growth and profitability in a "gracious way". At the company, humanistic capitalism manifests itself in a very specific set of policies and behavioral norms. Workers are paid wages that exceed 20% of the market norms; the workday (even for senior executive) is limited to the hours of 8:30 am to 5:30 pm; emails are not to be sent after hours or on weekends; lunch breaks are one and half hours long to allow workers to have lunch at home should they choose. There are also strong cultural norms emphasizing respect and dignity. As part of this culture, employees are expected to keep their workspaces clean; eating at desks is not permitted; water can only be drunk from cups (not bottles); speaking should be done in hushed tones so as not to disturb colleagues. None of these cultural norms, however, are explicitly described in any written documents. The company has adopted this model in both its Solomeo, Italy headquarters and in its North American headquarters located in New York City.

The case allows readers to explore the strengths and weakness of this company culture, leadership behavior, and human resource model in line with a sustainable business model. A particular focal point of the case concerns the question of such a leadership and human resource model impact on the business model and the brand identity. Does this model contribute to the brand's success or is "humanistic capitalism"? Is this model sustainable?

Over the past few decades, the Italian clothier Brunello Cucinelli has created a highly profitable, globally present, luxury fashion line while reading medieval monastics. Entrepreneurs and business ethicists might be intrigued to explore how this apparent paradox is resolved in Cucinelli's manner of running his company – a practice inspired, in part, by drawing widely from works in the Western humanistic and religious canon. From his study of St. Benedict and St. Francis, among others, Cucinelli has found ways of squaring particularly daunting circles: the correlation between luxury and quality, the meaning of labor for human dignity in an age of excessive production and consumption, the role of philanthropy in tandem with profit-making, and the transfiguration of the corporate CEO into an abstemious and caring abbot. By reading from Cucinelli's chosen philosophical touchstones and exploring the effects of that reading on his day-to-day operations, it is possible to gain insight into his particular understanding of luxury as it relates to his "humanistic enterprise" in the world of business, and to the specific demands such an undertaking makes on those who would be its leaders and stewards. The extent to which Cucinelli's business ethics might be translated beyond his Italian context, and in entrepreneurial initiatives other than high-end fashion, is also considered.

The aim of this case study is to analyze the leadership behavior of Cucinelli, and how his values and his subsequent behavior contribute to the long-lasting business success of his company. First, the appropriate theoretical leadership models are discussed in order to apply the leadership dimensions as the basis for a structured interview guide. Secondly, the empirical data are collected to give qualitative evidence for our final conclusions. Finally, we summarize our findings with theoretical and practical implications for future business leaders and CEOs to put their attention on the long-lasting business model in line with the sustainable goals by contributing to the sustainability, company culture, and human resources.

Theoretical framework

Choi (2021) investigates the impact of CEOs' sustainable leadership styles on employee wellbeing and organizational citizenship. She defined sustainable leadership behavior as an umbrella framework with servant, authentic, and ethical leadership elements, their common point being empowering and supportive behavior toward employees. The servant leadership turned out to be a highly effective behavior for the CEO to improve wellbeing in contrast to organizational citizenship, whereas the ethical style was the least efficient. The servant style is defined as taking on the role of a servant, a coach, and a developmental guide for employees.

Hallinger and Suriyankietkaew (2018) suggest that sustainable leadership behavior should highlight social care through a leader's responsibility for employees and society. Based on their review, the following features are summarized in a contextual model: sustainable leadership instead of unitary leadership, long-term vision and goals with organizational links to society, ethical behavior, social responsibility of leaders and the organization, stakeholder engagement, and innovation capacity for an open system. Di Fabio and Peiró (2018) supported Choi's approach (2021) by favoring human capital sustainability leadership as a concept integrating ethical, mindful, and servant leadership in an Italian study.

In line with Cucinelli's vision of human sustainability (2022), specifically "sustainability with creation, economic, moral and cultural", we bring into focus the servant leadership of Greenleaf (Greenleaf, 2002), which, nowadays, is an example of sustainable leadership. The servant leaders serve the employees to grow, develop, and feel well. Southwest Airlines serves as a successful example of suggested best practices for servant leadership and its impact business success and employee wellbeing (Greenleaf Center, 2022a, 2022b).

In their meta-analysis, Lee, Lyubovnikova, Tian, and Knight (2020) showed that the positive impact of servant leadership behavior on behavioral outcome, like performance, creativity, and organizational citizenship behavior, is partially mediated on individual- and team-level through trust in the leader, procedural justice, and leader–member exchange. Thus, Lee et al. (2020) conclude that a servant leadership style favors a culture that positively increases trust, fairness, and high-quality leader–follower relationships, therefore finally resulting in positive employee outcomes.

Del Baldo (2018) conducted a case analysis of Cucinelli, focusing on the impact of a servant leadership style on a sustainable business model. The findings highlight the impact of the values and ethical-based leadership of CEOs and entrepreneurs, such as sustainable and servant leadership. Del Baldo (2018) showed the overlap between Cucinelli's philosophy and business models and servant leadership by showing that there is an interplay of leadership, business vision, sales strategies, and social engagement between both. Some critical limitations occur as this case analysis is based on website statements. Del Baldo applied Laub's (2011) six pillars of servant leadership to Cucinelli's leadership behavior: valuing and developing people, building a community, displaying authenticity, NS providing and sharing leadership for 360-degree leadership feedback. However, we applied a qualitative investigative approach on Cucinelli by analyzing the interplay of sustainable business strategies, his values, and leadership behavior on the basis of servant leadership.

Moreover, Choi (2021) operationalized servant leadership on five dimensions by asking employees to judge their leader's behavior in her scientific study (see Table 8.1).

Table 8.1 Dimension of servant leadership

Dimensions	*Items in the employee survey*
Coordinating	Our company's CEO has listening/communicating/coordinating attitudes and makes effort to build empathy.
Assistance	Our company's CEO shows interest in healing the pains of organization members and supports capability development.
Service	Our company's CEO serves with a humble attitude and makes an effort to work together based on persuasion instead of blind obedience.
Presenting direction/vision	Our company's CEO provides alternatives through clear awareness and presents vision through broad thinking.
Assistance	Our company's CEO helps predict the future with keen insights and builds the community among organization members.

Source: Choi (2021).

Table 8.2 Ethical leadership

Dimensions	*Items in the employee survey*
Honesty	Our company's CEO does not lie or distort reality morally/legally/normatively.
Justice	Our company's CEO has principles of fairness and honesty morally/legally/normatively.
Respect	Our company's CEO always respects employees morally/legally/normatively.
Community	Our company's CEO pursues common interests (with the company, employees) morally/legally/normatively.
Integrity	Our company's CEO behaves with honesty and trustworthiness morally/legally/normatively.

Source: Choi (2021).

Finally, Lemoine, Hartnell, and Leroy (2019) compared different empowering leadership behavior in their scientific review. Positive leadership styles – such as transformational, ethical, authentic, and servant leadership – are observed to find the conceptual overlaps measuring the same latent construct. The intersection of all three discussed leadership styles is morality, which is a sustainable pillar of corporate social sustainability.

Next, we establish that ethical leadership is complementary to servant leadership. The ethical leadership focuses on the organizational level (i.e., organizational citizenship), whereas servant leadership keeps an eye on the individual and their wellbeing (Choi, 2021). Therefore, Choi (2021) defined ethical leadership as the ability to demonstrate normatively appropriate conduct through personal actions and interpersonal relations, and promoting such actions to organization members through communication, support, and decision-making. Zhang et al. (2019) revealed that ethical leadership impacted organizational citizenship on an organizational level, mediated via interactional justice rather than on an individual level.

According to Choi (2021), the ethical leadership should operationalized as follows, see Table 8.2, for an employee feedback survey.

Keeping the servant and ethical leadership behavior in mind, the successful case of Cucinelli is presented in order to later analyze Cucinelli's leadership behavior in line with his business model and draw conclusions for humanistic capitalism and sustainable business as a future outlook.

Brunello Cucinelli: The case study

Brunello Cucinelli is the son of a farmer who later became a worker in a cement factory. He went to secondary school and after graduating, enrolled in an engineering faculty to become a surveyor, from which he graduated without a degree in 1975. At that time, he frequented bars and described himself as a "slacker". At the same time, he claims to have learned more in bars and in the working class than on the university benches. In 1978, he started his entrepreneurial activity.

Cucinelli is one **of the most famous Italian luxury brands in the world**, whose story is told in the book *"Il sogno di Solomeo"* (published by Feltrinelli in 2018, dedicated to his daughters and all young people, heirs, and witnesses of artisan know-how and of the small hamlet, an architectural jewel nestled within medieval stones, built between the 12th and the 13th centuries (Cucinelli, 2018). I have entrusted my best memories to a book entitled *Il Sogno di Solomeo* (The Dream of Solomeo). "I was born in the country, to a family of sharecroppers, then I spent my youth at the local café, which I now consider my University of the Soul. I view these periods of my life as personally epic; in my eyes they are the greatest gifts, because the first taught me the steady values of timeless ideals and those of tradition, the second taught me to look at the future as a boundless horizon of possibilities". In 1982, he married Federica Benda, with whom he had two daughters, Camille and Carolina, currently in management positions inside the brand.

In 1978, he founded an Italian luxury brand that bears his name, known for its cashmere products, which is a company with high luxury products. His company has 783 employees and is located in Solomeo, a hamlet in the municipality of Corciano in Umbria, Italy. The first products marketed were cashmere jumpers for women. As such, he is known as the Prince of Cashmere. Brunello Cucinelli is also known in Italy as the "humanist entrepreneur" or the "Franciscan capitalist". After graduating from engineering school without a degree, he was described as a "failed engineer with a passion for philosophy". His passion for ancient philosophy led him to receive an honorary doctorate in philosophy and ethics of human relations from the University of Perugia in 2011. He says he is also passionate about yoga, music, and theatre. He has dreamed of being a monk and openly claims to be a student of St. Francis of Assisi, Aristotle, Seneca, and Kant. The American economist Theodore Levitt is also his inspiration. He is known for reconciling capitalism and ethics and for his concern for the welfare of his employees, who are paid 20% more than the industry agreement. In 2012, after his company went public, he decided to share his profits with his 783 employees, who each received a prime of 6,385 euros in December of that year. The businessman said: "It is a personal choice and a personal gift, to thank those who have helped us grow, thanks to their work".

As mentioned earlier, it is important for Cucinelli to develop a company ethic that illustrates how a worker should be treated, well paid and under what working conditions. It is about using his humanistic perspective to create a better workplace for his employees. Cucinelli believes that corporate ethics are essential and must be fully defined because it seems important to share common values within the same company in order to be more efficient and thus obtain better economic results. It seems important to share common values within a company to be more efficient and thus obtain better economic results. Indeed, Cucinelli believes that even a company that focuses on financial results should adopt a good business ethic by offering its employees a fair salary, comfortable working conditions, recognition, and responsibilities amongst others. Besides, in thinking about the future for young generations and "Made in Italy" techniques and skills not to disappear, Brunello Cucinelli created craftmanship schools in diverse expertise associated to fashion tailoring and knitwear. In addition to education, Cucinelli pays attention to the health sector, notably by donating to the construction of hospitals. In a society where the economic crisis is intersecting with a crisis of values, Brunello Cucinelli, the "Prince of Cashmere" as he is known in Italy, shows that it is possible to combine capitalism and ethics. That the well-being of employees – his employees are paid 20% more than the sector's contracts – is one of the keys to a company's success. As highlighted by Brunello Cucinelli himself on the website of the brand (Cucinelli, 2022): "In our company, thinking of those who work with us, we do this: we do not stamp the cards but we all strictly respect the timetable; we don't want him to stay connected after the work day and at the weekend; we want salaries to be slightly higher than average; we think that the lunch break should be as pleasant as a family break …". The definition of humanism is to focus on the well-being of the human being and to defend the freedom, human rights, autonomy, progress (including progressive policies), freedom of expression, and democracy. Cucinelli is also regularly active in various charitable contributions, where he exercises the "logic of giving". For example, he encourages educational philanthropy and believes that this cause should be supported more by the private sector. To this end, Cucinelli appears to be building a foundation and has contributed to the construction of a library. His humanistic capitalism includes that the brand only manufactures within the Umbria area and that some profit is devoted to Solomeo, village, the brand location, and social use. This is how the village saw the birth of a library, a theater, and an amphitheater, together with fixing ancient buildings while creating green areas. However, the territory was not the only to benefit from the brand profit.

Brunelllo Cucinelli continues to run at a high pace. The Italian luxury brand specializing in cashmere generated sales of 502.6 million euros between January and September 2021, up 9.4% (+12.2% at constant exchange rates) compared to the first nine months of 2019 with an acceleration in the last quarter. The increase jumps by 32.7% compared to the same period in 2020. These results enable it to forecast annual growth of 25% for 2021. In 2021, Brunello Cucinelli took part in the G20 summit in Rome and launched an appeal "full of hope and good intentions, to all generations for an economic renaissance under the sign of respect and balance of nature". In general, Cucinelli's profits are donated to the town of Solomeo, its craftsmen, the restoration of heritage sites, the town and the restoration of heritage sites, cultural activities (such as theatre, dance, and literary activities), and quality control. At Brunello Cucinelli, the environmental aspect is being developed. Indeed, Cucinelli is a luxury brand Made in Italy. In Solomeo, the industrial buildings were demolished to make way for new production units for the company. Brunello Cucinelli wanted to keep its production in Italy. Today, Solomeo is home to more than 300 artisans; an additional network of artisans extends across Umbria and numbers 3,000. Such is Cucinelli's belief in the traditions and craft excellence of 'Made in Italy' that in 2013 he founded La Scuola dei Mestieri (School of Crafts), inspired by the biographies and ideas of reformers William Morris and John Ruskin, two great names in the arts and crafts movement. According to Carolina, "Young minds can learn not only the techniques of binding, mending and tailoring for men and women, but also develop a passion for quality products and the traditional skills that have always been kept by our master craftsmen, now expanded and made contemporary by the use of technology.

The Brunello Cucinelli brand and global technology company Epson have partnered to launch PaperLab. This is an innovative and sustainable paper recycling system that enables businesses to fully embrace the circular economy of paper in their transition to sustainability. As the world's first secure, waterless paper recycler, Epson's PaperLab system allows businesses to recycle paper in a single process, providing a true circular solution that significantly reduces paper, water, and energy consumption and decreases forestry. Brunello Cucinelli not only recycles its paper, but also upcycles it in a single process. Recently, the brand launched a collection called "Never Ending Stories", the pieces in which will last over time thanks to a reusable linen cover. Another project is under consideration concerning the repair and recovery of their products to create other collections.

Cucinelli uses leather, wool, shearling, exotic animal hair, and down. However, the company does not use fur, exotic animal skin, or angora. In addition to its website, the brand is present on several social networks (e.g., Instagram: 254k – two hundred and fifty four thousand), to promote its new collections, LinkedIn: +83 (eighty three miles k), to share the brand's values, highlight inspiring people, and the notion of humanism that Cucinelli regularly addresses, Facebook: +10k (ten million followers, to promote its new collections). The environmental aspect as a challenge for the brand because Brunello Cucinelli's greatest assets, which are at the origin of its success, are the raw materials used, cashmere in particular. It would be therefore challenging for the brand to make such a "radical" change. However, today there are alternatives to these materials, excellent quality substitutes that allow the Brunello Cucinelli brand to preserve its image and the quality of its products.

Discussion

A typical business perspective in the last century was a common short-term perspective that focused on quickly growing the company's profit within a business year. A wise decision from the CEO might nowadays be to expand the business vision toward ecological and social sustainability for long-lasting company success in this disruptive 21st century. Going beyond this traditional business perspective might be extraordinary in the luxury fashion business.

In the context of family-owned companies, the risk for the company owner of focusing on long-lasting business success in line with the demands of the internal vs. external stakeholders must be lower.

In our case study about the company owner Cucinelli, his leadership behavior is in the focus of our case study as he strongly believes in humanism and social sustainability. Common goodness, sustainability, and corporate social responsibility (United Nations [UN], 2021 Carroll, 1979) are the foundations of humanistic value-driven companies, where these humanistic values are grounded in the inherent concept of positive psychology and meaningful lives (Seligman, 2003), favoring a general positive and developmental view on human beings instead of being purely a company's resource.

As a theoretical foundation for the case analysis of Cucinelli's leadership behavior, we argue that an empowering leadership behavior toward the employees and their dignity is crucial. Just like sustainable leadership for example, particularly ethical leadership, it enhances the organizational citizenship at an organizational level as well as servant leadership staff's wellbeing at an individual level (Choi, 2021; Lee et al., 2020; Zhang et al., 2019). In terms of sustainable business strategies, effective leadership that works with sustainable goals (UN, 2015) and sustainable development (Iqbal & Ahmad, 2021) are what make the difference from a short-term shareholder-driven business perspective.

Avery and Bergsteiner (2011) postulate and Del Baldo (2018, p. 228) argues that "the cultivating a way of being and acting immersed in sustainability values and a dynamic and collaborative process (Burns, Vaught, & Bauman, 2015) as a result of sharing the values of sustainability inside and outside of the company." Del Baldo (2018) summarized the successful impact of sustainable leadership on social value generation with external and internal stakeholders by focusing on the servant leadership of CEOs and entrepreneurs. This conclusion might be true for the case of Cucinelli. By using a valued based role model, the servant and ethical leadership behavior impact the employees' attitudes, capabilities, and finally their work behavior since this is a necessary requirement for sustainable business models (Bass, 2000; van Knippenberg & Sitkin, 2013).

Russo (2017) highlighted family supportive behavior of Cucinelli in his case analysis, considering work and private life as complementary facets of a personal meaningful way of life, where work vs. private life might benefit from each other. Furthermore, Russo (2017) argued that sustainable Human Resource Management (HRM) practices, such as implementing work–life balance ideas, is an investment in employee's retention, growth, and increased productivity. Cucinelli's company perspective on profit increase in luxury is extraordinary as he argued that 9% of profit increase p.a. is sufficient (Russo, 2017).

Conclusion

The results of our case analysis show evidence for Cucinelli's ethical and servant leadership behavior that is based on his strong humanistic value foundation as an entrepreneur. Thus, this value-based, positive, and empowering leadership style grounded on humanism drives his long-lasting business vision of sustainability and humanistic capitalism. From a management viewpoint, this accelerates his sustainable business models and leadership behavior, and finally it implements employee-oriented human resource management concepts which are defined as sustainable human resource management (Aust, Matthews, & Müller-Camen, 2020; Rank & Palframan, 2021) by the CSR approach. The concept of CSR with focusing on planet, people, and profit (Carroll, 1979) builds the theoretical foundation for sustainable HRM, which defines HRM strategy, policy, and practices to achieve the sustainable goals (UN, 2015). For example, this can go through implementing sustainable training concepts to increase the employee's awareness and their social or green behavior for charity or ecological projects (Piwowar-Sulej, 2021). However, this might just be possible as he is the sole company owner and believes in ethical, humanistic, and sustainable values. Considering these circumstances, he might be a positive leadership role model for sustainable business models of startups, whereas values and beliefs are strong accelerators for business success.

The lesson learned is to first invent a profitable *and* sustainable business model and then ground that on humanistic values that results in ethical and servant leadership behavior in daily business. But what might happen if the company is no longer successful in the near future? Thus, we conclude that there is high pressure on management being flexible, agile, open-minded, and finally innovative to succeed in their sustainable business model or new products substituting for organic materials. Therefore, the business thinking should not be antagonistic, but rather more holistic to combine new and sustainable business ideas with humanism.

References

Avery, G. C., & Bergsteiner, H. (2011). Sustainable leadership practices for enhancing business resilience and performance. *Strategy & Leadership, 39*(3), 5–15.

Aust, I., Matthews, B., & Müller-Camen, M. (2020). Common good HRM: A paradigm shift in sustainable HRM? *Human Resource Management Review, 30*(3), 100705.

Bass, B. M. (2000). The future of leadership in learning organizations. *Journal of Leadership Studies,* 7(3), 18–40.

Burns, H., Vaught, D., & Bauman, C. (2015). Leadership for sustainability: Theoretical foundations and pedagogical practices that foster change. *International Journal of Leadership Studies, 9*(1), 131–143.

Carroll, A. B. (1979). A three-dimensional conceptual model of corporate social performance. *Academy of Management Review, 4*(4), 497–505.

Choi, H.-J. (2021). Effect of Chief Executive Officer's sustainable leadership styles on organization members' psychological well-being and organizational citizenship behavior. *Sustainability, 13,* 13676.

Cucinelli, B. (2018). *Il sogno di solomeo.* Milano, Italy: Feltrillini.

Cucinelli, B. (2022). Bruno Cuccinelli. Retrieved from www.brunellocucinelli.com

Del Baldo, M. (2018). Sustainable business models through servant leadership: Theory and praxis. In L. Moratis, F. Melissen, & S. O. Idowu (Eds.), *Sustainable business models, CSR, sustainability, ethics & governance.* Berlin, Germany: Springer.

Di Fabio, A., & Peiró, J. M. (2018). Human capital sustainability leadership to promote sustainable development and healthy organizations: A new scale. *Sustainability, 10*(7), 2413.

Greenleaf, R. (2002). *Servant leadership: A journey into the nature of legitimate power and greatness*. Mahwah, NJ: Paulist Press.

Greenleaf Center. (2022a). *What is servant leadership*. Retrieved from https://www.greenleaf.org/what-is-servant-leadership/

Greenleaf Center. (2022b). *Servant leadership at southwest airlines*. Retrieved from https://www.greenleaf.org/wp-content/uploads/2014/09/Ridley-Keynote.pdf.

Hallinger, P., & Suriyankietkaew, S. (2018). Science mapping of the knowledge base on sustainable leadership, 1990-2018. *Sustainability, 10*(12), 4846.

Iqbal, Q., & Ahmad, N. H. (2021). Sustainable development: The colors of sustainable leadership in learning organization. *Sustainable Development, 29*(1), 108–119.

Lee, A., Lyubovnikova, J., Tian, A. W., & Knight, C. (2020). Servant leadership: A meta-analytic examination of incremental contribution, moderation, and mediation. *Journal of Occupational and Organizational Psychology, 93*(1), 1–44.

Lemoine, G. J., Hartnell, C. A., & Leroy, H. (2019). Taking stock of moral approaches to leadership: An integrative review of ethical, authentic, and servant leadership. *Academy of Management Annals, 13*, 148–187.

Laub, J. (2011). *Servant leadership*. Retrieved from http://www.olagroup.com/Display.asp?Page¼servant_leadership

Piwowar-Sulej, K. (2021). Core functions of sustainable human resource management. A hybrid literature review with the use of H-Classics methodology. *Sustainable Development, 29*, 671–693.

Rank, S., & Palframan, J. (2021). Internal corporate social responsibility preferences of young job seekers with regard to sustainable HRM: Are these CSR preferences related to their personal value orientations. *Journal of Intercultural Management, 13*(4), 34–62.

Russo, M. (2017). Brunello Cucinelli: An inspired leader who helps employees to have it all. In R. Koonce (Ed.). *Developing leaders for positive organizing* (pp. 43–54). Bingley, UK: Emerald Publishing Limited.

Seligman, M. E. P. (2003). Positive psychology: Fundamental assumptions. [Editorial]. *The Psychologist, 16*(3), 126–127.

United Nations (2021). *Sustainable Developmental Goals*. Retrieved from https://sdgs.un.org/goals

Van Knippenberg, D., & Sitkin, S. B. (2013). A critical assessment of charismatic—Transformational leadership research: Back to the drawing board? *The Academy of Management Annals*, 7(1), 1–60.

Zhang, Y., Long Zhang, L., Liu, G., Duan, J., Xu, S., & Cheung, M. W.-L. (2019). How does ethical leadership impact employee organizational citizenship behavior? *Zeitschrift Für Psychologie, 227*(1), 18–30.

9 Italian Luxury

Between Tradition and Storytelling: The Gucci Case

Mauro Ferraresi and Giulia Tonucci
IULM

Foreword

A caveat runs; this chapter aims to consider luxury as it is represented. The media representation of luxury and its narration in Italy is probably one of the self-determining factors of the Italian fashion system. In other words, industry qualitative excellence and aesthetic refinement are preferred among the macro-descriptors of the luxury phenomenon in Italian fashion. They carry with them other macro-descriptors such as pleasure and hedonism, exclusivity, high price, and even ostentation.

Qualitative excellence and aesthetic refinement are thus at the basis of the storytelling of Italian luxury, but it should be added that they alone would not be sufficient. There needs to be a glue that holds them together, and this glue will be brought to the reader's attention.

Studies on luxury can even be traced back to Greek philosophical thought when it was defined as megaloprépeia, meaning magnificence. Plato distinguished the physical from the soul. With very modern sensibilities, he went so far as to say that megaloprépeia was inseparable from economic implications: magnificence is manifested when there is substantial expenditure for public benefit. In fact, it seems that, at that time, magnificence was understood primarily as public luxury. It was Aristotle who addressed the issue in greater depth. The Greek philosopher, in the fourth book of the Nicomachean Ethics, argues that megaloprépeia consists of the virtue of great expenditure. It is defined as "the expedient way of spending big" (Eth. nic., IV, 2, 1122a 23). Aristotle identifies the core element of megaloprépeia as not only the large expenditure involved, which is nevertheless taken into account, but as the expenditure most appropriate to the circumstance. He elaborates on the philosophical theory of the "magnificent", and he links what we today call luxury to beauty, aesthetics, good taste, and, in addition, to the laws of economic availability. Today, the term luxury seems to have retained the link with aesthetics and certainly with economics, but it has moved away from the positive meaning that the Greeks seemed to associate with. Rather, the concept of luxury that we best understand today derives from the Latin term "luxus", which literally means "excess", "intemperance", "debauchery", and

DOI: 10.4324/9781003305095-12

"softness". The semantic meaning of the term also harbors negative connotations of "pomp" and even "magnificence", but they play a minor role. The Greeks' version of magnificence would not have received the criticism that contemporary luxury receives as it was less linked to the concept of wastefulness, although excess was certainly a feature of it. Magnificence was considered a virtue, as reported by some later reflections developed by Thomas Aquinas and Christian thought, and there is certainly a common thread that runs through the centuries and links the concept of Greek magnificence to beauty and, for example, to the splendor of courts and the arts. However, it can be speculated that it was precisely the splendor of the courts that began to bring negative connotations to the concept, allowing the great differences that existed between public and private magnificence to emerge and initiating the materialistic and hedonistic culture that lives on to this day.

Public luxury, private luxury

Luxury, both public and private, has always been present throughout history. In every human settlement and in every historical period, it is possible to trace that dose of "superfluity" used to embellish and adorn streets, squares, and palaces, going far beyond purely functional reasons. Indeed, it could be said that the transition from prehistory to history is seamless as far as luxury is concerned, although it is necessary to relate luxury to the specific types of wealth and technology possessed by those ancient societies. It seems that it was not even our ancestor, but rather homo erectus that made the Venus of Berekhat Ram found in Palestine in the Golan Heights and dating back more than 200,000 years. That find is an important example of prehistoric art that testifies to a very ancient link between religion, luxury, and beauty.

The reality of luxury is twofold: on the one hand, luxury in various forms and qualities has existed since prehistoric times (Treccani, 1929), and on the other hand, it has found important regulations within the religious and artistic spheres, so much so that, for a long time, a common path of managing luxury was built (Morand, 2012). Let us add that a third condition for the exercise of luxury is namely its sometimes more contrasted and debated connection with beauty. Is devoting time to constructing a useful statuette for a religious rite, expending vast amounts of energy and effort, using materials that were valuable for the time, an expenditure of value for a primitive pursuit of public luxury for religious reasons?

It is not incorrect to assume that the contemporary world tourism phenomenon of culturally artistic cities today is one of the consequences that public luxury developed in various eras of human history.

Private luxury, on the other hand, has to do with pleasure, voluptuousness, and taste. It is defined as that which makes life more pleasant and sybaritic, which led to the most popular perceptions and catchphrases regarding luxury precisely denouncing such pleasures. For what is devoting time to oneself, reading a book in peace, enjoying delicious food, or staying in beautiful and exclusive places, if not a manifestation of private luxury? (Lipovesky, 2007).

With each experience forms of private luxury, from the sybarite to the cenobite, albeit to varying degrees and because of different spending capacities and worldviews. One can be gaudy and voluptuous, or temperate and sober, but each is a small portion of luxury one indulges in for themselves. Like all complex phenomena, and because of the human inequalities provided by the differences in cultural, relational, symbolic, and economic capital discussed by Bourdieu (1997), private luxury also has different facets. For example, there are negative sides that speak of wastefulness, gratuitous uselessness, overspending, and distortion of ends, where attention to luxury far exceeds attention to humans (Lipovesky, 2007).

In this regard, Sombart differentiates between quantitative and qualitative luxury. Sombart links qualitative luxury to the consumption of goods typical of the upper classes, while quantitative luxury is strongly linked to wastefulness. Sombart believes that, in most cases, both types of luxury occur together, characterized by being superfluous. A little later, Sombart adds that qualitative luxury can give rise to elegant and aesthetically relevant objects, thus tying luxury to beauty as they entail the same need for refinement. Quantitative luxury, on the other hand, does not necessarily turn out to be refined and graceful. For the German sociologist, there is a difference between adorning an altar with pure gold and instead buying a very refined and expensive silk shirt. In the case of the former, one exhibits "vain superfluity", but it is somehow generous because it is donated in some way to the community. In the case of the latter, the individual and their selfish and voluptuous actions emerge. However, the categories of "generous" and "selfish" distinguish based on aesthetic-moral, if not political, judgments and conceptions. What is generous for one becomes selfish for the other, or otherwise benefits only one part of the community. An atheist, for example, would object to the fact that the pure gold altar is an act of generosity and would see a thousand alternative ways, certainly more useful and magnificent for him, to use the money. It is therefore advisable to stay within the more neutral distinction between public and private luxury.

A further element that Sombart highlighted relates to the relationship that luxury has with the necessary, where necessary means what an individual or a society needs in accordance with prevailing ethical and aesthetic values, and in accordance with physiological and cultural needs. But the concept of necessary is also ductile, porous, and changeable, depending on epochs and societies. So, Sombart (1967, 97) cannot define it further except in general sociological terms and by constructing both concepts, luxury and necessary, in relation to one another: luxury appears when it exceeds what is necessary. Fortunately, from the point of view of consumption, there is a rather precise definition of the necessary: "complex of goods and services comprising certain household items such as furniture, radio, television, refrigerator, and standardized brands of food and clothing". We could start from here to try to define luxury as that which exceeds the goods of citizenship, i.e., according to Alberoni's definition, that complex of goods and services that a given community feels is necessary to have in order for its members to feel like an integral part of the community (Alberoni, 1968). In contemporary Italian society, we could fearlessly advance the hypothesis that this includes the smartphone, without which no one would feel completely a citizen in his or her country, but instead an outcast who lacks the standard of goods to conduct his or her daily life worthily and fully. We are well aware that there are exceptions, and that there are and always will be people who will take pride in not owning a smartphone and in turn do not feel marginalized because of it. In fact, it is quite the opposite as they proudly might claim that they feel fully represented and empowered in the community in which they live even without relying on a cell phone. This is a most respectable position, to which one can only object that they are merely a minority not capable of undermining the truth of the package standard.

Finally, it should be noted that luxury and waste are not easily branded as absolute futility since absolute futility does not exist. Luxury can be superfluous, excessive, unjust, inadequate, inefficient, irrational, and hateful. But, in some ways, it is also the opposite: distinctive, adequate, rational and, as we shall see, pacifying, vital, and protective. In other words, volitional spending is a sociological rule, a kind of collective obligation to which we all subject ourselves to varying degrees. An obligation that, according to Lipovesky (2007, 25), even has its roots in magical and mythological concepts.

Luxury between de-tesaurization and representation

Why luxury? Lipovetsky offers a brief historical analysis to reach two conclusions (2007, 34ff). That is that luxury, when subjected to the gift economy, performs a fundamental de-exhausting function. The second explains that luxury contributes to the development of so-called "representational consumption". In primitive societies, where what anthropologists have called the "gift economy" was in force, waste and spending were aimed at restoring a situation of parity and economic equality among clans. From Mauss to Malinowsky to Sahlins and all those who have studied the potlatch and the gift economy, they have all come to the similar conclusion that the risk of completely losing one's possessions in the game of exchange where each gift must be superior to the gift received in a kind of contest of who spoils more and better, is actually a social strategy to seek peace. Exchanges, as Lévi-Strauss also observed, are wars resolved peacefully, and the gift serves to smooth out envy, grudges, jealousies as well as certain economic disparities.

De-tesaurization, that is, the waste and loss of one's possessions conducted by the gift economy, is to be regarded as a luxury of spending and superfluity. De-tesaurization was born before both the capitalist and commercial economies developed, at the time of great journeys and great discoveries. It is coeval with the very birth of communities. Luxury, therefore, has its roots in the rules of communities, which are useful for maintaining peace and prosperity. Luxury begins to manifest itself in the social over the individual, since the individual is, if anything, entitled to accumulation and possession while luxury, as we have seen, dispossesses.

As for the magical-cosmic implications, Lipovesky mentions that they too have strong roots in luxury, magnificence, and waste. Indeed, it must be noted that the game of gift and counter-gift creates bonds, unions, and understandings that are harbingers of peace. Such bonds, unions, and understandings are to be found in the world beyond. The relationship with one's ancestors is a feature of all cultures that, in different ways and in different capacities, seek to build forms of communication and relationship with the dead. The cult of the dead is a social fact, as Marcel Mauss puts it, present in all societies, from primitive to contemporary, from theocracies to modern, secularized democracies. Voluptuary spending therefore also extends to the deceased, thus creating a kind of alliance with otherworldly spirits and deities who are not of this world but who influence it. In this case, the so-called sumptuary madness is implemented because it can produce benevolence, divine protection, and spiritual aid that are continually felt to be needed. Sacrifices, for example, are an aspect of such beliefs. It is not erroneous to say that luxury arises from an inseparable interweaving of religious, mythical, and social needs, in a mix of otherworldly but also extremely earthly motivations if it is true that luxury manifests erotic needs as it expresses the desire to enjoy the world (1988).

Of course, all the above considerations should not make us forget that luxury is also the need for and the result of a symbolic challenge and struggle for the affirmation of the status of individuals, clans, and potentates.

If in early communities it served to build cohesion later, with the emergence of nation-states, its function would change decisively.

Indeed, the emergence of nation-states, among other things, increased the potential of the individual. With the transition from Gemeinschft to Gesellschaft, luxury increasingly played the role of status representation, and voluptuous expenditures become a sign of prestige and social difference. In modernity, luxury undergoes a twist in meaning that transforms it into an element of social differentiation. The collective bonds of community life fall apart in favor of individual affirmations of which luxury and superfluity become a specific and regular manifestation.

The analyses conducted thus far seem almost to reverse our definition of luxury into its opposite. The vulgate defines it as a process of differentiation and inequality, inequitable and dilapidating. In this brief examination, on the other hand, specific, even egalitarian characteristics of luxury emerge, as it follows the pattern of the potlatch. It was Baudrillard, above all, who noted in the volume "The System of Objects" (1968) that this link between luxury and the gift economy reflects the traditional pattern of potlacht where goods are squandered. In the same way, the wealthy squander part of their wealth to surround themselves with luxury, which in turn implements their partial egalitarian function.

Around the individual and his conquered importance, new types of luxury peep out (Lipovesky, 2007). Desire for collectibles and the search for precious artifacts develop, and the sense of esthetics grows through the careful selection of vestiges of the past. Fashion begins to set in motion its shifts that will speed up with time. In the 14th century, clothes became more fitted, laces and buttons were used, and trend and colors began to characterize garments. Slowly, the dynamic of change takes over from the previous static (Mafai, 2011). It is a slow process since some fabrics and brocades, for example during the Renaissance, are born and remain in fashion for dozens and dozens of years, but soon the process accelerates and becomes more complex following Simmel's (2001) famous reading of the phenomenon based on indicators such as imitation and change.

Some aspects of contemporary luxury

In 2021, the global luxury market is worth 1,140 billion euros, a figure that recovers about half of the 2020 losses, and thus approaches the pre-COVID value of 1,268 billion (Bain & Co, 2021).

If we look at the categories that make up this market, we find that they are difficult to define because all the companies and firms deal with high-cost goods. The sector includes companies that produce jewelry, companies that operate with luxury cars, and companies of haute couture and accessory brands. The sector also includes watches, furniture, personal care, yachts and private jets, high technology, exclusive foods, large hotels, starred restaurants, and the art market. Finally, there is also a place for many companies working with important assets, such as gold, silver, and diamonds, which have a high cost even as a gross product. Another independent consideration suggests the need for analyzing experiential luxury. This is the type of luxury that tickles the individual's voluptuousness most, and that focuses as never before on the experience of private luxury. Experiential luxury relates to an individual's lifestyle and the quantity and quality of luxury consumption experienced, even more than other types of luxury. Experiential luxury quilts the daily lives of those who can afford it: a very fine dinner, an exclusive relais, a first-class trip with champagne, orchids, or armchair beds. These are some examples of experiential luxury, often repeated to the point of daily excess. Such forms of experiential luxury add personalization, which is the idea that luxury can be perfectly tailored to personal needs.

Italian luxury and fashion

Fashion, as we understand it today, was born, as Belfanti states, when clothing ceased to merely be an element of distinction and rank but became part of a more articulate and mobile complex, driven by what Simmel called imitation (Belfanti, 2008, pp. 19, 42).

Italian high fashion in its modern reality was born specifically in 1951 in Florence from Giovanni Battista Giorgini. Giorgini, thanks to his contacts and relations, convinced U.S. buyers and the specialized press, busy as every year following the presentation of the Parisian collections, to extend their European stay and arrive on 12 February 1951, at Villa Torreggiani in Florence, Giorgini's home, to watch the first show of Italian tailoring creations.

It was probably this event, and Giorgini's ability to link Italian fashion to Florence, Tuscany, and the Renaissance, that gave rise to a genre of storytelling that is still in vogue today: the one that asserts that "Made in Italy" has its roots in the Renaissance culture of beauty and luxury, typical of the historical, cultural, and artistic movement (Corbellini & Saviolo, 2004).

Actually, Belfanti tends to dismantle this narrative by stating that the intangible attributes of "Made in Italy", that Italy does not exist in reality, even though "the effectiveness of the narrative has been so great and such that it has been extended to all consumer goods pertaining to "Made in Italy" (Belfanti, 2019, pp. 19–20). Belfanti states that this is cultural history and not material history, meaning that the Renaissance itself is a cultural invention, cultivated internationally since the 19th century at the height of the Romantic era. This invention does not align with the continuum of craftsmanship and production in modernity, since the way "Made in Italy" is produced today has little or nothing to do with Renaissance ways (Belfanti, ibid., p. 21). One hears in Belfanti's assertions historian Hobsbawm's concept of tradition. Hobsbawn (2002) suggests that an ad-hoc past is invented to validate the choices of the present. "Invented traditions" are a set of practices that tend to reaffirm certain values and attitudes, for example, how the West recognizes in Athens the home of democracy as it is understood in that part of the world. But it is the invention of tradition that advocates a continuity with the past and therefore upholds a legitimacy that comes from afar and is rooted more in myth than in history. The myth of the Renaissance and its invention are the narratives in which both "Made in Italy" and its characteristics of "beautiful, good and well made" are rooted (Ferraresi, 2014).

In the sectors of fashion, textiles, fashion accessories, shoes, eyewear, furnishings, and food, the country-of-origin effect has developed since 1951. It is a sedimented heritage of culture and knowledge capable of delineating the Italian commercial and productive profile with a relative image of the country based on two synergistic pillars: luxury and craftsmanship. In essence, "Made in Italy" is based on an invention, a false continuity with the past time, but this invention has led to the creation of an identity profile, a real brand.

The invention started continuous storytelling that links artisanal knowledge, attention to detail, quality choices in materials and ingredients, inventiveness, and creativity directly to the Renaissance. This is difficult to prove historically, but nevertheless, the Italian country of origin effect has occurred.

But what specifically are the characteristics of Italian luxury? According to Sofia Gnoli, luxury in fashion is irrevocably linked to haute couture. Gnoli explains that, in this sense, luxury is first and foremost French heritage, where haute couture was born (Belfanti, 2008, 176ff; Gnoli, 2020). The author also explains that Italian haute couture, on the other hand, was born later and almost at the same time as boutique fashion. Albeit, Italian fashion has a history beyond those years, with examples such as the five Fendi sisters specializing in haute couture furs since 1970 (Gnoli, 2020, p. 348), or even before that, the Fontana sisters who, in 1948, had already designed the wedding dress for Tyrone Power's wedding to Linda Christian (Gnoli, ibid., p. 152).

In Rome, we find Laura Biagiotti's master, Emilio Schuberth, whose sumptuous gowns certainly provided a boost to the luxury of Italian fashion. The creations of Roberto Capucci, Gattinoni, and other designers made Rome the capital of Italian haute couture (Gnoli, 2020, 157ff). Since then, the geography of Italian haute couture flows between Florence, Rome, and Milan, and we gladly refer to Gnoli's book for a more accurate review as we are more interested in focusing on what happened to Italian luxury.

Italian luxury in fashion received new life after the 1980s and after the rise of prêt-à-porter with one important characteristic: the concept of the couturier was born because he could design the right dress for the customer in front of him, and the dress is often unique and unrepeatable and cut specifically to the client's measurements, taste, and lifestyle.

The stylist, on the other hand, has to decide who his customers will be and design for potential buyers. Sometimes, he works for a fashion company whose production and distribution characteristics he must know. Sometimes, instead, he is the founder of the company himself, which began rising in popularity in Italy in the 1970s with the rise of Armani, Versace, and Ferré (cf. Gnoli, 2020, p. 268).

Italian haute couture has been revived in recent times after the successes of Italian prêt–à-porter. It restarted when Armani inaugurated haute couture with Armani Privé in 2005 and when Versace resumed its haute couture line produced under the name Atelier Versace in 2012. More examples are when Dolce & Gabbana recently collaborated with Alta Moda and Alta Sartoria, and when Prada made its bags and accessories even more exclusive.

To put all Italian luxury back in the hands of Italian haute couture or exclusive accessories is too simple, because Italian luxury is also defined and strengthened by two fundamental phenomena of contemporary fashion. The first is acceleration, the second is hybridization. In this regard, Sofia Gnoli says that, since 2000, many brands have inaugurated pre-collections so that new garments arrive in stores four times a year instead of twice. The "see now, buy now" formula inaugurated by Burberry in London made in-store availability of part of the collections that had just been shown on the catwalk trendy (Gnoli, 378). The phenomenon of capsule collections, small and limited collections that combine garments and accessories that offer a specific and complete look, helped increase the number of offerings.

This acceleration was certainly meeting market needs, but the quantity of supply necessary meant stressing the creativity of designers and decreasing the quality of ideas.

Hybridization, on the other hand, leads to an integration of precious materials and technological or even electronic materials; of ready-to-wear and haute couture. It also hybridizes formats, languages, and genres (Gnoli, 2020, p. 380).

Hybridization has made it possible to speak of luxury for Italian ready-to-wear as well, and acceleration has exacerbated this process.

In 2003, "Trading Up: The New American Luxury" by Michael Silverstein and Neil Fiske was released in the United States. The two authors talk about new frontiers in luxury and, most importantly, they analyze the emotional dimension of luxury where they depart from the classical idea of luxury that consists of a rare product, inaccessible to most, that becomes a status symbol and elitist.

In fact, if we can speak of a new luxury that increasingly increases the cost and prestige of luxury products, we can also speak of an emotional aura that luxury brings by involving consumers, who are willing to pay more for a perfume precisely because it belongs to a luxury brand capable of generating genuine emotion and a sense of belonging to an exclusive world. Of course, the emotional aspects must happily mix with the technical and performance aspects of the product in order to create a real difference from competitors.

The new concept of luxury analyzed in "Trading Up" involves consumers belonging to heterogeneous social classes who decide to choose and spend on one new luxury product while saving on others. An additional feature of great interest for the purposes of this chapter is that, according to the two authors, a luxury product requires characteristics and attention close to a handcrafted product but it must have an industrial-level production capacity, which is precisely the storytelling on which "Made in Italy" is based.

The characteristic of the new Italian luxury is therefore to provide the emotion of Italian-ness through the guarantee of craftsmanship, the care and quality of details, and the choice of fine materials. All this, however, is not so much the product of a careful craftsman as it is the specific industrial production of a brand or maison.

To recap: if classic luxury means buying an expensive item from the Armani Privé line, emotional luxury means buying a more affordable belt or Armani perfume. You spend more compared to a non-branded belt, but you participate in the world of Armani luxury. In the interview with Gucci that is collected and commented on in this same chapter by Giulia Tonucci, it emerges that luxury in Italy is always told and represented in the media through craftsmanship and manual labor. It is this aspect of luxury at play here. It is from this representation that the definition of Italian luxury is based: the luxury of manual labor.

Manual luxury is certainly found in every definition of luxury, as much in Italy as in France, and in all the states where luxury is produced, marketed, and promoted. But there is an Italian specificity in this definition, linked to the fragmentation of our industrial fabric and the great strength of the small and medium-sized business sector.

As Antonella Centra states, Italian luxury was born in this particular production context.

"Luxury in Italy is governed by a manufacturing sector of the highest level, characterized by an incredible capacity and resilience that is constituted through a fragmented world in which small-scale tailoring realities persist, both for leather goods and clothing. In Italian luxury, we find unique care and craftsmanship with respect to the making of products, passed down within small local productions that are pushed and supported by the presence of large realities".

On the other hand, Centra is very careful not to identify craftsmanship care with simple tradition: "... on the one hand we are strongly rooted in the territory, on the other hand, our production processes have evolved over time, not so much to the point of alienating mechanization-luxury for us still means what is handmade and here in Italy-but we have imported processes and innovations that allow this luxury to evolve".

This is evidenced by the connection that is, at first glance, arduous between artisanal care and digitization of production and marketing processes. According to Claudio Monteverde, this is why Gucci stands at the forefront. "The link between luxury and digital is evident in the relationship with the customer. For Gucci, digital tools are key to creating a unique customer journey that is as personalized as possible with respect to the needs of each individual customer. Among the most interesting examples is certainly the use of Artificial Intelligence, which has been implemented in two strategic areas: first, in distribution, with the aim of improving sales forecasts and defining stock replenishment volumes throughout the retail channel; and second, in marketing, to refine customer recognition based on past purchasing behaviors. Gucci 9, the House's Global Client Service, was created with the goal of differentiating Gucci from other luxury brands through a specific human touch, powered and enriched by technology".

A case study: Gucci

Under the creative direction of Alessandro Michele, Gucci has undertaken a decisive turn in terms of image and social commitment, becoming, in a very short time, one of the main representatives of a new approach to the fashion and luxury system in constant dialogue with the most pressing issues in our contemporary world.

Since 2015, Gucci has implemented a decisive re-positioning of the brand on several fronts, where style is only one part of it. These were necessary changes at a time when the brand was going through a phase of uncertainty, both from a commercial and an identity point of view. Gucci had an urgent need to find its own stylistic and creative connotation and to get a renewed boost toward the most urgent issues and dynamics of contemporary fashion.

The effective upswing that the new creative director has been able to achieve in recent years, together with the unconditional support of CEO Marco Bizzarri, is illustrated by the positive surge in the brand's sales curve on a global scale, also due to this fundamental repositioning.

The Equilibrium project, which has increasingly gained prominence in the definition of a brand identity aimed at 360 degrees of sustainability, has enabled Alessandro Michele to succeed in conveying, under the aegis of the iconic "Made in Italy" brand, the traditional values and post-contemporary mentality of Generation Z members. Gucci has thus become the resonant box of their social as well as environmental commitment and, at the same time, has undertaken practical actions with a ten-year plan in support of sustainability, which should reach the end of its first stage in 2025.

An Italian history

In Italy, Gucci, along with Ferragamo and Bulgari, is one of the names that symbolizes high quality and craftsmanship.

Keeping the family name for the corporate brand is an important trait for many luxury companies including Gucci. The family name indeed embodies a kind of legacy and brings with it the idea that products are reserved for a small and select circle of friends (Chevalier & Mazzalovo, 2021). We all recognize today in the intersecting double G logo an important, iconic brand that has succeeded, despite a thousand vicissitudes, course changes, and financial ups and downs, to gain the global spotlight, becoming the brand par excellence of a new "Made in Italy": globalized, revolutionized, and revolutionarily launched at full speed into a future of innovation, digital scenarios, and a new social consciousness.

The Gucci brand, headquartered in Florence, has a range of products including leather goods, shoes, accessories, clothing, jewelry, watches, make-up, fragrances, and a collection of furniture and decorative accessories. The brand's success dates back to before the generation of designers such as Versace, Armani, Moschino, and Ferré, who, between the late 1970s and the roaring 1980s, brought Italian fashion to the international spotlight. The history of Gucci begins many decades earlier and draws precisely on the traditions of the past that linked the success of the brand to the commercial genius of representing the family lineage.

The company was founded in Florence in 1921 by Guccio Gucci, but the story began a few years earlier when the young Florentine searched for his fortune in London. There, he worked as an apprentice at the capital's luxurious Savoy Hotel, coming into contact with the likes, whims, and trends of English high society. And it was from this experience that Mr. Gucci took note of all fashion-related details, including accessories and colors that would later characterize the style of the fashion house, inspiring himself from the late Victorian England high society, an aristocratic world that flaunted its elegance and goods in the opulent environments of the hotel. He immediately connoted his style with all the references that were part of his London experience: the stirrups, clamps, saddles, bridles, and harnesses, which became, in the following decades, an integral part of Gucci's heritage and iconography.

This experience prompted him, upon his return home, to set up his own handcrafted leather goods store, where he was able to artfully combine the foreign influence he had accrued with the best artisan traditions of leather-working in pure Tuscan style. It was a mix that immediately made a breakthrough in the fashion and homes of the Florentine aristocrats and upper middle class that quickly determined the success of this master leatherworker. It was a triumph of Italian craftsmanship combined with the skillful ability to pick up on the most sophisticated and elegant styles and trends that drove the buying patterns and desires of the wealthiest consumers, and not just Italians. Remembering the first step in the maison's long history is important now more than ever as it reacquaints us with the deeper value of luxury; what it comprises, what it represents and has represented from the beginning.

As iterated on the Kering group's website in the section dedicated to the Florentine fashion house, today "Gucci redefines the boundaries of luxury in the 21st century, an ambitious vision started in 2015 by Alessandro Michele, creative director, and Marco Bizzarri, president and CEO. [...] Through a skillful reinterpretation of cultural heritage and fashion, Michele's polyhedric approach successfully combines apparently opposite universes, such as dandy and Italian Renaissance styles, or Gothic aesthetics and DIY punk looks. Today more than ever, charisma, innovation, and commitment enable this brand to offer extremely modern garments" (Kering, 2022).

The griffe's iconic products, from the bamboo-handled bag (1947) to the Flora scarf (1966) to the Jackie O bag, distinguished an era still charmed by the idea of couture with a sartorial flavor, and in which "Made in Italy" fashion embedded internationals with similar feelings of a vacation on the clear waters of Capri, and the wonder of discovering the many artistic and architectural works spread along the Belpaese. But that era faded, along with the romantic images of black-and-white television, and left the room to technicolor and a new way of creating fashion.

Starting as a family business, Gucci evolved and was owned by the Anglo-Arab company Investcorp International in the late 1980s before becoming a public company in 1996. But for the general public, it was when Tom Ford relaunched the brand that there was a new polish and appeal to the leitmotifs of the collections offered (Gnoli, 2020). In the 1990s, the brand now extrapolated from its elitist dimension, along with other brands in the Italian fashion system including Prada, matured in its ability to strike a chord with the collective imagination, Vanni Codeluppi (2002) acknowledges. Gucci's evolution paralleled the shift in the fashion system from "proper", elegant, middle-class clothing to one closer to the trends of the youth of those years. If up to the 1980s Gucci still represented a snobbish world of luxury, it began to dress a freer, cosmopolitan, world citizen, minimalist, and refined person in the following years, thanks to the stylistic directives of Texan Tom Ford.

Tom Ford was succeeded in 2004 by Roman designer Frida Giannini, who, for ten years, until 2014, led the fashion house through a new hyper-feminized imaginary, distant from the aggressive and sexy verve of the previous creative director. This periodic change of styles and visions within the same brand can be recognized as what Sofia Gnoli has apostrophized as the "waltz of creative directors", a phenomenon that has been increasing since the 1990s in almost all luxury fashion houses, particularly those born at the beginning of the last century and linked at least initially to the couturier figure such as Balenciaga, Dior, Givenchy, Burberry, Valentino, and, indeed, Gucci. It is characterized by the turning from one brand to the next of their respective creative directors, constantly hovering between excessive brand "vampirization" and ever-shorter contractual relationships.

Since the end of the last century, many luxury groups have acquired brands with an important historical baggage on which they then build strong narratives. This is the case of Kering, which bought Gucci, Balenciaga, Alexander McQueen, and Bottega Veneta (Gnoli, 2020). For this reason, the ability to bring to the surface and enhance the roots of a brand becomes of fundamental necessity. This also opened the door to addressing another very important issue, namely that of the heritage, the need to keep alive and, at the same time, grow the artistic, cultural, and identity heritage of a brand. It is a fundamental and unchanging value, as opposed to this constant impetus for change in the fashion industry.

An aspect on which Gucci, since the very aftermath of the latest waltz that brought Alessandro Michele to the helm of the brand, continues today to pivot in an original and lively way, forming a continuous dialogue between tradition and the future, between references from the archives and new hybridizations. This issue was not affected, even following the acquisition of the brand by the French Kering group in 2004, a holding company described by Antonella Centra as "kind", precisely because of its corporate willingness not to enter into the autonomy of the different brands, but rather "the different companies can develop individually, without "cannibalization" from the top (full interview to follow).

A sustainable revolution

In the new millennium, the luxury world has had to come to terms with the issue of sustainability. Fashion, first and foremost, has some heavy and well-founded allegation, as being one of the world's most polluting industries, second only to the oil industry.

The unselfconscious euphoria of the 1980s, the economic growth followed by the financial crises of the 1990s and early 2000s, were all times when environmental protection seemed to be a topic with a little appeal, if not naïve features with little substance and far away from the prevailing consumerist frenzy. The change of course came when the increasing growth of the fashion industry, due primarily to the advent of the fast fashion firms, as well as the consequent frenzy of a ready-to-wear market ready to increase the pace of collections and productions, made evident how much this is causing consumption and waste of resources that can no longer be ignored.

Gradually, social awareness of these issues has increased, and fashion firms, as well as the holding companies that own them, have had to take action in response regarding not only the environment but also the issue of labor exploitation and social rights. The environmental aspect is in fact only one side of the coin and is comprehensive only if it is accompanied by the safeguarding of all the actors involved in the industry.

An example of good practices and concrete actions taken in this direction is that of Kering CEO François-Henri Pinault, who, for years, has been at the forefront in promoting important initiatives to raise awareness in the fashion and luxury world on issues related to social commitment and environmental protection. Indeed, as is reiterated on the group's official website, sustainability "has always been at the heart of Kering's strategy. Far more than an ethical necessity, it is a driver of innovation and value creation for the Group, its Companies Houses, and its stakeholders" (Kering, 2022).

Among the most important and most recent initiatives is undoubtedly the Fashion Pact, launched by Pinault himself at the behest of French President Emmanuel Macron and signed by about 250 luxury sector brands, committing all members to a common core of key environmental goals in three areas: stopping global warming, restoring biodiversity, and protecting the oceans. The ten-year plan to reduce emissions by 40%, a sustainability strategy inaugurated by the Kering group in 2015, which, as Antonella Centra recalls, has brought a radical change in Gucci's way of thinking and acting, with engagement at all company levels (interv.). It is fair to mention that, already in the early 2000s, even the then creative director Frida Giannini and the former CEO, Patrizio Di Marco, also worked to base Gucci on a socially and culturally responsible business model. In 2005, the company began a partnership with UNICEF, periodically donating a portion of its revenues on sales to the association and promoting its various social campaigns.

Around the same time was the "Schools for Africa" initiative in collaboration with the Nelson Mandela Foundation and Hamburg Society, a project that has been committed to bringing millions of children to school by supporting the construction and restructuring of schools, distributing educational materials for students, and conducting teacher training courses.

Then, in 2013, to protect women's rights, the fashion house created a charity called "Chime for Change" in collaboration with some of the most influential female personalities on the international art scene, including Beyoncé, to support the global campaign against violence on females.

Over the last decade, the expression "sustainable development" has become increasingly popular both in common parlance, but also, and especially, in the formulation of corporate business models. This combination of words, now so familiar and almost inescapable, was presented and defined only in 1987 in the United Nations Commission on Environment and Development report, as Chevalier and Mazzalovo (2021) remind us. It means "the ability to meet the needs of the present without compromising those of future generations. Its strength and originality lie in having integrated the concepts of humanity and intergenerational equity" (*Ibidem*, 2021). And if there is no ontological incompatibility between luxury and sustainability, Gucci's current creative director, together with CEO Marco Bizzarri, have dedicated the last seven years of the brand's work specifically to become as sustainable as possible for today's young generations as well as for future ones.

One could indeed say that the "gentle revolution", which took place with the change in the brand's management, started by asking why and how to make fashion, for whom, and for what purpose. Regarding the first question, Alessandro Michele's work is a search for beauty and a will to give it expression through multiple artistic-expressive languages, which go beyond the making of clothes to build a real universe of thought and action as this continuous will proceeds in parallel with the awareness of the protection of the environment and people. One might think that all creative work starts from the appreciation of the human being as a free and flowing individual, outside of any pre-established paradigm, and this deep and necessary relationship with reality and nature that surrounds us. As Alessandro Borghi recalls in a recent interview with Alessandro Michele, the latter has "completely reshaped the concept of beauty in such an elegant, smart and deep way that not all have been able to understand it".

From 2019, the Gucci Equilibrium project was born, "unifying the principles we uphold and the actions we pursue to treat our world and each other better, for our collective future" (Gucci, 2019), which becomes the core basis of the *culture of purpose* for which the brand stands. Equilibrium's online platform contains a collection of all the various sustainability projects the brand has activated over the years: from new ones that are ongoing, to those launched by the previous management yet continue to represent initiatives relevant to the brand's mission. They have been divided into the two categories "People" and "Planet". In the former, emphasis is given to initiatives concerning diversity, gender equality, and inclusiveness, starting from a strong and positive corporate culture. This includes the aforementioned "Chime for Change", which began in support of women and has now extended its voice to promoting Gender Equality.

With the campaign "To Gather Together" launched in 2019, Gucci appeals to the international community to overcome gender bias and does so by concerting different forms of expression and media, from artist MP5's murals to the short film "The Future is Fluid" by Jade Jackman and Irregular Labs. The film explores what the word "gender" means to Gen Z kids and shows the experiences of young protagonists from different parts of the world. On top of this is the first edition of Chime Zine, in digital format, which periodically features the contributions of activists, artists, and writers from all around the world.

In the second category of Equilibrium dedicated to the Planet, the many initiatives featured are dedicated to managing and preserving our planet's limited resources. In a way that Gucci himself calls holistic, what emerges by searching through the different projects is the desire to involve the entire supply chain and adopt climate-smart strategies to help protect and restore the nature for the future. In this whole project and ramifications of Equilibrium, there is not only the idea of being a showcase of "good deeds", but also the awareness of building a genuine and transparent dialogue with the different stakeholders of the brand; to share ongoing progress, achievements, and future goals; to involve the whole community in this collective and sustainable ideal.

Sustainable luxury, digital luxury

In this examination of the Gucci case, regarding a possible redefinition of contemporary luxury, it is necessary to consider factors different from those that determined luxury in the last century. While in Guccio Gucci's time luxury was mainly oriented toward exclusivity, preciousness, and product refinement, today what is required of luxury companies is also the construction of a narrative that leverages those principles and values that determine their positioning in the great debate on innovation and sustainability.

And Gucci, thanks to the corporate philosophy embraced and pursued, is among the luxury brands that are champions of innovation and engagement with the issues addressed above, and an undisputed promoter of a new idea of luxury. A luxury that, as we have said, simultaneously keeps the more traditional qualities linked to craftsmanship, the naturalness of the materials used, the authenticity of its own history, and the enhancement of its own heritage alive while knowing how to open up to the new possibilities offered by digital innovation.

As Elisabetta Rotolo writes, luxury brands must take part in "a digital future built on increasingly daring initiatives, toward more fluid multidimensional virtual realities" (Rotolo, 2022). And it seems that Alessandro Michele and his team do not want to move away from this mindset. On the contrary, the relationship between luxury and digital innovation is seen by the brand as an inescapable and symbiotic relationship. As early as 2000, Gucci had already begun its way down the e-commerce road by intensifying its digital investments and approaching the new tech industries. Then, in 2010, Gucci was the first to launch its own app, a platform that 'over the years has received numerous awards and recognitions for its content and the introduction of increasingly innovative features through Virtual and Augmented Reality' (Claudio Monteverde, interv).

Today, Gucci is still at the forefront of experimentation in gaming and digital innovation. For example, they created the Gucci Vault, a virtual online space made up of expressive and aesthetic contaminations that Michele described as a "container of wonders" in which vintage and iconic pieces of the maison are showcased alongside new products by emerging designers. These products can all be purchased online. Through the digital diffusion of its ethical, aesthetic, and creative universe, the brand has managed, for at least the past seven years, to get so close to Millennials and Gen Z that Gucci has become their true spokesman.

The reason for this success has certainly been the discovery of innovative ways to creating multi-party engagement while at the same time making the experience more uniform for those who approach the Gucci brand via smartphone and those entering a shop live. The golden rule of the *omnichannel* imperative is precisely this: the alignment of the brand's identity, its targets, and its communication that align with a single perspective. There are no multiple channels but one channel with multiple nuances, all in communication with each other.

References

Alberoni, F. (1968). *Citizenship goods.*

Bain & Co. Report, From Surging Recovery to Elegant Advance: The Evolving Future of Luxury, 20 December 2021. Retrived: https://www.bain.com/insights/from-surging-recovery-to-elegant-advance-the-evolving-future-of-luxury/

Barile, N. (2010). *Il made in Italy: da country of origin a metabrand, in Milano e moda.* Milano, Italy: IULM.

Belfanti, C. M. (2008). Was fashion a European invention?. *Journal of Global History, 3*(3), 419–443.

Belfanti, C. M. (2019). Storia culturale del Made in Italy. Società editrice il Mulino, Spa.

Bourdieu, P. (1997). The forms of capital. In A. H. Halsey, H. Lauder, P. Brown, & A. S. Wells (Eds.), *Education: Culture, economy and society.* Oxford, UK: Oxford University Press.

Chevalier, M., & Mazzalovo, G. (2021). *Luxury brand management. Una visione completa sulla natura e la gestione del settore del lusso, ai tempi del digitale e della sostenibilità.* Milano, Italy: Franco Angeli.

Codeluppi, V. (2002). Che cos' è la moda (pp. 1–110). Carocci.

Corbellini, E., & Saviolo, S. (2004). *La scommessa del Made in Italy.* Milano, Italy: ETAS.

Ferraresi, M. (2014). Il made in Italy reloaded: i processi dell'innovazione. *Bello, buono e ben fatto: il fattore made in Italy,* 133–140.

Gnoli, S. (2020). Moda. Dalla nascita della haute couture a oggi, Nuova Edizione.

Gucci. (2019). *Gucci equilibrium.* Retrieved from https://www.gucci.com/it/it/st/our-commitment

Hobsbawm, E. (2002). Inventando tradiciones.

Kering. (2022). *La storia.* Retrieved from https://www.kering.com/it/maisons/moda-e-pelletteria/gucci/storia/

Mafai, G. (2011). *Storia del costume dall'età romana al Settecento.*

Morand, P. (2012). *Les religions et le luxe. L'éthique de la richesse d'Orient en Occident.* Paris, France: Editions du Regard.

Mortara. (2004). *Sociologia del lavaro.*

Lipovetsky, G. (2007). La felicidad paradójica (p. 190). Barcelona: Anagrama.

Rotolo, E. (2022). "What's the future of luxury in the digital age?" Retrieved from: https://www.artribune.com/progettazione/new-media/2022/02/lusso-digitale/

Simmel, G. (2001). *La moda.* Milano, Italy: Mondadori.

Sombart, W. (1967). Liebe, Luxus und Kapitalismus. München: Deutscher Taschenbuch Verlag.

Treccani, G. (1929). *Treccani Enciclopedia: "Luxury".* Roma, Italy: Istituto dell'Enciclopedia.

10 Integrating Sustainability in Luxury Hospitality Experiences

The Italian Way of the Principe di Savoia

Elena Tinacci, Manuela De Carlo, and Martha Friel
IULM

Welcome to impeccable service and authentic Italian charm. With its exceptional standards of hospitality and care, Hotel Principe di Savoia embodies the true spirit of Milan, where it stands out as a landmark of true luxury.

(*Hotel Principe di Savoia,* n.d.)

Introduction

Luxury hospitality is defined as unique hotels of superior quality that provide excellent service and can symbolize the wealth and status of the owners (Peng & Chen, 2019). We believe the subject should be analyzed in terms of sustainability and corporate social responsibility (CSR) issues for several reasons.

A first, more general reason concerns the dimensional importance of the sector, as luxury hospitality represents the third largest market share in the global luxury goods industry (Amatulli, De Angelis, & Stoppani, 2021). A second more specific reason has to do with the structure and content of the offer. Indeed, if luxury can generally be seen more and more as a "consumer-defined approach, where the meaning of luxury is more self-driven, emotional, and emphasizing the experiences, quality, and enrichment of life" (Iloranta, 2022), in hospitality this becomes even more true as consumer experience and services are at its core. In fact, the direct relationship with the customer in hospitality takes on a particular centrality in the construction of the experience, and there is a direct transfer of values from the staff to the customers. The literature has indeed demonstrated how luxury hotels' ability to stimulate consumers' positive emotions and attachment is key to customers' repurchase intentions (Peng & Chen, 2019). Finally, the third reason concerns the growing emphasis that guests put on sustainability (Giardina, 2019; Jones, Hillier, & Comfort, 2016). Although academic literature has long suggested that commitment to sustainability could backfire on luxury hospitality brands because environmentally friendly practices could lower consumers' perception of the value of luxury hotel offerings, more recent

DOI: 10.4324/9781003305095-13

studies have instead suggested that consumers are increasingly receptive to luxury goods characterized by a sustainable approach (Amatulli, De Angelis, Costabile, & Guido, 2017).

This is supported by numerous industry reports; for example, the Fairmont Luxury Insights Report (2019) highlighted how 78% of luxury travelers consider hotels adopting environmentally sustainable practices important.

Furthermore, not only are guests in luxury hotels paying growing attention to sustainability issues, but this attention is not limited to ecological sustainability, also taking into account the other dimensions of sustainability, in particular social sustainability, evaluating the general integrity of hospitality brands and the consistency between how sustainability practices are communicated and implemented (Amatulli et al., 2021).

This has led many luxury hospitality brands to pay increasing attention to CSR practices in order to achieve value-based bonds with their consumers, stronger consumer–company identification, and therefore increased customer loyalty (Zhang, Yang, & Zheng, 2018).

In the development of these CSR programs, a key role is played by hotel employees, especially in luxury hospitality. It is generally true that CSR measures are decided by the management but are implemented by the employees, and therefore the staff always plays a central role in CSR practices (Nazir, 2020). But, in luxury hospitality, this takes on a particular value since employees are a fundamental source of competitive advantage and differentiation. Therefore, if we define luxury as the hotel's ability to relate to the customer and attend to his desires during his stay, the role of the employee becomes even more strategic. It requires a subtle and elegant transferring of the values at the core of CSR and the adoption of responsible practices in the relationship with the guest.

On this basis, the chapter intends to analyze how, in luxury hospitality, good CSR practices and the employees' commitment to them can be transferred into the relationship with the customer and therefore the strengthening of the overall brand experience.

Consistent with the objectives of this book, three main research questions are addressed:

- i How have "Made in Italy" hospitality luxury brands been able to integrate? sustainability into the product features and attributes that are relevant to their customers?
- ii Which are the characteristics that make this engagement real and not only a marketing tool?
- iii Is there an "Italian way" to create sustainable luxury hospitality? If so, which are its features?

In order to answer these questions, we conducted an in-depth single case study on the Hotel Principe di Savoia in Milan, Italy, a 5-star property belonging to the Dorchester Collection whose history and values well represent the "Italian way" of luxury hospitality.

We analyze the company's commitment to ecological sustainability, but most of all its commitment to improving its social sustainability, offering us a perspective on the Principe's CSR programs and how the focus on sustainability reinforces the relationship between the hotel and the guest, which in turn creates a competitive advantage.

Moreover, we analyzed the shift in the Principe's CSR practices during the COVID-19 pandemic, discussing how said practices have helped to keep employees' commitment strong, creating ideal conditions for a good recovery and an adaptation of the organizational structure to post-COVID needs.

After a review of the literature on CSR in the hospitality sector in the second paragraph and a methodological premise in the third, the fourth paragraph analyzes the case of the Hotel Principe di Savoia in depth through its history as a "Made in Italy" luxury brand and the development of their CSR strategies. Finally, the last paragraph suggests some further considerations regarding the future development of the company, and Italian luxury hospitality in general, in their approach to sustainability.

Literature review

CSR in luxury hospitality: Building a competitive advantage through shared values

For many companies in the services sector, creating and managing unique experiences has become vital. This is particularly true for luxury hospitality, as evidenced by the extensive analyses in hospitality and tourism literature (Alcántara-Alcover, Artacho-Ramírez, Martínez-Guillamon, & Campos-Soriano, 2013; Harkison, Hemmington, & Hyde, 2018).

Creating an experience, however, is a complex process in which the hotel staff plays a central role but also require the emotional involvement of the guest. This emotional engagement lies in the interactions between the guest and the company that triggers the co-creation of experiences through two-way interactions and the sharing of common values (Sørensen & Jensen, 2015).

The luxury accommodation experience, characterized by the inseparability of production and service, is therefore achieved through a process of co-creation that involves managers, employees, and guests (Harkison et al., 2018).

In this context, it is particularly important for employees to identify with the values, mission, and corporate culture of their organization, the uniqueness of which can then be passed on to the customer. This isn't just true for a company's cultural values in general, but even more so when fostering specific CSR strategies (Wells, Smith, Taheri, Manika, & McCowlen, 2016). Indeed, the role workers play in the CSR implementation has attracted the interest of many scholars involved in hospitality and tourism (Bohdanowicz, Zientara, & Novotna, 2011; Chou, 2014; Lee, Lee, & Li, 2012; Lynes & Andrachuk, 2008). For instance, Mackenzie and Peters (2014) analyzed the impact of managers' leadership styles and their perception of CSR on employee engagement during CSR activities within high- and medium-tier hotels in Hong Kong. After conducting a survey with employees in five mid to upscale hotel brands in China, Fu, Ye, and Law (2014) showed that these CSR measures consistently influenced organizational citizenship behavior (OCB) through the mediating effects of organizational identity and commitment.

A study conducted by Wang (2014) on the influence of the four dimensions of CSR – economic, ethical, legal, and discretionary – on the financial performance in the hospitality industry showed that ethical and sustainable initiatives positively affect "employee affective organizational commitment, organizational innovation and customer loyalty, while affective organizational commitment, innovation and customer loyalty all have positive effects on business performance" (Wang, 2014, p. 930). Kim, Rhou, Uysal, and Kwon (2017) also analyzed the relationship between CSR and the hotel Staff's Quality of Working Life (QWL) in addition to the dimensions of commitment, job performance, and OCB. QWL can be defined as the degree to which employees are able to ensure the satisfaction of personal needs – including health, safety, family life, social life, and self-actualization – through their professional performance achieving their organization's goals (Lee, Back, & Chan, 2015). Using data collected from hotel workers in upscale properties in South Korea, the study showed that "hotel employees' CSR perception of the firm positively influences their QWL, affective commitment, and OCB, which, in turn, enhance their job performance" (Kim et al., 2017, p. 26).

Indeed, when workers perceive their own value as aligned with those promoted by their organization, for example, CSR goals, their identification with their company increases (Brammer, He, & Mellahi, 2015; Tuan, 2017).

Martinez, Perez, and Rodriguez del Bosque (2014) pointed out that CSR is a powerful means to consolidate an organization's culture (Font & Lynes, 2018). The authors led a qualitative study on the Spanish hotel sector where they evaluated the influence of CSR in the conceptualization and definition of organizational identity. The results highlighted the importance of integrating CSR goals into firms' strategies. In addition, CSR is perceived as one of the main competitive advantages to establish a strong identity as it is a fundamental expression of corporate behavior. In particular, hospitality businesses have understood the direct and indirect power that CSR has on brand differentiation, through both how CSR values are shared with employees and guests as well as when customers' concern of the hotel's CSR activities demonstrate both their own social responsibility and their potential social influence (Zhang et al., 2018).

Many hotel brands thus invest many tangible and intangible resources to sponsor and advertise their CSR efforts, which in turn builds a strong organizational image.

COVID-19 driven CSR practices in luxury hospitality: A testing ground for future sustainability

This trend, already obvious before the pandemic, further increased during COVID-19 with the development of new specific programs aimed at reinforcing and accelerating the development of CSR programs to ensure greater sustainability and more resilience in the sector.

Filimonau, Derqui, and Matute (2020), for example, investigated organizational resilience, job security, and organizational commitment of senior hotel managers relative to a sample of senior executives in Spanish hotels in the context of COVID-19. The study showed that measures implemented by hotels to reduce the short-term detrimental effects of COVID-19 and any future measures put in place to minimize its long(er)-term impacts could potentially influence the organizational commitment of managers. These initiatives included the conversion of different hotels into temporary emergency hospitals which offered employees restricted and/or ad-hoc job opportunities or provided guests with "holiday vouchers" to be redeemed after the lockdown. In addition, the authors highlighted the distinction between compulsory measures such as social distancing and public hygiene protocols, and voluntary initiatives like donations or the increased use of digital technology to avoid human contact.

Hotels adopting more proactive and efficient CSR practices could not only increase their competitiveness in the domestic and international labor markets but also improve their levels of organizational resilience toward potential environmental changes.

Moreover, CSR practices during COVID-19 were proven to have reinforced perceived job security of managers which in turn determined their organizational commitment (Filimonau et al., 2020).

In sum, hospitality businesses were strongly encouraged to invest in CSR as it "can enable hotels to retain qualified staff, thus building their organizational capital and reinforcing their organizational resilience in light of external disruptions" (Filimonau et al., 2020, p. 10).

One of the most meaningful studies among the academic contributions exploring CSR during the pandemic is *Effects of tourism CSR on employee psychological capital in the COVID-19 crisis: from the perspective of conservation of resources theory* by Mao, He, Morrisson, and Coca-Stefaniak (2020). CSR was identified as a powerful means to improve employee psychological capital, which they defined as "the positive psychological status of employees in their development process, which is an important psychological resource and an inherent quality of individuals" (Mao et al., 2020, p. 4). Through the results of a survey of 430 employees in tourism in China, the authors demonstrated that CSR measures in face of the COVID-19 crisis had a positive impact on self-efficacy, hope, resilience, and optimism. The latter are the four main dimensions of employee psychological capital. Self-efficacy means that individuals have the confidence to make the required efforts to successfully deal with challenging work. Hope represents people's perseverance to achieve their goals and, if necessary, their capability of being flexible to guarantee success. Resilience is defined as employees' perseverance to succeed even when faced with difficulties and adversity. Lastly, optimism "refers to positive attribution of success at present or in the future" (Mao et al., 2020, p. 4).

Based on this review, it is widely evidenced that CSR influences hotels' business performances through work engagement, job and career satisfaction, organizational commitment, and OCB (Wang, Hu, & Zhang, 2020).

Methodology

The nature of our research question led us to adopt an in-depth single case study, which is motivated by the need to conduct an in-depth investigation on the issue of CSR in luxury hospitality. The aim is to answer the "how" and "why" questions relating to the development of business strategies through a variety of information sources (Dul & Hak, 2008; Yin, 2011).

This methodology was considered the most appropriate for this exploratory research which aims to observe and understand a specific phenomenon in its complexity and multiple facets. Through the case study, in fact, it is possible to grasp the complexity and particularity of the context, to the extent of understanding the specific circumstances within which the company's strategies were developed (Stake, 1995).

We have sampled the case of the Hotel Principe di Savoia as an illustrative case of a luxury hotel that, in recent decades, has been able to build a strong relationship with its customers and employees thanks to its important commitment to CSR and actions aimed at supporting the environmental and social sustainability of the company. Moreover, the Hotel Principe di Savoia was particularly proactive during the COVID-19 pandemic, developing specific CSR programs aimed at strengthening its cultural bond with its employees and with the surrounding area.

To further deepen the analysis, and in coherence with what is suggested by the literature (Patton, 1990; Yin, 2011), a strategy of diversification of sources was also adopted.

In particular, the first part of the research focused on a desk analysis of documentary sources relating to the history and to the development of the Hotel Principe di Savoia.

A second phase of the research was carried out through three in-depth interviews with the general manager, the human resources/CSR project manager, and with the marketing and communications manager. Interviews were designed to investigate the meaning given to CSR-specific strategies by the managers and employees of the Principe di Savoia as well as the alignment of these strategies to those relating to the construction of the brand experience for the customer.

The interviews were carried out following a three-step protocol. In the first part, we intend to explore both the relationship between the "Made in Italy" concept and the Hotel Principe di Savoia in tangible and intangible terms and to understand how the hotel faces today's challenge of finding an overlap between "Made in Italy" and innovation. The second section analyzed the role that sustainability has within the philosophy and values of the company. The third and final section aims at understanding the hotel's employee- and community-oriented CSR strategies.

Case study: Hotel Principe di Savoia

A historical overview

"Made in Italy" is intrinsically and historically associated with the manufacturing, design, fashion, and gastronomic sectors. However, it is crucial to shed light on its interesting and unique expression within the hospitality industry.

With its historic façade dominating Piazza della Repubblica in Milan, the Hotel Principe di Savoia dates back to 1896 when, decorated in Italian Art Nouveau style, it was known as "Hotel du Nord", characterized by its strategic proximity to the railway station and therefore attracting a business clientele.

1927 represented a turning point for the hotel when it was acquired by two well-known Milanese families, Principe and Savoia, who made it a landmark for celebrities, royalty, and popular artists performing at La Scala. Henceforth, the history of this iconic hotel is a mirror of the evolution of its destination, Milan. In response to the hotel's increasing popularity, two new wings were built in the 1950s, with two additional floors added later in 1958. This structural transformation was followed by the introduction, in the 1980s, of the current name "Hotel Principe di Savoia", or "The Principe" for short for the most loyal customers. From then on, it started hosting notable personalities and became the prime location to organize charity events.

Additional stories were added in the 1990s, including the tenth floor where the iconic Presidential Suite is located. At this point, the hotel started playing an important role in the successful development of the surrounding Porta Nuova district, becoming its reference point and an important contributor to the city's regeneration process.

The Hotel Principe di Savoia proudly joined the Dorchester Collection group of hotels in June 2003, the latter managing the world's top luxury hotels both in Europe and the USA, each of which reflects the distinctive culture of its destination. The current portfolio includes the following hotels (in order of them joining the group): The Dorchester, London; The Beverly Hills Hotel, Beverly Hills; Le Meurice, Paris; Hôtel Plaza Athénée, Paris; Hotel Principe di Savoia, Milan; Hotel Bel-Air, Los Angeles; Coworth Park, Ascot, UK; 45 Park Lane, London; and Hotel Eden, Rome.

In sum, the Principe grows in accordance with the evolution of the identity of Milan. This phenomenon generates a concept of responsibility, in the sense that every time the city hosts a special and important event, the Hotel Principe di Savoia conquers the scene, becoming a promoter and perfect host considering its excellent service, people, and magnificent spaces. For example, during the Expo in 2015, the hotel became the home of 54 state leaders.

This historical background helps us introduce the correlation between the Hotel Principe di Savoia and "Made in Italy". Indeed, the most relevant expression of "Made in Italy" in the context of this particular hotel is its natural tendency to reflect the Italian, and in particular the Milanese, spirit and identity through tangible and intangible elements. By entering the hotel, guests are welcomed with the typical "Buongiorno!" and can feel an authentic Milanese ambiance when observing the interior design, the lights, the sounds, the people, and the physical spaces. All these elements illustrate a perfect harmony between Italian tradition and modernity. A peculiar example is offered by the personnel's uniforms that have been carefully studied by a local designer with the goal of reflecting the Italian style but with a contemporary twist.

The precious furnishings and décor are all of Italian origin; sufficient to think about the Murano glass chandeliers. Renovation phases have always been dependent on the selection of Italian suppliers 95% of the time. The company considers these suppliers to be veritable partners: among them Acqua di Parma and Stefano Ricci. The Hotel Principe di Savoia provides its services and facilities to promote these brands' products. It is also important to point out that the Principe is part of Altagamma, namely a foundation born in 1992 that gathers high-end Italian cultural and creative companies in the fashion, design, food, jewelry, hospitality, automotive, and wellness sectors that are recognized globally as authentic ambassadors of Italian style. Its mission is to enhance the competitiveness of these companies and ultimately of the Italian economy.

The general goal is for these collaborations to promote mutual brand enhancement. For instance, the Principe partners with De Cecco to organize training sessions for the Food & Beverage team. Another example is the close cooperation with wine companies Ferrari Trento or Ca' del Bosco. Not only does the hotel promote its wines to guests, but the staff also has the chance to visit their cellars and discover the depths of their production line, philosophy, and territories.

The hotel has also forged partnerships with various fashion brands of the Quadrilatero della Moda, an upscale shopping area in the Centro Storico district of Milan. The guests who stay at the hotel for two or three nights can benefit from a shopping card that allows them to get a discount, a souvenir, or a glass of Champagne to pair with their shopping experience.

These are just a few examples of how the Hotel Principe di Savoia contributes to the promotion of "Made in Italy" through strategic brand alliances.

In addition to the aforementioned tangible dimension, it is crucial to highlight the intangible aspects through which the Hotel Principe di Savoia embodies the excellence of "Made in Italy". These elements represent a sustainable competitive advantage for the company.

First of all, the attitude of the staff naturally conveys the Italian spirit thanks to each of their individual personalities that are extremely valued by the company. Regardless of their nationality, the team members' personalities correctly illustrate the hotel's Italian soul and merge together to create a common identity. This is also possible thanks to the multiple People and Culture programs offered by the hotel, such as the induction course "Engage", that communicate the company culture and develop the employees' hard and soft skills. Personality is a key element in the Dorchester Collection's "We Care" philosophy, along with passion, respect, working together, and creativity.

The people animating the Principe become creators of an unforgettable experience for the guests through their unique capacity of establishing strong human relationships, which can also be interpreted as a distinctive Italian trait. This peculiarity makes the hotel experience highly personalized, enhancing brand appreciation and loyalty. In this vein, the Principe represents excellence as it treats the customer as a "person": the team members go above and beyond by genuinely anticipating, meeting, and exceeding the guests' needs, offering an experience rather than a mere service.

The "Italianess" is combined with the creativity, which plays a key role in the company's culture: all the employees are encouraged to find their own solutions to solve problems that cannot be found in the operating manuals. Indeed, the Staff is trained not to rely on manuals but to always analyze the context and find the proper solution based on their individual evaluation and inclination.

Furthermore, creativity is expressed in the team members' ability to identify guests' profiles, preferences, and needs before their arrival through investments in specific innovative IT system and programs focused on guests' centricity.

Hotel Principe di Savoia: Shaping a sustainable future for the hospitality industry

The Hotel Principe di Savoia is also a leading Italian brand in terms of adopting a conscious and sustainable approach to luxury. It is crucial to highlight that the Principe's commitment is far from embodying the concept of greenwashing but rather is made of small actions aimed at creating and communicating a culture of sustainability, which can also grow outside of the workplace.

Ecological commitment

Over the years, the Principe di Savoia has adopted several initiatives to reduce its ecological footprint and make a positive impact through important investments, including:

- Implementing a new lighting system with energy-saving light bulbs.
- Substituting old burners with new generation burners that bring about 30% of savings.
- Introducing induction burners in the kitchens.

- Using insulating materials, especially for windows and doors.
- Consistently reducing plastic-use following Dorcherster Collection's goal of completely eliminating it in the next three years.
- Using local, and generally Italian, materials during renovations phases, and of local produces in the Food & Beverage sector (the non-Italian products amount to only 5%).
- 100% differentiated trash collection.
- Choosing sustainable ways to consume food, i.e., not sponsoring the buffet option during large events or reducing to one day a week meat in the menu and introducing water refill points to discourage the use of plastic water bottles in the staff canteen.

It is worth mentioning that some of the structural investments have not been easy to implement considering that the Principe is a historical building.

It is also interesting to note that the hotel is part of the Central District Association of Milan, which includes multiple properties located near the Principe along Via Fara, Via Filzi, and Via Pisani. They organize some initiatives together aimed at revitalizing the area. For example, they arranged a jogging day while also cleaning the city.

Social and ethical commitment

The social and ethical CSR commitment of the company is perfectly aligned with the WE CARE philosophy and proves that the Principe is a main actor in the Milanese scene. This last concept helps us understand that the strong link between the Principe and "Made in Italy" is also the result of its large contribution through social actions within both the company and the local community.

The hotel regularly donates the staff's used clothes to recycling campaigns usually carried out in April and October.

The Principe actively partners with several associations and, over the years, the hotel has hosted many fundraising events.

Firstly, the Principe di Savoia believes it is important to hire people with disabilities into the hotel organization. Disability is not seen as an obstacle for the brand but an added value that enriches the team. They also collaborate with Dynamo Camp to support initiatives such as charity auctions that take place in the hotel's rooms that raise funds for the recreational therapy association. They offer free spaces for Dynamo Camp and Acqua di Parma to set up stands to sell products. Part of the earnings is donated to charity or, during the Christmas period, used to buy presents for children.

Another major partner of the hotel is the voluntary organization City Angels. Together, on Epiphany Day, they organize an event at the Principe where they offer lunch to the homeless in Milan. For instance, in 2020, before the pandemic, 200 homeless people had the chance to taste the vegetarian dishes prepared by Christian Garcia, the personal Chef of Prince

Albert of Monaco. They were served by 25 students and many institutional figures, actors, journalists, and TV presenters. Employees from the Principe di Savoia have also supported Pane Quotidiano – an organization founded in 1898 in Milan with the goal of providing basic food to those in need every day – working in their restaurant helping to serve meals to poor people.

The Rava Foundation is another Italian NGO that they collaborate with to organize fundraising events such as that aimed at supporting the maintenance of the St. Damien's Pediatric Hospital in Haiti.

The Principe also sponsors the LILT "Lega Italiana per la Lotta contro i Tumori" (Italian League for the Fight against Cancer).

Another important topic is the team's engagement in raising the awareness on social issues such as violence against women or immigration through events organized in collaboration with the local authorities where the team members are involved on a voluntary basis.

The Principe's conscious approach to luxury has been particularly relevant during the first phase of the COVID-19 pandemic. In fact, next, we will be analyzing the CSR commitment of the company in the context of this global crisis through a case study in the next chapter focusing on the impact on human resources.

Hotel Principe di Savoia: Making social sustainability a priority in the midst of the pandemic

Employee-oriented CSR approach

EMOTIONAL SUPPORT

First of all, the People and Culture team of the Principe di Savoia, adopting the WE CARE philosophy, offered emotional support to the employees during this uncertain time. This translated in periodical online meetings with the staff of every single department from the entry-level to the executive personnel. These online chats were aimed at bringing clarity and mental balance as reported by one of the respondents:

> We focused on their mental wellbeing [...]. Another meaningful initiative that we've pursued with the whole team has been to periodically meet online to find out how every single person in every single department was doing, half an hour for every single department repeated every two or three months. And the executive meetings obviously are much more frequent. For us it was important to call people, say hello, check on their situation, and understand if we could help in any way. [These online meetings aimed at] bringing clarity and mental balance since we were living in an era full of uncertainties. At a certain point, we didn't know what was going on, and from the initial fear came discouragement [...].

EMPLOYEE DEVELOPMENT PROGRAMS

Another CSR measure, instances of which have been often observed in the case of the Principe di Savoia and that is closely related to the provision of emotional support, is the implementation of employee development programs during the pandemic. This means that the hotel created many training programs dedicated to employees at all levels for their personal and professional growth. In particular, it has been observed that such programs mainly revolved around the new safety and hygiene protocols. Indeed, this measure has helped keep the hotel's human capital engaged. As reported by a respondent: "We focused on their mental wellness and mandatory training while always carrying forward the idea that this mandatory training has to become a culture, a way of life. It has to be something you learn in the hotel and take with you in your daily life. So, we have done all the COVID training with this logic, first round and second round because in the second wave there was a lot of confusion in Italy. With our competent doctor who is present in the hotel, and I must say that they were very interesting moments because people understood better what COVID was, what safe attitudes to adopt. So, this mandatory training became also personal training. The same goes for the second recall that we did in October–November. [...] We did this training activity called RE-ENGAGE [...] In 2021, we are thinking of programs that go in the direction of professional development. We are studying a program dedicated to leaders to be great leaders in the post-COVID era, to executives (what kind of future will we have in front of us) and some dedicated to the team (how to be guest-centric again in this era)".

INCREASED COMMUNICATION

Furthermore, the Principe di Savoia made increased timely communication a priority to cope with the challenges presented by the pandemic.

From the very first moments COVID-19 impacted the hotel business, Dorchester Collection's first newsletter – Legends@home – was launched. This led to phone trees being established in each property to ensure that every single one of the employees would be spoken to each week.

In general terms, effective communication has been defined by scholars as "crucial for tourism to survive and recover from global crisis" (Hang, Aroean, & Chen, 2020). Moreover, Coombs (2007) stresses the importance of focusing on stakeholders' emotions when communicating in times of crisis as emotions determine stakeholders' crisis responsibility attribution and their behavioral intentions. Hang et al. (2020) note that "crisis and disaster management research in tourism mainly focuses on recovery *after* crisis but offers little insights on communication *during a* sustained global crisis such as the coronavirus pandemic". In this vein, this study partially contributes to filling this gap as it sheds light on the communication strategies implemented by the hotel companies *during* the pandemic, as pointed out by one of our respondents: "During this time, we put in place a very intense communication plan, from more formal channels (email), to newsletters, and simple chats on WhatsApp. In this way we could engage people. With these three channels we reached everyone and urged everyone to participate".

Community-oriented CSR

In addition to monetary charitable donations, the hotel launched partnerships with local schools, NGOs, hospitals, and churches to provide food and care packages to those in need, as reported by our respondents: "We also helped those who could not celebrate Christmas, so we went in search of those associations that support families with children, in difficulty and who could not buy gifts for children. So, we worked on buying them in such a way that we could give them gifts. We worked on collaborating with the various communities to be able to carry out those small activities such as helping the neighbor, perhaps elderly in the first lockdown, to do the shopping. And a lot of our guys have been doing that, and we've been communicating all these initiatives internally".

Conclusion

Our analysis showed the importance of the role of CSR on two different levels. On the one hand, it showed how building a stronger workforce, characterized by high levels of engagement, OCBs, resilience, and optimism can help hotel organizations to better (i) strengthen staff awareness of the company's values and transfer them to customers and (ii) prepare for future economic and socio-cultural shocks like those that occurred during the COVID-19 pandemic.

On the other hand, what has been discussed up to now shows the importance of CSR programs for luxury hospitality in building relationships with the end customer.

In a world where even luxury consumers express the desire for more ethical and responsible consumption, with the consequent need for companies to be more transparent and willing to inform consumers about products and processes, the development of coherent CSR actions, and the adoption of protocols aimed at a more sustainable production of the service, takes on a new, core role.

This is even more true in the advent of post-crisis "silent luxury", where consumers pay more attention to the core content of luxury products, such as craftsmanship and tangible and intangible culture, rather than simply to aesthetic and status quo elements.

On this front, the experience of the Hotel Principe di Savoia is very representative of the valuable relationships that can be established with suppliers embodying excellence and sustainable quality; for example, we have the hotel's collaborations with Italian luxury brands and other important brands of "Made in Italy" wine & food. The integration of the relationship between the company, the place of origin, and their shared values within the product is in fact another central aspect giving the Principe di Savoia a competitive edge that highlights the content and the "Made in Italy" aspect of the offer.

This is because, on the one hand, the Italian "way of life" embodies the idea of sustainable living, of aesthetic quality, of original and artisanal products that harmonize well in a proposal of sustainable luxury (see Pasquinelli, 2022 in this book). On the other hand, it is enabled by the role that pro-social CSR activities have in helping consumers gain status (Zhang et al., 2018).

This contrast occurs within the Principle di Savoia where sustainable luxury and "Made in Italy" are integrated, reinforcing the very essence of the "Made in Italy" luxury services.

Finally, the efforts made by the Principe di Savoia hotel also show how CSR actions specifically aimed at employees can strengthen their belief in the company's values, which is then translated into the relationship with the guest.

References

Alcántara-Alcover, E., Artacho-Ramírez, M. A., Martínez-Guillamon, N., & Campos-Soriano, N. (2013). Purpose of stay and willingness to stay as dimensions to identify and evaluate hotel experiences. *International Journal of Hospitality Management, 33*(1), 357–365. https://doi.org/10.1016/j.ijhm.2012.10.006

Amatulli, C., De Angelis, M., Costabile, M., & Guido, G. (2017). *Sustainable luxury brands: Evidence from research and implications for managers*. London, UK: Palgrave Macmillan.

Amatulli, C., De Angelis, M., & Stoppani, A. (2021). The appeal of sustainability in luxury hospitality: An investigation on the role of perceived integrity. *Tourism Management, 83*, 104228.

Bohdanowicz, P., Zientara, P., & Novotna, E. (2011). International hotel chains and environmental protection: An analysis of Hilton's we care! Programme (Europe, 2006–2008). *Journal of Sustainable Tourism, 19*, 797–816. https://doi.org/10.1080/09669582.2010.549566

Brammer, S., He, H., & Mellahi, K. (2015). Corporate social responsibility, employee organizational identification, and creative effort the moderating impact of corporate ability. *Group & Organization Management, 40*(3), 323–352.

Chou, C.-J. (2014). Hotels' environmental policies and employee personal environmental beliefs: Interactions and outcomes. *Tourism Management, 40*, 436–446. https://doi.org/10.1016/j.tourman.2013.08.001

Coombs, W. (2007). Protecting organization reputations during a crisis: The development and application of situational crisis communication theory. *Corporate Reputation Review, 10*, 163–176. https://doi.org/10.1057/palgrave.crr.1550049

Dul, J., & Hak, T. (2008). *Case study methodology in business research*. Oxford, UK: Elsevier.

Fairmont Luxury Insights Report (2019). https://www.fairmont.com/offers/

Filimonau, V., Derqui, B., & Matute, J. (2020). The COVID-19 pandemic and organisational commitment of senior hotel managers. *International Journal of Hospitality Management, 91*, 1–13. https://doi.org/10.1016/j.ijhm.2020.102659

Font, X., & Lynes, J. (2018). Corporate social responsibility in tourism and hospitality. *Journal of Sustainable Tourism, 26*(7), 1027–1042. https://doi.org/10.1080/09669582.2018.1488856

Fu, H., Ye, B., & Law, R. (2014). You do well and i do well? The behavioral consequences of corporate social responsibility. *International Journal of Hospitality Management, 40*, 62–70. https://doi.org/10.1016/j.ijhm.2014.03.004

Giardina, G. (2019). Expo 2020 and sustainability: Luxury hotel properties challenges and future outlook. *Worldwide Hospitality and Tourism Themes, 11*(3), 314–326.

Hang, H., Aroean, L., & Chen, Z. (2020). Building emotional attaching during COVID-19. *Annals of Tourism Research, 83*, 1–4.

Harkison, T., Hemmington, N., & Hyde, K. F. (2018). Creating the luxury accommodation experience: Case studies from New Zealand. *International Journal of Contemporary Hospitality Management, 30*(3), 1724–1740.

Iloranta, R. (2022). Luxury tourism—A review of the literature. *European Journal of Tourism Research, 30*, 3007.

Jones, P., Hillier, D., & Comfort, D. (2016). Sustainability in the hospitality industry. *International Journal of Contemporary Hospitality Management, 28*(1), 36–67.

Kim, H. L., Rhou, Y., Uysal, M., & Kwon, N. (2017). An examination of the links between corporate social responsibility (CSR) and its internal consequences. *International Journal of Hospitality Management, 61*, 26–34. https://doi.org/10.1016/j.ijhm.2016.10.011

Lee, J.-S., Back, K.-J., & Chan, E. S. W. (2015). Quality of work life and job satisfaction among frontline hotel employees: A self-determination and need satisfaction theory approach. *International Journal of Contemporary Hospitality Management, 27*(5), 768–789. https://doi.org/10.1108/ijchm-11-2013-0530

Lee, Y.-K., Lee, K. H., & Li, D.-x. (2012). The impact of CSR on relationship quality and relationship outcomes: A perspective of service employees. *International Journal of Hospitality Management, 31*, 745–756. https://doi.org/10.1016/j.ijhm.2011.09.011

Levy, S. E., & Park, S. Y. (2011). An analysis of CSR activities in the lodging industry. *Journal of Hospitality & Tourism Management, 18*(1), 147–154. https://doi.org/10.1375/jhtm.18.1.147

Mackenzie, M., & Peters, M. (2014). Hospitality managers' perception of corporate social responsibility: An explorative study. *Asia Pacific Journal of Tourism Research, 19*, 257–272. https://doi.org/10.1080/10941665.2012.742915

Mao, Y., He, J., Morrisson, A. M., & Coca-Stefaniak, J. A. (2020). Effects of tourism CSR on employee psychological capital in the COVID-19 crisis: From the perspective of conservation of resources theory. *Current Issues in Tourism, 24*(19), 2716–2734. https://doi.org/10.1080/13683500.2020.1770706

Martınez, P., Perez, A., & Rodrıguez del Bosque, I. (2014). Exploring the role of CSR in the organizational identity of hospitality companies: A case from the Spanish tourism industry. *Journal of Business Ethics*, 124, 47–66. https://doi.org/10.1007/s10551-013-1857-1

Nazir, O., & Islam, J. U. (2020). Effect of CSR activities on meaningfulness, compassion, and employee engagement: A sense-making theoretical approach. *International Journal of Hospitality Management, 90*, 102630.

Patton, M. Q. (1990). *Qualitative evaluation and research methods*. London, UK: SAGE.

Peng, N., & Chen, A. (2019). Examining consumers' luxury hotel stay repurchase intentions incorporating a luxury hotel brand attachment variable into a luxury consumption value model. *International Journal of Contemporary Hospitality Management, 31–33*, 1348–1366. https://doi.org/10.1108/IJCHM-04-2018-0332

Sørensen, F., & Jensen, J. F. (2015). Value creation and knowledge development in tourism experience encounters. *Tourism Management, 46*, 336–346. https://doi.org/10.1016/j.tourman.2014.07.009

Stake, R. E. (1995). *The art of case study research*. London, UK: SAGE.

Tuan, L. T. (2017). Activating tourists' citizenship behavior for the environment: The roles of CSR and frontline employees' citizenship behavior for the environment. *Journal of Sustainable Tourism*, 1–26. https://doi.org/10.1080/09669582.2017.1330337

Wang, C.-J. (2014). Do ethical and sustainable practices matter? Effects of corporate citizenship on business performance in the hospitality industry. *International Journal of Contemporary Hospitality Management*, *26*, 930–947. https://doi.org/10.1108/IJCHM-01-2013-0001

Wang, C., Hu, R., & Zhang, T. (2020). Corporate social responsibility in international hotel chains and its effects on local employees: Scale development and empirical testing in China. *International Journal of Hospitality Management*, *90*, 1–14.

Wells, V. K., Smith, D. G., Taheri, B., Manika, D., & McCowlen, C. (2016). An exploration of CSR development in heritage tourism. *Annals of Tourism Research*, *58*, 1–17. https://doi.org/10.1016/j.annals.2016.01.007

Yin, R. K. (2011). *Applications of case study research*. London, UK: SAGE.

Zhang, L., Yang, W., & Zheng, X. (2018). Corporate social responsibility: The effect of need-for-status and fluency on consumers' attitudes. *International Journal of Contemporary Hospitality Management*, *30*(3), 1492–1507.

11 Luxury Household and Design

Kartell Loves the Planet

Michele Coletti and Matilde Rovai
Grenoble École de Management

When Design-Driven Innovation Is Also Sustainable: The Case of Kartell

Design-driven innovation

Let us use the adage "If I had asked people what they wanted, they would have said faster horses" attributed to Henry Ford. In terms of luxury retail, this brings up the issue of what companies should give to their customers and how they can figure it out. According to Verganti (2009), companies avoid the trap of blindly following customer requests by developing their own vision for radical innovation. He called this approach design-driven innovation (DDI).

This model argues that companies can create a competitive advantage by proposing new ways of satisfying consumer's emotional, psychological, and socio-cultural needs. DDI gives new meaning to products and services (Bellini, Dell'Era, Frattini, & Verganti, 2017).

The "meaning" is the "why" of a product, the psychological and cultural reasons for people to use a product. Meanings also have emotional and social dimensions: they relate to what the user feels when using the product, but also what the others think about the user of the product (Verganti, 2011). However, being too close to customers does not lead to significant innovation of meaning. A "technology epiphany" is reached when powerful meaning is enabled by new technologies. DDI starts by understanding emergent dynamics in sociocultural models and the use of new technologies to create radical design (Verganti, 2011). In this way, DDI overcomes the dichotomy between technology-push and market-pull innovation models (Bellini et al., 2017).

The Model T and the assembly line were the product and process innovations that allowed Henri Ford to sell cars at a reasonable price, changing the meaning of automobiles from a luxurious pastime for the lucky few to the mean of transport preferred by the American middle-class, and later even by the working class (Vlaskovits, 2011).

DOI: 10.4324/9781003305095-14

Kartell and the use of plastics in furniture design

Kartell is an Italian design company founded in 1949 by Giulio Castelli, a chemical engineer specialized in the then new polymers technology for which his teacher Giulio Natta was a pioneer and future Nobel Prize winner for Chemistry in 1963.

The first product was a ski rack made of plastics, but in 1951 they were already introducing injection molding to make home furniture. Castelli knew that designers were necessary to turn chemicals into objects (Lojacono, 2007). He launched a campaign to inform the public that Kartell products required a lot of R&D, both in terms of materials and production process. In the '60s, Kartell already used polythene to make a chair that was exhibited in places such as the Museum of Modern Art (MOMA, 1972) in New York, and a wastepaper basket designed by Gino Colombini that is still in production fifty years later. This basket was the first product to have a version in recycled plastics issued in 1993, but that did not last because the technology was still experimental (E. Storace, director of Kartell Museum, personal communication, 14 July 2021).

The wife of Giulio Castelli, Anna Castelli Ferrieri, was an architect. She became the Kartell internal designer in the late '60s, a perfect epoch to introduce colorful and cheerful products. This reflected customers' need for more informal furniture (Lojacono, 2007), appropriate for a multitude of contexts. Young people especially were searching for new lifestyles and new meanings for their lives and compact furniture that could be easily placed in different parts of the house satisfied these needs.

In 1967, Anna Castelli Ferrieri designed what at the time was the most innovative product in terms of aesthetic and material: the international award-winning "Componibili" series. The bright colors and the round-shaped plastic forms that characterized the "Componibili" line were at the core of the "Italy: the New Domestic Landscape" exhibition held at the MOMA in 1972. Moreover, their modularity encouraged a variety of possible combinations, increasing the sense of unicity (E. Storace, 14 July 2021).

The material chosen for the "Componibili" was Acrylonitrile-butadiene-styrene (ABS), innovative because of its mechanical and aesthetic characteristics. ABS is a composite material based on a thermoplastic matrix and a particulate rubber phase. Due to its two-phased nature, it has unique properties and can be considered as engineering plastic. The incorporation of the rubber gives high impact strength to ABS, also making it very versatile, so it could take a large range of forms and shapes. Moreover, its naturally glossy finish creates an advantage as it saves time on further polishing. Another advantage, especially for furniture, is its durability as it can last up to 30 years and more (Moore, 1973). The Lego bricks are a very famous example of a product made from ABS.

Plastic could have been proposed as an eco-friendlier material as it avoided the use of wood (see poster in Annex A). However, the popular features that shaped "the Kartell manifesto" in the '70s became a weakness in the '80s.

Colorful furniture and round shapes were no longer fashionable. By the late '80s, plastic was seen as a poor material and the industrial process to manufacture it was perceived as less prestigious than productions of small series artisan-like objects. The middle class wanted their furniture to look refined and unique. Opinion leaders started to describe Kartell's style as outdated and they criticized their basic range of colors (Lojacono, 2007).

In the late '80s, the change in ownership of the company marked a change in strategy, operations, and marketing, starting with including a wider number of colors for their products. Kartell became a diversified assembler company, offering a wide range of products, including lamps, chairs, bookcases, etc. ... based on the firm's core competency in plastic-manipulation technology. The company itself started focusing on design and marketing, whereas the production was externalized to suppliers, mostly in Northern Italy (Lojacono, 2007).

Nonetheless, Kartell has been a design-driven company from its creation. Since the beginning, the founder's technical competence and creativity combined with his close collaboration with technology experts and designers gave Kartell's furniture products a sense of modernity. The highly aesthetic reinterpretation of plastic transformed it to a noble material (Dell'Era, Marchesi, & Verganti, 2010). This is due to the frontier research conducted in Kartell's R&D department, a rare feature for a furniture company. Kartell's superior technological know-how can also be attributed to the Labware division. Created in 1958, they make equipment for laboratory and professional applications (Lojacono, 2007). Their core competence was the use of materials such as polypropylene, polystyrene, and polyethylene as valid alternatives to glass due to their lightness, strength, economy, and safety.

Leading entities of the target market can have extreme needs that require specific R&D to develop innovations that will only later be extended to wider market segments (Tidd & Bessant, 2009). Customers with tougher and more demanding requirements catalyze better and more robust designs, and usually this is a key factor for successful commercial exploitation in the long term (Gardiner & Rothwell, 1985). The Labware division is where the demands of the toughest consumers must be satisfied, leading to more innovative products in their future widely available lines.

Today, Kartell is the market leader in plastic household products, probably due to its focus on design, with a worldwide presence. Its traditional competence to work plastics has been enhanced by the firm's ability to manage its image and distribution, and the way it markets and sells products. New product development is carried out in collaboration with mold and chemical suppliers that help define the materials and molds that will be used in production. Most partners are located in Northern Italy to facilitate collaboration between company managers and suppliers, and because of the long-standing relationships, formal contracts are rarely necessary (Dell'Era et al., 2010).

It is extraordinary that Kartell maintained its leadership position in the industry despite the outsourcing of the manufacturing activity. Indeed, this is often a central issue when human skill and handicraft plays an important role in brand image. However, its collaborations with specialized suppliers are a key asset because they can leverage their specific expertise, the result of knowledge accumulated over decades and in some cases centuries (Filippetti & D'Ippolito, 2017).

The "Bookworm" is often described as the Kartell product that best represents a technology epiphany: designed by Ron Arad in the early '90s, the "Bookworm" is a bookcase that not only has full functionality but also has such a sculptural aspect that it serves as a piece of art on its own. Moreover, its flexibility gives the customer the ability to decide the final shape their bookcase will take. Both the wall and the sculptural object become the subject of personal interpretation, an extraordinary way to revolutionize the meaning behind a piece of furniture, explaining why the "Bookworm" has been a bestseller since 1994 (Dell'Era et al., 2010).

However, the "Bookworm" required long and complex R&D activity to find the most suitable materials and process. The technological solutions were chosen because of their ability to convey the meanings conceptualized by the designer. Design-driven companies deliver not only new meanings but they also develop the technologies that allow these values to be communicated. They push technological innovation to fit their design concepts, rather than the other way around (Dell'Era et al., 2010).

Kartell has been one of the heralds of the "Made in Italy" concept and of the so-called "Bello e ben fatto" paradigm, proposing products that are both beautiful and well made. However, customers increasingly require products that are also good for the environment and society. So, the question to ask is whether Kartell can deliver products that are still "belli e ben fatti", but also "buoni" (good). In other words, can is sustainability in Kartell's reach?

Sustainability as the emerging paradigm

Due to the increasing awareness regarding climate change and pollution, sustainability has become a key driver of innovation. Many companies fear that if they become more environment-friendly, they will be less competitive due to the additional costs. Managers treat sustainability as a corporate social responsibility issue rather than looking to incorporate it into business objectives (Nidumolu, Prahalad, & Rangaswami, 2009).

That is not Kartell's stance on sustainability, taking it seriously, starting with the durability of its products. Design-enhanced durability is one of the main actions to be taken to contribute to a circular economy (Lewandowski, 2016). Products with a strong meaning become objects of affection, leading to people keeping the symbolic products for much longer (E. Storace, 14 July 2021). Durability can reduce overconsumption, and consequently overproduction, especially when it is coupled with consumer education (Alonso-Martinez, De Marchi, & Di Maria, 2021). "Sustainability has been a key theme throughout Kartell's history", explains Lorenza Luti, the daughter of the current owner Claudio Luti. "Through our archives, we found several examples of sustainable material experiments from the 1950s, '60s and '70s" (Bertoli, 2021).

Indeed, key drivers of sustainability are the materials utilized for the products, although operations (i.e., logistics and production) still contribute, albeit partially, to the solution. Toxins and waste are built into the materials (Hopkins, 2010). In the past, architects and industrial designers vastly contributed to the pollution of this planet. Now they can and should work positively to improve product sustainability and change society (Müller-Kraenner, 2012).

Many consumers think that plastic is a low-quality material, giving it a negative connotation. They are in favor of recyclable alternatives, especially when it comes to packaging and single-use items. A recent study of Swedish consumers shows that plastic is perceived as worse for the environment than metal, while paper and glass are considered the most environmentally friendly materials (Otto, Strenger, Maier-Nöth, & Schmid, 2021).

Synthetic polymers like plastics and rubber are generally made of raw oil, though there are polymers that can be made from natural organic materials such as wood. It wastes a lot of energy and materials to make them in the first place (Moore, 1973). Burning oil-based polymers produce carbon-dioxide among other toxic substances, evidence that disposing of plastics is non-ecological.

Thermoplastic polymers are often seen as a better option, as re-melting is easy, melting temperatures being much lower than metals, leading to a much smaller energy consumption (Ljungberg, 2007). For this reason, the European Commission launched the Circular Plastics Alliance, which was signed by over 300 organizations, aiming to recycle 10 million tons of plastic by 2025 (Toloken, 2019).

The introduction of recycled material in a product requires redesigning it due to new specifications and technical trade-offs that must be dealt with. Indeed, material selection is a very difficult task given the quantity of options available, and particularly finding a replacement for plastics is a big challenge (Matos & Simplício, 2006). However, technical and physical requirements are not the only criteria to choose a material. Factors such as reputation, fashion, culture, and even feeling must also be considered (Ljungberg, 2007). Higher price is an element than can deter purchase, but brand reputation is important enough to mitigate it (Walia, Kumar, & Negi, 2020), though there is a limit on the additional price that customers are willing to pay to buy greener products (Rahman & Haque, 2011).

Today, plastic's biggest problem is its image: consumers think replacing plastic with other materials, whether it is paper, metal or wood is automatically better for the environment, which is an erroneous thought process (Loepp, 2021). Biodegradable plastics may not even be the best option. Indeed, most bioplastics are produced from crops such as corn, rice, or soybeans. This avoids the use of fossil fuels, but the produces are then less available for human and animal consumption. Moreover, the degradation of bioplastics in oceans and soils is not whole and mixing them with fossil-based plastics reduces the recyclability of both materials (Zhu & Wang, 2020).

The way forward for a more sustainable approach is to consider the entire material cycle and make sure that it is not only recyclable, but actually recycled, consistent with the Circular Economy principles (Cobra, Sanvezzo, & Branciforti, 2021).

The "Kartell loves the planet" manifesto

Despite all these difficulties, Kartell has decided to embrace the challenge with a new manifesto: Kartell loves the planet.

With this initiative, Kartell declares its commitment to sustainability and the environmental responsibility that comes with production. Because of their timeless design, Kartell pieces embody cultural values that transform them into symbols of treasured memories. Kartell uses entirely recyclable raw materials that can then give life to other industrial products. Their promise is that their materials have no negative impact on the environment and their packaging is made entirely of recyclable and reusable material.

The three axes at the center of Kartell engagement in sustainable materials and industrial processes are:

1. The first initiative was the introduction of wood in Kartell products. The wood comes from certified forests, with its consumption limited by a patented process that ensures that only a thin layer of material is necessary to create an innovative three-dimensional product.
2. The second action Kartell took was developing a new biodegradable material in their research department. Called Bio, it is made from the waste of farm production procedures that do not include food for humans or animals. This waste material is transformed into a biomass similar to plastic that can be injected and molded the same way other plastic materials can. The material is highly biodegradable in water and soil, and it has obtained prestigious certifications. Kartell was the first company in the furniture industry to test it, and since 2020, it has used it for the "Componibili" series, offering a new palette of pastel colors in addition to the traditional ABS colors.
3. The third axis involves a recycled thermoplastic polymer called Riciclato 100%. It is obtained from waste material that has not been contaminated by other materials. The technology behind it makes it possible to maintain the aesthetic quality and structural properties of the products, reducing the emissions required for production. This is a step that Kartell takes toward a circular economy as the use of recycled material eliminates waste from the environment by turning it back into raw material. The "Componibili" series has had several products made using Riciclato as well since 2020.

On top of these three axes to increase their sustainability, all Kartell's products have the GREENGUARD certification, which guarantees low levels of emissions, protecting indoor air quality.

"Componibili" were not the only Kartell products rejuvenated with new materials: the "Mobil" utility storage, another award-winning design, is now made of recycled materials from the automotive, furniture, and packaging industries. It took five years of research for Kartell to develop a material that guarantees the products' aesthetic and performance while being environmentally friendly. Half of the Kartell offer is today available with a green option. Other products based on recycled plastics are the "Re-Chair", designed by Antonio Citterio and the "A.I.", designed by Philippe Starck.

In 1999, Kartell became the first company in the world to make furniture in polycarbonate. The first product was "La Marie", a completely transparent chair with a modern, minimalist design. Transparent plastic became a distinctive element in Kartell's production thanks to products such as Starck's "Louis Ghost" chair and Laviani's "Bourgie" lamp, both of which are still bestsellers. Even these materials can become greener: Kartell developed a polycarbonate that combines a second-generation renewable polymer made from paper and cellulose waste (Bertoli, 2021). This material has a 75% reduced impact on the environment, with an imperceptible difference in the final product. Kartell's aim is to gradually replace existing materials with more sustainable options (E. Storace, 14 July 2021).

To achieve this objective, Kartell relies on internal expertise and on the competence of their suppliers, whether designers, material providers, or manufacturers. They also leverage new technologies such as Artificial Intelligence that enabled the design of the "A.I." chair with less material and energy than traditional methods. Kartell also recently introduced Aquaclean, an eco-friendly, heavy-duty, antibacterial, and easy-to-clean fabric without PFC.

Discussion

Despite being founded by an engineer, Kartell has always been very focused on design. Indeed, Giulio Castelli was also a co-founder of the Industrial Design Association in 1956. Since 1958, every two years (initially every three years), this association awards the prestigious Compasso d'Oro to the best products, with Kartell winning nine times.

In 1999, for the company's 50th anniversary, the Kartell Museum was established by its President, Claudio Luti, to not only conserve, promote, and enhance the company's value and intangible cultural heritage, but also to engage designers and customers in a discourse over products (E. Storace, 14 July 2021). The Kartell Museum won the Guggenheim Enterprise & Culture Award for the best business museum in 2000. Luti, who took over the ownership of the firm from Giulio Castelli and Anna Castelli Ferrieri during the '80s, kept a very hands-on approach and further developed the

DNA of Kartell, making it a champion of the "bello e ben fatto" and "Made in Italy" and one of the best examples of DDI (Dell'Era et al., 2010).

Kartell's success was due to the intuition that user needs were changing, and that rounder and colorful objects were going to replace dark, heavy furniture. Kartell was capable to sell objects made of plastics because of their solidity, durability, and higher perceived sustainability compared to other materials such as wood and metal. This required the development of strong manufacturing capabilities that are still crucial today as complementary assets for the company and its value network. Indeed, another advantage is that Kartell is located near Milan, the world capital of design that is at the center of an innovation ecosystem where most competences of the furniture supply chain are available.

Kartell has been a pioneer in the development of new materials and their application in the furniture industry thanks to strong internal R&D. A key role was played by the Labware division by working with very demanding customers, which acted as an accelerator of innovation. Kartell's unique ability to ennoble plastics was introduced to the living rooms of design-conscious people around the world. The monograph "Kartell – The Culture of Plastics" that Taschen published in 2012, the first dedicated to a design company, was a tribute to their unique history.

Today, plastic is under accusation because of its fossil origin and impact on sea and soil pollution. Moreover, it is perceived to be less valuable than wood or metal. This has pushed Kartell to offer greener alternatives to virgin plastics, such as recycled plastic and bioplastics, often at a premium price compared to its traditional lines, but also to introduce wood products and fabrics in their catalog. Indeed, material innovation is often the best driver of sustainability, though also applying the principles of circular economy would be effective rather than only replacing materials with other options, each of them having their own drawbacks. The principle behind a more integrative approach is to shift from eco-efficiency to eco-effectiveness (Müller-Kraenner, 2012).

Adopting new materials is a form of re-innovation that must be strategically managed to succeed (Rothwell & Gardiner, 1989), even more so when the material is symbolic of the company. This explains why Kartell is fully engaged in developing greener materials to show its commitment to sustainability, as the brand's strength lies in its innovative materials.

The "Kartell loves the planet" manifesto is practically tangible in the "Componibili" series, that after half a century on the market, is being created in new editions in recycled plastic as strong and durable as the original ABS, and in bioplastic, a biodegradable polymer obtained from agricultural waste. New colors and finishes have been introduced to expand and update the line that, over the years, has become more and more enriched from the artist's original conceived model (E. Storace, 14 July 2021).

Will the market consider these changes sufficient to give a new legitimacy to Kartell's products? Are customers willing to pay a premium price to purchase the greener versions of "Componibili"? Bio- and recycled plastics are generally perceived by customers as more environmentally friendly than the original material, with earthy colors potentially reinforcing the feeling, although they could induce doubts about product quality (Petersen & Brockhaus, 2017).

However, customers should understand that plastics are not necessarily evil, especially for products that last for decades, and that bio-alternatives may have hidden costs that keep them from being the best solution. Perception may be difficult to change and turning toward new materials such as wood could be interpreted as an implicit admission that plastics are ultimately unsustainable for the company.

A new technological epiphany may possibly be needed, and the emerging paradigm of a circular economy may hopefully inspire it. The technology that is most likely to enable this new epiphany is digital, potentially being the necessary future evolution for Kartell and, more generally, for DDI.

Conclusion

We have seen how over the years Kartell has been successful thanks to its DDI approach. The technological epiphanies represented by products such as the "Bookworm" and the "Componibili" series are the result of aesthetic visions proposed by extraordinary designers and made possible by the outstanding engineering capabilities of Kartell R&D department and their manufacturing suppliers. A key innovation activity is carried out in the Labware division, a "gym" where the most demanding needs are addressed, and the knowledge developed becomes an asset for the entire firm.

On the other hand, plastics are under attack these days because of their perceived negative impact on the environment as they are made from oil and gas. Kartell products are beautiful and well built, but plastics are their core material and most importantly at the core of their brand. The firm has responded to this threat by introducing wood-based products for the first time in its history, but also by proposing their existing product lines made from "green" options such as recycled plastics and biomass-derived polymers.

The traditional idea of Italian design products as "Belli e ben fatti" needs to evolve in "Belli, buoni e ben fatti". There is little doubt that Kartell will find the most suitable technical solutions. However, this challenge has a strong marketing and communications dimension: will the old and new customers accept the same design in new materials while paying a premium price for it, or are broader innovations needed to satisfy the expectations of customers who do not want to compromise on their values? While the market will give the ultimate answer, the authors' belief is that, while material is at the core of a sustainability effort, more comprehensive action may be required to convince the market segment more sensitive to this issue. Greener materials on their own cannot achieve sustainability, just as faster horses were not the answer to the mobility challenge.

Annexes

Kartell key timeline

1949: **Giulio Castelli** a young chemical engineer, together with his wife **Anna Ferrieri, founded Kartell** in Milan.
1950: the **Car Accessories Division** was born.
1953: the **Household Products Division** was established, and Kartell started the production of **plastic articles using industrial molds.**
1955: the **covered round bucket designed by Gino Colombini won the first Compasso d'Oro or Kartell.**
1958: the **Labware Division** was created, followed by the **Lighting Division in 1959.**
1963: the **Habitat Division** was formed to produce **plastic furnishing products**. In this period, the company strengthened its identity with **the help of external designers such as Marco Zanuso and Joe Colombo**.
1964: **the first seat worldwide made of plastic** won the **Compasso d'Oro.** In 1969, **Anna Castelli Ferrieri** designed the **round version of the Componibili modular furniture line**.
1972: Kartell participated in the **exhibit MOMA "Italy: The New Domestic Landscape"** bringing the **three living modules designed by Ettore Sottsass, Marco Zanuso, and Gae Aulenti**, entering the permanent collection of the prestigious American museum.
1973: the **team Centrokappa** was established to **develop the design and communications project**s aimed at promoting Italian design.
1988: **Claudio Luti** took over Kartell and became **the new President**. He created a creative team with the collaboration of **designers such as Philippe Starck, Antonio Citterio, Vico Magistretti, Ron Arad, and Ferruccio Laviani**.
1994: **Ron Arad** designed **Bookworm**, the first free-form bookshelf, consisting of a flexible plastic band that can be fixed to the wall in the desired shape.
1997: **the first Kartell flagship store opened in Milan.** In 1999, **Philippe Starck** designed **the La Marie chair, the first transparent polycarbonate chair in the world**.
2000: **the Kartell Museum** was awarded the **Guggenheim Business & Culture Award for Best Company Museum**.
2002: the **book "Kartell. 150 Items, 150 Artworks"** a collection of contributions from 150 photographers and artists, was published **by Skirà**.
2006: the new division for accessories **"Kartell à la mode"** was established.
2012: **Taschen** published the **first monograph** dedicated to a design company: **"Kartell – The Culture of Plastics".**

2014: the sofa **Uncle Jack by Philippe Starck** becomes **the largest piece of transparent polycarbonate ever injected in a single mold**, and won the **Red Dot Award Best of the Best 2016.**

2017: **Philippe Starck** designed **Sir Gio, the first table with a central polycarbonate leg.**

2019: as part of **Kartell's 70th birthday celebrations, "The art side of Kartell"**, was an exhibition showing the story of the brand from the arts perspective. Kartell **Smart Wood Collection** was introduced. **The first design object conceived by artificial intelligence** was launched on the market. The manifesto **Kartell loves the planet** comes to light.

2020: The Componibili series were proposed also in bioplastics and recycled plastics.

References

Alonso-Martinez, D., De Marchi, V., & Di Maria, E. (2021). The sustainability performances of sustainable business models. *Journal of Cleaner Production, 323*, 129145. https://doi.org/10.1016/j.jclepro.2021.129145

Bellini, E., Dell'Era, C., Frattini, F., & Verganti, R. (2017). Design-driven innovation in retailing: An empirical examination of new services in car dealership. *Creativity and Innovation Management, 26*(1), 91–107. https://doi.org/10.1111/caim.12184

Bertoli, R. (2021) *Kartell's industrial manifesto puts sustainability front and centre*. Retrieved from https://www.wallpaper.com/design/kartell-sustainable-design-focus

Cobra, R., Sanvezzo, P., & Branciforti, M. (2021). Circular technology roadmapping (TRM): Fostering sustainable material development. *Sustainability, 13*(13),1–13.

Dell'Era, C., Marchesi, A., & Verganti, R. (2010, March–April). Mastering technologies in design-driven innovation. *Research Technology Management, 53*(2) 12–24.

Filippetti, A., & D'Ippolito, B. (2017). Appropriability of design innovation across organisational boundaries: Exploring collaborative relationships between manufacturing firms and designers in Italy. *Industry and Innovation, 24*(6), 613–632. https://doi.org/10.1080/13662716.2016.1263888

Gardiner, P., & Rothwell, R. (1985). Tough customers: Good designs. *Design Studies, 6*(1), 7–17.

Hopkins, M. (2010). How sustainability fuels design innovation. *MIT Sloan School of Management Review*, October.

Lewandowski, M. (2016). Designing the business models for circular economy—Towards the conceptual framework. *Sustainability, 8*(1), 43.

Ljungberg, L. Y. (2007). Materials selection and design for development of sustainable products. *Materials and Design, 28*(2), 466–479. https://doi.org/10.1016/j.matdes.2005.09.006

Loepp, D. (2021) Plastics doesn't have a recycling problem; it has an image problem. *Plastic News*. November 11. Retrieved from.

Lojacono, G. (2007). The Italian furniture industry and the Kartell case study. In R. Jerrard (Ed.). Design management: exploring fieldwork and applications (1st ed.). London, UK: Routledge. https://doi.org/10.4324/9780203825969

Matos, M. J., & Simplício, M. H. (2006). Innovation and sustainability in mechanical design through materials selection. *Materials and Design, 27*(1), 74–78. https://doi.org/10.1016/j.matdes.2004.09.023

Moore, J. D. (1973). Acrylonitrile-butadiene-styrene (ABS) – a review. *Composites, 4*(3), 118–130. https://doi.org/10.1016/0010-4361(73)90585-5

Müller-Kraenner, S. (2012). Reform of global sustainable development institutions. Friedrich-Ebert-Stiftung.

Museum of Modern Art (MOMA). (1972). Italy: The new domestic landscape – MOMA 1972. In E. Ambasz (Ed.). Greenwich, CT: New York Graphic Society.

Nidumolu, R., Prahalad, C. K., & Rangaswami, M. R. (2009). Why sustainability is now the key driver of innovation. *Harvard Business Review*, (September).

Otto, S., Strenger, M., Maier-Nöth, A., & Schmid, M. (2021). Food packaging and sustainability – Consumer perception vs. correlated scientific facts: A review. *Journal of Cleaner Production*, 298, 126733. https://doi.org/10.1016/j.jclepro.2021.126733

Petersen, M., & Brockhaus, S. (2017). Dancing in the dark: Challenges for product developers to improve and communicate product sustainability. *Journal of Cleaner Production*, 161, 345–354. https://doi.org/10.1016/j.jclepro.2017.05.127

Rahman, K., & Haque, M. (2011). Exploring price sensitivity of a green brand: A Consumers' perspective. *World Review of Business Research, 1*(2), 84–97.

Rothwell, R., & Gardiner, P. (1989). The strategic management of re-innovation. *R&D Management, 19*(2), 147–160.

Tidd, J., & Bessant, J., (2009). Managing innovation: Integrating technological, market and organizational change (4th ed.). Chichester, UK: Wiley.

Toloken, S. (2019). European Commission official: No 'plastics bashing,' but industry must step up recycled content. *Plastic News*, October 16.

Verganti, R. (2011). Radical design and technology epiphanies: A new focus for research on design management. *Journal of Product Innovation Management, 28*(3), 384–388. https://doi.org/10.1111/j.1540-5885.2011.00807.x

Verganti, R. (2009). Design driven innovation – Changing the rules of competition by radically innovating what things mean. Boston, MA: Harvard Business Press.

Vlaskovits, P. (2011). Henry ford, innovation, and that "Faster horse" quote. Harvard Business Review. Retrieved from https://hbr.org/2011/08/henry-ford-never-said-the-fast

Walia, S. B., Kumar, H., & Negi, N. (2020). Impact of brand consciousness, perceived quality of products, price sensitivity and product availability on purchase intention towards 'green' products. *International Journal of Technology Management and Sustainable Development, 19*(1), 107–118. https://doi.org/10.1386/tmsd_00018_1

Zhu, J., & Wang, C. (2020). Biodegradable plastics: Green hope or greenwashing? *Marine Pollution Bulletin, 161*(PB), 111774. https://doi.org/10.1016/j.marpolbul.2020.111774

12 Place Heritage and Corporate Heritage as Levers for Sustainability

The Ferragamo Case

Cecilia Pasquinelli[1] *and Serena Rovai*[2]
[1]Università degli Studi Napoli Parthenope
[2]EXCELIA Business School

Introduction

Sustainability strategies and practices have rapidly become a common ground for luxury fashion firms' development and evolution. Empirical evidence has to further ground and better explain consumers' preference and effective search for sustainable products, but the buzz on sustainability in luxury reveals the commitment of several companies to turn sustainability into an approach to product, process, organization, and brand innovation.

Although growing literature is analyzing and describing fashion and luxury fashion strategies focused on sustainability (Bendell & Kleanthous, 2007; Dean, 2018; Joy, Sherry, Venkatesh, Wang, & Chan, 2012; Kapferer & Michaut-Denizeau, 2014), most interest is focused on the environmental pillar of sustainability. In the practice, however, the intertwining of the social and territorial dimensions with the environmental dimension of sustainability seems to make rapid advancements. In this regard, theoretical and empirical studies are missing and there is a need to frame the emerging holistic notions of sustainability. Conceptualized in abstract terms, sustainability may find in the luxury fashion industry a meaningful field for developing applicative frameworks.

In this regard, there is a need to focus on the practices of sustainability and systematic case analysis can help this exploration. What are, in the practice, the emerging approaches to sustainability? How and to what extent the social and territorial dimensions, in connection with the environmental one, make firms' strategies distinctive, credible, and competitive? This chapter presents the analysis of the Ferragamo case showing how the capacity to lever and reinterpret the corporate heritage and its valuable connections with the place heritage (Faroudi, Cuomo, Foroudi, & Katsikeas, 2020) shape an integral approach to sustainability, which is distinctive and rooted into the company's history and path of evolution.

DOI: 10.4324/9781003305095-15

Sustainability in the luxury fashion industry: A literature review

The term sustainable luxury started circulating in the luxury fashion industry since the beginning of 2000 (Bendell & Kleanthous, 2007). However, the field remains far from consolidated (Joy et al., 2012; Kapferer & Michaut-Denizeau, 2014). Ostentation, overconsumption, indulgence, and leisure intrinsic to conventional notions of luxury create inconsistencies between the generally perceived notion of luxury and sustainability. The research highlighted how in the past evidence was gathered demonstrating sustainability was irrelevant for fashion brands (Henninger, Alevizou, Tan, Huang, & Ryding, 2017; Hu, Henninger, Boardman, & Ryding, 2019; Joy et al., 2012) and that luxury and sustainability were not compatible (Dean, 2018). If luxury is the epitome of personal indulgence and pretentious social identity, sustainable consumption is associated to equality and ethics (Naderi & Strutton, 2015). As a result, until recent evolutions, scholars disregarded the connection associated to luxury and sustainability (Kapferer & Michaut-Denizeau, 2014).

Strategies and practices of sustainability have however progressively exemplified the path of change and innovation in luxury firms, with considerable ventures in green manufacturing and supply chain management (Karaosman, Perry, Brun, & Morales-Alonso, 2020), starting from raw materials acquisition and traceability. Product and process innovation started twining ecological and social factors influencing product design and responding to growing customers' expectations about the environmental protection. Such expectations grew also in relation to the connection and contribution of firm activities with local communities. Luxury and fashion sectors significantly exploit the country and place images to create brand value (Kapferer, 2009; Lee, Chen, & Wang, 2015). Although the country (and place) of origin remains a controversial concept (Aiello et al., 2009; Godey et al., 2012; Ko & Megehee, 2012), in practice, fashion companies do rely on place identities, and national and local cultural heritage (Power & Scott, 2004) to impose a premium price in the market (Carcano & Lojacono, 2019). Studies are needed to frame how and to what extent place/country image and place/country of origin can be exploited as a lever to construct distinctive sustainability approaches.

If for Kapferer and Michaut-Denizeaut (2014), a "sustainability silence" was discernible in the luxury industry, recent evolutions – accelerated by the pandemic context – increased awareness of social, territorial, and ecological issues across the globe. The consumer perspective on sustainable luxury products has been under scrutiny in the academic debate. Initially, academia emphasized that sustainability was not taken into account by luxury shoppers in the purchase decision-making process (Davis et al., 2012; Gardetti & Torres, 2017). Luxury shoppers seemed not to consider positively the idea of purchasing products made from recycled textiles because recycling did not yield a connotation of rarity and prestige. However, further empirical studies revealed the profiles of luxury clients with respect to their sustainable consuming choices: on the one hand, there are those who substantiate their sustainable engagement through a decreasing consumption; on the other hand, there are those who prefer to be more selective in their luxury products choices by choosing recycled, regenerated or "pre-loved" (reused) luxury and vintage products (Ryding, Henninger, & Blazquez Cano, 2018; Zamwel, Sasson-Levy, & Ben-Porat, 2014). Gabriel and Lang (2015) defined the sustainable luxury client as a "consumer citizenship", behaving considering an opinion shaped by seeking information that orient the selection and choice.

Products' rarity and scarcity (in quantitative terms) are deeply connected to the notion of luxury when coming to the idea of elitist consumption of unique and highly personalized products (Han, Seo, & Ko, 2017; Janssen, Vanhamme, Lindgreen, & Lefebvre, 2014). Rarity in resources, including human resources (Ranfagni & Guercini, 2014), is intrinsic to craftsmanship and local district know-how. Luxury is about quantity and quality and from these two perspectives many companies started tailoring their sustainability paths.

Eco-fashion conceptualizes the contribution of luxury fashion to the preservation of natural resources (Godart & Seong, 2014) of timeless long-lasting products. As Kapferer (2009) argued, luxury and sustainability are characterized by durability and evidencing how both of them chase natural environment preservation through product duration and longer lifecycles.

In addition to manufacturing process and product design, distribution catalyzed significant attention in sustainability strategies. Store design must mirror luxury firms' sustainability, with the central role of the staff trained to social and environmental concerns (Arrigo, 2018).

Methodology

The research adopted a case study qualitative method. The methodological choice of the present article relies on Glaser and Strauss (1967) case-study research strategy related to the empirical investigation of a specific contemporary phenomenon through a multiplicity of context-related sources of evidence (Robinson, 2014). In this analysis, the authors decided to focus on a case study (Eisenhardt, 1989; Yin, 2004) from the luxury fashion, leather, and accessories brand that thanks to their entrepreneurial path offer specific insights to a new perspective on how luxury firms may shape their sustainability approach and programs.

Primary and secondary data were collected and analyzed, relying on the company's official reports, websites, online news archives on specialized magazines, and interviews with the sustainability department and also with customers to have a diversified perspective. Primary and secondary data were used to frame the sustainability strategy and its main components. The collected text materials were coded to find consistency in the data collected which were then analyzed accordingly. Semi-structured interviews involved the Ferragamo Sustainability department through various contacts and exchanges of information on the subject. In this regard, it has to be evidenced that a professional biography method was adopted (Fillis, 2006), allowing to integrate in this chapter a specific company managers' accounts of the sustainability approach and evolution.

Case study: Ferragamo

Ferragamo heritage is important, relevant, and interesting also in the present sustainable emergence. It recalls the story of how the innovative ideas and the vision of a young Italian boy grows into a luxury brand of reference at the international level, made of legacy, heritage, and innovation. Later on, the story of a family that, relying on the excellencies of its territory and innovation in the heritage of "Made in Italy" clusters.

Today, the Ferragamo brand is not simply well-known for its distinctive, elegant, and luxurious fashion style. It is the symbol of a luxury "Made in Italy" and its distinctive and innovative traits, particularly nowadays in the new sustainable context. Nowadays, the Ferragamo group is not only a reference in leather and accessories, but it is the symbol of "Made in Italy" in personal goods, varying from women's and men's footwear and accessories to silk scarves and accessories, from refined women's and men's fashion and apparel to perfumes and jewelry.

After spending more than 13 years in the United States, Ferragamo returned to Italy, in 1927 deciding to establish himself in Florence, where he founded his workshop where he kept on designing and manufacturing those handmade shoes with his emphasis on the specificities of women's footwear. He also began using the expertise of the local craftsmen as they were readily available.

This was the beginning of the Ferragamo brand. In this workshop, he designed and produced

However, the limiting of manufacturing raw material – affected by the World War II – gave Salvatore Ferragamo's genius the possibility to test easily accessible materials which were not restricted. This led him to design and create innovative iconic footwear. Ferragamo also began applying for patents for visionary designs but in 1960, Ferragamo passed away prematurely and his wife, Wanda Ferragamo, took over the management of the brand with later his six children sharing the responsibility of managing the fashion house and in so doing ensuring a smooth legacy and transition to the brand and its heritage.

One of his iconic pair of shoes was "The Rainbow", sandal designed for American actress and singer Judy Garland for her song "Over the Rainbow" in 1938. The shoe was innovatively made in the heel and platform from slab-shaped corks covered in suede and the same shoe was about to become in our days one of the iconic symbols of Ferragamo sustainable engagement.

Since when, in the summer of 1927, Salvatore Ferragamo returned from the United States and settled down in Florence, enraptured by the beauty of the Tuscan capital and fascinated by the skill of the local craftsmen he never moved his workshop. Since then, the link with the city of Florence has remained unbroken and has been strengthened through the company's support for significant restoration projects and numerous charitable initiatives for many local causes. In addition to the Group's direct commitment to making a positive contribution to the area in which it operates, the activities of the Fondazione Ferragamo and the Museo Salvatore Ferragamo are also part of this context.

Ferragamo Group relies on a procurement structure with a high level of technical preparation and works with historic companies, with which it has established an ongoing collaboration. This structure highlights the Group's strong connection to the local community and, considering the geographic distribution, it has a high percentage of Italian raw material suppliers, equal to around 97% of procurement in 2021. Moreover, Tuscan contract manufacturers accounted for almost 53% of the turnover of finished product processing, while Campanian contract manufacturers accounted for approximately 24%; the remaining part of this 2021 turnover is allocated to the other Italian regions. With respect to contract manufacturers, the Ferragamo Group works exclusively with highly specialized manufacturing companies that meet the most demanding quality standards. Virtually all of them are located in Italy.

Furthermore, on the digital platform, Ferragamo wanted to give visibility to specific insights into the responsible products included in the Brand's collections, also engaging in dialog, and giving voice to some of the Group's local suppliers, with the intent of sharing stories of craftsmanship, innovation, and circularity that are characteristic of Made in Italy. The platform offers thematic insights that embrace all-around sustainable thinking, where new ideas on responsible projects and activities come to life, also thanks to an international network of contributors with different levels of sensitivity and experiences, ready to harmoniously address the continuous evolution of sustainable issues: from social justice to sustainable supply chains, from climate change to innovative materials with a low environmental impact. Various personalities were invited to express their views on the changes and innovations that the planet is undergoing today.

Sustainability strategy

For Ferragamo Group, investing in sustainable development means respecting the values handed down by the Founder and believing that the use of innovative materials, the connection with the local community, and the respect for the environment and its own people are key to success, not only of the business but of all stakeholders. Sustainability is a positive challenge that the Salvatore Ferragamo Group decided to adopt and interpret in favor of future generations, committing to place social responsibility at the center of its decision-making process and pursuing economic growth objectives that also take into account the positive and negative impacts of its operations on society and the environment.

Ferragamo Group has been, from the very beginning, a byword for top quality and "Made in Italy". Over the years, the company has implemented numerous initiatives aimed at communicating the activities and corporate culture of sustainability to the public. In 2014, the Group drafted the first internal Sustainability Report, which was made public in 2015. Subsequently, the sustainability website was launched, entirely dedicated to the communication of the Group's sustainability projects. More recently, the Group started to structure its sustainability contents on social platforms such as LinkedIn and Instagram.

The integration of the digital world into the communication methods completes the Group's brand experience and supports the conveyance of sustainability messages to the public. A great deal of communication and awareness work in the field of sustainability and environmental responsibility has been done through the Sustainable Thinking Platform, which aims to provide food for thought on such an important issue for the future.

As evidence of its commitment to efficiency and protecting the environment, in recent years the Ferragamo Group has endeavored to obtain the most important environmental certifications for its facilities. The efforts to obtain certifications have also involved the retail area; the Group obtained the LEED Gold certification for the following stores: Beijing China World, Canton Road in Hong Kong, Copley Place in Boston, Madrid, and Hong Kong City Gate. It obtained the LEED Silver certification for the following stores: Seasons Place Beijing, Pacific Place in Hong Kong, Troy in Michigan, and the Ginza flagship store. In 2021, the process was started to obtain the LEED certification for the stores in Barcelona and Amsterdam.

The commitment to sustainability, intended as a behavioral model to be followed without compromise, has been structured over the years and draws inspiration from the values that underlie the history of the Ferragamo Group: a passion for world-class craftsmanship, creativity, and innovation. Understanding and respecting these values translate into ethically correct behaviors, both inside and outside the Group, supporting it in terms of economic growth and credibility.

Italian craftsmanship has been an essential value at the basis of every creation of the brand: it is not just a question of manual skills but also of experience, utmost care, and attention to detail, continuous research into materials and technologies, to be incorporated into a handcrafted and, at the same time, innovative product. At Ferragamo, operating in the luxury industry, the company management believes in the utmost quality of the products and superior craftsmanship, which is handed down from one generation to another. On these aspects, the company collaborates with our carefully selected suppliers to develop innovative solutions and to introduce low climate impact materials in our collections.

Raw materials

Creating better products also means starting from the early stages of the supply chain, paying close attention to the fibers and raw materials used. These initiatives are complementary to the many innovative and low environmental impact materials included in Ferragamo's collections: from organic cotton to regenerated nylon yarns, from post-consumer recycled silk and cashmere to metal-free and vegetable-tanned leather.

To facilitate the choice of innovative and responsible materials and ensure the highest quality, a guideline document has been drawn up defining characteristics, certifications, standards, partnerships, and preferred sources of procurement to respect the environment, people, and the planet. The guidelines are an evolving document, designed to ensure constant updating as materials continue to innovate. The Founder never set limits to the fields in which to research and experiment. The continuous research and experimentation were not only for leather and embroidered uppers but also for poorer materials which had never been used for shoes in Ferragamo's time: paper, bark, raffia, fish skin, and cellophane.

Today, the interest and drive to experiment remain, making the constant search for innovation a key value for the Brand. In 2020, the Group further consolidated its tradition of experimentation by setting up a cross-functional work team dedicated to the discovery and inclusion of alternative, regenerated and circular materials in its collections.

In order to tackle the challenges our industry faces, collaboration across the entire sector is key to create change and make an impact. For this reason, in 2019, our Group decided to join the Fashion Pact, a coalition made up of over 250 leading fashion and textile brands to set out strategic and concrete targets for reducing the environmental impact of this important industry. Following the signing of the Fashion Pact, in 2020, to prevent the most damaging effects of climate change, we have set science-based targets to reduce our Scope 1, 2, and 3 emissions by 42% by 2029.

For this reason, the Company decided to replace some of its basic components with more responsible materials: starting with the Fall-Winter 2021 collection, all leather soles used for the Brand's footwear have been purchased from suppliers certified according to the UNI 11427 Ecological Leather Standard; moreover, starting from the Pre-Spring 2022 collection, for all leather creations, from footwear to accessories, a 100% recycled polyester yarn from post-consumer sources has been used; finally, from 2022, the viscose used for the Vara bows will be replaced with a viscose that respects the well-being of forests and local communities.

Communities and craftsmanship

Ferragamo Group is made up of highly skilled people that show their love and dedication to their work every day. Realizing people's potential at all stages of the production chain is a priority for Ferragamo, which strives to attract new talents and rewards those who contribute every day to the Brand's success with their passion. The Company believes in equal opportunity and invests in the professional development of its resources, encouraging employee initiative to create the conditions for managerial and technical growth – all in accordance with its historic values. Diversity is considered a key value for the Group, which is committed to ensuring that its employees can grow in a working environment where they can feel free to express themselves and where particularities and individuality generate experimentation and positive comparisons.

The Group's commitment to diversity issues was formalized with the adoption and publication in 2019 of the Inclusion Policy that aims to support multiculturalism, considered essential for the development of innovative and distinctive elements that can increase the Brand's competitiveness and for promoting equality and equal opportunities, combatting all types of discrimination and condemning any form of harassment. The Policy sets the goal of promoting meritocracy and fair treatment at all levels, facilitating the development, expression, and enhancement of individual potential. Ferragamo considers training a priority, as it is necessary to ensure the professional growth of employees and the development of the key competencies lying at the basis of the Company's heritage. Ferragamo Sustainability department highlighted how Ferragamo focuses on social sustainability for their internal community in considering training a priority, as it is necessary to ensure the professional growth of employees and in particular the development of the key competencies lying at the basis of the Company's heritage. An example of the attention Ferragamo pays to protecting artisanal skills and to the so-called "talenti del fare", in the company's know-how is the Manovia, the historic prototyping and manufacturing unit set up in 1967 where material cutters, sewers, and assemblers work. Recently renovated at the Osmannoro site, the Manovia – which consists of approximately 20 artisans – mainly creates samples and prototypes and fine-tunes the structure's stretchers, heels, insoles, and soles for the new models and, since 2021, a limited production of sneakers. In the Manovia, the place where the unique know-how of Ferragamo's craftsmen takes shape, the models of the Ferragamo's Creations line are manufactured in limited quantities, numbered, and entirely handcrafted using the techniques, materials, and finishing details of the Founder. All Ferragamo's Creations shoes feature the Brand's historic logo, designed by Lucio Venna in 1930, and provide the opportunity to explore Ferragamo's creative tradition, celebrating his pioneering vision and know-how. In 2021, thanks to their craftsmanship, the Manovia craftsmen contributed to the creation of the Ferragamo Icon-Up capsule collection, making, and fitting the bows deriving from silk products recovered from the Maison's stock.

Another place where the excellence of technique and the creativity of those who research the materials, create the style, and make the Ferragamo product are celebrated is the Modelleria division for Men's and Women's Leather Goods, an operational workshop since 2017 designed for the transmission of know-how from leather craftsmen to new talents. Staying true to its Italian tradition and craftsmanship, the Group wants to celebrate the "Ferragamo touch" in the world of leather goods, with infinite possibilities for testing innovative types of leather and materials during the processing stages as well as improving the quality and efficiency of development processes. Together, the Manovia and Modelleria are key to preserving the know-how passed on by the Founder and carried on by the skilled craftsmen of the Ferragamo Group.

Sustainability is also part of the Group retail's staff training activities. Through the Group's internal learning platform, digital learning courses, relating also to sustainability are assigned to the retail team.

Stakeholder engagement

The numerous aspects of the sustainability journey undertaken by the Ferragamo Group are based on an approach focused on transparency, integrity, and reliability, with the aim of engaging stakeholders in the economic, social, and environmental goals of its business. The Group does not simply promote initiatives as part of business ethics, social and environmental responsibility but recognizes the value of sustainability as part of its corporate strategy and puts forward innovative proposals for its stakeholders.

In 2021, the Group launched "Sustainable Thinking", a digital platform integrated within the Brand's eCommerce website. The platform offers thematic insights that embrace all-around sustainable thinking, where new ideas on responsible projects and activities come to life, also thanks to an international network of contributors with different levels of sensitivity and experiences, ready to harmoniously address the continuous evolution of sustainable issues: from social justice to sustainable supply chains, from climate change to innovative materials with a low environmental impact. Various personalities were invited to express their views on the changes and innovations that the planet is undergoing today.

As the interviewee manager stated, "At Ferragamo we say that in order to act sustainable, we must think sustainable". Sustainability is deeply integrated into the Business strategy. The numerous elements to the sustainability path undertaken by the Group are based on an approach focused on transparency, integrity, and seriousness, with the aim of involving stakeholders in the economic, social, and environmental objectives of the Business.

Operating responsibly translates into being aware of our impact, while looking for creative, innovative, and serious solutions to mitigate it. The fashion industry has a huge impact on the environment, and it is our responsibility to make sure we act to protect and safeguard our planet. To do so, it is important to set quantitative targets and collaborate with the entire value chain to mitigate the dangerous side effects of our current "business as usual".

Respecting the values of quality and "Made in Italy", the Group has always been committed to supporting the development of local communities, promoting Italy's world-class manufacturers, and carefully purchasing products and services almost exclusively from Italian suppliers. The Group relies on a wide network of carefully selected and qualified contract manufacturers known for their outstanding craftsmanship. Many of them have been working with Ferragamo for years now.

Discussion and conclusion

The case analysis suggests a sustainability framework that intersects two dimensions. The first is composed of three themes framing Ferragamo *sustainability architecture*, which are integration, experimentation, and engagement. The second regards the transversal role of corporate heritage and its connections to place heritage in grounding the three abovementioned sustainability themes.

Integration concerns the vision of the firm's top management who saw the need to consider sustainability not as marginal or additional programs on top of the existing business model and organization. Instead, sustainability is understood as penetrating and changing "the business as usual" into a "behavioral model to be followed without compromise". The basis for turning sustainability into an integral approach to business management is founded in the corporate heritage mobilizing values that the company consolidated in history: these refer to craftsmanship, creativity, and innovation that, conceived as the premises for sustainability, intertwine the corporate heritage with the place heritage of local manufacturing and the Florentine and Made in Italy districts.

Experimentation concerns the propensity to innovate through research and venturing new production modalities. Particularly, the interviewees reported about experimentation in raw materials, a cornerstone in pursuing sustainability as discussed in the literature. The use of alternative, poorer, and recycled materials is a field for experimentation on diverse perspective, from the most technical experimentation to design and marketing the final products in the luxury market. Also in this case, sustainability goes parallel with the firm's "tradition for experimentation" rooted in corporate heritage. Know-how and awareness of the importance of material innovation drove the company to set up a dedicated team assembling skills and mindsets from the different organization units of the group. Not only the corporate heritage but also location heritage is the basis for the experimental approach to innovative and responsible materials. Experimentation, in fact, is viable and integrated with the rest of the functional company units (from design to production and marketing) thanks to the connections of the company with the Made in Italy know-how pools and, particularly, with the craftsmanship that flexibly intervenes in the experimentation process.

Engagement concerns the need to pursue sustainability through stakeholder involvement, meaning internal and external stakeholders. Internally, the continuous training and investments in employees' professional growth made these essential parts of the experimentation approach described above. On the other side, the interviewees stressed how sustainability cannot be pursued only by one firm: networking and engagement of supply chains, consumers, and, generally, a wide range of stakeholders are necessary conditions. Again, on this dimension, corporate heritage and its connections with the place heritage play a significant role for the reputation of the company, globally and in the local community where it is physically present and operating, and the networking capacity earned over time and history enabling an effective stakeholder engagement.

These findings suggest scholars to engage with further conceptualizations of sustainability in luxury, focusing on the framing of sustainability architectures adopted by luxury firms. The sustainability architecture allows framing the strategized intertwining of the different sustainability pillars, economic, social, environmental, and reflecting on the cultural and territorial dimensions. Integration, experimentation, and engagement can be considered backbones of the sustainability architecture since transversally framing the different actions the firm can undertake (such as green manufacturing, eco-design, sustainable retailing, etc.). If this is relevant for all companies approaching sustainability, it is even more so for luxury firms that struggle in building distinctive and credible sustainability strategies for the need to repositioning the same notion of luxury in global consumers' and operators' minds. Furthermore, corporate and place heritage and their points of contacts are another promising dimension of the sustainability architecture of luxury firms. "Made in Italy", district history, and local craftsmanship can be turned into levers for luxury firms to think, design, and explain their sustainability vision to customers, building on their corporate and place heritage.

References

Aiello, G., Donvito, R., Godey, B., Pederzoli, D., Wiedmann, K. P., Hennigs, N., ... & Singh, R. (2009). An international perspective on luxury brand and country-of-origin effect. *Journal of Brand Management, 16*(5), 323–337.

Arnould, E. J., & Price, L. L. (2000). Authenticating acts and authoritative performance. In S. Ratneshwar, D. G. Mick, & C. Huffman (Eds.), *Why of consumption: Contemporary perspectives on consumers' motives, goals and desires* (pp. 144–163). New York, NY: Routledge.

Arrigo, E. (2018). Social media marketing in luxury brands: A systematic literature review and implications for management research. *Management Research Review.*

Arsel, Z., & Thompson, C. J. (2011). Demythologizing consumption practices: How consumers protect their field-dependent capital from devaluing marketplace myths. *Journal of Consumer Research, 37*(1), 791–806.

Ashman, R., Patterson, A., & Brown, S. (2018). 'Don't forget to like, share and subscribe': Digital autopreneurs in a neoliberal world. *Journal of Business Research, 92*, 474–483.

Belk, R. W., & Costa, J. A. (1998). The mountain man myth: A contemporary consuming fantasy. *Journal of Consumer Research, 25*(3), 218–240.

Belk, R. W., Ger, G., & Askegaard, S. (2003). The fire of desire: A multisited inquiry into consumer passion. *Journal of Consumer Research, 30*(3), 326–351.

Bendell, J., & Kleanthous, A. (2007). Deeper luxury. *WWF-UK, Godalming.*

Bendell, J., & Thomas, L. (2013). The appearance of elegant disruption: Theorising sustainable luxury entrepreneurship. *Journal of Corporate Citizenship, 2013*(52), 9–24.

Beverland, M. B. (2005). Crafting brand authenticity: The case of luxury wine. *Journal of Management Studies, 42*(5), 1003–1030.

Beverland, M. B. (2006). The "real thing": Branding authenticity in the luxury wine trade. *Journal of Business Research, 59*(2), 251–258.
Beverland, M. B. (2009). *Building brand authenticity? 7 habit of iconic brands*. Basingstoke, UK: Palgrave MacMillan.
Beverland, M. B., & Farrelly, F. J. (2010). The quest for authenticity in consumption: consumers' purposive choice of authentic cues to shape experienced outcomes. *Journal of Consumer Research, 36*(5), 838–856.
Beverland, M. B., Lindgreen, A., & Vink, M. V. (2008). Projecting authenticity through advertising: Consumer judgements of advertisers' claims. *Journal of Advertising, 37*(1), 5–16.
Bevolo, M., Gofman, A., & Moskowitz, H. (2011). *Premium by design*. Aldershot, UK: Gower.
Biraghi, S., Gambetti, R., & Pace, S. (2018). Between tribes and markets: The emergence of a liquid consumer-entrepreneurship. *Journal of Business Research, 92*, 392–402.
Brown, S. (2001). *Marketing – The retro revolution*. Thousand Oaks, CA: SAGE.
Brown, S., Kozinets, R. V., & Sherry, J. F. (2003). Teaching old brands new tricks: Retrobranding and the revival of brand meaning. *Journal of Marketing, 67*(3), 19–33.
Bruner, E. M. (1994). Abraham Lincoln as authentic reproduction: A critique of postmodernism. *American Anthropologist, 96*(2), 397–415.
Caniato, F., Caridi, L., Crippa, L., & Moretto, A. (2012). Environmental sustainability in fashion supply chains: An exploratory case based research. *International Journal Production Economics, 135*, 659–670.
Carcano, L., & Lojacono, G. (2019). *Made in Italy Industries: Managerial issues and best practices*. EGEA spa.
Carrigan, M., McEachern, M., Moraes, C., & Bosangit, C. (2017). The fine jewellery industry: Corporate responsibility challenges and institutional forces facing SMEs. *Journal of Business Ethics, 143*, 681–699.
Carson, P. P., & Carson, K. D. (1998). Theoretically grounding management history as a relevant and valuable form of knowledge. *Journal of Management History, 4*(1), 29–42.
Carù, A., & Cova, B. (2003). Revisiting consumption experience: A more humble but complete view of the concept. *Marketing Theory, 3*(2), 267–286.
Chalmer, T. D., & Price LL. (2009). Perceptions of authenticity in advertisements: Negotiating the inauthentic. In A. L. McGill & S. Shavitt (Eds.), *Advances in consumer research* (Vol. 36, pp. 73–74). Duluth, MN: Association for Consumer Research.
Cohen, E. (1988). Authenticity and commoditization in tourism. *Annals of Tourism Research, 15*(3), 371–386.
Collins, E., Lawrence, S., Pavlovich, K., & Ryan, C. (2007). Business networks and the uptake of sustainability practices: The case of New Zealand. *Journal of Cleaner Production, 15*, 729–740.
Davies, I. A., Lee, Z., & Ahonkhai, I. (2012). Do consumers care about ethical-luxury?. *Journal of business ethics, 106*, 37–51.
Dean, A. (2018). Everything is wrong: a search for order in the ethnometaphysical chaos of sustainable luxury fashion. *The Fashion Studies Journal*, 1–18.
Dicks, B. (2002). Postgraduate programs using action research. *The Learning Organization, 9*(4), 159–170.
Eisenhardt, K. M. (1989). Building theories from case study research. *Academy of management review, 14*(4), 532–550.
Faroudi, P., Cuomo, M. T., Foroudi, M. M., & Katsikeas, C. (2020). Linking identity and heritage with image and a reputation for competition. *Journal of Business Research, 113*, 317–325.

Fillis, I. (2006). A biographical approach to researching entrepreneurship in the smaller firm. *Management Decision*.

Firat, A. F., & Venkatesh, A. (1995). Liberatory postmodernism and reenchantment of consumption. *Journal of Consumer Research, 22*(December), 239–267.

French, S. (2009). Action research for practicing managers. *Journal of Management Development, 28*(3), 187–204.

Gabriel, Y., & Lang, T. (2015). *The unmanageable consumer*. SAGE.

Gardetti, M. A., & Torres, A. L. (Eds.). (2017). *Sustainable luxury: Managing social and environmental performance in Iconic brands*. London: Routledge.

Geraghty, L. (Ed.). (2015). *Popular media cultures: Fans, audiences and paratexts*. Houndmills, UK: Palgrave Macmillan.

Gilmore, J. H., & Pine, B. J. (2007). *What consumers really want: Authenticity*. Boston MA: Harvard Business Press.

Giron, M. E. (2010). Inside luxury, LID editorial, Madrid.

Gladwell, M. (2000). *The tipping point: How little things can make a big difference*. Boston, MA: Little, Brown and Company.

Glaser, B., & Strauss, A. (1967). *The discovery of grounded theory*. Hawthorne, NY: Aldine Publishing Company

Godart, F., & Seong, S. (2017). Is sustainable luxury fashion possible? In *Sustainable luxury* (pp. 12–27). Routledge.

Godey, B., Pederzoli, D., Aiello, G., Donvito, R., Chan, P., Oh, H., ... & Weitz, B. (2012). Brand and country-of-origin effect on consumers' decision to purchase luxury products. *Journal of Business Research, 65*(10), 1461–1470.

Grayson, K., & Martinec, R. (2004). Consumer perceptions of iconicity and indexicality and their influence on assessments of authentic market offerings. *Journal of Consumer Research, 31*(2), 296–312.

Greenwood, M. (2007). Stakeholder engagement: Beyond the myth of corporate responsibility. *Journal of Business Ethics, 74*, 315–327.

Håkansson, H. (1982), *International marketing and purchasing of industrial goods: An interaction approach*. Hoboken, NJ: Wiley.

Han, J., Seo, Y., & Ko, E. (2017). Staging luxury experiences for understanding sustainable fashion consumption: A balance theory application. *Journal of Business Research, 74*, 162–167.

Handler, R., & Gable, E. (1997). *The new history in an old Museum*. Durham, UK: Duke University Press.

Handler, R., & Saxton, W. (1988). Dissimulation: Reflexivity, narrative and the quest of authenticity, in "living history". *Cultural Anthropology, 3*(3), 242–260.

Henninger, C. E., Alevizou, P. J., Tan, J., Huang, Q., & Ryding, D. (2017). Consumption strategies and motivations of Chinese consumers: The case of UK sustainable luxury fashion. *Journal of Fashion Marketing and Management: An International Journal, 21*(3), 419–434.

Hietanen, J., & Rokka, J. (2015). Market practices in countercultural market emergence. *European Journal of Marketing, 49*(9/10), 1563–1588.

Holt, D. B. (1998). Does cultural capital structure American consumption? *Journal of Consumer Research, 25*(1), 1–26.

Holt, D. B. (2002). Why do brands cause trouble? A dialectical theory of consumer culture and branding. *Journal of Consumer Research, 29*(1), 70–90.

Hu, S., Henninger, C. E., Boardman, R., & Ryding, D. (2019). Challenging current fashion business models: entrepreneurship through access-based consumption in the second-hand luxury garment sector within a circular economy. In *Sustainable Luxury* (pp. 39–54). Singapore: Springer.

Janssen, C., Vanhamme, J., Lindgreen, A., & Lefebvre, C. (2014). The Catch-22 of responsible luxury: Effects of luxury product characteristics on consumers' perception of fit with corporate social responsibility. *Journal of Business Ethics, 119*(1), 45–57.

Joy, A., Sherry Jr, J. F., Venkatesh, A., Wang, J., & Chan, R. (2012). Fast fashion, sustainability, and the ethical appeal of luxury brands. *Fashion theory, 16*(3), 273–295.

Kapferer, J. N. (2009). Kapferer's Brand-Identity Prism Model. *European Institute for Brand Management, 24*, 2014.

Kapferer, J. N., & Bastien, V. (2009) *The luxury strategy: Break the rules of marketing to build luxury brands.* London, UK: Kogan Page.

Kapferer, J. N., & Michaut-Denizeau, A. (2014). Is luxury compatible with sustainability? Luxury consumers' viewpoint. *Journal of Brand Management, 21*(1), 1–22.

Karaosman, H., Perry, P., Brun, A., & Morales-Alonso, G. (2020). Behind the runaway: Extending sustainability in luxury fashion supply chains. *Journal of Business Research, 117*, 652–663.

Keller, K. L. 2003. *Strategic brand management: Building measuring, and managing brand equity.* Sydney, NSW: Prentice Hall.

Ko, E., & Megehee, C. M. (2012). Fashion marketing of luxury brands: Recent research issues and contributions. *Journal of Business Research, 65*(10), 1395–1398.

Kozinets, R. V. (2002). Can consumers escape the market? Emancipatory illuminations from burning man. *Journal of Consumer Research, 29*(1), 20–38.

Lawrence, S. R., Collins, E., Pavlovich, K., & Arunachalam, M. (2006). Sustainability practices of SMEs: The case of New Zealand. *Business Strategy and the Environment, 15*, 242–257.

Lee, H. C., Chen, W. W., & Wang, C. W. (2015). The role of visual art in enhancing perceived prestige of luxury brands. *Marketing Letters, 26*(4), 593–606.

Lewin, K. (1946). Action research and minority problems. *Journal of Social Issues, 2*(4), 34–46.

Lowenthal, D. 1992. Authenticity? The dogma of self-delusion. In Jones M (Ed.), *Why fakes matter: Essays on problems of authenticity* (pp. 184–192). London, UK: British Museum.

Lubin, D., & Esty, D. (2010). The sustainability imperative. *Harvard Business Review, 88*(5), 42–50.

MacCannell, D. (1973). Staged authenticity: Arrangements of social space in tourist settings. *American Journal of Sociology, 79*(3), 589–603.

Murray, J. B. M., & Ozanne, J. L. (1991). The critical imagination: Emancipatory interest in consumer research. *Journal of Consumer Research, 18*(September), 129–144.

Naderi, I., & Strutton, D. (2015). I support sustainability but only when doing so reflects fabulously on me: can green narcissists be cultivated? *Journal of Macromarketing, 35*(1), 70–83.

Ozanne, J. L., & Saatcioglu, B. (2008). Participatory action research. *Journal of Consumer Research, 35*(October), 424–438.

Peirce, C. S. (1998). *Collected papers of Charles Sanders Peirce* (Vol. 8). In C. Hartshorne and P. Weiss (Eds.). Bristol, UK: Thoemmes.

Penãloza, L. (2000). The commodification of the American West marketers' production of cultural meaning at the trade show. *Journal of Marketing, 64*(October), 82–109.

Perry, P., Wood, S., & Fernie, J. (2015). Corporate social responsibility in garment sourcing networks: Factory management perspectives on ethical trade in Sri Lanka. *Journal of Business Ethics, 130*(3), 737–752.

Peterson, R. A. (1997). *Creating country music: Fabricating authenticity.* Chicago, IL: University of Chicago Press.

Pettigrew, A. M. (1990). Longitudinal field research on change: Theory and practice. *Organization Science, 1*(3), 267–292.

Phillips, R. (1997). Stakeholder theory and a principle of Fairness'. *Business Ethics Quarterly*, 7(1), 51–66.

Postrel, V. (2003). *The substance of style: How the rise of aesthetic value is remaking commerce, culture, and consciousness.* New York, NY: HarperCollins Publishers.

Power, D., & Scott, A. J. (Eds.). (2004). *Cultural industries and the production of culture* (Vol. 33). London: Routledge.

Ranfagni, S., & Guercini, S. (2014). On the trail of supply side authenticity: Paradoxes and compromises emerging from an action research. *Journal of Consumer Behaviour, 13*(3), 176–187.

Reason, P., & Bradbury, H. (2001). Introduction: Inquiry and participation in search of a world worthy of human aspiration. In P. Reason, & H. Bradbury (Eds.), *Handbook of action research* (pp. 1–14). Thousand Oaks, CA: SAGE.

Robinson, O. C. (2014). Sampling in interview-based qualitative research: A theoretical and practical guide. *Qualitative Research in Psychology, 11*(1), 25–41.

Ryding, D., Henninger, C. E., & Blazquez Cano, M. (2018). Introduction to vintage luxury fashion—Exploring the rise of the secondhand clothing trade. In *Vintage Luxury Fashion* (pp. 1–10). Cham: Palgrave MacMillan.

Rose, L. R., & Wood, S. L. (2005). Paradox and consumption of authenticity through reality television. *Journal of Consumer Research, 32*(2), 284–295.

Rossignonli, F., & Lionzo, A. (2018). Network impact on business models for sustainability: Case study in the energy sector. *Journal of Cleaner Production, 182*, 694–704.

Spradley, J. P. (1979). *The ethnographic interview.* Belmont, CA: Wadsworth Pub Co.

Stubbs, W., & Cocklin, J. C. (2008). Conceptualising a sustainability business model. *Organization & Environment, 21*(2), 103–127.

Thompson, C. J., Rindfleisch, A., & Zeynec, A. (2006). Emotional branding and the strategic value of the doppelganger brand image. *Journal of Marketing, 70*(1), 50–64.

Tura, N., Keranen, J., & Patala, S. (2019). The darker side of sustainability: Tensions from sustainable business practices in business networks. *Industrial Marketing Management, 77*, 221–231.

Van Maanen, J. (1979). Reclaiming qualitative methods for organizational research: A preface. *Administrative Science Quarterly, 24*(4), 520–526.

Verhoef, P. C., Reinartz, W. J., & Krafft, M. (2010). Customer engagement as a new perspective in customer management. *Journal of Service Research, 13*(3), 247–252. https://doi.org/10.1177/1094670510375461

Yin, R. K. (2004). *The case study anthology.* SAGE.

Zamwel, E., Sasson-Levy, O., & Ben-Porat, G. (2014). Voluntary simplifiers as political consumers: Individuals practicing politics through reduced consumption. *Journal of Consumer Culture, 14*(2), 199–217.

13 Sustainable Luxury Trajectories for "Made in Italy" Wine Businesses

The Cantine Ferrari Case

Jacopo Cammeo,[1] *Elena Casprini,*[2] *and Lorenzo Zanni*[3]
[1]European University Institute
[2]Università degli Studi di Siena
[3]University of Siena

Introduction

The concept of "luxury" applied to the world of wine is certainly not new, even if in managerial literature it has been mainly studied from the point of view of the price lever and consumer perception (Heine, Phan, & Atwal, 2016; Lockshin & Corsi, 2012; Wolf, Morrish, & Fountain, 2016). The study of the wine sector as one of the pillars of "Made in Italy" is not innovative either (Fortis & Sartori, 2016; Pomarici, Corsi, Mazzarino, & Sardone, 2021) as wine is a leading product in Italian exports where quality, tradition, and innovation have coexisted for years, allowing "Made in Italy" brands to compete in the highest segments of the market.

More recent is the interest in the theme of "sustainable luxury", a term that implies reconciling two very different worldviews, with the first referring to a philosophy that aims to conserve the environment, protect our society, and last over time, while the second focuses on exclusivity, what is not necessary, and is aimed at demarcating prestige and personal pleasure (Athwal, Wells, Carrigan, & Henninger, 2019; Ranfagni & Guercini, 2016). However, the two concepts are deeply interlinked when considering their attributes of durability and uniqueness (Ranfagni & Guercini, 2016). As Athwal et al. note, "luxury is synonymous with skill, quality and endurance, which may be easily aligned with sustainability" (2019, p. 405).

Similarly to industries such as fashion, cars, fine art, traveling, and retail (Kunz, May, & Schmidt, 2020), the concept of sustainable luxury is important in the wine industry. This sector has been traditionally characterized by world-leading luxury products, such as Champagne in France or premium wines such as Sassicaia in Italy, while also having invested an increasingly greater attention to sustainability issues (Pucci, Casprini, Galati, & Zanni, 2020).

Extensive research on sustainable luxury has focused on the consumers' perspective, investigating, for example, sustainable luxury consumption by specific

DOI: 10.4324/9781003305095-16

consumer segments, such as Millennials (Islam, Wang, Ali, & Akhtar, 2021; Kapferer & Michaut-Denizeau, 2020), the willingness to pay for sustainable luxury products, and how consumption values influence purchasing intentions across countries (Wang et al., 2021). Less is known about the organizational perspective, where scholars have analyzed aspects related to marketing, in particular focusing on the threats coming from counterfeiting as well as what and how companies communicate, on corporate social sustainability and sustainable activities along the value and the supply chains, and on the role of stakeholders in sustainable luxury. However, it seems that previous studies have neglected to study how a company can create a sustainable luxury value offering.

Investigating from a resource-based view (Barney, 1991), this paper aims to fill this gap, answering the following overarching research question: *how can a company develop a sustainable luxury wine?* We conducted an in-depth case study of Cantine Ferrari, a leading Italian winery that has been able to position its sparkling wine as a sustainable luxury product at both the national and international levels. According to Athwal et al. (2019), "*from an organizational perspective, we need to understand better what the characteristics of a sustainable luxury product, service or experience are*" (p. 417). Therefore, we started our inquiry by exploring what sustainable luxury means in the wine industry. Next, we investigated what challenges wineries faced and are facing in developing and positioning a "Made in Italy" sustainable luxury wine. In particular, we looked at the role that tradition and innovation play in such a challenge. Finally, we concluded by exploring the role that sustainability may play in the luxury strategies of Italian wineries.

Luxury wine: Definition and relevant variables

Over the last decades, both the production and consumption of luxury wine have experienced a notable increase (Donzé & Katsumata, 2021). Despite the relevance of the topic from the practitioners' perspective, studies on luxury wine have often resulted in scattered research (Wolf et al., 2016) due to theoretical challenges. Therefore, the definition of the concept is complex and not uniform (Beverland, 2004), similar to the general interpretation of the dynamics that can foster the development of a high-quality brand (Kapferer & Michaut-Denizeau, 2017). Fine wine incorporates the three core concepts of a luxury product – feelings and sensual experiences, going beyond the necessary, and high prices – but at the same time, its consumption is considerably different from other luxury products (Wolf et al., 2016).

When analyzing the development trajectories of a product such as wine, we will be considering two aspects. On one hand are all the factors that could influence consumer behavior (for a review see Sogari, Casprini, Devigili, & Pucci, 2018). Unlike other goods, wine is a complex product since its quality is difficult to assess before consumption (Rainer, 2021). Consumers tend to rely on extrinsic cues, such as packaging and label design (Sáenz-Navajas, Campo, Sutan, Ballester, & Valentin, 2013), and on intrinsic characteristics, such as wine bouquet and taste (Rahman & Reynolds, 2015). In terms of marketing strategies and consumer behavior, the interlinked role played by income and culture in the consumption of luxury products such as wine is widely recognized (Dubois & Duquesne, 1993). Consequently, a suggested managerial approach to luxury wine could be based on the purchasing power of consumers, premium price strategies, and selective distribution channels. Another possible approach is based more on cultural changes that influence luxury goods' consumption ("democratization"), the hedonic consumption, and the extended self-personality model that involve the values and social codes connected to a specific luxury brand. Following this approach, we have divided the luxury wine market in two interconnected segments (Dubois & Duquesne, 1993) based on:

- Authenticity, absolute quality, in which wine brands act as a standard of excellence.
- Model and social codes, where wine brands represent symbols related to culture and values.

Other scholars have provided interpretations that help to understand the competitive advantage of wine companies and tried to identify other elements that could determine the success of a luxury wine brand. As part of the agro-food industry, wine grapes' production undergoes natural cycles and its quality is affected by the environment (Merloni, Camanzi, Mulazzani, & Malorgio, 2018), determining a unique and original product depending on the geographical location. Some studies highlighted the relevance of **wine territorial characteristics**, such as country of origin and region of origin (Pucci, Casprini, Rabino, & Zanni, 2017; Gilinsky, Atkin, & Bayar, 2021; Pomarici et al., 2021). Wine firms' **geographical proximity** is another significant determinant to achieve a competitive advantage, thanks to relationships on the territory (Fortis & Sartori, 2016) and their role in providing services (Nosi & Zanni, 2004), knowledge dissemination, and innovation processes (Doloreux & Lord-Tarte, 2013).

On the other side, the firm's chosen growth pathway is influenced by all the unique resources managed by the firm and its structural characteristics, such as governance. According to Alonso and Bressan (2016), **the development trajectory of a wine company is influenced by its endowment of valuable, rare, imperfectly imitable, and non-substitutable** resources. So, in the framework, there are four main attributes of resources. These characteristics are based on the theoretical aspect of the resource-based view, according to which a firm's performance and competitive advantage are related to the endowment and the use of its tangible and intangible resources (Barney, 2001; Wernerfelt, 1984). This is particularly important when it comes to natural resources (Hart, 1995).

The first idea is that the resources at a firm's disposal must be valuable in terms of quality, services related to the product, innovative practices compared to competitors, and the control market (Barney, 2001). The possession of a valuable resource is then characterized by the rarity of said resource, for example having in-depth knowledge of the wine sector, difficult to find on the market, and specific executive business-related strategies (Alonso & Bressan, 2016). In the theoretical framework, the valuable and rare resources cannot be transferred to another firm as a firm is also imperfectly imitable in terms of history, reputation, and consumers' perception (Kraaijenbrink, Spender, & Groen, 2010). The fourth and last element contributing to a firm's competitive edge is the non-substitutability of the resources (Barney, 2001). This characteristic refers to several categories of resources such as the equipment of technology and specific machinery (Wernerfelt, 1984), elements of the production process, but also the strategic geographical position thanks to which the resources that characterize the product cannot be replaced, only imitated.

Few studies focused on the **knowledge** needed by wineries to evolve (Giuliani & Bell, 2005). In this approach, geographical and territorial characteristics are no longer the determining factors in the chosen growth path of the firm, and they must be used efficiently by companies to gain a competitive advantage. Other scholars have shed light on the importance of the governance of a winery. Several businesses in the wine sector are, in fact, **family firms**, similar to "Made in Italy" brands. In general, the family model is viewed as strong in organization (e.g., corporate culture, employee engagement), marketing (e.g., customer orientation, trustworthiness), and branding dimensions (e.g., tradition and continuity, authenticity, and credibility) (Astrachan, Prügl, Hair, & Babin, 2019). In the wine industry, holding the title of a family business is indeed a key element in brand construction (Faraoni, Devigili, Casprini, Pucci, & Zanni, 2020), and vital to transmitting knowledge across generations. In some cases, this ability to transmit firm values and oenological competences is a centuries-old tradition, considering that luxury wines are based on the concept of "long-lasting wineries" (Zanni, Devigili, & Cordero di Montezemolo, 2009). Moreover, family wineries seemed to obtain better economic-financial results (return on assets, operating margin, and debt ratio) than non-family wineries (Soler, Gemar, & Guerrero-Murillo, 2017). They might be more efficient in following a convergent path between tradition and innovation (Vrontis, Bresciani, & Giacosa, 2016).

So, in the literature, there are several contributions determining wine companies' development model's characteristics. The interpretation provided by the resource-based view (RBV) approach applied to family businesses seems to be the most appropriate to give a solid theoretical contribution to analyze the growth path of a wine firm. However, there is a research gap in the analysis of the evolutionary trajectories that characterize the creation of a luxury wine brand (Vecchio, Gergaud, & Pomarici, 2021). Focusing on previous studies, this chapter analyzes how a family business was able to transform its trajectory from a small, local, family firm to a medium-large, global company with a complex governance structure. Furthermore, we uncover the firm's strategy in market positioning as a luxury wine, its innovative capacity, and the company's future scenarios in the light of the epochal changes we are experiencing, such as the digital transformation and desire for sustainability (Flores, 2018; Wamba & Queiroz, 2022).

Case study: Cantine Ferrari

Methodology

The explorative nature of our research question led us to adopt a single in-depth case study (Yin, 1994). A single case study is suitable to answer "what" and "how" questions and it is appropriate to properly grasp the nuances of a phenomenon in its context. We theoretically sample the firm of Cantine Ferrari as an illustrative case (Siggelkow, 2007) of a family (Lunelli) winery that, in the last decades, has been able to develop a luxury brand, nowadays known worldwide.

Data collection

Data was collected through an in-depth interview with Dr. Simone Masé, the managing director of Lunelli Group, as well as data gathered from secondary sources, in particular press releases. The interview protocol consisted of a few open-ended questions. The interview lasted 60 minutes and it was recorded and transcribed.

Data analysis

Data was coded in three steps (Miles, Huberman, & Saldaña, 2014). The first one's aim was to answer the "what" question, exploring the meaning of the concept of "luxury" in wine. In this case, we analyzed how our informant described luxury in the wine sector. Bearing in mind the key themes reviewed in the literature, such as feelings and sensual experiences, going beyond the necessary, and high prices (Wolf et al., 2016), we searched for a deeper meaning of the term.

Second, we zoomed into "how" Cantine Ferrari developed its brand over time. In doing so, we distinguished the main events characterizing the history of the company and we were able to identify multiple time periods along which Cantine Ferrari has become a world-wide recognized brand.

Finally, we looked at the elements that enabled and are enabling this development that can be summarized in terms of segmentation and positioning, innovation, and sustainability, and eventually in the future national and international scenarios due to new consumption behaviors in the wine industry.

A brief history

The company known as Cantine Ferrari, its exact name being Ferrari Fratelli Lunelli SpA, was founded in 1902 thanks to the intuition of entrepreneur Giulio Ferrari. The story starts with the production of a wine from Chardonnay, a French type of grapes already used at that time for sparkling wine, in the area of the current province of Trento. The entrepreneur returned from a few years of training in France where he learned the classic methods of preparing Champagne. He saw potential in the encounter between Chardonnay and the Trentino region, pursuing a quality-driven business model. Over the years, the brand has gained traction, so much that for a period it was able to boast the appellation of Champagne wine.

After decades of entrepreneurial development, interspersed with the First and Second World Wars, in 1952, the founder Giulio decided to entrust the reins of the company to wine merchant and long-time collaborator Bruno Lunelli. Ferrari wine had, in the meantime, called its product sparkling wine, following the introduction of specific legislation on the appropriate naming of products. In the transition phase between Giulio Ferrari and Bruno Lunelli's management, it was decided to keep the Ferrari brand name and to change the business model by increasing production, thus expanding the target of consumers but keeping the quality of the final product unchanged.

Thus, the company began to establish itself as an Italian leader in the production of sparkling wine, continuing to deliver remarkable performances while maintaining the structure and relationships characteristic of family businesses. In fact, from the early 1970s, Giulio's sons Franco, Gino, and Mauro followed in his footsteps as the leaders of Cantine Ferrari, in line with the typical mechanisms of family entrepreneurship. The second generation of Lunellis is continuing down the path started by their father in affirming the Ferrari brand. This is when the renowned products such as Ferrari Rosé and the Riserva sparkling wine, commemorating the founder Giulio Ferrari, arrived on the market. Ferrari was also the first wine brand to adopt an alternative communication strategy by creating partnerships with famous "Made in Italy" brands (e.g., Prada and Maserati).

From the early 2000s, the company's leadership was passed on to the third generation of the Lunellis, thanks to the appointment in 2011 of Matteo, Giorgio's son, as President of the Group. In the meantime, the brand saw significant expansion, incorporating within it brands of grappa, mineral water, other types of wines, and the ownership of some accommodation facilities. Alongside Matteo at the helm of Ferrari, numerous members of the family are involved in the business, such as Marcello, Franco's son, and the agronomist and oenological director of production; Camilla, Mauro's daughter, and head of communication for the whole company; and finally, Matteo's brother Alessandro, and the managing director of Tenute Lunelli. Simone Masè, managing director of the Group since 2019, completes the picture of the Ferrari's governance. Masè has an international background in management and he is not a family member, but he knows the territory well, having been born in the province of Trento.

Nowadays, Cantine Ferrari is a group that has more than 300 employees, with a turnover of about 270 million euros and a net profit that amounts to more than 13 million euros by 2020 (a year of decline due to the pandemic crisis). The production of millions of bottles per year does not seem to have negatively affected the quality of Ferrari's product, which has been certified for the third time in its history as the "*World Sparkling Wine Producer of the Year*" in 2021 during the most important international competition for the sector, called "The Champagne and Sparkling Wine World Championship", in which it has also won several further prizes and awards.

Cantine Ferrari can therefore be considered the most famous Trentodoc wine producer in the world as well as one of the most important sparkling wine brands at an international level. On top of this, the company plays an important social role in the province of Trento by organizing events to promote the area as well as training activities in schools.

Current strategies

The company is not only a national but also an international leader that plays the game of luxury in the highest segments of the market. During its development to an international brand, it has followed segmentation and positioning strategies typical in the world of wine, relating to the construction of a brand characterized by exclusivity, authenticity, and territoriality (Fortis & Sartori, 2016; Pomarici et al., 2021).

The most significant evolutions that took place in Cantine Ferrari were in reference to the control market, company size, and governance structure.

First, the initially local market based on a niche production until the 1950s, expanded to become international and **the firm entered the global market**. This transformation has occurred in other companies in the wine sector where firms took advantage of globalization mechanisms to expand their markets, but, in this case, it happened thanks to partnership strategies with luxury "Made in Italy" brands from the fashion and car industry that allowed the wine to be promoted on a global scale. As the General Manager Simone Masè pointed out, in recent years, the firm has increasingly focused on international development, both by leveraging the fact that Ferrari wine is an Italian luxury product (the so-called made-in effect) and focusing on the growing interest of the market toward "wine with bubbles" (Vecchio et al., 2021), as evidenced by the important increase in sales on a global level.

Secondly, the development of the reference market was understandably accompanied by the **growth in size of the company**, which, in a few decades, went from being a small firm to a medium-large company with hundreds of employees and an impressive turnover. The evolutionary dynamics of Ferrari is not unique in the national panorama of the wine industry, where some historic companies have managed to establish themselves on the market by increasing their economies of scale (Pomarici et al., 2021; Zanni et al., 2009). Italy is now the first sparkling wine producer in the world, overtaking Germany and France (Area Studi Mediobanca, 2021). However, as it evolved, Cantine Ferrari has tried, with some success, to increase its presence on the market and its company size while maintaining a high-quality standard both real and perceived, in terms of brand exclusivity and following an affordable luxury strategy.

Third, the **firm's governance structure has changed over time**. The traditional model of family entrepreneurship has been replaced by a mixed governance model in which an important operational role is covered by an external general manager. As recalled by the manager itself:

> *For more than three hundred employees, there are four family members in the company, and they cannot do everything. The leap in quality in a higher and larger competitive arena, at an international level, would not be feasible for the company if it did not integrate professionalism and skills, including external ones.*

However, the family business dimension remains a fundamental factor in terms of product and process knowledge, company reputation, and relationship with stakeholders:

> *The Lunelli family has an international vision, but it is rooted in the territory. It is an expression of Italian entrepreneurship and has an excellent reputation locally too. The family and managerial dimensions are not in contrast but are two elements that must integrate and evolve together.*

The **triple-factor transition** from a small family business operating on the local market to a medium-large global company with an external manager reinforced the image of the Ferrari product as a luxury Italian sparkling wine.

In the definition of luxury, there are three strong elements identified by the manager in the corporate strategy: **excellence**, **scarcity**, and **relationships with stakeholders**. Masè said:

> *For us at Ferrari, luxury is first of all related to the word* **excellence**. *This excellence refers to the production processes, the choice of raw materials, the presentation of the product, and the packaging. Furthermore, the distribution locations of the product and those where it is drunk (for example, Michelin-starred restaurants) are part of this mechanism. This way, the pursuit of technical excellence is accompanied, in the case of Ferrari, by investments in niche-product promotion, effectively conveying the concept of luxury. Thus, the attractiveness of the product for customers comes from the luxury of being able to drink something refined and exclusive.*
>
> (Rainer, 2021)

A second keyword in the definition of luxury for Ferrari, according to Masè, is **scarcity**. In management, scarcity is one of the basic competitive advantages, both in terms of skills and exclusive knowledge of production processes (Barney, 2001), and wine territorial characteristics, which determine the non-replicability of the product (Pucci et al., 2017). In Ferrari's case, territorial factors are relevant for scarcity:

> *For geographic reasons and availability of raw materials, and for issues linked to the denomination of our wine within the Trento Doc consortium, we make a product that is limited and not always available in large quantities. Therefore, the scarcity of raw materials is due to the geographical limits that the company must respect to fall within the designation of origin are the primary factors. There is a roller coaster effect on the quantity of grapes and consequently on production capacity and prices.*

A third strategic element that has helped the Ferrari brand on its path toward luxury is its **relationship with stakeholders**, with a specific attention on price formation. The idea is to position Ferrari sparkling wine as an accessible luxury product in order to attract a good number of intermediaries and customers, "*interested in trying an excellent sparkling wine without spending very high amounts of money*", said Masè. This happens simultaneously with trying to place some very expensive types of wine on the market (e.g., Ferrari Riserva del Fondatore®, Ferrari F1 Podium®, etc.), thus differentiating the offer. Another type of stakeholder relationship handled by Ferrari on its trajectory toward luxury is the commercial relations with other brands. The company has been a pioneer in building partnerships with other luxury companies, ranging from the high fashion sector to collaborations with elite sports such as Formula 1®, that, starting in 2021, has chosen Ferrari Trento as its official partner to celebrate the drivers' victories on the podiums.

In addition to the three key elements identified, the definition of luxury cannot ignore the two current mega trends of **sustainability** and **technological innovation,** intended as factors that influence the quality of the product. As a company, in 2021, Ferrari presented its first corporate sustainability report named "Cultivating excellence", in which the three dimensions of sustainability – protection of the natural environment, healthy human development, and solid economic growth – are incorporated. Organic vineyard certifications, a broad company welfare plan, and a strong collaboration with the local community of the place of origin (province of Trento) are among the elements that confirm the company's efforts toward sustainability. In this regard, Masè stated:

> *Being sustainable is the first condition for being able to exist unless we are dealing with products that are strongly oriented towards chemistry*", saying that "*for us, naturalness is fundamental. In our view, sustainability and excellence converged, and we have much stricter quality controls than those required by law for what concerns the Trento Doc.*

The manager confirms that the concepts of sustainability and luxury are not only compatible (Kapferer & Michaut-Denizeau, 2017), but often interlinked

(Ranfagni & Guercini, 2016). In addition, taking into account the economic, environmental, and social dimensions represent a good luxury marketing tool (Athwal et al., 2019). A sustainable orientation is not determined only by intrinsic goals, such as a generally more natural product or being increasingly ethical (Osburg, Davies, Yoganathan, & McLeay, 2021): consumer behavior is also becoming a significant factor as wine consumers are increasingly demanding greater compliance with sustainability criteria from companies (Flores, 2018; Zanni & Cammeo, 2021). On top of this, the company is aware of the importance of environmental sustainability as a communication lever but highlighted the customer's lack of awareness of the concept of social sustainability. In this regard, the general manager recalled that there is contradictory evidence regarding consumers' perception of sustainability as a development driver for a luxury brand:

> *We talk about sustainability to our interlocutors, we have organic certifications, and we try to communicate our sustainability efforts as well as possible, even if it remains a topic that is* ***not too relevant for some stakeholders****, such as some intermediaries and final consumers.*

While it is true that in terms of excellence, sustainability, and the related certifications, it is an important dimension (Athwal et al., 2019), but this trend is still at a preliminary stage and is recognizable in the market only for certain demographic segments (Kapferer & Michaut-Denizeau, 2020). Nonetheless, as mentioned, Ferrari is continuing to invest in sustainability on several fronts, which is partly thanks to technological innovations created to manage the impact of production on the environment, such as electric energy systems from renewable resources, vineyards irrigation machineries for the optimization in water consumption, low-polluting tractors with which treatments are distributed with minimum dispersion coefficients, or innovative systems for processing wine in the cellars. Innovation is a driver for being more sustainable and a strategic goal in the company's development plan: they must convey both **respect for traditions** and **elements of innovation**.

> "*In the world of wine, it must be said that the concept of innovation has a little less importance because it pays more attention to what has always been done in the past than what could be done in the future. However, in this case I am happy to say that we believe in innovation*", asserted Masè.

Openness to change and R&D applications are not limited to the scope of innovation for sustainability. For example, there are product innovations, such as the research aimed at perfecting a non-alcoholic sparkling wine, conceived with the intention of meeting the demands of new international markets and new generations, without compromising the quality of the final product. There are also the networks of relationships necessary to reduce the distance to the frontiers of innovation, such as those guaranteed by cooperation with the research centers of the universities of northern Italy:

> "*We collaborate with the Politecnico di Milano and, for some productive aspects, with the Mach Foundation of the University of San Michele all'Adige in the province of Trento. Then we had a collaboration with the University of Padua*", said the manager.

According to Masè, the company aims to increase the number of collaborations with local universities with the goal of identifying significant and incremental innovations that do not alter the business model and existing strategies.

Future scenarios

The process and product innovations mentioned in the previous paragraph represent an important part of the company's managerial strategies to face the entrepreneurial challenges of the near future. Among these challenges, the Ferrari manager highlights two main issues: the **company's attractiveness to the new generations** and the **expansion into international markets**.

Firstly, young consumers are asking for sustainability, evaluating waste reduction, reducing carbon footprint, providing sustainable packaging, committing to ethical work practices, and respecting human rights as fundamental practices (Pomarici, Asioli, Vecchio, & Næs, 2018). The quality of the product itself and its belonging to the luxury segment is evaluated by the so-called millennials (Kapferer & Michaut-Denizeau, 2020). In the wine industry, for young generations, sustainability adds value to the product (Pucci, Casprini, Nosi, & Zanni, 2019). According to Ferrari, the natural and authentic aspects of the product are strengthened by enriching the purchase process with **experiential opportunities**, such as visits to the cellar, which are increasingly occurring and requested by young customers. At the same time, the company has made a **major shift toward digital communication**:

> "*This has never based its strategy on advertising investments in television, radio, newspapers ... it was a right choice that again refers to the concept of luxury to be visible and present only in certain contexts and places*", stated the manager Masè. At the same time, "*we have increased our presence on social channels, mainly Instagram and Facebook, to reach a wide spectrum of potential consumers in a 'trendy' way*".

Investments in sustainability and digitalization are not the only avenues for further development for the company: new marketing experiential strategies pursued by Ferrari aim to strengthen its position in the **affordable luxury market**, for example, with the initiative called "pizza and bubbles". This combination does not seem to be typical of traditional luxury in the sparkling wine industry. In the idea of pizza, the perception of sophisticated consumption by the few is transformed. However, the initiative lays its foundation by considering the association between Ferrari sparkling wine and an aperitif/dinner in a fine dining restaurant where Italian food is typically consumed:

> "*Let's say that it is a derivation of the made in Italy, of the Italian spirit*", said Masè.

The plan to continue to **focus on "Made in Italy"** is part of a broader set of strategies aimed at promoting the internationalization of the brand, such as the aforementioned partnerships with other brands or alcohol-free product innovations. In this case, what really matters for the company is using the made-in image and nationality positive bias related to the quality of the wine and to the Italian way of life, especially in terms of international markets. At the same time, the company will have to continue to manage the **dichotomy** between belonging to the **Trentino** regional cluster and the promotion of the brand as a typical **"Made in Italy"** company.

Findings and discussion

The analyzed case made it possible to investigate several of the issues that emerged during the literature review regarding the **definition of luxury wine, the development trajectories of wine firms, sustainability, and innovation as drivers for expansion and better performances**.

However complex the definition of luxury wine (Donzé & Katsumata, 2021), the importance of the elements **excellence**, **scarcity**, and **relationships with the stakeholders** has been confirmed. Excellence in the sparkling wine industry is related to factors such as the high quality of production processes, choice of raw materials, presentation of the product, and packaging (Dubois & Duquesne, 1993; Rahman & Reynolds, 2015; Sáenz-Navajas et al., 2013). **Scarcity** concerns the company's endowment of natural (Merloni et al., 2018, Joy et al., 2021) and knowledge-based (Alonso & Bressan, 2016; Barney, 2001) resources that are valuable, rare, imperfectly imitable, and non-substitutable.

Relationships with the stakeholders are about the efficient building of a network of stable relationships based on trust, exploiting the geographical and/or cognitive proximity with other entities (Doloreux & Lord-Tarte, 2013; Fortis & Sartori, 2016). The company is **embedded within the "Made in Italy" cluster** thanks to its belonging to the culture of long-lasting wineries (Zanni et al., 2009). Among the stakeholders, in the case of Ferrari, a fundamental role in terms of **knowledge dissemination** (Giuliani & Bell, 2005) is played by the actors **in the territory** to which the company is linked, in this case in the province of Trento.

The path of evolution followed by the company deserves some consideration. The transition from a small family business to a medium-large global enterprise with a hybrid governance model, which took place over the decades of corporate history, is not unique in the wine industry landscape (Pucci et al., 2017). What the case analysis helped clarify is the development trajectories that characterize the building of a luxury wine brand that can compete in the high-luxury market segments (Gilinsky, Atkin, & Bayar, 2021), and how the Ferrari company managed to co-evolve the increase in production and the strengthening of its position in the luxury market.

This research shows that the remarkable results achieved by the company are derived from a **delicate balancing strategy on several fronts**: the family governance structure that has been opened to non-family members, the maintenance of a strong bond with the companies and institutions in the local area, and the construction of partnerships on the international market. Likewise, in terms of investments in sustainability and technological innovation, Ferrari has tried to bring together both traditional and innovative elements (Vrontis et al., 2016).

The in-depth analysis did not fully clarify some aspects relating to **sustainability** in luxury wine. On one hand, it has clearly emerged that sustainability is of **fundamental importance for the present and future development of the company**, due to the necessary research for the creation of a more natural product, and in light of the consumers' request for organic wine certifications (Maesano, Di Vita, Chinnici, Gioacchino, & D'Amico, 2021). On the other hand, it is meaningful that, according to the manager of the company, sustainability, especially in its social dimension, is still **not a discriminating factor for many intermediaries and customers**, as evidenced by previous empirical research (Zanni & Cammeo, 2021). Luxury and sustainability are two elements that do not contradict each other (Ranfagni & Guercini, 2016), even if some difficulties in identifying consumers' perception of sustainable luxury products remain (Kapferer & Michaut-Denizeau, 2020; Amatulli, De Angelis, & Donato, 2021).

The **balance between tradition and innovation** is evident in Ferrari's plans of increasing the internationalization of the brand. In this case, the company is going to offer **product innovations**, such as non-alcoholic sparkling wine, which meet the demands of developing foreign markets (Shahid, Islam, Farooqi, & Thomas, 2021).

Conclusion

The analysis of the Cantine Ferrari case allows us to trace initial summary reflections on the issue of sustainable luxury for "Made in Italy" wine, highlighting some distinctive features and development trajectories that are useful from both academic and managerial points of view. In particular, we would like to focus our attention on answering **three research questions**.

What are the specificities of "luxury" in the wine industry and who are the main business actors in this peculiar segment of the Italian wine sector?

The specificities of luxury in the wine industry have not changed much from the past. At the same time, **elements connected to culture are**

increasingly relevant, like the experiential nature of the purchasing process with high emotional interactions and the new reference values (democratization, sustainability). The luxury interpretation of Italian wine companies has brought some new elements in terms of relations with stakeholders. The protagonists of this segment of the Italian wine industry are **medium-large family businesses** that have made their governance evolve by hiring external managers and increasing their size. The analysis of the Cantine Ferrari case confirmed that the competitive advantage of Italian wine is often based on several small-sized firms geographically concentrated in some wine clusters, but inside these territories such as Trento doc, few firms emerge as "leading actors" not only in terms of firm dimensions (medium-large companies) but mainly regarding the endowment of internal resource and competence and in terms of the quality of their external relation (social and economic networks).

What are the strategic levers and repositioning strategies that are implemented in the case analyzed? More specifically, what challenges arise for a "Made in Italy" luxury wine aiming to balance tradition and innovation?

The strategies that emerged in the case study concern not only price mechanisms and rare endogenous factors but also assets created and designed to differentiate the experience, such as **strategic commercial partnerships** with other luxury brands (e.g., Formula 1, fashion brands, starred restaurants). In addition, the business dimension is increasingly linked to the territorial dynamics through collaboration networks. The **coevolution between the "Made in Trentino" and "Made in Italy"**, if properly defined to avoid any possible confusion, actually strengthen the "Made in Italy" strategy, suitable for the Italian context but also in the international markets, in line with the high positioning of "Made in Italy" regional products in the global markets. The Italian wine luxury firms are different from international competitors, given that "Made in Italy" wine is the bearer of social values of the territory and, before that, of the family owner, unlike the luxury segments of the great French brands (Gilinsky, Atkin, & Bayar, 2021), or of American global companies (Vecchio et al., 2021). In the Italian wine clusters, elements of cooperation and competition often coexist: the territory is not a simple marketing lever but represents a set of unique oenological characteristics and economic-social relations. It is the original nature of this marriage of values and wine culture – sociality, community, territory – which are the foundations of the "*luxury ecological transition*" of Italian wine. When leading companies and territories know how to build, guide, and communicate this virtuous path, they avoid the risk of becoming commodities and are able to stand out on the global market. The success of these strategies depends not only on the company's adaptability and resilience to respond to exogenous contextual factors (pandemics, wars, and ecological crises) but on Ferrari's ability to attract future generations of consumers and to enter new international markets with new digital solutions (e-commerce, social media strategies).

What role does sustainability play in the luxury strategies of Italian wineries?

Sustainability is, at this point, a fundamental factor in the wine industry (Flores, 2018). However, the path toward full economic, environmental, and social sustainability is long. **Being sustainable is a gradual process** that can be affected by contextual factors such as global health emergencies or humanitarian crises. Understandably, the company prioritized economic sustainability, that is vital in the current period of severe turbulence (financial crises, COVID-19, Russian invasion of Ukraine, climate change), and environmental sustainability that is used as a differentiation lever. The firm tried to fill the general gap in terms of application and communication of social sustainability principles (Zanni & Cammeo, 2021) with the publication of its first Sustainability Report in 2021, in which the social dimension is strongly considered. Still, this dimension does not aim to assume the main role as a marketing strategy, due to the lack of consumer demand so far. Awareness that a holistic **vision of sustainability in its triple dimension** adds value for future generations is a key element that will allow the company to continue to pursue its path to success as a sustainable luxury wine brand.

References

Alonso, A. D., & Bressan, A. (2016). A resource-based view of the firm and micro and small Italian wine firms. *International Journal of Wine Business Research, 28*(4), 349–368.

Amatulli, C., De Angelis, M., & Donato, C. (2021). The atypicality of sustainable luxury products. *Psychology & Marketing, 38*(11), 1990–2005.

Area Studi Mediobanca. (2021). *Vino e spirits: le sfide di un'eccellenza italiana.* Italy: Milano.

Astrachan, C. B., Prügl, R., Hair, J. F., Jr, & Babin, B. J. (2019). Marketing and branding in family business: Assessing the landscape and charting a path forward. *Journal of Family Business Strategy, 10*(1), 3–7.

Athwal, N., Wells, V. K., Carrigan, M., & Henninger, C. E. (2019). Sustainable luxury marketing: A synthesis and research agenda. *International Journal of Management Reviews, 21*(4), 405–426.

Barney, J. B. (1991). Resource-Based theories of competitive advantage: A ten-year retrospective on the Resource-Based view. *Journal of Management, 17*, 99–120.

Barney, J. B. (2001). Resource and sustained competitive advantage. *Journal of Management, 27*(6), 643–650.

Beverland, M. (2004). Uncovering "theories-in-use": Building luxury wine brands. *European Journal of Marketing, 38*(3/4), 446–466.

Doloreux, D., & Lord-Tarte, E. (2013). The organisation of innovation in the wine industry: Open innovation, external sources of knowledge and proximity. *European Journal of Innovation Management, 16*(2), 171–189.

Donzé, P. Y., & Katsumata, S. (2021). High-end luxury wine demand and income inequality. *International Journal of Wine Business Research, 34*(1), 112–132.

Dubois, B., & Duquesne, P. (1993). The market for luxury goods: Income versus culture. *European Journal of Marketing, 27*(1), 35–44.

Faraoni, M., Devigili, M., Casprini, E., Pucci, T., & Zanni, L. (2020). Branding your identity online! The importance of the family dimension for Italian family wine businesses' foreign turnover. *Italian Journal of Management, 38*(2), 151–164.

Flores, S. S. (2018). What is sustainability in the wine world? A cross-country analysis of wine sustainability frameworks. *Journal of Cleaner Production, 172*, 2301–2312.

Fortis, M., & Sartori, A. (2016). Food & wine: Quality, tradition and innovation. In *The pillars of the Italian economy* (pp. 283–317). Cham, Switzerland: Springer.

Gilinsky, A., Jr, Atkin, T., & Bayar, S. (2021). The champagne industry in 2020. *Wine Business Journal, 4*(1), 22300.

Giuliani, E., & Bell, M. (2005). The micro-determinants of meso-level learning and innovation: Evidence from a Chilean wine cluster. *Research Policy, 34*(1), 47–68.

Hart, S. L. (1995). A natural-resource-based view of the firm. *Academy of Management Review, 20*(4), 986–1014.

Heine, K., Phan, M., & Atwal, G. (2016). Authenticity and prestige: What luxury brands could learn from the wine industry? *Luxury Research Journal, 1*(2), 177–190.

Islam, T., Wang, Y., Ali, A., & Akhtar, N. (2021). Path to sustainable luxury brand consumption: Face consciousness, materialism, pride and risk of embarrassment. *Journal of Consumer Marketing, 39*(1),11–28. doi: 10.1108/JCM-09-2020-4099.

Lockshin, L., & Corsi, A. M. (2012). Consumer behaviour for wine 2.0: A review since 2003 and future directions. *Wine Economics and Policy, 13*(1), 2–23.

Kapferer, J. N., & Michaut-Denizeau, A. (2017). Is luxury compatible with sustainability? Luxury consumers' viewpoint. In *Advances in luxury brand management* (pp. 123–156). Cham, Switzerland: Palgrave Macmillan.

Kapferer, J. N., & Michaut-Denizeau, A. (2020). Are millennials really more sensitive to sustainable luxury? A cross-generational international comparison of sustainability consciousness when buying luxury. *Journal of Brand Management, 27*(1), 35–47.

Kraaijenbrink, J., Spender, J. C., & Groen, A. J. (2010). The resource-based view: A review and assessment of its critiques. *Journal of Management, 36*(1), 349–372.

Kunz, J., May, S., & Schmidt, H. J. (2020). Sustainable luxury: Current status and perspectives for future research. *Business Research, 13*(2), 541–601.

Maesano, G., Di Vita, G., Chinnici, G., Gioacchino, P., & D'Amico, M. (2021). What's in organic wine consumer mind? A review on purchasing drivers of organic wines. *Wine Economics and Policy, 10*(1), 3–21.

Merloni, E., Camanzi, L., Mulazzani, L., & Malorgio, G. (2018). Adaptive capacity to climate change in the wine industry: A Bayesian network approach. *Wine Economics and Policy, 7*(2), 165–177.

Miles, M. B., Huberman, A. M., & Saldaña, J. (2014). *Qualitative data analysis: A methods sourcebook* (3rd ed.). Thousand Oaks, CA: SAGE.

Nosi, C., & Zanni, L. (2004). Moving from "typical products" to "food-related services": The slow food case as a new business paradigm. *British Food Journal, 106*, 779–792.

Osburg, V. S., Davies, I., Yoganathan, V., & McLeay, F. (2021). Perspectives, opportunities and tensions in ethical and sustainable luxury: Introduction to the thematic symposium. *Journal of Business Ethics, 169*(2), 201–210.

Pomarici, E., Asioli, D., Vecchio, R., & Næs, T. (2018). Young consumers' preferences for water-saving wines: An experimental study. *Wine Economics and Policy, 7*(1), 65–76.

Pomarici, E., Corsi, A., Mazzarino, S., & Sardone, R. (2021). The Italian wine sector: Evolution, structure, competitiveness and future challenges of an enduring leader. *Italian Economic Journal*, 7(2), 259–295.

Pucci, T., Casprini, E., Nosi, C., & Zanni, L. (2019). "Does social media usage affect online purchasing intention for wine? The moderating role of subjective and objective knowledge. *British Food Journal*, *121*(2), 275–288.

Pucci, T., Casprini, E., Rabino, S., & Zanni, L. (2017). Place branding-exploring knowledge and positioning choices across national boundaries: The case of an Italian superbrand wine. *British Food Journal*, *119*(8), 1915–1932.

Pucci, T., Casprini, E., Galati, A., & Zanni, L. (2020). The virtuous cycle of stakeholder engagement in developing a sustainability culture: Salcheto winery. *Journal of Business Research*, *119*, 364–376.

Rahman, I., & Reynolds, D. (2015). Wine: Intrinsic attributes and consumers' drinking frequency, experience, and involvement. *International Journal of Hospitality Management*, *44*, 1–11.

Rainer, G. (2021). Geographies of qualification in the global fine wine market. *Environment and Planning A: Economy and Space*, *53*(1), 95–112.

Ranfagni, S., & Guercini, S. (2016). Beyond appearances: The hidden meanings of sustainable luxury. In *Handbook of sustainable luxury textiles and fashion* (pp. 51–72). Singapore: Springer.

Sáenz-Navajas, M. P., Campo, E., Sutan, A., Ballester, J., & Valentin, D. (2013). Perception of wine quality according to extrinsic cues: The case of burgundy wine consumers. *Food Quality and Preference*, *27*(1), 44–53.

Shahid, S., Islam, J. U., Farooqi, R., & Thomas, G. (2021). Affordable luxury consumption: An emerging market's perspective. *International Journal of Emerging Markets*, (ahead-of-print).

Siggelkow, N. (2007). Persuasion with case studies. *Academy of Management Journal*, *50*(1), 20–24.

Sogari, G., Casprini, E., Devigili, M., & Pucci, T. (2018). Sensory and consumer sciences: What is their role as a business tool in the wine sector? In C. Santini & A. Cavicchi (Eds.), *Case studies in the wine industry* (pp. 49–60), Duxford, UK: Woodhead Publishing – Elsevier.

Soler, I. P., Gemar, G., & Guerrero-Murillo, R. (2017). Family and non-family business behaviour in the wine sector: A comparative study. *European Journal of Family Business*, 7(1/2), 65–73.

Vecchio, R., Gergaud, O., & Pomarici, E. (2021). Sparkling wines' future in the USA: Insights from the industry. *International Journal of Entrepreneurship and Small Business*, *44*(2), 138–154.

Vrontis, D., Bresciani, S., & Giacosa, E. (2016). Tradition and innovation in Italian wine family businesses. *British Food Journal*, *118*(8), 1883–1897.

Wamba, S. F., & Queiroz, M. M. (2022). Industry 4.0 and the supply chain digitalisation: A blockchain diffusion perspective. *Production Planning & Control*, *33*(2/3), 193–210.

Wang, P., Kuah, A. T. H., Lu, Q., Wong, C., Thirumaran, K., Adegbite, E., ..., Kendall, W. (2021). The impact of value perceptions on purchase intention of sustainable luxury brands in China and the UK. *Journal of Brand Management*, *28*(3), 325–346.

Wernerfelt, B. (1984). A resource-based view of the firm. *Strategic Management Journal*, *5*(2), 171–180.

Wolf, H. L., Morrish, S. C., & Fountain, J. (2016). A conceptualization of the perceptions and motivators that drive luxury wine consumption. *International Journal of Wine Business Research*, *28*(2), 120–133.

Zanni, L., & Cammeo, J. (2021). Work and social sustainability in the world of wine. Luci sul Lavoro 2021, Gambero Rosso-Equalitas, Italy.

Zanni, L., Devigili, L., & Cordero di Montezemolo, S. (2009). Managing succession in family business: Successful lessons from long lasting wineries in Tuscany. In M. Faraoni & C. Santini (Eds.), *The wine business in California and Tuscany: A cross country analysis*. Milan, Italy: McGraw Hill.

Section III

14 Luxury "Made in Italy" Start-ups and the Sustainable Innovation Challenge

Dennis Valle
Corneliani CMO, Former VP, Dolce & Gabbana

The 20th century has been an era of unparalleled industrial development and social improvement, which has headed to extremely relevant increase in energy exploitation, natural resource reduction, and growth of wide-ranging challenges involving sustainability. The consequent negative impact on the environment has led to an increased recognition about the critical value of sustainability and the appearance of a contemporary call among luxury brands to reduce their ecological footprints. Even though luxury and fashion brands are perceived as one of the main sources of the current social and environmental concerns, and the cause of lack of sustainability in society, they still have the opportunity to act as change agents by championing a responsible approach to business. With this shift in company mindset and consumer preferences, the demand for sustainable goods and services has increased.

Nowadays, luxury manufacturers are doing their best to integrate both concepts – luxury and sustainability. In fact, this integration of luxury brands strategy is not a spontaneous movement made only to differentiate themselves from their competitors, but this is oriented to reach a new segmentation in the sector. These clients are involved with the concern of the public on three pillars – environment, social, and economy. Therefore, the luxury industry is having a great burden and pressure in order to change their business in a sustainable manner (Li & Leonas, 2019), forcing luxury brands to conform and immerse in sustainable goals.

According to the United Nations and the World Commission on Environment and Development (WCED, 1987, p. 41), sustainable development is a "development that meets the needs of the present without compromising the ability of future generations to meet their own needs. It contains within it two key concepts. The concept of 'needs', in particular the essential needs of the world's poor, to which overriding priority should be given; and the idea of limitations imposed by the state of technology". Following the summit of the United Nations in 1987 and when 196 United Nations States signed the Paris agreements in December 2015, the 17 Sustainable Development Objectives were created to promote prosperity while protecting the planet (United Nations, 2022). Scholars have proposed various firm measures and programs relevant to green manufacturing and the green supply

DOI: 10.4324/9781003305095-18

chain, which can be identified as core elements: green product development and green practices integrated in the supply. However, in the luxury fashion industry, luxury fashion brands are starting to adopt different sustainable strategies and practices so as to pursue green manufacturing and supply chains to evidence brand image and competitiveness. However, luxury products don't only see product eco-sustainability but also the ethical and social factors as a matter of clients' expectations with environmental protection.

Despite the consequences of the pandemic and the need – in some contexts – to redefine the global and domestic strategy, luxury brands have continued to benefit from a growth – even if limited and different depending on the sectors. If in the past, the increase was mainly driven by the growing demand in some geographical markets, in particular, in the fast-growing ones (Kiss, Danis, & Cavusgil, 2012), the last years have testified a growth – even if limited due to the consequences of the COVID pandemic – offered from the changes in the retailing strategies and the new metaverse orientation but also by innovative new creations from a growing number of responsible luxury start-ups. Certainly, with not all of these new luxury ventures thriving but with some proposing innovations in the market.

Sustainability and Innovation have started to represent a critical component of "Made in Italy" identity and strategically demanded for its positioning internationally. Luxury "Made in Italy" is globally recognized for its inimitable heritage, unique expertise, and outstanding creativity, but certainly sustainability was not one of its main defining characteristics. As the main global Italian luxury brands were fighting to add alternative ways to reduce their negative effect on the planet and preserve human lives, a network of contemporary brands started recently to manufacture high-quality products and to embrace a comprehensive sustainable identity.

The goal of living in a luxury environment has become increasingly relevant for some consumer markets as the fast-growing ones. And even though the luxury industry is still prerogative of the most privileged ones, owning at least a few luxury products or living a luxury experience is a must for some new segments of consumers in sought of a newly acquired social status. However, as the interest in luxury increases, at the same time the consumer market is facing new challenges as what applied to be identified as a luxury in the past is not necessarily the same for the new millennials and generation Z. Similarly, customers in the luxury "Made in Italy" are modifying their principles when shopping luxury. Are there new options that are considered, new expectations? If the origin of the materials is sustainable or the operations are in line with responsible certifications?

The new need of responsible luxury and the relationship between customers and brands in the process is a crucial challenge for global heritage brands in the luxury industry, and it is offering new openings for entrepreneurs interested in the luxury industry. Millennials and Gen Z are savvier shoppers, taking into account not only the quality, exclusivity, or style of a product or a brand but they are also giving significant attention to the origin, raw material choices, and production processes. In the new luxury responsible orientation, times are changing. Customers have begun to be more oriented towards more conscious shopping options, making the luxury industry more responsible for its manufacturing operations and particularly their goods' lifecycle. Those brands were considered accountable for their engagement not only from an environmentally friendly perspective but also from a societal one. Consequently, because of the change of perspective in the consumer market, retailers and luxury brands were also responding to the new sustainable orientation, progressively promoting their sustainability agendas, by creating a sustainable selection of goods of their own exclusive products, a fashion recycling program for new garments or resurging authentic responsible processes.

The call for sustainable consumption is innovating the "Made in Italy" luxury and their brands' identity and characteristics, impacting their manufacturing operations and social engagement. "Made in Italy" brands have consequently started to introduce more information in their reports about their operations with respect to their engagement for people, planet, and profit. The new orientation has given birth to an innovative entrepreneurship orientation composed of young or family-run "Made Green in Italy" start-ups. Young luxury consumer segments think that manufacturers should be obliged to integrate sustainable characteristics in their manufacturing and retailing strategies. And in response to their call, the new most innovative Italian luxury start-ups are not simply integrating a more responsible approach to their operations, and in the main "Made in Italy" clusters they find a new brand definition and value through sustainability.

As a result of the new luxury consuming sustainable orientation, luxury "Made in Italy" brands have come up with innovative solutions to implement sustainability in their supply chain as well as in their ecosystem. In so doing, luxury brands have started to redefine the values associated with luxury through the adoption of sustainability among luxury brands and customers in a disruptive business model innovation as described. In the Italian scenario embedded in the expertise of the "Made in Italy" clusters and traditional handcrafting, there are innovative start-ups that are presenting tech-enabled solutions, or rediscovering excellence processes and traditions to contribute to the development of a more sustainability evolution in the luxury and fashion industry. Those start-ups – presented in this chapter – are supporting the circular economy in decreasing carbon emissions and waste throughout various stages of the product lifestyle, for example through renewable textiles, second-hand, recycled materials and processes, or authentic craft core operations. All of these teams were founded in Italy in the last 3–5 years and show promising growth and positive response from the consumer market.

As some of the luxury sectors – in particular the personal goods sector with its fashion and apparel or leather and accessories areas – are classified as heavily contributing to environmental pollution with respect to their waste generation on the planet, a specific emergence for a more sustainable luxury industry started to appear as fundamental in the market. The ecological impact is seen through the different steps of its product's life cycle: "from fiber growth and manufacturing, dyeing and printing, transportation to stores and selling, to end of the garment life disposal" (Hill & Lee, 2012).

Raw materials, clothes waste, and water treatments are considered the most impactful sustainable issues in the product life cycle from the environmental perspective. Luxury and fashion brands are growing increasingly aware of the importance of sustainability and are actively looking for innovative solutions. Sustainability can push innovation by integrating various means from those ecological and environmental related to those improving societal conditions as well as norms and values up to a comprehensive circular economic approach. Sustainability involves additional importance in the innovation framework. While it is certainly relevant to debate over sustainability as an increasingly relevant driver in luxury value creation, the differentiation in luxury products and services will represent the most critical determinant for the brand in the consumer market. In the current responsible-oriented luxury consumers' context, the sustainable-driven innovation represents the main source of differentiation.

Either from a people, planet, or profit perspective, sustainability can modify the scenario for luxury brands by driving innovation and in so doing modifying traditional processes and operations or rediscovering them. In fact, it can also suggest outdated sustainable processes that innovation can redefine and positively apply to the new context. This can be the case for waste and reuse manufacturing techniques as reported in some of the cases in this chapter or it can also be a rediscovery and disruptively using a heritage handcrafting technique. In fact, innovative efforts can be sustaining or disruptive, both providing added value to the brand, its identity, and its positioning in the market. Both innovation perspectives drive new horizons that have not been thought and providing a new competitive advantage in the field of sustainable positioning.

The emphasis on decreasing waste, differently using manufacturing techniques, or rediscovering "forgotten" materials can be a powerful driver for creating innovative products and operating models for new start-ups in the field.

References

Hill, J., & Lee, H. H. (2012). Young generation Y consumers' perceptions of sustainability in the apparel industry. *Journal of Fashion Marketing and Management: An International Journal, 16*(4), 477–491.

Kiss, A. N., Danis, W. M., & Cavusgil, S. T. (2012). International entrepreneurship research in emerging economies: A critical review and research agenda. *Journal of Business Venturing, 27*(2), 266–290.

Li, J., & Leonas, K. (2019). Trends of sustainable development among luxury industry. *Sustainable Luxury*, 107–126.

United Nations. (2022). *Sustainable development goals*. Retrieved from https://www.un.org/sustainabledevelopment/

WCED. (1987). Report of the world commission on environment and development: Our common future. Oxford University Press.

15 Rifò and Prato Recycling Capital

Daniela Toccafondi
Università degli Studi di Firenze

The place where tradition meets the future: The anomalies that made Rifò an interesting case study for the textile district of Prato

Introduction

The concept of sustainability is becoming increasingly important, not only for the apparel industry. But as everyone knows, fashion is based on trends and the product has, as a result, a short life cycle. The emergence of ready-to-wear fashion has also shortened clothes' life cycle and made the quantities produced larger with a significant reduction in consumer prices. The consequence is a progressive accumulation of unsold and discarded clothes: waste. The precise negative environmental impact of the fashion industry remains unknown. Thanks to trade liberalization, globalization, and enduring cost pressures, most well-known brands outsource final production. McKinsey has recently estimated that the carbon impact of the industry is 4% of overall global carbon emissions (Pucker, 2022).

In the fashion system, a product is considered sustainable not only because it is made with sustainable, raw materials but substantially more if it is the result of a sustainable process. Furthermore, sustainability is not only synonymous with attention to the environment through suitable products, but also with respect for production processes, working conditions, workers' rights, and supporting communities in need. Sustainability is a dynamic and continuous process; it is not an immutable state but one that is constantly evolving. Sustainability starts at the beginning of the supply chain and the early stages are the most vital.

Contextual framework

Prato has always been a place where attention to sustainability is very strong due to the unique nature of the typical local product: carded wool yarns and fabrics and regenerated wool productions. Nowadays, the following statement is widely agreed upon by experts, journalists, and professionals: the concept of reuse is rooted in the culture of the territory, as demonstrated by

DOI: 10.4324/9781003305095-19

the theatrical performance "Stracci" (*Rags*) developed in 2008 by the talented director Tommaso Santi and performed inside the production warehouse. Repurposed in 2014, thanks to funding achieved through crowdfunding, Silvia Gambi and Tommaso Santi produced a docufilm ("Stracci") that was screened in the warehouse for all interested sector operators in the Premiere Vision Exhibition in 2022.

One of the most important Prato academics, Giacomo Becattini, emphasized the great peculiarity of Prato's organizational model, made up of a myriad of small- and medium-sized family-owned companies specializing only in certain phases of the supply chain (Bettiza & Patruno, 2020).

The Municipality of Prato, with its approximately 194,000 inhabitants, is in fact the third-largest city in central Italy, after Rome and Florence. The Prato manufacturing system has a long-standing tradition in the textile sector with the medium market and high range, but, in recent years, the clothing sector has been validated thanks to a large immigration of Chinese citizens who are loyal to ready-to-wear fashion (products of low price that have the characteristic of being reabsorbed in a very short time). The Prato district extends well beyond the boundaries of the province of Prato, going all the way to areas belonging to the provinces of Pistoia and Florence. Prato has 7,000 textile and apparel companies – 2,500 textile companies and 4,500 clothing companies – each with a hyper-specialization according to a specific supply chain phase. Over the years, that typical organization, based on phases satisfied by the operation of many independent companies, has gained the attention of economic operators and guaranteed very large, specific investments.

At the Italian level, Prato is the territory with the highest number of people employed in textiles – 18,520 in 2019 (Confindustria Toscana Nord, 2022). It is simultaneously the province with the highest number of employees in apparel – 24,447 in 2019 according to the indications of Confindustria. Istat data tells us that there were 19,169 employed in apparel in 2017, representing 11.2% of the total apparel workforce with an increase from 2001 to 2017 of +296.8%. Prato is also the Italian district that exports the most textile products (yarns, fabrics, clothing, etc.) for a total amount of 2.8 million euros approximately a year (Confindustria Toscana Nord, 2022). With this consistent manufacturing endowment, the city remains in the middle of the league table in the analysis that Legambiente carries out every year on Italian cities (Becattini, 2001). There are various reasons for this, in part linked to the environmental characteristics of the area (very windy, rich in water, close to uncontaminated mountainous areas, etc.), but also in part linked to the right choices and environmentally friendly economic policies since the birth of the district. An important example is represented by the public-private joint-stock company GIDA SpA, founded in 1981 for the purification, treatment, and recovery of civil and industrial wastewater. It is estimated that every day GIDA SpA avoids the production of 1,982 tons of carbon dioxide.

But the issue that is of most interest to frame the territory is that Prato has a strong characterization among traders as a place where wool is produced by recycling rags, packaging scraps, and production leftovers. This has been their claim to fame since the 1950s. Prato began to specialize in textiles in the 12th century, but it was at the end of the 19th century that industrial expansion came, with the introduction of mechanization and geographic concentration. A reason for this significant expansion was the lower costs of carded wool processing caused by the gradually increasing production of recovered wool obtained from shredding old clothes and industrial scarps. It is not just a question of sustainability of processes: for many years, in the Prato district, the issue of circular economy has been successfully tackled in many production processes. In short, in Prato, there was a circular economy long before the concept of circular economy spread among consumers all over the world.

According to the Ellen MacArthur Foundation, one of the world's leading institutes, the circular economy is defined as: "an economy designed to be able to regenerate itself. The circular economy is a system in which all activities, starting with extraction and production, are organized so that someone's waste becomes a resource for someone else". The textile district of Prato is the place where the circular economy was present in everyday life from its genesis.

This is the framework in which Rifò was established in 2017. The company does not keep this truth hidden; on Rifò's website, we found the announcement "we believe in our territory that since many generations held a huge textile know-how". It is a sort of recognition of the importance of being in Prato, one of the most important textile districts in Europe.

Case description

When Niccolò Cipriani, Rifò's young leader, thought of a company involved in the sustainability aspect of manufacturing for the first time, he was far away from Europe. It was probably due to his own culture and sustainability awareness that he was impressed by the effects of ready-to-wear fashion on the whole world.

He was born in October 1990, just around the corner of Prato in Florence, the cradle of the Renaissance, only 15km from Prato. When looking at these two places from the sky, a single large city is all that can be observed, with no distinction and no visible borders. Niccolò was still a boy when he moved to Prato with his family and went to school.

During his Erasmus program in Rennes, he realized for the first time the importance of the concept of the circular economy. Thinking about the companies located in Prato, he realized that there was hard work to do to communicate how sustainable fabrics and yarn made by Prato's manufacturers were. The heart of the matter was (and still is) to create a much more marketing-oriented company to better inform the consumer. As most young students who came from Prato, he usually spent his school holidays and summers doing an internship in some local company, which, in Niccolò's case, meant his uncle's company, a finishing and dyeing company specializing in fabrics. Therefore, Niccolò knew a lot about fabrics, yarns, knitwear, weaves, and cloth (Becattini, Bellandi, Del Ottati, & Sforzi, 2003).

During his work for a charity in Tanzania, he could see the huge amount of clothes coming from industrialized countries. As everyone probably knows, some international circuits sort secondhand clothes. Generally, winter clothes and a part of summer clothes (in very good condition) remain in Europe where they are sold in charity shops. Summer clothes are sent to Africa to be sold to the local population at a very low cost. However, about 25% of garments are not reusable at all and they will be recycled and transformed into new fiber. A small part – about 10% – is destined for energy recovery (Confidustria Toscana Nord, 2022).

It was exactly at that moment – in 2012 – that Niccolò Cipriani first came up with the idea of a fashion company that launched a clothing collecting initiative. Together with three Spanish students, he established a plan of action to create a start-up within his Erasmus project. The program included a separate collection of used clothes, door to door. It was an extraordinary way to collect secondhand clothes, completely unique and out of the norm. But the project was noticed. BNP Paribas awarded them a prize and supported the project. This was a small attempt that will be resumed and expanded a while later, after Niccolò finally graduated from the University of Florence and, some years later, in 2014, received his master's degree from Bocconi, Milan.

The further he got from university, the more autonomous he became, and he soon realized that there were hidden potential opportunities in the green economy. At the end of 2015, after a period of hard work in a buyer's office for the world exhibition Expo, Niccolò won the ONU Fellowship Program for Technical Cooperation Capacity Building and Human Resources Development. This important initiative is financed by the Italian government and management through the Ministry of Foreign Affairs together with United Nations Social. It offered young graduates up to 28 years old the opportunity to carry out a professional training course in developing countries (Laurenti & Trentin, 2021).

This international experience is a rare opportunity compared to the experience of many young entrepreneurs in Prato who, before starting their own business, only trained in local companies after having attended a technical high school or receiving their master's degree. For the young Cipriani, the destination was Hanoi, the capital of Vietnam, where he remained until 2017. The program aimed to improve, microcredit, and open up more financial services to poor people in that country. In the initial phase of the project, Niccolò was involved in microfinance, a sort of social entrepreneur, for a country that deeply needed it. Despite international and national support, Vietnam's microfinance sector still continues to underperform compared to its peers in Asia and elsewhere (Bevacqua, Nguyen & Lambert, 2021).

In that time period, companies were born to be global. Entrepreneurs do not automatically buy raw materials from nearby suppliers or set up factories close to their headquarters. They were looking for the planet's best manufacturing locations. In the fashion industry, many production chains were located in the East where costs were significantly lower. This led to an obvious increase in the consumption of goods at lower costs which, in turn, triggered overproduction and, finally, an excess of supply. Many well-known brands, even those in the medium-high segments of the market, moved their production centers to low-cost labor countries with an intensification of international trade in semi-finished products and a substantial displacement of the center of gravity of the manufacturing industry. The main countries involved were Bangladesh, Vietnam, India, and Sri Lanka. The phenomenon in itself would not have been so significant if the investment choices had not been based on the logic of short-term efficiency rather than on the desire to establish roots in the territory to bring economic stability. In some cases, these choices led to inhumane situations of violation of workers' rights, who were underpaid, overworked, and with healthcare benefits.

During his stay in Hanoi, Niccolò became aware of the problems related to the overproduction in the clothing industry, the huge traffic of clothes sold in that country at very low prices while the large quantities of surplus were sent to the landfill or incinerator. He figured there was hard work to be done: providing a valid alternative to the global trade in second-hand fast-fashion clothes to stop the outsized affluence of the goods in poor countries and finding an alternative business model to that adopted by the established companies.

When he returned to Italy, it was time to start an autonomous entrepreneurial path based on a new model of sustainable production in fashion. Niccolò tried everything to implement his idea. First of all, he found comfort in the ideas and friendship of an old friend, who was eager to start a small production in a very short amount of time, basing himself on the traditional experience of many companies located in the Prato district. They had once played water polo together, but they could not find the same harmony that they had developed in sports within their own business.

Niccolò was very determined to consolidate his unconventional business idea, which involved the possibility of recovering 100% of the raw materials from used clothing and knitwear, limiting the need for creating new fibers. In Prato, most companies offered recycled products at the end of the Second World War. Today, there are still a considerable number of them, but, generally, the articles offered have a much higher proportion of new fibers to give stability to the fabrics, especially for those intended for outwear (coats, jackets, etc.). Niccolò studied the practicability of his project, visiting the so-called "cenciaioli" who are highly experienced professionals in the sorting of used clothing, able to differentiate each item by weight, color, and fabric composition only by touch. Present in Prato for decades, these people have been in the workforce for many years, in search of true generational change. With their precious indications, he strengthened the idea of reinterpreting the way of selecting clothes. Finally, he prepared a crowdfunding campaign with Clarissa, Michele, and Fiammetta that would allow them to start their beautiful entrepreneurial adventure. The crowdfunding started and, in just 30 days, about 11,500 euros were collected, thanks to Rifò supporters.

Although there is a strong sensibility to the circular economy in wool production in the Prato district, Niccolò credits his experiences in East Asia where he was particularly interested in the sustainability of cotton products, which use large tracts of land and need large quantities of water to bring the plant to maturity. For this reason, as well, fashion is believed to be one of the most polluting industries in the world. Rifò's sensitivity to the world of organic cotton started from the promotion of new T-shirts. In April 2018, the crowdfunding campaign for the "100% Regenerated T-shirt" is launched: more than 300 t-shirts are sold in just one month. With this idea, Rifò beat the new marketing campaign promoted by Zara – which is committed to offering 100% recycled clothes by 2025 – by a landslide.

Despite the first evident successes, the confirmation on social networks, and the increasing number of followers, Rifò was lacking the capital needed to start a company and it was starting to become urgent to find new sources of funding. Fortunately, Rifò was included in a start-up acceleration program created some years before by the Fondazione Cassa di Risparmio di Firenze to finance the innovative ideas of talented young people in the area (Hubble program). It is a 16-week acceleration program and it consists of four months of pure venture building. It supports each entrepreneurial project with a grant of up to 50,000 euros, an in-class training program of over 90 hours, digital services with the main players in the market, international and high-profile mentorship, and dedicated workshops. The idea is a project where training requires the work to be carried out by each team on its idea in parallel: learning by doing. Hubble takes shape through the collaboration of Nana Bianca, the first start-up studio and certified digital incubator in Italy, together with Fondazione Cassa Risparmio di Firenze (Banca Intesa San Paolo) and Fondazione per la Ricerca e l'Innovazione.

Rifò obtained a 50,000-euro loan from Banca Intesa SP. At the end of the year, it set up a limited liability company with the intention of dealing with sustainable production and began a collaboration with Niccolò Corsi of Mashup Lab, which has a wide and consolidated network of relations with companies in the area. After the personal education of the leader, the initial credit for the business is the second anomaly in Rifò's story. Guaranteeing initial credit to new businesses is a matter of great interest in evaluating the potential of a territory. In post-war Italy, and even before the economic boom of the sixties, many young people started up their businesses by resorting to credit from friends and family.

In Prato, a special mechanism called "intertwined credit" was used for a long time so that young people with brilliant ideas but no money available could use bank loans based on guarantees from friends, family members, or their customers (Dei Ottati, 1994). The way to re-pay these debts with the customers was to work for free using the scheduling of deliveries (the Italian expression "sconto Lavoro"). Many companies in the industrial districts, but above all many companies from Prato, began their history in this way; they are now household names and successful brands in the fashion system. This very important role of local banks, capable of giving credit to ideas and promoting young people, was an undoubted advantage that has generated rapid and intense growth across the whole territory. In more recent years, with the adaptation of the banking system to international agreements and the self-regulation of credit by the Basel Committee that set itself the objective of identifying and establishing common standards, and with the disappearance of local banks and the grouping of banking institutions, everything changed. We can say that, now, there are many more entry barriers for young people and start-uppers. However, there are also valid alternative and very powerful methods of financing, such as crowdfunding campaigns or participation in acceleration programs by business incubators that are linked to leading banking institutions.

Today, knowing how to identify new ways of accessing credit is an advantage that distinguishes successful young entrepreneurs. The Rifò team, whose leader is Niccolò Cipriani, has amply demonstrated its ability to access these innovative forms of financing. In February 2020, the first round of investors brought 30,000 euros of capital to the startup. These are companies that believe in the value of sustainable fashion: the accelerator Nana Bianca, the Fondazione Cassa di Risparmio di Firenze, Encelado, and Economa. In the first months of 2022, there was a new investment round of 1.5 million euros with eight partners. In addition to the previous ones, which confirm that they believe in the potential of Rifò, new investors arrived: GM Investimenti of the historic Miroglio textile family in the Alba area; Filpucci, a leading company in the Prato area in the field of fancy yarns of the Gualtieri family; A/impact; and Abnormal. This funding is intended to expand clothing collections based on regenerated fibers and to strengthen the collection service of used clothing to transform waste into resources. In addition, a part is intended to strengthen e-commerce sales and strengthen the presence of Rifò products in international markets: Germany followed by Switzerland and Austria. Combined with in-depth marketing and management studies, this access to credit represents the second distinctive element of Rifò's compelling story.

On the strength of the funding obtained and with an established network of relationships, Rifò began its real story, and, in June 2019, Martina became the company's first employee in the role of a content creator. The company now has 14 permanent employees, with an average age of 29, who carry out service functions, from marketing to time to market, fashion designers, and communication specialists. We are starting to think of "Rifò" as a real brand, regardless of the product. Production is 100% carried out in the district, in manufacturing companies of various sizes and with various specializations.

In 2019, by the principles of the circular economy, the first jumper regenerated from jeans, 100% Italian, was launched. This is how the collaborative circular economy project "Rethink your jeans" was born, involving consumers in the act of returning old jeans garments that can be used in a regeneration process. From the point of view of product realization, the project is made possible thanks to the collaboration with a company that processes used clothing, Recooper, which also deals with fraying and fiber extraction. There is also a strong partnership with Pinori Filati, an important yarn manufacturer that has been operating in the Prato district for over 50 years. Under the motto "bring denim alive", Pinori Filati has been reinventing yarns from used jeans for over ten years and has produced an iconic yarn for the circular economy. From the point of view of circularity and market supply, the project is made possible thanks to the collaboration with the NaturaSi chain of shops that focuses on sustainable consumption, the fight against food waste, and the protection of biodiversity (119 shops are involved in the project) and has placed cardboard drums in its shops for the collection of clothes. The jeans handed in for recycling give the consumer the opportunity to obtain a discount voucher valid for two years for the purchase of a Rifò garment. The result is a product that is marketed right in Naturasi, online, under the "Oso" brand, a 100% green fashion brand, made by young people for young people.

It is a project in which different realities come together, united by a strong commitment to ethics and sustainability. The collections are designed and produced by social tailors coordinated by Rifò in Italian territory engaged with projects of inclusion and job placement. Rifò works with reliable manufacturers who can provide international certifications. Only vegetable raw materials are used, whose production has a minimal impact on the environment, they are long-lasting, and can be disposed of without producing toxic waste. Natural fibers such as organic cotton, seaweed, and bamboo fabric are used to create environmentally friendly garments. The entire production process of the supply chain is outsourced to specialized process step companies located within a 30km radius of Rifò. With Rifò's philosophy, after the globalization phase, fashion returns to the value of being a production located, localized, and anchored to the territory and its competencies (Figure 15.1).

The last anomaly that distinguishes Rifò from the other companies in Prato is regarding the possibility to be recognized by the final consumer as a brand, thanks above all to the commitment to use new information technologies to reach the consumer in real time. Sustainability and digitalization are the predominant drivers of the company's expansion. The approximately 18,500 items of clothing made during 2021 by Rifò with regenerated materials are 100% "Made in Italy" and are sold in over 100 stores around the world, as well as directly online thanks to a collaboration agreement established with Zalando. It provides free delivery throughout Italy for purchases over 100 euros. All these pieces of information are well highlighted in an extremely articulate "Sustainability Report" for the year 2020 that Rifò has produced to inform all its past and future customers. It has been published in full on the company's website. Reading that report, people learn that last

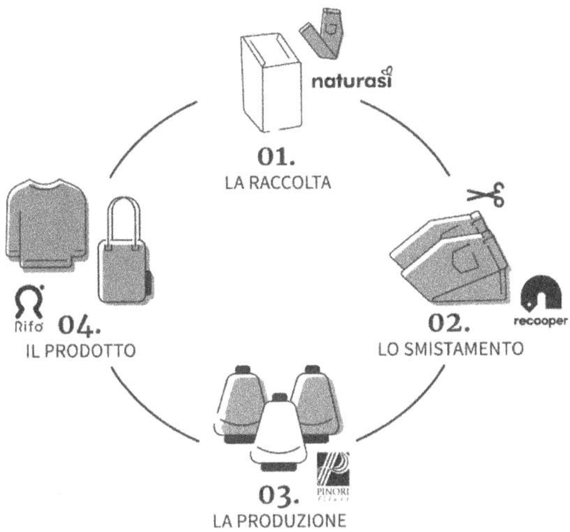

Figure 15.1

year, about 8,500 old cashmere sweaters were transformed into new fibers for Rifò's products (Table 15.1).

The report also mentions the difficult task that is fiber procurement. Wool and cashmere are fibers that fall into the post-consumer category as they are derived from used or discarded clothing from North America and Southern Europe. Cotton, on the other hand, is a pre-consumer category fiber that is derived from industrial waste to be disposed of. It is more difficult to recover cotton from used garments because it is normally found with other man-made fibers in a mixed composition that is mainly synthetic.

The absolute transparency of Rifò's information characterized the company's communication style. For incentivizing the aspects related to marketing communication, Rifò took part in Wem Park Laboratory at PIN, the Prato center of the University of Florence. This allowed the creation of a website in direct contact with supporters and awareness campaigns that have increased the number of young people gravitating toward the brand. There is a large group of approximately 2,000 supporters on Facebook. A "fidelity" program

Table 15.1 Percentage of regenerated and virgin fibers on total production 2020 Rifò (Rifò, 2022)

Regenerated cashmere	62
Regenerated cotton	27
Virgin cotton	05
Virgin wool	03
Regenerated polyester	02
Other regenerated fibers	01
Total	100

will soon be launched to acquire information and keep up to date on the most faithful customers.

On the website, there is a blog updated in real time with all the information about the brand, Rifò's participation in conferences and events (Cipriani, 2020), and useful insights about the theme of sustainability in fashion with various distinctions between natural fibers, animal fibers, and artificial fibers. This is an excellent way to educate the consumer about Rifò's philosophy, which is to produce only what is needed to avoid overproduction.

The appropriate and progressive use of e-commerce has helped the company to overcome the difficult times of the coronavirus pandemic, which practically paralyzed Italian manufacturing that suffered very substantial consequences from the forced closure of stores and sales outlets. There are now almost 15,000 clients, 70% in Italy and 30% abroad. The online sales platform is not the only marketing channel for Rifò's products: there are also connections with 250 stores, 50% in Italy and 50% abroad, mainly in Germany, Austria, and Switzerland.

That's why all Rifò's numbers are marked positive (employees, turnover, etc.), even during the pandemic. The establishment of the Rifò brand came during the 2021 Christmas Holidays when Intesa San Paolo banking group, which had financed the start-up a few years earlier, decided to donate to its consultants all over Italy a 100% recycled cashmere scarf made by Rifò: 8,000 scarves were produced for this new prominent customer.

This direct relationship with the evolved consumer, sensitive to respect for the environment and people's rights, represents another distinctive feature of Rifò's brand. The success of the company shows us that the road taken is the right one, compared to the average of companies in the Prato district, used to working continuously without necessarily keeping customers and consumers informed. Rifò, on the other hand, finds itself in the embarrassment of having to grow in size but at the same time having to economize on production in order not to fall into the trap of overproduction. This paradox is experienced by the leader Niccolò Cipriani with the commitment of those who work as if they were "walking on a high wire". Certainly, it will be possible to contain this paradox as long as production quantities are contained. But the company's philosophy is inspired by the "Less is more" motto.

Discussion and conclusion

In 2021, the European apparel and textile confederation Euratex (2022) realized a comparative study to establish the sectoral skill strategy for textile, clothing, and leather, projecting the situation of the industry in 2030. They developed five scenarios to establish a set of recommendations and strategies for the stakeholders – education, industry, and policymakers. According to that potential reality, Rifò could be one of the main characters of the medium scenario, called "Renaissance of the craft", in which the company will combine heritage with technological developments for a range of goods of different price levels produced locally. The scenario considers the change in consumer behaviors, which have become more conscious and sustainable, giving rise to local models of recycling based on traditional concepts that are enhanced by technology (Uomo, 2022). In this scenario, the main characteristic that moves the new consumer is a great awareness of sustainability and circular economy. This is exactly what Rifò is doing now with its transparent, detailed, and comprehensive marketing strategy.

Rifò's line also includes attention to product packaging and distribution. All packaging is sustainable and uses recycled and recyclable materials such as cardboard. However, in the company's plans, there is a desire to replace cardboard with packaging made directly from recycled fabric from the Prato district. In addition, the company proposes a repacking service, which reuses the external package (RePack, 2022).

For all these reasons Rifò, since its establishment, has participated in all editions of the "Fashion Revolution Week", a very important annual event for sustainable and ethical fashion. Organized by Fashion Revolution is a global non-profit present in over 100 countries in the world, founded in 2013 after the tragic events of the Rana Plaza in Savar, Bangladesh, where thousands of people lost their lives in precarious working conditions for the collapse of an old building used as a manufacturing factory. They were all working for the world's top fashion brands. Fashion Revolution's annual event aims to make consumers aware of many untold stories about manufacturing processes and hopes to involve international fashion brands in raising awareness of sustainability.

Rifò was also present at the first Fashion Revolution week, organized in Turin in 2018, where the motto was "Be curious. Find out. Do something".

In the 2022 edition, which will take place, as every year, in the last days of April in memory of the tragic events, there will be a guided tour of the companies in the Prato district that normally collaborate with Rifò to illustrate to a wide audience the concept of the circular economy through a project called "Open Factories".

The company Rifò has received an honorable mention in the ninth edition of the "Premio Santo Stefano per il Lavoro", an award strongly desired by the local institutions that, every year, give a certificate to some deserving companies that are ethically irreproachable and environmentally friendly. The motivation for Rifò was based on its project of enhancing the circular economy, perfectly eco-sustainable, according to the ancient tradition of reuse that has made the city of Prato great over the years.

One of the last characteristics of Rifò consists of their commitment to professional training. Rifò is the main actor in a training project based on the "cenciaiolo" figure. The project involves various local actors for good causes such as teaching people who have had difficulties with work and giving them new job opportunities. As usual, some leading companies of

Prato joined Rifò and financed the project: Beste, Filpucci, Lanificio Mario Bellucci, Milior, and M&A joined with a total amount of 10,000 euros. Rifò itself financed the project with a further 15,000 euros. The municipality of Prato, the artisan association Cna, Astri Consortium, Fil (education and training office), Consorzio Detox, and Opera Santa Rita are also partners of the project, which is intended for vulnerable subjects such as asylum seekers or victims of labor exploitation. This new initiative marks a further acceleration in Rifò's ecological strategy which has chosen to strengthen ethical sustainability on top of environmental sustainability. "Nei nostri panni. Cenciaioli si diventa" is the funny name of the project that plays with the meaning of the words: "In our shoes, to become cenciaiolo". It is a symbolic commitment since training courses have been developed for only five people, which will be hosted by historic rags sorting companies. But the meaning deserves great praise because some unfortunate foreigners are ennobled in the Prato district and because they try to solve a real problem for the local industry: the need for a valid generational change in the key areas of the supply chain. If this project leads to good results quickly, there will be a possibility to repeat the experience, thinking of other professions whose absence has been felt in recent times: spinners and weavers, for example.

The company also pays great attention to social issues. With the "2loveprato" campaign, Rifò has allocated two euros for each garment sold to some non-profit local associations reaching more than 6,000 euros in donations in 2020. A significant part of these donations went to Santo Stefano hospital in Prato for the purchase of masks and other necessities caused by the pandemic.

In 2020, the new Rifò headquarters were inaugurated, a 750 square meter co-working space on two levels where it is possible to visit the collection and bring back used clothes to be put into the production cycle. A recent agreement with Muji shops in Milan has enabled the company to expand its collection points in Italy (Muji, 2022).

Since 2020, Rifò has been certified as a B Corporation. It means that it is a company that generates a positive impact on the environment, respect of social standards, responsibility, and transparency.

Rifò is an artisan company associated with CNA Toscana Centro that has decided to join the extraordinary Astri Consortium, a transversal group of more than 130 companies born in 2000 and located in Prato: ferrymen to old rag-and-bone men, dealers, finishing, wool mills, and dyeing groups. They make the circular economy a daily commitment.

In the future, Rifò is thinking about a totally sustainable look that goes from a series of products to packaging and communication via App. In this way, Rifò proves to be a very modern company, with strong roots in the Prato district but with great dedication to the digital economy. But there is also a dream that, with recent funding, could come true: a series of innovative textile products for the home furnishing sector. Nicolò Cipriani

Figure 15.2

represents an authentic Tuscan entrepreneur, an innovator that looks ahead with the awareness of his own culture. That is exactly what we understand by "Tuscany is a magical landscape where everything around is kind; everything is both ancient and new" (Curzio Malaparte) (Figure 15.2).

References

Becattini, G. (2001, January 1). *Caterpillar and butterfly*. Mondadori Education.

Becattini, G., Bellandi, M., Del Ottati, G., & Sforzi, F. (2003). *From industrial districts to local development*. Cheltenham, UK: Edward Elgar Publishing.

Bettiza, S., & Patruno, P. (2020, December 16). *Prato: The Italian town turning rags into new clothes*. Retrieved from https://www.bbc.co.uk/news/av/world-europe-55267992

Bevacqua, R., Nguyen, D., & Lambert, D. (2021, November). Reimagining Vietnam's microfinance sector: Recommendations for institutional and legal reform. Working Paper no. 20. *Asian Development Bank*. http://dx.doi.org/10.22617/WPS210385-2

Cipriani, N. (2020). *Circular Fashion: ritorno alle emozioni*. Retrieved from https://www.ted.com/talks/niccolo_cipriani_circular_fashion_ritorno_alle_emozioni

Confindustria Toscana Nord. (2022). Retrieved from https://www.confindustria.toscana.it/?doing_wp_cron=1659109628.3289508819580078125000

Dei Ottati, G. (1994). Trust, interlinking transactions and credit in the industrial district. *Cambridge Journal of Economics*, *18*(6), 524–546.

Euratex. (2022). *The voice of the European apparel and textile industry*. Retrieved from https://euratex.eu/

Laurenti, M., & Trentin, M. (2021). *Ecosistema urbano: Rapporto sulle performance ambientali delle città 2021.* Retrieved from https://www.legambiente.it/wp-content/uploads/2021/11/EcosistemaUrbano2021.pdf

Muji. (2022). *Muji.* Retrieved from www.muji.com

Pucker, K. (2022, January). *The Myth of Sustainable Fashion.* Retrieved from https://hbr.org/2022/01/the-myth-of-sustainable-fashion

RePack. (2022). *Gentle on the planet. Tough on waste.* Retrieved from www.originalrepack.com

Rifò. (2022). *Rifò: Circular Fashion Made in Italy.* Retrieved from www.rifo-lab.com

Uomo, P. (2022, January 12). *Il Futuro dell'industria della Moda.* Retrieved from https://www.pin.unifi.it/eventi/879-12-gennaio-il-futuro-dell-industria-moda-innovazioni-scenari-strategie-e-competenze-nel-tessile-abbigliamento-pelle-calzatura

16 How to Combine Sustainability and Authenticity in Luxury Brands

An Insight into the Case of La Milanesa

Silvia Ranfagni[1] *and Giada Salvietti*[2]
[1]Università degli Studi di Firenze
[2]Università degli Studi di Parma

Introduction

In recent years, sustainable luxury, especially in the fashion domain, has become increasingly valued and demanded by consumers (Amatulli, De Angelis, Korschun, & Romani, 2018). It has also been one of the key drivers for the long-term success of brands (De Angelis, Adıgüzel, & Amatulli, 2017). Its importance is also stressed in McKinsey's 2022 State of Fashion report, which states that advances in sustainability will be the sector's biggest opportunity for recovery and renowned growth in the wake of the COVID-19 pandemic.

Worth noting, and as pointed out by Athwal et al. (2019), the concept of "sustainability" has struggled to be clearly declined within the luxury context. Sustainable luxury comprises "the scope of design, production and consumption that is environmentally or ethically conscious (...) and oriented towards correcting various perceived wrongs within the luxury industry" (2019, p. 406) As such, luxury brands have engaged in a wide variety of sustainable initiatives that they take on while trying not to alter their brand values. It is therefore useful for them to understand how to convey sustainability to their customers while preserving their luxury brand identity. More specifically, authenticity is turning out to be a valuable competitive lever (Beverland, 2005). For sustainable luxury brands, it can imply credibility of their sustainable actions through brand consistency built around brand attributes amongst which the high quality of the product stands out (Napoli, Dickinson-Delaporte, & Beverland, 2016).

Understanding how brand authenticity intertwines with sustainability is intriguing. This means shedding light on how brand authenticity can activate a virtuous process that fuels brand sustainability and vice-versa. The effect that this process can generate is twofold: (1) it contributes to social well-being, and (2) it reinforces the consumer's brand perception.

DOI: 10.4324/9781003305095-20

In this chapter, the relations between brand authenticity and sustainability are explored through the case study of La Milanesa, an Italian sustainable luxury start-up, which combines the recovery of materials and artisanal competencies from the past with ethical initiatives targeting women in distress. The case study illustrates how an environmental and social sustainability can interact and integrate with brand authenticity pursued above all through the attributes of the perceived brand heritage and the perceived product quality (Rose et al., 2016).

Sustainability and brand authenticity as cornerstones of luxury brands

The concept of luxury is complex and multifaceted (Heine, 2012). Luxury is value: the offer of a luxury brand consists of very expensive goods and excellent quality. Luxury is culture: luxury brands embed ways of living, values, and ethical issues. Luxury is also art: gifted designers and manufacturers are involved in creating products of luxury brands. Finally, luxury is exclusivity: luxury brands are perceived as rare, as something that only a few people can possess (Kapferer, 2015). Today, luxury brands are trying to go beyond these connotations and increase their perceived value among consumers by pursuing the traits of sustainability and authenticity. Both are seen as traits that enable luxury brands to differentiate and increase their competitiveness in the global markets.

Sustainability and luxury

Due to appearing to be opposites, sustainability and luxury seem to be two concepts that cannot be integrated (Achabou & Dekhili, 2013). Luxury is something inessential, superfluous, exclusive, and ostentatious: it is a personal object of desire. Since the degree of luxury consumers ascribe to that object depends on how much they consider it a luxury product, luxury is also a subjective construct. Conversely, sustainability is something indispensable: it is linked to the conservation of common goods. Moreover, since sustainability translates into behaviors which, if implemented, have a social impact, it is an ideological and collective phenomenon.

Despite these differences, scholars show how, in reality, sustainability in its environmental form and luxury can relate to each other via the features of durability and rarity that define both of them (Kapferer, 2012). The conservation of natural resources is the main objective of environmental sustainability. Similarly, luxury has an everlasting existence and does not pass as fashion changes (Hoffman & Coste-Manière, 2012). Luxury is also a rarity (Ricca & Robins, 2012): its products are unique. The value of its products depends as much on the use of rare craftsmanship as on the use of rare resources (skins, leather, pearls, etc.). By preserving the environment, environmental sustainability preserves these resources and their rarity. Therefore, while it contributes to generating luxury perceived value due to being durable over time, luxury limits the use of natural resources contributing to environmental sustainability (Winston, 2016).

If it is environmental, sustainability induces companies to respect the environment by activating an efficient use of natural resources. However, as Seidman points out, "sustainability is about more than our relationship with the environment: it is about our relationship with ourselves, our communities, and our institutions" (2007, p. 58). Sustainable behaviors can be aimed at preserving certain territorial resources including the culture, traditions, and values of local communities. Such behaviors connote another form of sustainability that luxury companies can pursue, namely cultural sustainability.

Both environmental and cultural sustainability can combine with another form of sustainability, the social one. Based on actions aimed at promoting an egalitarian society, it contributes to reducing poverty and disparity in the access of resources for consumption and unfair working conditions (Closs, Speier, & Meacham, 2011). Regardless of the type of sustainability, each sustainable action is more likely to be successful when sustainability is embedded in the firm's ideology, and when it fosters a business philosophy forming on the basis of emotionally charged beliefs, values, and norms that bind people together (Trice & Beyer, 1993).

Many global fashion companies are mainly addressing environmental sustainability by developing eco-friendly product lines (e.g., Armani), seeking sustainable sourcing and manufacturing (e.g., Vivienne Westwood; Gucci's "fur-free" initiative), and fueling dedicated funds (e.g., LVMH's LIFE project for supporting biodiversity and fighting against climate change). However, recently, luxury brands have become increasingly more socially and ethically committed, resulting in having to balance the issue of positively contributing to social causes while maintaining the quality, skill, and exclusivity of their products (Kunz, May, & Schmidt, 2020; Osburg, Davies, Yoganathan, & McLeay, 2020). To achieve this, on the one hand, brands have focused on the development of internal capabilities, promoting the preservation of unique skills and competences. And on the other, they have undertaken community development projects, supporting one or more social causes, either directly (e.g., donations, subscriptions) or indirectly (e.g., social media campaigns, partnerships).

Authenticity and luxury

Authenticity is inevitably a part of luxury. Since luxury is "true" when not counterfeit, the authenticity that characterizes it is "pure" or "indexical" (Grayson & Martinec, 2004), that is, it can be found in something that is believed to be the original and real thing. But authenticity defining luxury can also be "iconic" (Grayson & Martinec, 2004): it is acknowledged in luxury brands connoted by attributes that are not real but stylized and evocative of places, myths, and historical periods. Thus, it can be found in a blended reality consisting of a mix of both real and fantasy elements (Rose & Wood,

2005). This is because authenticity is also a socially and personally based construct stemming from self-negotiating acts consumers implement to reveal their true self (Arnould & Price, 2003).

Authentic brands are a "form of expressive culture no different in principle from films and television programs, or rock bands" (Holt, 2002, p. 87): consumers dialogue with them, establishing an almost intimate personal relationship "as useful ingredients to produce the self as one chooses" (Holt, 2002, p. 81). Companies can build a perceived brand authenticity by implementing communicative actions with the aim of creating a brand aura that "pertains to the presence of a powerful sense of authenticity that original works of art exude" (Brown, Kozinets, & Sherry, 2003, p. 24), and that expresses a self-brand authentication around a brand's core values (Postrel, 2003). According to Beverland (2006, 2009), the self-authenticating brand attributes which reveal self-consistency are quality commitment, pedigree, stylistic consistency, heritage, relationship with traditional production practices, and territories.

While quality and pedigree are indexical cues, offering guarantees in terms of product genuineness (2006), the other attributes are also iconic cues, fostering a consumer's self-authentication through connections with place and time.

Among the traditional production practices, handcrafted productions are characterized by feeding a consumer's self-authentication via connections to moral personal values. It is therefore no coincidence that attributes such as quality, heritage and craftsmanship are at the basis of brand authenticity that luxury brands like Chanel, Christian Dior, Prada, and Ferragamo build (Turunen & Laaksonen, 2011; Watanabe & Horiuchi, 2021).

Authenticity, however, does not merely translate to self-consistency pursued over time and conveyed through certain attributes. In this respect, as pointed out by Bishop (2013), authenticity can be seen as a self-consistency pursued over the years by interacting with the environment and time. More specifically, authentic individuals act in response to a purpose of being, but to quote philosopher Heiddeger (1962), one of the most outstanding scholars on the subject of authenticity, they are not only "das Ein", that is, beings which relate to their ethical values but also "das-Ein-in-der-Welt": they immerse themselves in the environment, inhabit it and project themselves into it. They embed the environment in their beliefs and actions.

This is not so much individually based as a collectively based perspective of authenticity can be found in some of Beverland's studies. It emerges that, behind luxury wine brands, there are not only brand attributes that express their brand authenticity. Underlying these brands are also entities that pursue their self-consistency, behaving as if they were authentic individuals. They define themselves and their consistency over time by embedding a "terroir" as a synthesis not only of physical aspects (climate, soil, terrain) but also of territorial cultures (Chartes et al., 2017). These cultures characterize their wine production.

A collectively based perspective of authenticity concentrates not so much on how self-consistency can be individually pursued and expressed to the market, but on how it is ethically constructed through interaction with the environment and its values and cultures (Ranfagni, 2022). Luxury fashion brands can also be explored according to this prospective. They can embed ways of living developed by a community and passed down from generation to generation, including customs, practices, places, objects, and artistic expressions. In other words, they pursue brand consistency by taking care of cultural heritage. Defined as a composite of history, coherence, and continuity of a group or society's distinguishing characteristics (Arantes, 2007), a cultural heritage makes up their brand identity and is found as a distinctive element in their collections. Ferragamo is renowned for embodying the manufacturing practices typical of the handicraft productions of the city of Florence (Carù, Ostillio, & Leone, 2017), where the company was born and has its headquarters. In the same way, Chanel and Christian Dior evolved by incorporating the elegance typical of the French culture of luxury (Mendes & Rees-Roberts, 2015). A brand that builds its brand consistency by interacting with the environment also interacts with time. Authentic beings explore the past to understand why they think and behave the way they do; and their past associations emerge as enmeshed in connection with others. It is thanks to this set of connections that just like a brand, an authentic being can also realize how it evolves, what its aspirations are, and how these can influence its interactions with consumer targets.

It is worth investigating how sustainability and authenticity can interact with each other within the luxury brands. Brand authenticity, understood as self-consistency, can make certain sustainability actions more credible. Brand authenticity as an embedding of self-consistency can foster a cultural sustainability by preserving collective resources (terroir, traditions, values), thus contributing to the collective well-being. It is more difficult to prefigure how sustainability can contribute to brand authenticity. The fact that sustainable actions are oriented toward preserving natural and rare resources used in luxury productions leads us to believe that they can contribute to creating an indexical brand authenticity and making the product really authentic. How then sustainability in more detail combines with the brand authenticity's attributes is an issue that needs investigating. Our objective is to study how brand authenticity and sustainability interact through the case study of La Milanesa, a luxury Italian start-up emblematic for its socially sustainable behavior and its efforts to pursue brand authenticity mainly through the recovery of artisanal manufacturing techniques from the past.

Methodology

From a methodological point of view, we tried to answer the research questions through the case study of La Milanesa (Yin, 1981), a family-run enterprise in Milan (Northern Italy), that produces luxury handcrafted bags and accessories reflecting traditions of a local artisanal tradition. The case was constructed through secondary data collection (Stewart & Kamins, 1993), netnographic analysis of online communities, and in-depth interviews.

Secondary data included narrations extracted from the company website (lamilanesa.it) and social media pages, and interviews given by the company's founder in national newspapers and at fashion events. The netnographic analysis focused on online communities (Kozinets, 2015), the members of which were customers who talked about their relationships with the company and its products. The interviews (a total of two lasting no more than three hours), which involved the marketing consultant and the owner of the company (Eisenhardt & Graebner, 2007), investigated the following aspects: (a) the company's history and market positioning, (b) sustainability behaviors and the attributes of brand authenticity, (c) the interaction basis bridging sustainability and brand authenticity, and (d) the marketing policies guiding the company's interactions with consumers. In identifying the forms of sustainability and how they are combined with brand authenticity, we shed light on how combinations of sustainability and brand authenticity can act as the engine of the company's growth process in Italy and on international markets.

The case of "La Milanesa"

Company origin and entrepreneurial passion

Many luxury companies have emerged in the last few years based on new sustainable business models that aim to enhance their diversity and authenticity. La Milanesa is one of these. Founded in Milan in 2018, the company's quest for authenticity is intertwined with attention to sustainability. Its founder Cinzia Macchi went through a difficult period due to a serious disease that left its mark, after having worked for years as a project manager in the vocational training sector. After overcoming her illness, she decided to give reign to her desire to "create something for the others" by organizing concrete charitable initiatives. La Milanesa was founded out of her intention to help women in need combined with her passion for fashion and "artisanal creativity". The business idea in fact originated when, upon visiting a friend's antiques shop, she saw an old wool blanket made with the traditional crocheting technique and decided to reuse it for crafting modern luxury bags. Crocheting is a very old sewing technique used in households to produce woolen items for personal use, much appreciated by Cinzia ever since she was young. She chose the city of Milan, and in particular the "5 Vie" district, as the company's headquarters, as it is the oldest area in the center of the city where craftsmen in their workshops make their products using old artisan techniques.

Socially sustainable projects and the recovery of artisan manufacturing techniques

La Milanesa is a family-run business that uses old crocheting techniques to produce blanket squares used to create innovative bags designed for the luxury markets. A year after being founded, the company was able to participate in a particularly relevant event, the "White Milano", a contemporary fashion show held annually during the Milano Fashion Week. This acted as a springboard for La Milanesa's business development: the crocheted bag concept was praised by important international buyers who ordered 500, a larger quantity than the company was able to produce at the time.

In order to meet this request, Cinzia searched for a network of suppliers of crocheted blankets squares. All those she identified corresponded to particular organizations, including healthcare centers and nursing homes where the elderly with crocheting know-how became involved in the La Milanesa's manufacturing process. Their engagement generates a dual positive social effect. Firstly, it provides the elderly who are deprived of social stimuli, with a sense of renowned dignity and utility. Secondly, it keeps them mentally active. In this regard, neurologists have discovered that crocheting is good for health as it helps prevent neurovegetative illnesses such as Alzheimer's and Parkinson's.

Other suppliers of crochet-square blankets are organizations that support socially marginalized women (either unemployed or in distress). La Milanesa is very active in this sector. As Cinzia points out, it is a brand "from a woman for women". As part of this mission, the company has collaborated extensively with "Fare Per Bene Onlus", an association that supports female victims of domestic violence and abuse, and it has taken part in the "Fabbricatori di Sogni" project. Since September 2021, with the financial support of banks and ONGs, it has been promoting the social reintegration into the labor market of women victims of violence through training courses aimed at teaching how to crochet. The six-month training course is aimed at assisting these women during their recovery, while also providing psychological and economic support. Some of those who finished the project have been engaged as external workers in the La Milanesa bag production.

Two clarifications are needed here: (1) the company's profits are partly or entirely devolved to the organizations acting as suppliers, and (2) all the women involved in the production of crochet blanket squares have complete freedom in the choice of colors and patterns. In giving free reign to their own creativity, they create original and unique crochet squares. Once received, these are disassembled by the company's designers and rearranged in a different order to create new esthetic solutions and bags perceived as "one of a kind" in the season's collection.

La Milanesa also supports other social causes in developing dedicated capsule collections. In this respect, it is worth mentioning La Milanesa's social commitment to a project destined for children in pediatric units. Conceived by Cinzia, it involved printing a book telling the life history of her friend, Brother Giulio Savoldi, in the form of a tale that was sold with a shopping bag to raise funds. Similar initiatives concern projects aimed at supporting The Children for Peace, an international NGO that helps HIV-positive children in third-world countries. La Milanesa's social commitment was very active during the COVID pandemic when it collaborated with the San Donato

Foundation – an Italian NGO promoting scientific research to cure and prevent cardiovascular diseases through fundraising with the development and sale of bag charms.

A sustainability bridging with brand authenticity

The crocheted bag is La Milanesa's most iconic product and at the core of its offer. Social projects revolve around its production, allowing La Milanesa to preserve a production technique (crocheting) inherited from the past. This technique, if evoked in the brand communication, helps nourish the brand authenticity via the perceived attributes of the brand heritage. Brand authenticity derives from sustainability which, at La Milanesa, is both a social and an environmental commitment.

The crocheted bag itself is created by adapting the crochet blanket squares on a structure which, in line with the principles of the circular economy, is made with natural and recycled raw materials. They use jute and artificial fibers made of recycled plastic bottles and leather has been banished and replaced entirely with "gomau", an innovative material resembling suede made of cardboard and recycled plastic. Even the packaging of the bags purchased by consumers, both offline and online, is made of cardboard and recycled paper. To be perceived as unique, it can be enhanced with a spray of a fresh perfume.

Just as all the La Milanesa bags are certified as sustainable according to the European regulations, the company itself has also been declared "zero-impact" in line with the United Nations directives. In creating its bags, in addition to the crocheted squares, La Milanesa also uses raw materials that are territorially rooted and therefore part of a local culture. Since they are no longer used in production processes, they are resources that tend to become extinct and increasingly scarce. One example of such materials is the wool of La Garfagnana that La Milanesa uses in its productions. La Garfagnana is a territory in Tuscany (Italy), and its local wool was used by households in the past to make hand-knitted sweaters.

It follows that at La Milanesa's, brand authenticity exists through perceived brand heritage deriving from: (a) reviving manufacturing techniques of the past (crocheting), and (b) valorizing raw materials as an expression of cultural traditions. Through point (a), La Milanesa promotes social sustainability aimed at generating the social integration of women in difficulty, thus contributing to the collective well-being. Through point and (b), La Milanesa also promotes territorial integration aimed at preserving the local culture and correlated natural resources. Social sustainability actions are taken by recovering a manufacturing technique, which is an expression of local traditions. At La Milanesa, social sustainability also helps foster a cultural sustainability. It is a brand that combines sustainability with the recovery of a cultural heritage.

Socially and environmentally sustainable, La Milanesa exploits manufacturing traditions for creating innovative bags. More specifically, its bags are bearers of a past that resides in a modern concept of a product destined for a sustainable luxury market. The resulting effect is that of a sustainable brand filled with a nostalgic appeal. This effect is amplified by the image characterizing the city, Milan, where La Milanesa is located. Milan is modern, dynamic, and cosmopolitan, and one of the centers of the fashion industry. In fact, the word "Milano" is explicitly evoked in the brand name. The choice of "La Milanesa" as a brand name reflects the strong linkage Cinzia has with this city. Thanks to Milan, she had the opportunity to start a new life as an entrepreneur, expressing her passion for craftsmanship and fashion, igniting her entrepreneurial intuition which led her to create a new luxury bag for women.

Given its medium-high market positioning, the consumer targets are women who have adequate purchasing power and are attracted by the nostalgia the brand emits. Cinzia is aware that the bag produced by La Milanesa is the "extra bag that women can treat themselves to, the one that complements the others", a unique object that can both delight and surprise women because of its social and cultural meaning. However, she states that sometimes she feels "a midget" compared to other luxury and fashion brands. Despite her modesty, it is undeniable that La Milanesa has been able to trigger a new fashion trend; this is proven by the many crocheted bag replicas (so-called Granny bags) produced by improvised artisans and commercialized online at affordable prices.

Company organization, distribution, and communication choices

Today, La Milanesa has a simple but well-defined organizational structure. The company outsources all the components of the bags in the collection. They are assembled within the workshop by designers who work in close contact with the owner. According to the company organization chart, Cinzia supervises a marketing director, a commercial director, and an administrative director in managing their respective functions.

In terms of distribution, La Milanesa had initially planned to sell its bags in offline multi-brand stores in partnership with fashion retailers. However, upon carrying out business during the first lockdown period (March 2020) due to COVID-19 pandemic, it had to change its distribution strategy. It thus decided to promote its first collection on social networks and to launch it on the market through e-commerce and luxury e-tailers, such as Yoox and Farfetch. It anticipated the digital development La Milanesa would inevitably need and had positive effects in terms of sales and a growing number of social media followers. Today, the brand counts around 70,000 and 12,000 followers on Instagram and Facebook, respectively.

Only recently has La Milanesa launched the openings of offline flagship stores, mostly located in touristic destinations. The first store was opened in Milan (Italy) and the second in Marbella (Spain), followed by two pop-up stores in Italy, specifically in Noto in July and Bologna in September 2021.

Despite its recent debut, the active engagement of the brand on the social networks has attracted fashion experts: La Milanesa's bags have been featured in international magazines such as Vanity Fair, Vogue, and Cosmopolitan. The brand is strong in the European markets while also increasing its sales in the Middle East and Asian markets which are mature with respect to the luxury sector (e.g., Japan).

In terms of communication policies, La Milanesa prefers advertising focused on the celebration of conscious lifestyles and authentic values. Its style is informal and direct while staying personal and intimate. The social media accounts are the most widespread means of communication and their content is edited directly by the owner. They tell the stories of the brand, emphasizing its social commitment and continuous quest to create innovative bags by embedding past memories. In addition to transmitting energy and positivity to consumers, these stories tend to make people emotional and excited, and therefore strengthen brand perception around the social and cultural brand benefits. The social media posts are usually integrated with photos or videos showing certain initiatives, such as the crochet technique's training sessions, which provide evidence of the brand's social commitment.

Discussion

La Milanesa is a sustainable luxury company, basing its product on environmental sustainability. This is reflected in all its collections, which are made using natural or recycled materials. Environmental sustainability is combined with social sustainability, pursued through projects aimed at socially reintegrating women living in marginalized conditions.

But La Milanesa's history also shows that it integrates cultural sustainability. In its production, it uses raw materials (e.g., wool) rooted in the local territory as an expression of local values and traditions. These are raw materials that no longer have an economic purpose. By using them to cover the bags it produces, the company reduces the risk of their extinction while preserving the intangible heritage of the local culture they embody. This heritage is collective: it belongs to everyone without distinction. However, the local culture that La Milanesa preserves can also be found in the use of artisanal production techniques. The company deserves credit for having relaunched crocheting as an ancient production technique through social sustainability actions. Precisely because of the effects they produce in terms not so much of social integration as of protection of local cultures, they in turn act as a means of cultural sustainability.

At La Milanesa, environmental sustainability is integrated with the other two forms of sustainability. By nurturing product rarity through actions aimed at conserving natural resources (Dekhili, Achabou, & Alharbi, 2019; Wang, Sung, & Phau, 2021), environmental sustainability contributes to the perception of product quality. Social sustainability and cultural sustainability combined with the construction of a perceived brand heritage, which, together with perceived brand quality, act as the basis of brand authenticity. Specifically, this case shows how (1) a perceived brand heritage pursued through the recovery of past production traditions (crocheting) interacts with social sustainability actions aimed at integrating socially marginalized women and is based on the transfer of certain manufacturing skills, meaning brand heritage feeds on social sustainability and vice-versa, and (2) a cultural sustainability aimed at favoring the preservation of local traditions and pursued through the use of territorially rooted raw materials interfaces with a perceived brand heritage, meaning brand heritage feeds on cultural sustainability and vice-versa.

The use of artisan techniques and natural resources evocative of a local culture increases product rarity and therefore also increases the perception of product quality. It follows that the perceived brand heritage nurtured by social sustainability and cultural sustainability strengthens brand authenticity in terms of higher perceived product quality. Moreover, the preservation of natural resources residing in a local area that cultural sustainability activates increases the perception of the company's commitment to environmental sustainability.

Since perceived brand heritage derives from both social sustainability and cultural sustainability, by nurturing it, La Milanesa contributes to generating social welfare in terms of social integration (social sustainability) and territorial integration (cultural sustainability). This case shows how perceived brand heritage acts as a bridge between social sustainability and cultural sustainability, and luxury (see Figure 16.1). More precisely, it brings them into dialogue with the traits of rarity and durability of luxury (Kapferer, 2010): actions in favor of social integration and territorial integration that recover the past (productive or cultural) contribute to creating a timeless brand (durability) and a unique brand (rarity).

La Milanesa is a start-up that bases its brand authenticity on brand consistency built around the brand values of quality and brand heritage (Beverland, 2006). Such brand consistency is created by acting from a collective rather than an individual perspective (Vannini & Williams, 2016). It is built by

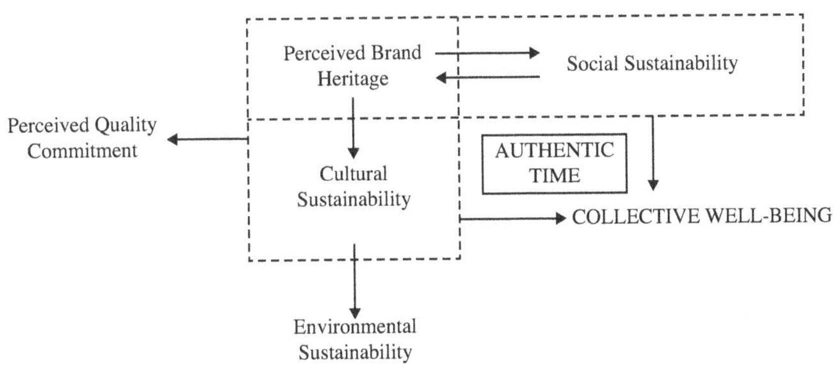

Figure 16.1 The interface of brand authenticity and sustainability in La Milanesas.

embedding (a) manufacturing traditions (crocheting) through social sustainability actions, and (b) local traditions (natural resources) through cultural sustainability actions. Both (a) and (b) become part of the product of La Milanesa, and they define it.

Its brand heritage is not an iconic or indexical trait expressive of self-consistency. It is a trait that conceals an embedded self-consistency; therefore, it connotes an ethically authentic brand. It is not so much an iconic cue as an indexical cue. In pursuing an embedding self-consistency, the brand lives an authentic time (Bergson, 1960), i.e., it lives the past in the present. It actualizes it in everyday life and uses it as a guide for future choices. The past (of artisan production and local traditions) lives again in the modernity of La Milanesa bags and helps to dictate the production guidelines to be pursued in the future. Tradition and innovation combine in a product charged with a nostalgic effect.

The authentic time in which the brand seems to be immersed is the same time that the owner lives in. Cinzia had vivid memories of crocheting work and decided to relaunch it. In doing so, she lives her past in the present, of when she was young and when certain production techniques were widespread. This dimension of inner time came to Cinzia at the end of a particularly difficult period of her life which led her to be more sensitive to certain social issues. It drives her entrepreneurial passion. Authentic time transferred to the brand makes it able to combine present and past by making communication and distribution choices, also innovative and based on digital technologies. The authentic brand that interacts with sustainability can therefore use digital technologies to nurture and transfer an embedded self-consistency. It is, in our opinion, the study of self-consistency in its interaction in time and environment (Beverland, 2014) through new digital technologies that open up new keys to understanding the relationship between sustainability and brand authenticity.

At this point of the research, it becomes interesting to reflect on how the company can employ "brand authenticity" (emerging from a brand-embedded self-consistency) to reinforce a socially and culturally sustainable brand and vice-versa. La Milanesa shows how an environmentally sustainable brand can reinforce brand authenticity via perceived quality and vice-versa. It also provides evidence on how a heritage, socially sustainable, and culturally sustainable brand can symbiotically enhance their credibility.

Owning a heritage brand means being linked to the past (traditions, values, culture) and taking action to preserve it. Just as the past that the brand embeds is a collective good, so too is the well-being derived from actions aimed at pursuing social integration. In order to create a connection between brand heritage and social sustainability, it makes sense to stress the dimension of brand-embedded self-consistency, i.e., to communicate the brand as an entity which, living in history, makes the past a resource that it maintains as a collective good by taking on a social commitment. To make brand heritage and cultural sustainability connective, it is necessary instead to stress the brand's link with traditions, values, and culture as ingredients of the past that it preserves. If there are natural resources (like wool) underlying these ingredients, communicating the link between natural resources that the brand preserves as a result of cultural heritage preservation, makes brand heritage and environmental sustainability interact.

In short, it emerges that 1) environmental sustainability feeds brand authenticity through the development of a perceived product quality, and 2) authenticity can be fed through: a) the dialogue between social sustainability and brand heritage triggered by a brand showing its social commitment to preserving the past as a source of collective well-being, b) the dialogue between cultural sustainability and brand heritage triggered by a brand showing its connection to a preserving cultural heritage, and c) the dialogue between environmental sustainability and brand heritage triggered by a brand showing its connection to preserving natural resources through the preservation of a cultural heritage.

Conclusion

La Milanesa has proven to be an emblematic case study, showing how sustainability and authenticity can interact. Both perceived brand quality and perceived brand heritage have emerged as possible points that connect brand authenticity deriving from an embedded self-consistency and sustainability. Authenticity is a complex construct. It has an individual dimension (self-consistency) and a collective dimension (embedded self-consistency). Investigating in greater detail how these two dimensions of authenticity interact with sustainability in their different forms (environmental, social, and cultural) would be very intriguing. In this sense, it would also be worthwhile to investigate how the use of digital marketing tools (social networks, e-commerce, etc.), as a new basis for creating value for consumers, is combined with brand authenticity and in turn with sustainability. It is on these topics that we will try to continue our research, aware that today, at a time when philosophers and sociologists are debating digital humanism, it is increasingly more important to understand how the human factor can maintain its centrality with respect to the use of technology as an effect of modernity. Questioning how to be ethically authentic through sustainable choices could be a way to understand how an entrepreneur can evolve with technology without bowing to it. All this could serve to identify a new entrepreneurial species that combines a kind of homo sapiens and homo technologicus.

References

Achabou, M. A., & Dekhili, S. (2013). Luxury and sustainable development: Is there a match? *Journal of Business Research*, *66*(10), 1896–1903.

Amatulli, C., De Angelis, M., Korschun, D., & Romani, S. (2018). Consumers' perceptions of luxury brands' CSR initiatives: An investigation of the role of status and conspicuous consumption. *Journal of Cleaner Production*, *194*, 277–287.

Arantes, A. A. (2007). Diversity, heritage and cultural politics. *Theory, Culture & Society, 24*(7–8), 290–296.

Arnould, E. J., & Price, L. L. (2003). Authenticating acts and authoritative performances: Questing for self and community. In *The Why of Consumption* (pp. 140–163). London, UK: Routledge.

Athwal, N., Wells, V. K., Carrigan, M., & Henninger, C. E. (2019). Sustainable luxury marketing: A synthesis and research agenda. *International Journal of Management Reviews, 21*(4), 405–426.

Bergson, H. (1960) *Time and free will: An essay on the immediate data of consciousness*, Trans. by F. L. Pogson. New York, NY: Harper and Row.

Beverland, M. (2005). Brand management and the challenge of authenticity. *Journal of Product & Brand Management, 14*(7), 460–461.

Beverland, M. (2006). The 'real thing': Branding authenticity in the luxury wine trade. *Journal of Business Research, 59*(2), 251–258.

Beverland, M. (2009). *Building brand authenticity: 7 habits of iconic brands*. Berlin, Germany: Springer.

Beverland, M. (2014). Building brand authenticity (pp. 110–132). In K. Kompella (Ed.), *The definitive book of branding*. Thousand Oaks, CA: SAGE.

Bishop, W. H. (2013). Defining the authenticity in authentic leadership. *The Journal of Values-Based Leadership, 6*(1), 7.

Brown, S., Kozinets, R. V., & Sherry, J. F. Jr (2003). Teaching old brands new tricks: Retro branding and the revival of brand meaning. *Journal of Marketing, 67*(3), 19–33.

Carù, A., Ostillio, M. C., & Leone, G. (2017). Corporate museums to enhance brand authenticity in luxury goods companies: The case of Salvatore Ferragamo. *International Journal of Arts Management, 19*(2), 32–45.

Charters, S., Spielmann, N., & Babin, B. J. (2017). The nature and value of terroir products. *European Journal of Marketing*, 51(4), 748–771.

Closs, D. J., Speier, C., & Meacham, N. (2011). Sustainability to support end-to-end value chains: The role of supply chain management. *Journal of the Academy of Marketing Science, 39*(1), 101–116.

De Angelis, M., Adıgüzel, F., & Amatulli, C. (2017). The role of design similarity in consumers' evaluation of new green products: An investigation of luxury fashion brands. *Journal of Cleaner Production, 141*, 1515–1527.

Dekhili, S., Achabou, M. A., & Alharbi, F. (2019). Could sustainability improve the promotion of luxury products?, *European Business Review, 31*(4), 488–511.

Eisenhardt, K. M., & Graebner, M. E. (2007). Theory building from cases: Opportunities and challenges. *Academy of Management Journal, 50*(1), 25–32.

Grayson, K., & Martinec, R. (2004). Consumer perceptions of iconicity and indexicality and their influence on assessments of authentic market offerings. *Journal of Consumer Research, 31*(2), 296–312.

Heine, K. (2012). The concept of luxury brands. *Luxury Brand Management, 1*(2), 193–208.

Hoffman, J., & Coste-Manière, I. (2012). *Luxury strategy in action*. London, UK: Palgrave Macmillan.

Holt, D. B. (2002). Why do brands cause trouble? A dialectical theory of consumer culture and branding. *Journal of Consumer Research, 29*(1), 70–90.

Kapferer, J. N. (2012). Abundant rarity: The key to luxury growth. *Business Horizons, 55*(5), 453–462.

Kapferer, J. N. (2015). *Kapferer on luxury: How luxury brands can grow yet remain rare*. London, UK: Kogan Page Publishers.

Kozinets, R. V. (2015). *Netnography: Redefined.* Thousand Oaks, CA: SAGE.

Kunz, J., May, S., & Schmidt, H. J. (2020). Sustainable luxury: Current status and perspectives for future research. *Business Research, 13*(2), 541–601.

Mendes, S., & Rees-Roberts, N. (2015). New French luxury: Art, fashion and the reinvention of a national brand. *Luxury, 2*(2), 53–69.

Napoli, J., Dickinson-Delaporte, S., & Beverland, M. B. (2016). The brand authenticity continuum: Strategic approaches for building value. *Journal of Marketing Management, 32*(13–14), 1201–1229.

Osburg, V. S., Davies, I., Yoganathan, V., & McLeay, F. (2020). Perspectives, opportunities and tensions in ethical and sustainable luxury: Introduction to the thematic symposium. *Journal of Business Ethics, 169*, 201–210.

Postrel, V. (2003). *The substance of style: How the rise of aesthetic value is remaking commerce, culture and consciousness.* New York, NY: Harper-Collins Publishers.

Ranfagni, S. (2022). Cultural-based authenticity and luxury as a bridge to cultural sustainability, social well-being, and innovation: The case of Giuditta Brozzetti's textile workshop. In W. Batat (Ed.), *The rise of positive luxury: Transformative research agenda for well-being, social impact, and sustainable growth.* Routledge.

Ricca, M., & Robins, R. (2012). *Meta-luxury: Brands and the culture of excellence.* Berlin, Germany: Springer.

Rose, G. M., Merchant, A., Orth, U. R., & Horstmann, F. (2016). Emphasizing brand heritage: Does it work? And how?. *Journal of Business Research, 69*(2), 936–943.

Rose, R. L., & Wood, S. L. (2005). Paradox and the consumption of authenticity through reality television. *Journal of Consumer Research, 32*(2), 284–296.

Seidman, D. (2007). *How we do anything means everything.* Hoboken, NJ: Wiley.

Stewart, D. W., & Kamins, M. A. (1993). *Secondary research: Information sources and methods* (Vol. 4). Thousand Oaks, CA: SAGE.

Trice, H. M., & Beyer, J. M. (1993). *The culture of work organizations.* Upper Saddle River, NJ: Prentice Hall.

Turunen, L. L. M., & Laaksonen, P. (2011). Diffusing the boundaries between luxury and counterfeits. *Journal of Product & Brand Management*, 20(6), 468–474.

Vannini, P., & Williams, J. P. (2016). *Authenticity in culture, self, and society* (pp. 17–34). London, UK: Routledge.

Wang, X., Sung, B., & Phau, I. (2021). Examining the influences of perceived exclusivity and perceived rarity on consumers' perception of luxury. *Journal of Fashion Marketing and Management: An International Journal.*

Watanabe, S., & Horiuchi, T. (2021). Modeling perceptions using common impressions: Perceptual "authenticity," "luxury," and "quaintness" for leather. *Textile Research Journal, 91*(1–2), 73–86.

Winston, A. (2016). Luxury brands can no longer ignore sustainability. *Harvard Business Review, 8*(2), 1–3.

Yin, R. K. (1981). The case study as a serious research strategy. *Knowledge, 3*(1), 97–114.

17 ACBC and the Impossible Challenge of Quality Non-Leather "Made in Italy"

Jinju Hu[1] *and Mark Esposito*[2]
[1]Chanel Innovation Advisor
[2]Harvard Business School

Let's walk the new talk: All can be changed and so did ACBC

Introduction

Around the world, the innovation landscape is varied and comprised of many realities. When we talk about "innovation", we tend to think of large tech giants in the Silicon Valley or manufacturing conglomerates in Europe, India, or China. Moreover, we generally view innovation as a game of the few, rather than an activity applied by and related to the many. While the broader constructs of innovation continue to hold true, the past few years, if not the past decade, have brought a grassroots-based diffusion of innovation practices. This movement has involved, for instance, microentrepreneurs in Bangladesh who introduced innovations in the dairy industry (Lawson-Lartego & Mathiassen, 2016), and the innovative use of GoPro cameras in Africa as an effective way to monitor traffic and inspire crowdsourced applications aimed at reducing congestion (Radjou, 2014). Innovation today is more of an open system to which millions of doers and thinkers contribute (Chesbrough, 2012) than a centralized form of discovery camouflaged under industrial IP protocols and the red tape that accompanies them.

Innovation is also being manifested and organized in relation to different types of value facilitation, which are classified based on what they aim to achieve (Kogabayev & Maziliauskas, 2017). We find ourselves in the presence of multiple forms of innovation and innovation directionality. Internally driven innovation aims to improve efficiency and effectiveness within the firm itself. The evolution from internal to external occurs when we elaborate a consumer-facing innovation to examine how goods and services are engaging with consumers and their mounting demands for more equitable products (Wan, Liu, & Wang, 2020). If "internal" and "external" tend to refer to the focal direction of innovation in relation to the value proposition and the production of physical goods or services, we can also find different types of incremental innovations. These innovations aim at preserving market share through tweaks that retain consumers through habits, branding, and loyalty (Setijani & Sugito, 2019). Since almost three decades already, as argued by

DOI: 10.4324/9781003305095-21

Banbury and Mitchell (1995), incremental innovation does not necessarily alter the philosophy of the products but focuses on their progressive evolution over time. However, one kind of innovation tends to change the chemistry of the market – disruptive innovation, which displaces the market dynamics in favor of new paradigms (Christensen, McDonald, Altman, & Palmer, 2018; Christensen, Raynor, & McDonald, 2013).

The abovementioned forms of innovation (i.e., internal, external, incremental, and disruptive) are widely recognized by both academics and practitioners as some of the most commonly pursued mechanisms of value creation. However, they are not the only value-creation mechanisms that resonate with ACBC, which is an agent of architectural innovation. ACBC crafted a new system of reference for a given product through its rewiring of the footwear industry. This architectural innovation unleashed a series of subsequent modular innovations in which the thinking about and production of the components became as important as the overall strategy of the footwear industry's value chain. ACBC built a new paradigm around its own products. Interestingly, it applied this paradigm in a new way through its modular approach and the strategic meaning that modularity has for this firm.

Although modularity is at the center of this case, we will not discuss it just yet. Eventually, ACBC, our protagonist in this story, will teach us the heuristics of modularity and how this start-up dared to change the industry by thinking big. However, we first need to understand that innovation in some parts of the world, like Italy, is not a novel practice. Innovation is what has differentiated this country's fortunes from its misfortunes and what allowed the world to benefit from *italianità* – Italian ingenuity. We might refer to this as the "Italian Genius Bar" – a reference to the Apple Store offering where experts provide advice on the best use of Apple products.

Italy has been home to some of the most impressive business-model innovations in the food, luxury, fashion, wine, culture, and arts sectors. It is a key place for innovators, who then often flee abroad and prosper elsewhere. If there is one Italian region in which this trend has been particularly notable throughout the industrial era, it is Veneto, an area in Italy's north, which was a global leader in innovation in shoe manufacturing during the golden age (1950–2010). Italian shoemakers and manufacturers who work with leather are still recognized around the world, and hordes of tourists still visit leather factories in Florence or find themselves enchanted by the many leather-derivative products offered at the open-air markets and by leading retailers. However, shoe manufacturing in Italy started to decline with the emergence of Chinese competitors since the late 1990s, who brought products to the market in larger volumes with faster production cycles and impressive logistical turnaround times. China grew into an advanced player in the manufacture of leather products and became a direct competitor to Italian companies, which lost significant market ground after the turn of the century. Many firms closed, or simply sold their remaining assets and moved elsewhere.

This historical context offers an important lesson. What we are about to examine is not the rebirth of a phoenix from the ashes. ACBC did not alter the destiny of the market's incumbents by changing the market's direction. Instead, through innovation based on modularity, it created a space for science, novel production, circular models, and new materials to co-exist in a new working paradigm. Inspired by other examples of modularity, it redefined shoes not as "walkable" items but as concepts of our century.

The idea of modularity builds on the assumption that production is not vertical, but involves the integration of multiple, comparable pieces. For example, Lego, the Danish giant, reinvented the toy industry through its modularity and inspired a new form of management with the Lego Serious Game, which is used by thousands of managers to understand managerial practices and the leadership challenges faced by their teams. Modularity builds on the idea that several producers can contribute to the production of any item, such that its disposability cannot be siloed into a whole product, but only into the pieces that need to be replaced or disposed.

Concepts of this nature help us understand that if we think of production differently, we can build more resilient forms of value that can be assimilated into components, recollections, materiality journeys, traceability, and, ultimately, a journey of sustainable modeling. Sustainable production is the core philosophy behind our story in which circularity is a necessity.

Sustainable production revolves around the tenets that the cost of materials, the carbon used for production, and the associated costs of transportation and logistics may be accounted for and, ideally, re-integrated into the value chain. This may involve a closed-loop re-integration, where the value does not leave the production cycle, or an open-loop reintegration in which a given component at the end of its life in the value chain is procured by someone else – somewhat like organ donors, who extend others' lifetimes in the ultimate act of generosity as their lives end. While this example may seem dramatic, the idea of sustainable production implies processes that can withstand the test of time and neutralize the external factors associated with production that, if ignored or hidden in the cost structure, may render products inequitable. In other words, the focus is on processes that can create carbon neutrality.

ACBC's business model blended ingenuity with material science to generate sophistication in consumers' abilities to think of shoes in modular terms. It then went further by reinventing its supply chain to allow for micro-disposability while advancing the design of its shoes into one of the most successful forms of circular innovation. This innovation approach suggests that this is just the beginning of where this Italian start-up may go in its initial flight in terms of inspiring firms to meet new needs as they work within our planet's boundaries while unleashing remarkable forms of creativity in products for use in everyday life.

Building a company based on sustainability is a daunting task. There are differences in many dimensions of the value chain and finding convergence in a complex supply chain may be an impossible task. Consider, for example, the labor regulations that exist in the different countries that produce components for ACBC, or consider certifications and government frameworks and the ways in which they differ. Although ACBC is based on principles of sustainable production, bottlenecks, stumbling blocks, and hurdles must be expected when pursuing a truly sustainable model.

Despite the challenges, ACBC's story is not only exceptional but also part of a new cultural context involving a new generation of innovators. These innovators are likely to introduce new zeroth principles in terms of the way we produce, consume, and dispose of goods.

We start by looking at the story of this incredible firm and its founders. We believe that ACBC can serve as an inspiration for the many in Italy and around the world who admire the Italian Genius Bar.

The founders

The relationship between fashion and Giorgio Giacobbe, the founder of ACBC, can be traced back to 2005 when, soon after graduating from college with a degree in economics and strategy, he began offering consultancy services to clients of such fashion houses as Foot Locker, Prada, Ecco Scarpe, and Tommy Hilfiger. Born in Sanremo on the Ligurian Riviera in Italy, Giacobbe's Italian heritage helped him understand what it takes to exercise excellency and innovation in the fashion industry. Moreover, his passion allowed him to continue driving his career path toward success at an early age. If his experiences at fashion houses like Tommy Hilfiger and Peuterey nurtured his passion, his work as a business analyst at the German company BASF sharpened his ability to look at business models from multiple angles and to seek solutions to business challenges with a more analytical mindset. We might say he has an accomplished STEM (Science, Technology, Engineering e Mathematics) profile, given the integration of the social sciences and analytical skills with his entrepreneurial DNA.

Given his great passion in combination with his rich experiences in multiple regions ranging from Germany to Italy to Shanghai, Giacobbe became a managing director for the Italian luxury brand, Trussardi, where he was responsible for the Asian market, including China, Hong Kong, and Japan, all before he turned 30. At the time, China was in the mid of significant growth and found its role shifting from the world's factory toward a harvester of innovation. China was no longer at the receiving end of western fashion companies' ideas and designs, which it was expected to produce. It had become a sandbox in which an increasing number of local Chinese companies experimented with and introduced numerous innovative ideas to the market. Moreover, it had a huge consumer base that few countries could match. All of this and more can be considered as contributing to the creation of an innovator in Giacobbe. These experiences were coupled with his ingenuity and his understanding of the markets, their global appeal, and their movements.

Giacobbe was a global player with a global mindset. His experience of the world shaped his thinking and, more importantly, the thread that established the bigger picture of where the markets' sensitivities were shifting. An understanding of emerging trends as well as certain needs that have not yet been formally expressed by potential customers is an important entrepreneurial skill. It requires an ability to strategize through business modeling to create new processes, which is a key differentiating factor for ACBC. For this firm, this is more of a credo and a belief than a simple attempt to participate in the market.

As such, Giacobbe was ready to step into the venture that led to the impressive growth of ACBC, as his ethos was forged by the opportunities materializing around him and by a world in transition. He wanted to capture one idea, which emerged when he met Edoardo Iannuzzi, the co-founder and chief sustainability officer of ACBC. A designer by trade, Edoardo loved footwear, and he had designed and patented an innovative closure for shoes that allows travelers to travel in a lighter but more fashionable way owing to its simplicity and modularity. Moreover, as he had been exposed to multiple regions and various cultures through his work in Asia, New York, and Europe, Iannuzzi had gained a deep understanding of global customers and insights into major trends that were shaping the industry. Consumers' increasing focus on sustainability resonated with his long-standing desire for a more sustainable future. His first patented design, the modular shoe with a special closure, is now a signature characteristic of ACBC's products and serves to demonstrate the firm's strong identity as a sustainability advocate.

It did not take long for Giacobbe to agree to embark on the journey together with Iannuzzi after Iannuzzi approached him with his innovative design, ideas, and technology. Their aim was to create a business that would serve their desire for a better future. Iannuzzi's modular design opened a door to the possibility of solving the overproduction problem in the shoe industry without forcing consumers to compromise on their desire to wear different styles. Their story is important for understanding the humanistic side of this organization and how sustainability is at its core in terms of, for example, the sourcing of materials.

Sourcing

Corn, apples, grapes, algae, hemp, cactus … imagine overhearing two people talking about these products. You would most likely assume that they work for a food company. In fact, most people would not envision the possibility that these two people might work for a shoe manufacturer. This is how innovation can sometimes take us beyond our own imaginations – by providing us with ideas, products, and solutions that are shaped around new norms rather than what we already know. This relates to our story because it reflects the core idea of how sourcing became part of ACBC's success. Its vegan leather has become the name of the game.

Like other industries, the fashion industry is not immune to fast-changing consumer habits and demands, largely driven by technology advancements, new ideas, and unique offerings born out of the struggle to innovate. In previous works, we have argued for the need for legacy and modernity in order to strike a balance and find a new path forward. Luxury is in an epic battle with itself, trying to reconcile its historical heritage with the push for upgrades and modernity. These reconciliation efforts are the future of the luxury industries. ACBC fits into this mold of co-habitancy, as it has integrated a sense of exclusivity generated by fresh and novel thinking about production into its offering. Sourcing is one of its unique value propositions (UVP).

Many experts in the shoe industry face common challenges owing to the high complexity of shoe design and production, which not only seem to be a major hurdle in attempts to level up the game but also leave little room to innovate. A shoe – a relatively small product – is comprised of several different materials, often including some form of leather, and its production requires the complex assembly of components and a sophisticated process. In a shoe, leather is much more than just a sole or an exterior part of the product and its finishing. Leather is about comfort, touch, durability, perspiration and, most importantly, aesthetics. Therefore, when we talk about leather in the context of shoe manufacturing, its relevance goes beyond a single product component. It is, to some extent, the product itself.

Business modeling and the challenges ahead

ACBC's business model sparkles with innovation. Research into this start-up demonstrates that one of the best ways for innovators to push the envelope of what is considered "conventional" lies in the way ACBC has transformed the business. Its UVP is found in the ideation of the product and its entire production value chain, from sourcing to engagement with responsible consumers. If we were examining how firms contribute to the UN's Sustainable Development Goals, ACBC would score high on multiple fronts. Its positioning on the market is also clear. It has a prime brand, premium positioning, and a transformative product.

What could go wrong? Innovative companies exist throughout the world. They benefit from a crux of technologies that are increasingly becoming streamlined with the collaborative set-up of people, assets, and ideas that are shared daily on a global scale. This is where the magic happens. However, market access, the challenges of scaling at a price point that makes sense for everyone, and the sustainability of a niche supply chain pose numerous challenges for these companies. The impressiveness of the business model and its UVP cannot suffice unless they become eco-systemic.

Footwear manufacturing is a major business. IBISWorld, a data-research firm, estimates its size at a bit over USD200 billion globally, with slightly more than 3% growth projected for 2022. How much of this market will innovators be able to transform? Likely little if they are working alone. Therefore, we need a series of "collaborative innovation models" (a term used by the World Economic Forum to describe the relationship between start-ups and scaling through multinational companies) that can expose more vendors, firms, and consumers to the shift in the mindset surrounding a given product. This is not impossible or out of reach. It requires an active process of the landscaping of the business environment. For ACBC, this will involve more than just a great UVP – it will demand a habitat in which growth can expand beyond the company's boundaries into the wider market.

Technology

The general consensus is that no modern business can be considered technology free. From the simple use of mobile payment solutions to the reliance on messaging services to organize and execute food delivery, technology seems to be a new transversal normal. Some may resist the idea that this is true for footwear companies, but ACBC is a tech-led firm that is changing the nature of the footwear industry by infusing technological solutions and new forms of materials into the production cycle and beyond. The understanding of the value that ACBC brings to the market must transcend a simple description of its products. While its UVP is clear and implicit in terms of both the product and the overarching concept, we should aspire to look at the bigger picture of where the true innovation dwells. We are not arguing that the innovation is far removed from the footwear itself, but that it is part of a larger network of technological developments that are worth exploring.

Like many industries around the world, the footwear industry has been dominated by few large companies that push products out across their complex supply chains. The technologies usually associated with these activities are driven by the efficiency of production and the selection of the materials that determine the composition of the product in the end. In simpler terms, these companies rely more on an industrial benchmark than on innovation. However, ACBC has been able to blend three emerging technological trends that are likely to become important in the coming years: alternative natural fibers, gene-edited fiber crops, and bio-fabricated leather.

Alternative natural fibers involve a new method of cultivating fibers, which is characterized by a reduction in water usage and an improvement in the agricultural process that produces the raw materials. For instance, hemp requires less water than cotton and has superior permeability when worked. This has also to do with the enzymes used and the impact of green chemistry on the overall balance among chemical components, deforestation, and land degradation.

Gene-edited fibers use a technological approach that is widely utilized in the food industry. The properties of the fibers are genetically modified to render them less susceptible to pests while manipulating their natural characteristics. This has a major positive impact on the environment and significantly reduces greenhouse gases, creating a better source of fiber than is available from traditional agricultural processes.

Bio-fabricated leather, which is one of the most recent developments in the industry, is a lighter, thinner, and more durable form of leather, which lends itself to the production of leather products without the consequences associated with traditional, animal-based leather. Not only does this have a major impact on the slaughtering of cattle for the purpose of collecting their hides but it also reduces greenhouse gases and simplifies the supply chain, making it much more tech-driven and less controlled by drivers of intermediacy and "middlemanship", which generally characterize the industry today. While bio-leather previously suffered from a lack of biodegradability due to its synthetic components, ACBC has developed a superior form of bio-leather that has all of the benefits of bio-leather and offers environmental stewardship. As such, it represents a major breakthrough.

ACBC's 100% animal-free approach to leather production has special meaning for ACBC as an Italian brand given Italy's worldwide recognition for excellent quality, exquisite design, and craftsmanship in leather products. For leather, "Made in Italy" serves as a mark of quality around the world. As mentioned earlier, China has increasingly been capturing the fashion markets with its enormous production volumes, lower costs of business, easier access to economies of scale, supply chain power, and other advantages. However, the excellence of leather products made with the skills and knowledge found in Italy is not something that any country can easily reproduce in a short period of time.

Can Italy rest comfortably and continue with business as usual? Although the current situation gives Italy more time to compete in the market, leather itself is facing a new challenge. Traditional leather production still harms animals and is not environmentally friendly. Stricter scrutiny is demanded by customers and governments, and fashion companies are under the microscope in this regard. The need to integrate sustainable technologies in order to produce cruelty-free materials is rising, which is creating more pressure on Italian leather producers. ACBC has suggested a solution to this long-standing problem and proved that leather manufacturers around the world do not have to compromise on leather's aesthetics, quality, or comfort. It represents an effective integration of Italian leather craftsmanship and excellence with new technologies for vegan-leather production – non-leather "Made in Italy".

These three developments are at the core of the technology that ACBC has been championing in the market. Not only has this start-up lived up to the expectations of these Fourth Industrial Revolution technologies and the way they augment human capacity, but it has taken the entire concept to the next level, allowing for superior applications of these technologies. In ACBC, we find the most sophisticated practice of sustainable footwear currently available in the market, which directly reaches consumers. This, in itself, is a major milestone that must be acknowledged.

Modularity

With the widespread adoption of social network services, sharing photos with people who are connected has become a new standard. Platforms like Instagram and Facebook recognized people's desire to show and share their journeys with others. The incentive to share on social media fits well with the desire to use modularity as a new, fashionable trend, which is spreading as a new competitive edge for firms. Examples of this can be seen in the apparel and fast fashion industries, which are dominated by large clothing brands like Under Armour and Patagonia, where modular designs are becoming relevant. Moreover, we have seen modularity in electronics and computers, where modular pieces and accessories have dominated adjacent industries and are now worth billions of dollars. However, modularity in footwear was a missing piece of a puzzle that continues to enchant, as we are seeing a profound transformation in expectations of the footwear industry of the future. This is the shift that ACBC has recognized, and it is therefore leveraging a first-mover advantage over brands that never imagined that footwear could become modular.

If social media has played a role on its own, the race toward mobility and the models of Globalization 1.0 have brought us into a world in which mobility is being widely improved more than any time in our history. Traveling and mobility make it possible for fashion to move quickly and to reach consumers around the world. Although the COVID-19 pandemic has greatly affected and reduced mobility, we are already witnessing a return to pre-pandemic levels in some parts of the world. These global movements and the convergence of trends are creating new momentum and traction.

The outlook

A company like ACBC could represent the onset of a bright and revolutionary future, not only for the industry itself but also for the gravitas of the innovation movement, which is gathering significant momentum. Our assumptions and our speculations about the future highlight three possible paths for ACBC.

The first avenue is the *expansion* of the current business model into a more scaled and proven format. This might, for instance, involve more strategic partnerships, wider participation by a number of vested stakeholders, and a more robust and well-defined innovation ecosystem in which ACBC can play a primary role and expand its products and ideas on a global scale. We view this option as a direct extrapolation of the current situation. It may be the most plausible future for this innovation powerhouse.

The second avenue, which qualitatively differs from the first, would position ACBC as an **advanced landscaper** of innovation beyond its current R&D activities, moving it into the scouting of new materials. Working closely with start-ups, which are often not cognizant of the value of their innovations, ACBC might consider platforming their ideas into streams of production that could constantly loop into the innovative outputs of firms, translating them into new products that could constantly disrupt the markets and move the markets' centers elsewhere – likely upward on the scale of significance.

The third avenue focuses on the **frontier** and pushing the envelope further. It revolves around the idea that the science of materials may be taken to the next level, beyond the mere production of footwear into billion-dollar ideas and opportunities to rethink main consumables, such as plastics and other kinds of carbonized fibers, many of which contribute to the external costs of production for our natural environment. In this regard, we envision ACBC taking on a new role as a beacon in redefining the horizon of new materials. By pioneering new tenets of green advanced chemistry, biotechnology, and advanced genomic engineering, ACBC can become a frontier company in material sciences rather than an innovative footwear company.

We are not arguing that any of the above will be the journey ACBC actually takes. Moreover, we are aware that its future will likely be different from our above flight of fancy. Perhaps its reality will be a combination of options across the three scenarios or, perhaps, our imagined timeline will prove conversative in relation to the potential the company yields and aspires to in the coming years. Although we cannot predict the future, we know that ACBC finds itself at one of the most interesting intersections in the sustainability discourse in modern history. It has the possibility to reinvent production aligned with the aspirations of a human-centric society. Compelled by planetary boundaries, ACBC has the ability to unleash the best potential of our innovators: their ingenuity.

Welcome to the era of the Italian Genius Bar.

References

Banbury, C. M., & Mitchell, W. (1995). The effect of introducing important incremental innovations on market share and business survival. *Strategic Management Journal, 16*, 161–182. http://www.jstor.org/stable/2486774

Chesbrough, H. (2012). Open innovation: Where we've been and where we're going. *Research-Technology Management, 55*(4), 20–27. https://doi.org/10.5437/08956308X5504085

Christensen, C. M., McDonald, R., Altman, E. J., & Palmer, J. E. (2018). Disruptive innovation: An intellectual history and directions for future research. *Journal of Management Studies, 55*(7), 1043–1078. https://doi.org/10.1111/joms.12349

Christensen, C., Raynor, M. E., & McDonald, R. (2013). *Disruptive innovation*. Brighton, MA: Harvard Business Review.

Kogabayev, T., & Maziliauskas, A. (2017). The definition and classification of innovation. *HOLISTICA–Journal of Business and Public Administration, 8*(1), 59–72. https://doi.org/10.1515/hjbpa-2017-0005

Lawson-Lartego, L., & Mathiassen, L. (2016). Designing and orchestrating embedded innovation networks: An inquiry into microfranchising in Bangladesh. *Social Science Research Network*. https://doi.org/10.2139/ssrn.2866960

Radjou, N. (2014, October). *Creative problem-solving in the face of extreme limits* (video). Ted. Retrieved from https://www.ted.com/talks/navi_radjou_creative_problem_solving_in_the_face_of_extreme_limits?language=ha

Setijani, E., & Sugito, P. (2019). Mediating customer relationship management on the effect of incremental innovation on product life cycle. *International Journal of Scientific and Technology Research*, *8*(9), 59–64.

Wan, W., Liu, L., & Wang, X. (2020). How user-driven innovation and employee intrapreneurship promote platform enterprise performance. *Management Decision*, *58*(12), 2705–2723. https://doi.org/10.1108/MD-06-2019-0701

18 Sustainably Small, Successfully Slow

Artisanal Excellence and the New Made in Italy – The Case of Bespoke Tailoring

Fabio Duma
Zurich University of Applied Sciences

Introduction

Not only since Goethe's Wilhelm Meister Italy is evocative of beauty, art, and culture. The country is renowned for its rich cultural heritage and design-based products (Bertacchini & Borrione, 2013). Craftsmanship is one of the backbones of the Italian cultural and creative industries (Aiello, Donvito, Ranfagni, & Grazzini, 2013, p. 321) and makes a vital contribution to "Made in Italy's" soft power (Micelli, 2014, p. 11). And yet, craft-related industries are underrepresented in the creative industries debate (Bertacchini & Borrione, 2013), and potentially undervalued in the search for more sustainable forms of production and consumption in a post-Fordist economy.

For this study, the extreme luxury niche of bespoke tailoring was chosen as a research context to represent the craft-related sectors. Bespoke is a key aspect of the luxury market that invokes the human element as well as ideas of time, patience, and one-of-a-kind. It is about the customer, but also about the maker and it takes highly skilled craftspeople using traditional methods and tools to create a unique product (Frater & Hawley, 2018, p. 301). Tailors are the epitome of refined traditional Italian artisanal craftsmanship and artisan entrepreneurship. Swimming in a "sea of sameness" (Silverman, cited in Cheng, 2018), consumers in post-modern societies have expressed an increasing interest in singular (Reckwitz, 2017, p. 131) and unique products (Crafts Council & Morris Hargreaves McIntyre, 2010). Demand for handmade goods (Cheng, 2018; Waytz, 2019), products made with love (Fuchs, Schreier, & van Osselaer, 2015; Gray, 2012), and a high degree of personalization, such as bespoke creations that are made with only the buyer in mind and according to their specifications (Lahey, 2019), has been rising over the past decades. Classic sartorial craftsmanship is one of the many artisanal traditions that are still cultivated in Italy. According to the Chamber of Commerce of Milano, Monza Brianza, and Lodi, there are nearly 9,000 artisanal sartorial enterprises in Italy, employing roughly 13,000 people (2019). In classic sartorial menswear, the bespoke tailors are considered the absolute luxury segment. With several hundred bespoke

DOI: 10.4324/9781003305095-22

tailors, Italy still ranks top among the European countries that have a tailoring tradition, such as Great Britain, France, Germany, or Spain (Grunwald, 2018). While the number of bespoke tailors has been in decline, and despite the economic, structural, and political challenges, there is a new generation of passionate tailors and entrepreneurs that builds upon the rich tradition and decades-, if not century-old techniques developed over generations. Italian bespoke tailors are expanding their geographical reach across Europe and beyond. Besides training aspiring tailors from Italy and abroad, these artisans create awareness for Italian artisanal excellence one suit at a time but also by intensively using social media and digital communication channels to reach their discerning international clientele.

The fashion industry is one of the worst polluters on earth and is frequently related to exploitative production methods. De Castro has poignantly described contemporary fashion as "made in misery, bought in haste, worn for one night (if that) and then chucked in the bin" (2021). The bespoke tailor's approach to creating garments is radically different, valuing quality over quantity, elegance and durability over trendiness, slow craft time (Sennett, 2008) over speed, and perfect technical execution over cost. Consequently, a bespoke suit might cost several times the amount of a mass-produced model, but the expense is relative when compared to comfort and life span. While it is certainly not a feasible alternative to the modern fashion system in toto, the tailor's ethos and the desire to do a job well for its own sake (Sennett, 2008) are worth exploring in terms of social and environmental sustainability and with regard to the handcrafts' contribution to individual well-being. In the present study, this is done based on the personal accounts of five tailors from five different regions across the Italian peninsula. The participants shared their perspectives on craft, the motivations for choosing their profession, and talked about the challenges and opportunities related to it. They were also asked about the role of sustainability and their view of bespoke tailoring and "Made in Italy", at present and in the future. The study is of inductive nature and the findings embedded in the context of the participants and their perception. To relate them to the broader context of luxury "Made in Italy" and its evolution toward more sustainable business practices, they are discussed in relation to theory.

Literature review

The theoretical foundation of the study is mainly built on the literature on "Made in Italy" as a country of origin (COO) label and its effect, on sustainability in luxury and fashion, and on craftsmanship and artisan entrepreneurship and their potential with regard to sustainability and well-being.

Luxury "Made in Italy": An image crafted over centuries

Luxury is a multifaceted and dynamic phenomenon and as such difficult to define. Most definitions include aspects like heritage, know-how, culture, territory, and COO, in addition to high price, exclusivity, or uniqueness (Duma,

Hallier Willi, & Steinmann, 2015, p. 13; Kapferer & Bastien, 2012, p. 46). At its fundamental level, as Singh (2015) states, luxury consists of craftsmanship, exclusivity, skill, and time. Luxury products are often the result of production processes that are based on artisanal skills and craft techniques that are strongly rooted in certain geographical areas and local communities (Aiello et al., 2013). Manufacturers, through their creations, contribute to the image of their region and COO and, in turn, benefit from their geographical locations' reputation.

There is a considerable body of literature on COO. The COO effect, a subfield of consumer behavior research (Kotabe & Jiang, 2009) and international marketing research (Homburg & Krohmer, 2003), is one of the most significant phenomena impacting the evaluation of foreign products. It acts as a competitive factor in the commercialization of goods and services in foreign markets (Vianelli & Marzano, 2012). COO can be defined as a form of stereotype. The COO effect is related to images that consumers have about a country or the goods produced in that country (Suh, Hur, & Davies, 2016). It is an important cue in consumer choice behavior as it has a significant effect on consumer product evaluation (Aichner, 2014; Al-Sulaiti & Baker, 1998; Schooler, 1965) by simplifying information processing, reducing risk aversion, and thus assisting consumers in the purchase decision (Anholt, 2003; Beverland & Lindgreen, 2002; Cheah, Zainol, & Phau, 2016; Kim, Shin, Cheng, Lennon, & Liu, 2015). This is important in an environment where product variety is high, as it is the case in many luxury categories that have grown significantly and where new classifications, such as premium, masstige, made-to-measure, or uber-luxury, have proliferated to provide some degree of differentiation. Customers are ready to spend more money for a branded product from a COO with a more favorable country image (CI) (Bernhard, 2014; Koschate-Fischer, Diamantopoulos, & Oldenkotte, 2012) since COO is often interpreted as a signal of quality. According to Aichner (2014), the dimensions of quality that are influenced by the customer's individual perception of the COO include the product's esthetics, conformance, durability, performance, and reliability. Aichner mentions several examples, for example, German cars which are considered very durable and reliable, Italian cars that are seen as more esthetic, French cosmetics with sophisticated formulas and prestigious ingredients, and handmade mechanical timepieces from Switzerland. These products are generally believed to be of high quality, just because of their origin (Aichner, 2014; Götze & Brunner, 2019).

While Italy is home to over one-fourth of the hundred largest luxury companies in the world (Deloitte, 2021), small- and medium-sized companies (SMEs) make a major contribution to the economy (Aiello et al., 2013, p. 322) and are often suppliers to their larger and more prominent counterparts. SMEs constitute 99.9% of Italian enterprises of which most are micro-SME with nine or less employees. Overall, they provided 44.9% of employment in 2019 and, unbeknown to many consumers, they form the invisible backbone of the cultural and creative industries in Italy. On a global level, artisan entrepreneurs make a significant contribution to the economy and society (Pret, 2019). Likewise in Italy, artisanal know-how has been defined as the foundational element of what "Made in Italy" stands for (Micelli in Cavalli, Comerci, & Marchello, 2014), namely elegance, culture of design, tradition, and refined style (Aiello et al., 2013, p. 321). Innovative artisans, making use of new communication channels and combining ancient techniques with modern technology and new business models, are vital to the economic success of the Italian economy and to the country's image abroad (Micelli, 2016, p. 14). The favorable image evoked by the COO label contributes to Italian manufacturers' perceived quality and luxuriousness abroad and vice versa.

Sustainability & luxury: Changing customer expectations and the need to catch-up

Despite their claims of quality, origin, and tradition, Kapferer and Michaut-Denizeau (2014) have shown that in the recent past, abandoning the "stringent principles of a luxury strategy" (Kapferer & Bastien, 2012), many luxury companies have grown by expanding operations to low-cost factories and seeking volume by selling trendy, high margin accessories. The luxury market has come to epitomize our current dominant social paradigm (DSP) in which economic growth and technological advancement are prioritized over other outcomes, and that therefore favors a growing consumer society and the pursuance of hedonic benefits (Kilbourne, Beckmann, & Thelen, 2002; Osburg, Davies, Yoganathan, & McLeay, 2021). The era of mass luxury evokes the idea that happiness is a by-product of owning things, which creates ethical issues and major challenges in sustainable development terms, as the pursuit of higher volume puts more strain on the communities, ecosystems, and species along the supply chain (e.g., rare species preservation, origin of raw ingredients, working conditions in factories, etc.) (Kapferer & Michaut-Denizeau, 2014, p. 6). This increasingly leads to suspicion and provokes scrutiny by sustainability advocates and journalists (Ciancio & Wendlandt, 2021) who started paying more attention to luxury brands' business practices.

The sustainability of the luxury sector has only been covered comparatively recently by companies, media, and academics, because "in luxury markets we are (…) dealing with a high-profile context with a large number of societal and environmental issues to be addressed, but limited consumer drive for change" (Osburg et al., 2021, p. 202). There is indeed a divergence in consumer responses to sustainability across industry and product characteristics such as the value of the purchase, or whether the purchase is a necessity or an indulgence (Belz & Peattie, 2009). And Davies, Lee, and Ahonkhai (2012) found that ethical conditions of production were significantly less important in luxury purchase decisions than in commodities. However, in recent years the pressure on luxury brands to adapt their priorities has increased. D'Arpizio, Verde Nieto, Davis-Peccoud, and Capellini (2021) have declared that in luxury "the sustainability decade is underway" (p. 1), as Generation Z, but increasingly also older consumers, reward brands with a positive impact on the environment and society and disconnect from those that do the opposite.

The literature on COO and sustainability is still rather scarce. Studies have investigated perceived country sustainability as a dimension of COO or CI (Bassi Suter et al., 2018), such as Götze & Brunner's exploration of COO and sustainability perception of Swiss food among Swiss consumers, or Renko, Petljak, and Stulec's study on the CI of Croatia and "green dimensions" (2017). According to a recent study by Thøgersen and Pedersen (2021), consumers use a country's environmental image as a cue to the credibility of environmental claims. This can give exporters from countries with a favorable environmental image a competitive advantage, while those with an unfavorable environmental image need measures to compensate. Hence, countries that do not join the international efforts to counter the negative effects of economic activity and overconsumption might harm their competitiveness and the attractiveness of their exporters, thus a country's image related to its perceived sustainability is a factor to be considered when cultivating CI and ensuring positive COO perception.

Effort, accomplishment, and well-being: The value of bespoke tailoring and artisan entrepreneurship beyond money

As consumers are looking for authenticity and uniqueness, the demand for handmade goods is growing and so is the interest in courses where people can learn craft techniques and acquire manual skills. The re-appraisal of the crafts may signal has been interpreted as a potential signal of a paradigmatic change in contemporary economies. Mignosa and Kotipalli (2019) hypothesize that after "an instrumentalist period with the emphasis on increasing quantities of all kinds – such as the quantities of income, production, GDP, profit, jobs – interest turns to qualities of all kinds – such as the quality of work, of goods, of communities, of family life" (p. vi). However, at present, of the 100 largest luxury companies, the top ten incorporate 51.2% of sales and more than 70% of net profit (Deloitte, 2020). Since the early 1990s, most family-owned luxury houses have been acquired by luxury groups (Hoffmann & Coste-Manière, 2012; Turngate, 2009) to the point where independent companies have been declared an "endangered species" (Hoffmann & Lecamp, 2015). The Italian luxury landscape is no exception in this regard (Ciancio & Wendlandt, 2021) and is home to 26% of the world's largest luxury companies (Deloitte, 2021). Much of the existing literature in the fields of luxury and sustainability is focused on how to make large corporations more sustainable, while less attention has been paid to the majority of micro-, small- and medium-sized companies. These small companies, thanks to their creative power, innovation, flexibility, and pragmatism, can be a source of inspiration and innovation for better ways to manufacture and do business (Cavalli et al., 2014, p. 14). Moreover, craft-based sectors and creative systems of design in Italy tend to locate in small and non-metropolitan centers (Bertacchini & Borrione, 2013). They form an important part of the economic potential (e.g., tourism, education) and social fabric in regions outside of the Metropolitan areas, which are the main concentration points of the creative economy which further underlines the importance of putting them on the map of sustainability research. It is also noteworthy that some of the most successful representatives of craft-based luxury follow business philosophies that are different from the mainstream. As described by Ricca and Robins (2012), "meta-luxury" business models are based on the pillars of craftsmanship, focus, history, and rarity. Instead of volume growth and profit maximization, they are geared toward unique achievement. This counter-institutional identity, which stands in opposition to the growth- and profit-focused DSP, does not always lead to the rejection of firm growth (Solomon & Mathias, 2020), but revenues, costs, or profit for artisan entrepreneurs are rather seen a means to an end and only important inasmuch as they make the pursuit of unique achievement sustainable. Profit will be sacrificed for the benefit of excellence as long as business continuity is not endangered (p. 169).

This approach toward business and artisanal excellence resonates with what Sennett (2008) defined as craftsmanship, namely "an enduring, basic human impulse, the desire to do a job well for its own sake" (p. 9). Sennett's identification of craftsmanship and the development of skill as a source of confidence and serenity (2009) also provides a link to sustainability defined in a broader sense that includes, besides economic and ecological aspects (Elkington, 1994), social and, in the case of craftsmanship, individual ones such as gratification and well-being. Gropius, in his famous Bauhaus manifesto, not only underlined the significance of craftsmanship for creative design and art but also to develop excellence:

> *When a young person who senses within himself a love for creative endeavor begins his career, as in the past, by learning a trade, the unproductive "artist" will no longer be condemned to the imperfect practice of art because his skill is now preserved in craftsmanship, where he may achieve excellence.*
>
> (Gropius, 1919)

Gropius identified excellence as a source of meaning and purpose. Seligman (2011, 2018) linked meaning, accomplishment, positive emotions, engagement, and relationships to the sense of well-being. And more recently, de Castro, although with the amateur maker in mind, confirmed:

> *(...) another aspect of sewing, knitting, crocheting, embroidering, and making that we have forgotten to love is the mindful relaxation and sense of well-being that comes with it. Crafting often brings with it a sense of being immersed in the moment – soothing gestures that bring the physical contentment that comes from owning a lovely product, the pride of having made it, and the abstraction of thoughts that occurs when undertaking this kind of manual work. Basically: bliss.*
>
> (2021, p. 65)

De Castro's observation supports research showing that when consumers make something themselves, by hand, they become emotionally attached to the fruit of their labor (Norton, Mochon, & Ariely, 2012) and insights from the psychology and organizational behavior literature (Baum & Locke, 2004; Locke, 2000) where the producer's love and passion for his or her work has been identified as a main motivational source (Fuchs et al., 2015). Since the process of commissioning a bespoke garment involves personal interaction between the craftsperson and the customer, one can assume it has the potential to increase the latter's well-being as well. As Almond (2011) writes, the luxury of the traditional tailoring process is in the time, craft, and experience instilled into each garment. He describes the bespoke tailor as a sculptor whose medium is cloth. The tailor basically molds a shell out of this cloth that refines and accentuates the human form of his client. As the garment is made to their exact size specifications, particular attention is given to the detail, quality, and excellence in the work (Almond, 2011). The human contact and the sense of effort (Buell & Norton, 2011), as well as human intention perceived by the customer, tend to make their experience more purposeful – and meaningful (Waytz, 2019), which contributes to pleasure (Gray, 2012). Moreover, products that are connected to people, places or the past can make customers feel more emotionally grounded which, among other effects, increases happiness and well-being (Eichinger, Schreier, & van Osselaer, 2021). Given the potential of craftsmanship as a source of individual well-being for both, the makers, and the buyers, it appears worthwhile examining bespoke tailoring and business models rooted in handwork and artisanal entrepreneurship, in the context of a holistic understanding of sustainability.

Methodology

The empirical part of the present study is designed to create a deeper understanding of the realities of Italian bespoke tailors and their professional context. This includes their personal view on "Made in Italy" and reflections on tailoring and its future. The insights are based on an open, flexible, and iterative research process of step-by-step learning, reflection, and understanding of the researched phenomenon. A combination of qualitative data collection methods was used. Online interviews (Flick, 2014, p. 233), based on an interview guide with mainly open-ended questions (Seidman, 2006, p. 10; Schostak, 2006, p. 9 ff.; Weiss, 1994, p. 9 ff.), represent the main data source. Additionally, the analysis included publicly available information, such as company information on websites and social media profile biographies (including follower counts or profile likes), to provide context and support deeper understanding (2014, p. 360). The multi-step data collection process and different sources of empirical data provided a texture-rich and context-appropriate understanding of the research topic (Rubin & Rubin, 2012, p. 3; Kubicek, 1977, p. 23).

The sample consists of five tailors (see Table 18.1) who agreed to share their personal views and represent different tailoring businesses across Italy. The sample selection was a purposive (Flick, 2014, p. 175, 236) and pragmatic one, based on existing contacts and established rapport through the authors'

Table 18.1 Italian Sartorial businesses studied (own illustration, 2022)

Interviewee no. & date of interview	*Year of found-ation*	*Location of company*	*Ownership*	*No. of full-time employees*	*Geographical markets*	*Online presence (January 2022)*
Aristide Tofani (T1), Sartoria Tofani **Aug. 2021**	1954	Campania	Family-owned (second and third generation)	2–4	• Europe (ex-Italy) • USA • Asia • Italy	• Company website • Company Instagram profile: 155,000 followers • Company Facebook page • Personal Instagram profile: 562,000 followers • Additional personal profiles on LinkedIn, Youtube, and TikTok
Carlo Ostellari, Laura Mantovani (T2), Ostellari Sartoria **Sep. 2021**	1952, new entity since 2017	Lombardy	Privately owned (second generation)	4–6	• Italy • Europe (ex-Italy) • USA • Asia (Hong Kong)	• Company website • Company Instagram profile: 2,551 followers • Company Facebook page • Company LinkedIn page • Personal profile on LinkedIn
Gianmarco Mola (T3), Sartoria Molvissimo **Dec. 2021**	1940	Apulia	Family-owned (third generation)	5	• Italy, • Europe (ex-Italy)	• Company website • Company Instagram profile: 913 followers • Company Facebook page • Personal profile on Instagram: 937 followers • Additional personal profile on LinkedIn and Facebook

(Continued)

Table 18.1 Italian Sartorial businesses studied (own illustration, 2022) *(Continued)*

Interviewee no. & date of interview	*Year of found-ation*	*Location of company*	*Ownership*	*No. of full-time employees*	*Geographical markets*	*Online presence (January 2022)*
Riccardo Verolo (T4), Sartoria Lemmi Jan. 2022	1948	Umbria	Family-owned (second generation)	8	• Italy • UK • CH • USA • Germany • Europe (ex-Italy & Germany)	• Company website • Company Instagram profile: 14,500 followers • Personal profile on Instagram: 69,400 followers • Additional personal profile on LinkedIn and Facebook
Leonardo Simoncini (T5), Liverano & Liverano Dec. 2022	1948	Tuscany	Family-owned (first generation)	15	• Europe • Hong Kong • Japan • USA • Asia (Thailand, South Korea)	• Company website • Company Instagram profile: 41,700 followers • Company Facebook page • Personal profile on Instagram: 6,674 followers • Additional personal profile on LinkedIn and Facebook

research interest in small artisanal niche players in luxury over the past years (p. 235). All participants were identified through social media are working in private or family-owned companies and offer bespoke tailoring services. Except for one, they were founded in the 1940s and 1950s and on average manufacture between 60 and 350 garments per year in a price range starting at roughly 1,700 euros with an average of around 2,500 euros, depending on fabrics and other details. The selected tailors are based in different regions (Lombardy/Veneto, Tuscany, Umbria, Puglia, Campania) to represent the diversity of sartorial traditions and different clusters across Italy, even though not all participants claimed to follow a distinct sartorial style. All companies included in the sample cultivate a digital presence and are active online through their company website and a variety of social media platforms, mainly Instagram and Facebook. Except for one, all tailors have personal social media profiles tied to their profession (e.g., they count between roughly 1,000 and 500,000 followers on Instagram).

The question of how many interviews is enough to reach saturation has been addressed by many researchers and often answered with "it depends" (Baker & Edwards, 2012). Depending on the research aim (Charmaz, 2006), epistemological, methodological, and practical issues, recommendations go from 6–7 (Guest, Namey, & Chen, 2020) to 25–30 (Dworkin, 2012) and more interviews (Mason, 2010). In the present study, after five interviews, the number of additional codes and themes diminished, suggesting a point of saturation where only marginal insight is created by adding more data to the sample. The purpose of the study was to gain a fair understanding of the world of bespoke tailoring in the context of "Made in Italy" across the Italian peninsula and its potential contribution to social, ecological, and economic sustainability. Other than generalization, the data had to allow for an acceptable level of rigor and inductive theorizing (Punch, 2014, p. 170) and was meant to allow transferability to similar contexts or further exploration of the issue based on a broader dataset.

After initial consultation and explanation of the study by means of online communication (e.g., e-mail, Instagram direct messaging) six participants agreed to participate in the study. Due to time constraints of participants, geographical distance, and travel restrictions during the data collection period, they were sent the interview questions via e-mail (Flick, 2014, p. 233). The document included detailed instructions and mainly open-ended questions both in English and Italian. The participants were able to choose the language that made them feel most comfortable and had the possibility to answer the questions at a time of their convenience and, due to the written form, were able to read and reflect (2014, p. 235) on the researcher's questions. They also had the possibility to ask for clarifications in written or oral form at any time during the data collection period. Five participants answered and returned the questionnaire within the given time frame. The data was analyzed using MaxQDA 2020 employing a two-stage coding process (Rädiker & Kuckartz, 2020). The interviews were first openly coded one by one. Emerging codes were described in more detail in researcher memos. In the second stage, the transcripts were subjected to additional coding based on the generated code list, where codes were compared across the transcripts to identify common patterns, differences, and nuances of meaning. Where feasible, codes were consolidated into second-order themes or categories (Charmaz, 1990). These where then compared with existing literature and illustrated using direct quotes that which are either representative of a general tendency found in the data, or mark perspectives and insights of particular interest, or that contrast other points of view where interviewees did not share the same opinion.

Findings

The insights are presented with a focus on the main objectives of the study, which is to explore the bespoke tailor's perspective on COO and "Made in Italy", the future of their craft, and their contribution to social, economic, and ecological sustainability and well-being.

Country of origin: "Made in Italy" and the role of craftsmanship

"Made in Italy", in the view of the participants, is a globally recognized COO label, or rather a quality guarantee (T1), that stands for *passion, taste, craftsmanship,* **heritage**, and **tradition**. It has also been defined as the maximum representation "di bellezza e di ben fatto" (T3), which could be loosely translated as **beauty,** and something made well, or job well done **(quality).**

Even though history and the achievements of the past form a significant part of the participant's definition of "Made in Italy", their perspectives are oriented toward the future, and craftsmanship is portrayed as a **source of creativity and innovation**. It is seen as a process of constant evolution and adaptation. Asked about the importance of handcraft for Italy and its country-of-origin brand, T5 said:

> *(...) it is a huge differentiator of the Italian economy guaranteeing a net advantage in terms of competence and tradition conservation. Secondly, it is a great premise for innovation and inspiration for the whole economy (...).*
>
> (T5)

The views of the participants might be explained by their rather young age with most of them ranging between their mid- to early-20s to mid-30s which does not correspond with the popular image of the tailor as "an old man working in his small workshop" (T3).

While the participants felt rather optimistic about the **future potential of "Made in Italy"**. T1, in line with the fears expressed by other participants, argued that it was becoming more a brand rather than a quality guarantee. His criticism is referring to the commercialization of the COO label which, in his view, is sometimes being exploited by industry players that are capitalizing on the monetary value of it, however without abiding to what is believed to be the necessary standard of quality and beauty. In contrast, the representatives of 'true "Made in Italy"' (T2), as he explains, are

> *(...) still trying to defend those values of passion, tradition and ethics that distinguish Italian production, which is increasingly threatened by the fast and mass production that has developed in recent decades to keep up with the frenetic pace of modern times.*
>
> (T2)

To defend its reputation and cachet in the future, some participants felt that "Made in Italy" should be better protected, e. g. by **regulations** (T1 and T6) and through a shared effort by all the players in the ecosystem (T5). Artisans and small artisan businesses are regarded as essential contributors to this endeavor:

> *(...) it is necessary that artisan realities continue to carry on tradition with pride and passion, trying to innovate to keep up with time. Institutions, for their part, must continue to support the small artisan businesses that uphold the value of "Made in Italy" around the world.*
>
> (T2)

What also became clear is that for craftsmanship to remain a central pillar of "Made in Italy" the access of younger generations and aspiring artisans to **formal education** and **on-the-job training** in artisanal businesses should become easier and not depend solely on the private initiative of far-sighted individuals and master artisans who want to pass on their knowledge to the next generation. While there is a growing number of technical and professional schools offering education and training to young apprentices (T2), T5 explained that

> *it's not easy for young people to approach to the world of bespoke tailoring, mainly because many companies prefer to have experienced (...) tailors, but at* [company name] *for instance, Maestro* [name] *has decided to invest in young tailors and lately set up a school for the next generation or for the people who want to have a contact with the world of bespoke tailoring.*
>
> (T5)

The future of craft also depends on societal and economic priorities and the role and social status of manual labor, as it determines what young people want to learn and which career paths they pursue. The once common culture of choosing an artisanal profession and learning a craft from a master, acquiring not only the technical skills but growing personally by listening to their advice and hearing about the experiences which these artisans have accumulated over the years, got somewhat lost over the past century (T2 and T3).

All participants have had exposure to their craft in their childhood and youth. The journey of T4, for example, began in his youth and led to a formal education: "I started sewing with a seamstress in my village at the age of 14, then I specialized at the CEDAS in Rome, and learned the secrets at some tailor's shops" (T4). Other participants grew up in an artisanal entrepreneurial context and spent their childhood observing and playing in the workshop. T1 explained:

> *(...) as a little kid I used to visit my grandfather's shop after school. My mom used to bring me there just to visit my father and my grandfather. During these visits, I was always very attracted by their job and the things they were doing, (...) my grandfather used to teach me the basics as a game, so even if I was a little kid, I started to learn very important things of the job that for me were as fun as a game.*
>
> (T1)

Through this early contact with their family members performing the craft participants developed an interest and fascination for tailoring which eventually made them start their own artisanal journey. According to T1, Italy should do more to raise broader **awareness** about careers in craftsmanship and the attractive prospects in a global market environment where demand for handmade authentic goods is increasing:

> *I think that handcrafts are the goldmine of Italy, and it would be extremely wise, if the government supported more the young people who'd like to join these careers. Unfortunately, nowadays it is not as easy as before and most of the young people don't want to follow these careers, so we risk that many of those ancient arts will disappear in the close future.*
>
> (T1)

The lack of young talents leads to the crafts' main weakness and limitation to growth which lies in the difficulty of increasing manufacturing capacity: "We have a hard time finding trained youth who can help us. It is not by chance that we decided to do our own in-house training" (T4).

However, T3 points out that "the world of employment is changing rapidly, and it seems like artisanship and **craftsmanship** are **gaining more prestige and appreciation**" (T3). There should be incentives for experienced artisans to take on apprentices (T1 and T5), as "the cost of hiring an apprentice in Italy can be very overwhelming" (T1). One participant pointed out that

> *(...) governments must keep the flame of craftsmanship alive, making it grow from schools and then helping small companies and new start-ups in order to carry on the traditions with an eye open to innovation.*
>
> (T5)

While many governments, such as the UK (T5), have put programs in place to support contemporary craftsmanship, in the view of some participants Italy is not yet doing enough:

> *Little is being done to bring young people closer to learning an artisan craft, such as our tailoring craft, and little is being done to help young people who courageously decide to start a business by taking up an artisan job.*
>
> (T2)

Artisan's contributions to immaterial cultural heritage, a sustainable "Made in Italy" and individual well-being

While their **economic contribution** to the Italian GDP compared to other sectors might be limited, tailors clearly see themselves as playing an important role "not only for the economy but also for the preservation of a cultural heritage of a long tradition" (T2). And since cultural heritage is a main characteristic of Italy's COO image, it appears that tailors, through their embeddedness in local and regional **communities and ecosystems**, and via collaborations, are also having a positive impact on other important contributors to the Italian economy, such as **tourism**. T5, for example, mentions the fact that their clients often travel to Florence to order a new suit and T2 shares that they collaborate with retailers, shoemakers, hatters but also with personal shoppers and tour operators. Capitalizing on the online popularity he gained by showing his artisanal journey, T1 started collaborating with hotels and other business partners at home and abroad, thus not only promoting them and himself but also the COO to an audience around the world:

> *(...) lately I've found myself developing very good collaborations with businesses in the tourism industry. Many luxury hotels are happy to invite us to host one of our trunk shows in exchange of the huge exposure we can provide on our social media channels.*
>
> (T1)

To ensure the economic success of tailors as craftspeople and artisanal entrepreneurs, and thus to make a sustainable contribution to the economic output, **collaboration** and working in national and international **ecosystems** of like-minded partners is seen as becoming more important, not only to create wider awareness beyond the tailors' own reach, but to generate new business contacts, find inspiration, and create new offerings for clients:

> *(...) it is really important to be able to work in ecosystems in our sector because it enriches, generates work and puts a greater offer on the market for end customers. Putting our experience and potential at the service of other activities multiplies the resonance of our work exponentially and helps "Made in Italy" to preserve*

and expand its strength for the benefit of the whole country. (...) we work in close contact and in strong relationship with the Italian companies that produce the excellent fabrics we use, and it is also thanks to them that we often find outlets and customers in the national and international markets. We, for our part, are committed to letting our customers know about their careful research into innovation and sustainability that they propose in each new collection.

(T2)

Concerning their contribution to the **ecological sustainability** of "Made in Italy", the interviewees showed a tendency toward seeing their craft as being inherently sustainable: "Tailoring has always been a profession that respected the planet" (T4). However, all participants were aware that there is potential for further improvement. While none of them recalled ever having been asked by a client about the sustainability of their product, they talked about the transparency of manufacturing the garment and, because they usually know their suppliers personally, about the provenance of the materials and fabrics they use.

Our work, like that of our suppliers, is completely transparent and the result of years and years of research and respect for tradition. We like to work without ever exploiting what nature gives us as well as protecting the work and health of the people who work with us. It is a perfect balance that we have the responsibility to maintain.

(T2)

Overall, the interviewees rated the sustainability of their business and products rather high, pointing out that not much material is wasted in the process and referring "to the long-term usage of (...) garments" (T5). In what could be interpreted as an act of clear dissociation with the contemporary fashion and luxury industry, bespoke tailoring was related to the category of "***slow fashion***" (T5) that gains in relevance with the increasing demand for authentic quality goods, manufactured at a more moderate, human pace, using artisanal techniques. The participants see tailoring as a sustainable form of fashion production and consumption, decidedly different from the "fast fashion" approach that changed the industry over the past decade and influenced corporate strategies beyond apparel. Participants, however, see a growing consciousness among consumers that favor the value proposition of bespoke tailoring:

(...) after years in which the fast fashion has spread, massively saturating the market with products of low value, not only [in] economic [terms], but also and above all ethical and sustainable, tailoring has always been present and is back in the limelight precisely because of the quality and values that has always preserved and brings with it. (...) people have begun to appreciate beauty again.

(T2)

All participants shared this view, believing that "bespoke tailoring will always be relevant" (T1) and observing how "the world is starting to take some distance from the fast fashion and the big brands", as many people start to recognize, "that sometimes for a fraction of the cost they can get something that is specifically handmade [for them] with a luxury fabric of their choice and that will last for a lifetime" (T1).

Related to the aspect of durability, the participants agree that **quality** is paramount. They share the tendency to strive for perfection through continuous improvement: "It's no coincidence that it takes almost 60 hours to make a suit" (T4). In the context of business expansion, quality was mentioned as a central pillar of an artisan's reputation that is not to be compromised by growth:

> *Naturally we strive for growth, but [we] need to be careful with quality assurance. (...) as all high-end luxury brands, our brand equity is almost exclusively in the hands of our clients, so any decision of any kind must take [into] consideration their reaction and behavior. There is an extremely thin margin of mistake and the response from the clients for change is immediate.*
>
> (T5)

With regards to **societal sustainability** and **individual well-being**, the participants' common use of the word **family** when referring to all people involved in the company seems noteworthy. T2, for example, explained: "We work as a big family protecting our workers and respecting our customers with whom we establish a bond more than professional but of confidence and friendship." The role of **community**, beyond company boundaries and stretching out to regional and increasingly international partners, also became evident across the interviews. When asked about their contribution to social sustainability, T5 specifically mentioned the fact that they offer **training** and employ highly competent personnel. He also pointed out, however, that they have to "improve in terms of diversity. The sartorial world is mainly followed by men."

Another aspect that emerged from the data is **employee well-being** and the concern for the workers in the artisanal workshop, as "a bespoke suit means not only wearing something unique that reflects our personality but also helping the planet by not feeding and supporting the kind of mass production that does not protect either the environment or the workers who are part of it" (T2). In a similar fashion, T4 confirmed that they want to improve their sustainable contribution especially with regards to employees' well-being: "(...) because when the serenity of an employee is lacking, the quality of a product is also lacking" (T4).

The participants were also asked about the sources of satisfaction and dissatisfaction in their job. It became evident from their responses that craftsmanship and the path to mastery are indeed being perceived as a deeply **gratifying experience** and a **source of pride and individual well-being**.

The striving for perfection has been mentioned both, as a source of great gratification but also dissatisfaction when it is not (yet) achieved (T4). T5, who is still learning the craft from the master, explained that:

> *(...) looking back and remembering where I have started from, I see how many things I've learned and still need to learn, [it is] so challenging. And of course, the satisfaction comes from the "perfection" of small details, such a clean pocket or a beautiful facing on a jacket.*
>
> (T5)

The joy in the eyes of clients (T2 and T3) was mentioned as a main source of personal **satisfaction**: "my grandfather used to say, the success, the joy of our work is when after working for so many days on a single piece you can finally see your client wearing it with a big smile of approval" (T1). While the lack of awareness and appreciation for the artisan's handwork has been mentioned as an occasional source of dissatisfaction (T3).

Commissioning a bespoke suit is to be perceived as a **holistic experience** as has become evident through statements like the following:

> *To our customers we always say that today before selling a product, we sell a service. This is because we are ready to leave (...) Italy to reach our customers in their homes/offices in foreign countries. In this way, in addition to selling a unique suit (...), we also sell an experience with real professionals.*
>
> (T4)

The **personal encounter** is indeed something that has been mentioned as being fundamental to the tailoring experience: "Tailoring is based on relationships between people" (T4). And the establishment of a **relationship** over a **process** of conception and production of a completely personalized garment has been highlighted as a mutual source of satisfaction when "(...) seeing the idea of a dress that they had in mind come true slowly from the first fitting until the finished garment" (T3) and "being aware of the whole process of transforming a simple piece of fabric into a masterpiece garment" (T2).

Discussion and conclusion

The exploratory findings of this study paint a rich and promising picture of bespoke tailoring in Italy and confirm the notion of craftsmanship as a central pillar of "Made in Italy" and a source of individual well-being. Craftsmanship might be undervalued as a source of inspiration for more human and more sustainable ways of producing and consuming.

Artisans and artisan entrepreneurs are an important innovative and creative power (KPMG, 2016) around the world and in Italy (Cavalli et al., 2014; Micelli, 2016). They contribute to and benefit from the global reputation of their COO's image and the "Made in Italy" brand. However, the study also suggests that with the current focus on volume growth and efficiency of the more prominent players, there is a risk of the COO label being exploited and negatively impacted to the detriment of other actors with different ambitions and measures of success. The findings are in line with previous research which demonstrated that artisan entrepreneurs' success is intertwined with their geographical and cultural context, as it depends on heritage, which is a main characteristic of "Made in Italy". Research set in the geographical contexts of Scotland (McAuley & Fillis, 2005) and Madeira, Portugal (Teixeira & Ferreira, 2018) identified the pivotal role that artisanal labor and entrepreneurship play in a region's culture, society, and economy. Tailoring positively contributes to the image and tourist appeal of the tailor's home regions (Pret, 2019). The findings from the present study support this, for example, when looking at the participants' links to the tourism ecosystem, e.g., by collaborating with tour guides, personal shoppers, retail partners, or hotels. The tailors' embeddedness in the local culture, society, and economy adds to a destination's attractiveness and competitiveness.

As indicated by previous research (e.g., Bouette & Magee, 2015; Tregear, 2005), supporting artisans and artisan entrepreneurs results in mutual benefits for the destination and the craftspeople. The findings from this study suggest that while the offer of formal craft education has increased in Italy over the past years, thanks to public and significant private initiatives, there is a need for wider support structures. While government-approved programs of education and formation, and the possibility of receiving an officially recognized diploma help to increase the interest of younger generations in pursuing artisanal careers and their prospects of success, on-the-job training and apprenticeships need to be further encouraged and supported. Especially small companies often struggle to turn the hiring of young, less experienced, and thus less efficient craftspeople into an economically feasible endeavor. By providing financial and other resources to support on-the-job training, the government and private actors can create employment opportunities for young craftspeople and thus make a sustainable contribution to the economy, society, and the preservation of immaterial cultural heritage (Almond, 2011).

The present study does not provide a full lifecycle assessment of the sustainability of bespoke garments. While the findings suggest that further improvements to the sustainability of fabrics and other materials used in bespoke tailoring are being made by the textile producers, the full impact on environment and animals involved needs to be taken into consideration and transparency in this regard is further increased. This includes the environmental impact of international trunk shows, fittings, and client visits that involve an increase in travel. However, statements like the one by Carlo Andreacchio of A. Caraceni, a traditional tailoring house in Milan, are reminiscent of a mindset, that we might have to reconsider to return to a balanced and sustainable lifestyle. Andreacchio, during an interview and not without pride, mentioned that the blazer he was wearing "*is thirty-eight years-old, it was created in 1982*" (Attanasio, 2020). His statement is representative of values and an ancient form of manufacturing that were present up until the 1980s even in industrialized Western metropolitan cities focused on substance and not speed (de Castro, 2021, p. 56), inspired by techniques and patterns (Almond, 2011), and not trends and short-lived hypes. Other than efficiency and optimization of margins, the ultimate objective lies on absolute quality of material and manufacture (Almond, 2011), perfect fit, and longevity (de Castro, 2021, p. 53).

The positive relationship of craftsmanship and individual well-being has been suggested earlier in the literature (Fancourt, cited in de Castro, 2021, p. 65). Given the significance of artisanal techniques as immaterial cultural heritage, the number of artisans in Italy and their contribution to the perception of "Made in Italy", the link between bespoke tailoring as a craft and individual well-being of tailors is worth exploring further. The observation from the data is in line with complementary insights by researchers in different fields, such as Sennett (2008) in sociology; Seligman (2011, 2018) in positive psychology, or Ricca and Robins (2012) in branding and management. Statements such as the following corroborate the role of craftsmanship as a potential personal source of pride, gratification, and well-being: "*There is no specific reason that led me to the choice of being a tailor. When you're lucky enough to have a passion, you realize it after many years of practice and that it has become an integral part of your life*" (T4). The participants experience is supported by findings by Baum and Locke (2004) and Locke (2000) that link the producer's love and passion with motivation (Fuchs et al., 2015). It is further consistent with findings by Norton et al. (2012), and resonates with what Sennett (2008) concluded about craftsmanship. He identified evolving mastery as an individual source of pride and satisfaction: "Craftsmen take pride most in skills that mature. This is why simple imitation is not a sustaining satisfaction; the skill has to evolve. The slowness of craft time serves as a source of satisfaction; practice beds reflection and imagination – which the push for quick results cannot" (p. 295). Besides the maker, handmade and especially bespoke products can also enhance the well-being of the customer, as Almond suggests: "A well-cut, made-to-measure suit can deceive the eye by flattering and enhancing; it can also instill a confidence and elegance in the wearer through its flattering silhouette or style" (2011). An observation consistent with what the participants mentioned as being one of their main sources of satisfaction, namely the happiness in the eye of their customers when trying the finished suit.

The findings suggest that, depending on contextual factors and on the agility of the artisanal company and openness of its owners to change, there are economically, environmentally, and socially sustainable ways of doing business in traditional sectors of artisanal labor, even in an environment where handwork is being replaced by technology (Almond, 2011). Craftsmanship is at the root of much of what we call luxury today (Singh, 2015) and it is a source of inspiration and innovation (Cavalli et al., 2014) for businesses and entrepreneurs in and beyond the cultural and creative sectors. Studying craftsmanship and craftspeople helps us to look beyond the dominant measures of success in our current Social Paradigm. While artisanal products and small businesses in the sector might not be more sustainable per definition, the values embedded in craftsmanship, and the guiding purpose of artisans and artisan entrepreneurs can serve as examples of how to balance economic objectives with contributions to well-being along the value chain, much like Schumacher suggested already five decades ago (Schumacher, 1973).

However, what also becomes clear is that, despite the recent increase in interest in craft by consumers (Cheng, 2018) there is a persisting lack of awareness (Crafts Council, 2016) and appreciation of skilled manual labor in the broader public which might contribute to the underestimation of its future potential in a world obsessed with technology, speed, and efficiency. Politicians and educators tend to undervalue the work of the hand and the personal satisfaction that comes with it, as well as the positive social effect on communities and economies. Given the adverse effects of our current economic system on individuals, societies, and the planet, the insights from the present study, albeit exploratory and limited in scope, suggest a need for a closer examination of the way we look at and include skilled manual and creative labor and fine artisanal work in our strategies for a socially, environmentally, and economically sustainable future. Or, to conclude with the words of Vivienne Westwood, who in the late 1980s and early 1990s pushed the look of tailoring and the craft traditions of bespoke to the forefront of directional fashion, which provoked a resurgence of interest in the craft (Almond, 2011):

> *I don't understand this desperate need to always move forward. To strive for the new is the most conformist thing you can do. Everyone can tell you about what is new and clever, but no-one can tell you what is good! There is a myth that the past is irrelevant, that progress is the only thing.*
>
> (cited in Holgate, 1998)

References

Aichner, T. (2014). Country-of-origin marketing: A list of typical strategies with examples. *Journal of Brand Management, 21*, 81–93. https://doi.org/10.1057/bm.2013.24

Aiello, G., Donvito, R., Ranfagni, S., & Grazzini, L. (2013). Luxury SMEs networks. In K.-P. Wiedmann & N. Hennigs (Eds.), *Luxury marketing – A challenges for theory and practice* (pp. 321–339). Wiesbaden: Springer-Gabler.

Almond, K. (25–27 March 2011). Bespoke tailoring: The luxury and heritage we can afford. (Unpublished). The International Conference of Technology, Knowledge and Society, University of Basque Country, Spain. Retrieved from http://eprints.hud.ac.uk/id/eprint/10817/

Al-Sulaiti, K. I., & Baker, M. J. (1998). Country of origin effects: A literature review. *Marketing Intelligence and Planning, 16(3)*, 150–199.

Anholt, S. (2003). *Brand new justice: The upside of global branding.* Oxford, UK: Butterworth-Heinemann.

Attanasio, F. (2020). *Guide to Milanese tailoring*. Retrieved from https://therake.com/stories/guide-to-milanese-tailors/

Baker, S. E., & Edwards, R. (2012). *How many qualitative interviews is enough? National Center for Research Methods*. Retrieved from http://eprints.ncrm.ac.uk/2273/

Bassi Suter, M., de Moura Engracia Giraldi, J., Mendes Borini, F., Ferranty MacLennan, M. L., Crescitelli, E., & Fernandes Polo, E. (2018). In search of tools for the use of country image (CI) in the brand. *Journal of Brand Management, 25(2)*, 119–132. https://doi.org/ 10.1057/s41262-017-0062-4

Baum, R. J., & Locke, E. A. (2004). The relationship of entrepreneurial traits, skill, and motivation to subsequent venture growth. *Journal of Applied Psychology, 89(4)*, 587–98.

Belz, F. M., & Peattie, K. J. (2009). *Sustainability marketing: A global perspective*. Chichester, UK: Wiley.

Bernhard, E. (2014). Welche volkswirtschaftlichen Auswirkungen hat der Schutz der Herkunftsangabe 'Schweiz'? *Die Volkswirtschaft–Das Magazin für Wirtschaftspolitik, 10*, 11–13.

Bertacchini, E. E., & Borrione, P. (2013). The geography of the Italian creative economy: The special role of the design and craft-based industries. *Regional Studies, 42(2)*, 135–147. https://doi.org/10.1080/00343404.2011.628652

Beverland, M., & Lindgreen, A. (2002). Using country of origin in strategy: The importance of context and strategic action. *Journal of Brand Management, 10(2)*, 147–167.

Bouette, M., & Magee, F. (2015). Hobbyists, artisans and entrepreneurs: Investigating business support and identifying entrepreneurial profiles in the Iris craft sector. *Journal of Small Business and Enterprise Development, 22(2)*, 337–351.

Buell, R. W., & Norton, M. I. (2011). The labor illusion: How operational transparency increases perceived value. *Management Science, 57(9)*, 1564–1579.

Cavalli, A., Comerci, G., & Marchello, G. (2014). *Il valore del mestiere. Elementi per una valutazione dell'eccellenza artigiana*. Venezia, Italy: Marsilio.

Charmaz, K. (2006). *Constructing grounded theory: A practical guide through qualitative analysis*. Thousand Oaks, CA: SAGE.

Charmaz, K. (1990). 'Discovering' chronic illness: Using grounded theory. *Social Science and Medicine, 30*, 1161–1172.

Cheah, I., Zainol, Z., & Phau, I. (2016). Conceptualizing country-of-ingredient authenticity of luxury brands. *Journal of Business Research, 69*, 5819–5826.

Cheng, A. (2018). *No more of the same: Why mass production is actually a boon for Etsy, Amazon Handmade*. Retrieved from https://www.forbes.com/sites/andriacheng/2018/08/08/your-rebellion-against-mass-produced-goods-promises-growth-for-etsy-amazon-handmade/?sh=57cea9b727e2

Ciancio, A., & Wendlandt, A. (2021). "MADE IN ITALY INC." gets organized. Italian luxury manufacturers join forces to become more competitive and sustainable. Retrieved from https://www.misstweed.com/detail-article.html?id=46

Crafts Council. (2016). *Studying craft 16 – Presentation of findings*. Retrieved from https://www.craftscouncil.org.uk/about/research-and-policy/studying-craft-16

Crafts Council, & Morris Hargreaves McIntyre, M. H. (2010). Consuming craft: The contemporary craft market in a changing economy. Retrieved from https://www.craftscouncil.org.uk/documents/858/Consuming_craft_2010.pdf

Davies, I. A., Lee, Z., & Ahonkhai, I. (2012). Do consumers care about ethical-luxury? *Journal of Business Ethics, 106*, 37–51.

D'Arpizio, C., Verde Nieto, D., Davis-Peccoud, J., & Capellini, M. (2021). *LuxCo 2030: A vision of sustainable luxury*. Bain & Company/Positive Luxury. Retrieved from: https://www.bain.com/globalassets/noindex/2021/bain_brief_luxco_2030_a_vision_of-sustainable-luxury.pdf

De Castro, O. (2021). *Loved clothes last. How the joy of rewearing and repairing your clothes can be a revolutionary act*. Dublin, UK: Penguin Life.

Deloitte. (2020). *Global powers of luxury goods*. Retrieved from file:///C:/Users/dumf/AppData/Local/Temp/gx-consumer-business-gplg-2020-report.pdf

Deloitte. (2021). *Global powers of luxury goods*. Retrieved from: https://www2.deloitte.com/global/en/pages/consumer-business/articles/gx-cb-global-powers-of-luxury-goods.html

Duma, F., Hallier Willi, C., & Steinmann, C. (2015). *The business of luxury*. Zürich, Switzerland: vdf Hochschulverlag.

Dworkin, S. L. (2012). Sample size policy for qualitative studies using in-depth interviews. *Archives of Sexual Behavior, 41*, 1319–1320. https://doi.org/ 10.1007/s10508-012-0016-6

Eichinger, I., Schreier, M., & van Osselaer, S. M. J. (2021). Connecting to place, people, and past: How products make us feel grounded. *Journal of Marketing, 1*, 16. https://doi.org/10.1177/00222429211027469

Elkington, J. (1994). Towards the sustainable corporation: win-win-win business strategies for sustainable development. *California Management Review, 36*, 90–100. https://doi.org/10.2307/41165746

Flick, U. (2014). *An introduction to qualitative research*. London, UK: SAGE.

Frater, J., & Hawley, J. M. (2018). A hand-crafted slow revolution: Co-designing a new genre in the luxury world. *Fashion, Style & Popular Culture, 5(3)*, 299–311. https://doi.org/10.1386/fspc.5.3.299_1.

Fuchs, C., Schreier, M., & van Osselaer, S. M. J. (2015). The handmade effect: What's love got to do with it. *Journal of Marketing, 79(3)*, 98–110.

Götze, F., & Brunner, T. A. (2019). Sustainability and country-of-origin. How much do they matter to consumers in Switzerland? *British Food Journal, 122(1)*, 291–308. https://doi.org/10.1108/BFJ-06-2018-0401.

Gray K. (2012). The power of good intentions: Perceived benevolence soothes pain, increases pleasure, and improves taste. *Social Psychological and Personality* Science, *3*(5), 639–645. https://doi.org/10.1177/1948550611433470

Gropius, W. (1919). *Program of the Staatliche Bauhaus in Weimar*. Retrieved from https://bauhausmanifesto.com/

Grunwald, T. (2018). *Bespoke tailors have become travelling tailors*. Retrieved from https://sartorialnotes.com/2018/10/03/travelling-tailors/

Guest, G., Namey, E., & Chen, M. (2020). A simple method to assess and report thematic saturation in qualitative research. *PLoS ONE, 15*(5).

Hoffmann, J., & Coste-Manière, I. (2012). *Luxury strategy in action*. New York: Palgrave Macmillan.

Hoffmann, J., & Lecamp, L. (2015). *Independent luxury: The four innovation strategies to endure in the consolidation jungle*. Hampshire & New York: Palgrave Macmillan.

Holgate, M. (1998). *The prime of Miss Vivienne Westwood*. London, UK: Vogue.

Homburg, C., & Krohmer, H. (2003). *Marketingmanagement: Strategie – Instrumente – Umsetzung –Unternehmensführung*. Wiesbaden, Germany: Gabler.

Kapferer, J.-N., & Bastien, V. (2012). *The luxury strategy – Break the rules of marketing to build luxury brands*. London, UK: Kogan Page.

Kapferer, J.-N., & Michaut-Denizeau, A. (2014). Is luxury compatible with sustainability? Luxury consumers' viewpoint. *Journal of Brand Management, 21*, 1–22.

Kilbourne, W., Beckmann, S. C., & Thelen, E. (2002). The role of the dominant social paradigm in environmental attitudes: A multinational examination. *Journal of Business Research, 55*(3), 193–204.

Kim, H.-S., Shin, E.-Y., Cheng, A., Lennon, S.-J., & Liu, W.-S. (2015). Influence of design, workmanship, and familiarity on perceptions of country-of-origin apparel brands: A study of consumers in the US, China and Japan. *Journal of Global Fashion Marketing, 6*(4), 265–277.

Koschate-Fischer, N., Diamantopoulos, A., & Oldenkotte, K. (2012). Are consumers really willing to pay more for a favorable country image? A study of country-of-origin effects on willingness to pay. *Journal of International Marketing, 20*(1), 19–41.

Kotabe, M., & Jiang, C. X. (2009). Contemporary research trends in international marketing: The 2000s. In A. M. Rugman (Ed.), *The Oxford handbook of international business* (pp. 447–501). Oxford, UK: Oxford University Press.

KPMG. (2016). *Innovation through craft: Opportunities for growth. A report for the Crafts Council.* Retrieved from https://www.craftscouncil.org.uk/documents/875/Innovation_through_craft_executive_summary_2016.pdf

Kubicek, H. (1977). Heuristische Bezugsrahmen und heuristisch angelegte Forschungsdesigns als Elemente einer Konstruktionsstrategie empirischer Forschung. In R. Köhler (Ed.), *Empirische und handlungstheoretische Forschungskonzeptionen in der Betriebswirtschaftslehre* (pp. 3–26). Stuttgart, Germany: Poeschel.

Lahey, S. (2019). *Bespoke is coming to a product or service near you.* Retrieved from https://www.zendesk.com/blog/bespoke-coming-product-service-near/

Locke, E. E. (2000). *The prime movers.* New York, NY: Amacom.

Mason, M. (2010). Sample size and saturation in PhD studies using qualitative interviews. *Forum: Qualitative Social Research, 11*(3), 8.

McAuley, A., & Fillis, I. (2005). The Orkney based craft entrepreneur: Remote yet global. *Journal of Small Business and Enterprise Development, 14*(4), 498–509.

Micelli, S. (2016). *Fare è innovare. Il nuovo lavoro artigiano.* Bologna: il Mulino.

Micelli, S. (2014). Foreword. In A. Cavalli, G. Comerci, & G. Marchello (Eds.), *Il valore del mestiere. Elementi per una valutazione dell'eccellenza artigiana* (pp. 11–12). Venezia, Italy: Marsilio.

Mignosa, A., & Kotipalli, P. (2019). *A cultural economic analysis of craft.* Cham, Switzerland: Palgrave Macmillan.

Norton, M. I., Mochon, D., & Ariely, D. (2012). The IKEA effect: When labor leads to love. *Journal of Consumer Psychology, 22*(3), 453–460.

Osburg, V.-S., Davies, I., Yoganathan, V., & McLeay, F. (2021). Perspectives, opportunities and tensions in ethical and sustainable luxury: Introduction to the thematic symposium. *Journal of Business Ethics*, 169, 201–210.

Pret, T. (2019). Artisan entrepreneurship: A systematic literature review and research agenda. *International Journal of Entrepreneurial Behavior & Research, 25*(4), 592–614.

Punch, K. F. (2014). *Introduction to social research. Quantitative & qualitative approaches.* London: Sage.

Rädiker, S., & Kuckartz, U. (2020). *Focused analysis of qualitative interviews with MAXQDA: Step by step.* Berlin, Germany: MAXQDA Press. https://doi.org/10.36192/978-3-948768072

Reckwitz, A. (2017). *Die Gesellschaft der Singularitäten.* Berlin, Germany: Suhrkam.

Renko, S., Petljak, K., & Stulec, I. (2017). The basic postulates of the green image of a country: The case of Croatia (pp. 1–39). In Renko, S. and Pestek, A. (Eds.), *Green economy in the Western Balkans.* Bingley, UK: Emerald. https://doi.org/10.1108/978-1-78714-499-620171001

Ricca, M., & Robins, R. (2012). *Meta-luxury: Brands and the culture of excellence*. Springer.
Rubin, H. J., & Rubin, I. S. (2012). *Qualitative interviewing: The art of hearing data*. Thousand Oaks, CA: SAGE Publications.
Schostak, J. (2006). *Interviewing and representation in qualitative research*. Maidenhead, UK: Open University Press.
Seidman, I. (2006). *Interviewing as qualitative research. A guide for researchers in education and the social sciences* (3rd ed.). New York, NU: Teachers College Press.
Seligman, M. (2011). *Flourish*. New York, NU: Simon & Schuster.
Seligman, M. E. P. (2018). PERMA and the building blocks of well-being. *The Journal of Positive Psychology, 13(4)*, 333–335. https://doi.org/10.1080/17439760.2018.1437466
Sennett, R. (2009). Richard Sennett on Art and Craft, Lecture, the Getty Center, December 3, 2009. Retrieved from https://www.youtube.com/watch?v=LH1aX_6-xkY
Sennett, R. (2008). *The craftsman*. New Haven, CT: Yale University Press.
Schooler, R. D. (1965). Product bias in the Central American common market. *Journal of Marketing Research, 2(4)*, 394–397.
Schumacher, E. F. (1973). *Small is beautiful. Economics as if people mattered*. New York, NY: Harper Perennial.
Singh, R. (2015), *Redefining luxury the V&A way in 2015, Forbes/Asia*, Retrieved from http://www.forbes.com/sites/ranisingh/2015/04/28/what-is-luxury/#6ca420686cce
Solomon, S. J., & Mathias, B. D. (2020). The artisans' dilemma: Artisan entrepreneurship and the challenge of firm growth. *Journal of Business Venturing, 35, 5*. https://doi.org/10.1016/j.jbusvent.2020.106044.
Suh, Y. G., Hur, J. Y., & Davies, G. (2016). Cultural appropriation and the country of origin effect. *Journal of Business Research, 69*, 2721–2730.
Teixeira, S. J., & Ferreira, J. J. M. (2018). Entrepreneurial artisan products as regional tourism competitiveness. *Journal of Entrepreneurial Behavior & Research, Special Issue, 25(4)*, 652–673. https://doi.org/10.1108/IJEBR-01-2018-0023
Thøgersen, J., & Pedersen, S. (2021). The importance of the export country's environmental image for consumer responses to an imported environmentally friendly product. *International Marketing Review, 38(6)*, 1217–1241. https://doi.org/10.1108/IMR-05-2020-0085
Tregear, A. (2005). Lifestyle, growth, or community involvement? The balance of goals of UK artisan food producers. *Entrepreneurship & Regional Development, 17(1)*, 1–15.
Turngate, M. (2009). *Luxury world: The past, present and future of luxury brands*. London, UK: Kogan Page.
UN Global Compact (n.d.). *Social Sustainability*. Retrieved from https://www.unglobalcompact.org/what-is-gc/our-work/social
Vianelli, D., & Marzano, F. C. (2012). *L'effetto country of Origin Sull'intenzione D'acquisto Del Consumatore: Una Literature Review*. Trieste: EUT Edizioni.
Waytz, A. (2019). When customers want to see the human behind the product. *Harvard Business Review*. Retrieved from https://hbr.org/2019/06/when-customers-want-to-see-the-human-behind-the-product
Weiss, R. S. (1994). *Learning from strangers: The art and method of qualitative interview studies*. New York, NY: The Free Press.

Conclusion

Luxury "Made in Italy" and Sustainability

Ian Phau
Curtin University

Introduction

The luxury industry is going through a massive transformation. It is clear that conspicuous consumption is overshadowed by conscious consumerism. Customer experience is radiating toward online with millennials and Gen Z leading market trends and as such accelerating the growth of new technologies. Bain & Co. research purports that online shopping is forecast to reach 105–115 billion euros by 2025 to exceed 30% of the market, making digital the main channel for luxury purchases. Luxury brands have taken up the new role of producing and broadcasting content for their market. In spite of the aforementioned prospect, luxury experts in industry and academia have called for research on the future of luxury. In a rapidly changing world, and shifting consumer attitudes, what experiences and values do consumers expect from luxury brands? How do luxury brands recalibrate their strategies to compete in a future market where traditional ideas of luxury are changing? How can luxury brands maintain their desirability in the constantly changing marketspace?

Clearly what is synonymous with luxury is the "Made in Italy" label. This endowed respect of craftsmanship, exclusivity, and authenticity spans across a breadth of products and services. It is not uncommon to see a description of a product label that beams "Made in Italy" followed by a tagline "synonymous with quality and design creativity". This sums up the consensus of the halo effect of the country-of-origin label of "Made in Italy". What is also interesting in luxury is the escalating voice of the term sustainability. Sustainability is considered a key factor that influences the luxury consumers as they are motivated by environmental, animal, and moral concerns related to manufacturing. Current literature provides little evidence on this aspect of luxury consumer behavior. In particular, research suggests that second-hand luxury shopping is a symptom of the up-and-coming circular economy, which may be defined as the "closed-loop" system giving a product multiple life cycles in efforts to minimize the waste of materials. What are the scopes of examining the type of sustainable practices followed by luxury firms and the challenges faced by luxury fashion retailers to adapt to sustainable practices?

Will the circular economy dilute the elite-ness and become part of the masses for secondhand luxury? What are the consequences to the desirability for luxury in part even with the "Made in Italy" label? And more importantly, many perspectives from contributing authors of the chapters in this book have uncovered the relevance of sustainability and luxury and ultimately the "Made in Italy" label.

The overarching essence of this book hinges on how the concept of sustainability is being embedded with the "Made in Italy" label for luxury brands. Three themes are clearly defined with many perspectives from the contributing authors, through case studies, interviews with industry experts, and findings from empirical research. A series of provoking questions are posed and researched through a myriad of methodologies including case studies and interviews have certainly provided valuable lessons and shared in the discussions.

Theme 1

The first theme looks at the luxury industry in transition and the challenges to "Made in Italy". This theme starts with a case of Diesel. The resale revolution by celebrating a re-buy initiative of old jeans, reconditioning them, and proudly launching a new initiative – the birth of Secondhand Diesel. This clearly puts their stamp in the circularity movement. Diesel actively invites customers to participate in the sustainability strategy "For responsible living" and builds a bond with the customers to set specific objectives by 2030 in terms of environmental protection, attention to the product, and social commitment. An engaging interview with Andrea Rosso only sealed the audience in awe with his commitment to the sustainability initiative across all functions of Diesel. He wears the pride of Diesel and the mark of sustainability in his sleeves.

In a similar vein, the chapter and case study on 10 Corso Como provides an uncommon example of luxury that can encourage and motivate other retailers to integrate sustainable strategy in their offerings and brand image. 10 Corso Como provides a good directive that luxury and sustainability can successfully coexist despite several challenges as expressed by academic and industry reports. 10 Corso Como has a heritage built meticulously over time and hinges strongly on the "Made in Italy" concept. The latter, however, still needs to implement sustainable strategies to remain competitive in the global market. As concluded in the discussion of the chapter, the "Made in Italy" brand has integrated sustainable values contributing to social and environmental causes into the luxury brand's concept without jeopardizing the prestige and premium quality. This mandate is communicated through a number of channels with several first of its kind in this format. Merchandise-wise, they are carefully curated focusing on high quality and sustainability, and produced in smaller quantities thus less production waste. Sustainable orientation of the brand is communicated to consumers and stakeholders through art exhibitions inside the venue. Private and public events are organized to trigger word-of-mouth and draw media attention to social media accounts.

Gucci has always been in the forefront of the sustainability transition, building awareness on social commitment and environmental protection in the luxury industry. It has also curated a reputation of that this is not just an ethical necessity but also a driver of innovation and value creation. We recognize the intersecting double G logo as an iconic brand now transiting to a new "Made in Italy" representing a future of innovation, digital scenarios, and new social consciousness. One of the most signature initiative, as described in the chapter is the Equilibrium Project. This is the epitome of this initiative lies in the sight of 360 degrees of sustainability. This has gained resounding momentum unifying the principles that Gucci uphold and the actions to pursue to treat our world and each other better for a sustainable collective future. The Equilibrium's online platform excels through excellent story telling of the plethora of sustainability projects that the brand has activated over the years clearly depicting clear relevance and resonance to the brand's mission. The Equilibrium comprised of two arms namely "People" and "Planet". "People" focuses on diversity, gender equality, and inclusiveness, starting from a strong and positive corporate culture. Initiatives such as "Chime for Change" was designed in support of women and promoting gender equality and "To Gather Together" was designed to appeal to the international community to overcome gender bias and does so by integrating all forms of expression and media. The other arm, "Planet" consistently focuses on the management and preservation of the limited resources on earth. The essence of the Equilibrium involves different projects looking at the entire supply chain and adopting climate-smart strategies to help protect and restore the nature for the future. The Equilibrium positions Gucci in the forefront and challenges the successfully curated genuine and transparent dialogue with different stakeholders. Storytelling is best designed involving the whole community in this collective and sustainable ideal sharing warm achievements, projected progress, and foreseeable future goals. The interview in the Gucci chapter, clearly depicts the transition from luxury of exclusivity, preciousness, and product refinement to a new era of innovation and sustainability.

Theme 2

The second theme focuses on sustainable engagement of "Made in Italy" luxury brands and shows evidence that conscious luxury approach does not necessarily mean there is a need to sacrifice ethics for aesthetic. There is an increasing emphasis on local roots, tradition, and craftsmanship consistent with the perception of a productive system that inherently pays more attention to issues like natural materials, sustainable production processes and authenticity of artisan skills.

The yachting and sailing industry embrace every attribute that defines luxury in the likes of elegance, sophistication, creativity, and innovation. The

Ferretti Group, a renowned player of the Italian boating industry, prides itself in building their boats bearing all these attributes but also adhering to the sustainable criteria of quality and traceability with the assurance that it does not harm the environment. Ferretti Group adopts the Triple Bottom Line concept as its business philosophy to analyze sustainable performances building on three key pillars: (a) Profit which refers to financial performances, that is a company willingness to persist operationally in the long term, (b) People which refers to the consideration the societal impact has on business activities, and (c) Planet, which refers to the ecological dimension such as waste disposal, energy use, and the management of scarce resources. Ferretti Group is one of the very few companies to publish a sustainability report. This association with ethical and responsible lifestyles not only enhances their image and exhibits positive contemporary values but also motivates other players to engage with sustainable development.

The commitment of Salvatore Ferragamo to issues pertaining to diversity fully supports multiculturalism, which is perceived as essential for the development of innovative and distinctive elements to increase equal opportunities, combating all types of discrimination, and condemning any form of harassment. The sustainability initiative considers training as a top priority ensuring the professional growth of employees and the development of the key competencies of the brand heritage. In particular, the protection of artisanal skills, Italian tradition, and craftsmanship in the Manovia, which is the historic prototyping and manufacturing unit where material cutters, sewers, and assemblers work create prototypes and fine-tunes the structures of their shoes and sneakers. Salvatore Ferragamo is one of the first few luxury brands that have produced a sustainability report, and this facilitated the launch of "Sustainable Thinking", a digital platform on their website which presents sustainable thinking initiatives from social justice to sustainable supply chains and from climate change to innovative materials with a low environmental impact. This conforms to one of the management mottos, "in order to act sustainable, we must think sustainable". Adhering to the values of quality and "Made in Italy", Salvatore Ferragamo supports the development of local communities, promotion of Italian manufacturers, and using products and services almost exclusively from Italian suppliers. Salvatore Ferragamo clearly embodies "Made in Italy", district history and local craftsmanship and turned these into levers for luxury and as a result, successfully achieved sustainability vision through corporate and place heritage.

This theme also spotlights the perspective of "Bespoke Tailors" on "Made in Italy" and the future of their craft and their contribution to social, economic, and ecological sustainability and well-being. Through expert interviews, bespoke tailoring is perceived as always being relevant. The consensus is "Made in Italy" is defined as passion, taste, craftsmanship, heritage, and tradition that translates into an epitome of Italian beauty and quality. The Italian craftsmanship is portrayed as a source of creativity and innovation and in constant evolution and adaptation. There is the consensus as in other chapters in this theme that the future generation of aspiring artisans must have access to formal education and on-the-job training in artisanal businesses to sustain this art form. In addition, there is also the call for Italy to raise more awareness about careers in Italian craftsmanship especially when there is an accelerating demand for ethically produced and handmade authentic goods. Perhaps the key to enhancing this bespoke craftsmanship should involving innovation in sustainable ways of producing and consuming.

With the banner "Kartell loves the planet", Kartell revolutionizes the aesthetic of its predominantly plastic-made products and replacing them with recycled plastic and bioplastics made from agricultural waste. This as described in the case study is an important foresight as their products are always aesthetically appealing and well built, but plastics, with a negative connotation, is their core material. The move to using recycled and bio-plastics and even challenge themselves to include using wood fully embrace the vision of the circular economy. Kartell's products are accredited with the GREENGUARD certification which guarantees low levels of emissions safeguarding indoor air quality. It is still early to tell if consumers are willing to pay more for the higher cost of sustainable raw materials. Kartell has however embraced the vision of care for the environment, and not compromising on quality and aesthetic keeping the luxury attributes of "Made in Italy".

In the same vein of the innovative use of recyclable plastics, the swimsuit line of EDIT, "Made in Italy" Yamamay, embraces the concept of circularity, with an eco-designed innovative textile. The EDIT line is made with a mono-polymer fabric, 100% recycled and 100% recyclable created from plastics retrieved from the ocean; a nice ring with swimwear and builds connections of storytelling of the ocean. Yamamay has been a partner of the One Ocean Foundation with a strong and longstanding commitment to the creation and propagation of models that concretely demonstrate the commitment to reducing the impact of the fashion industry on the oceans. This is in support of the "Save the Ocean" campaign promoted by the foundation. Further, manufacturing partnership with Tiba Tricot further guarantees total recyclability at the end of the swimsuit's life cycle. The prints are reworked from maritime-themed designs by fabric designer Beppe Spadacini, taken from the homonymous historical archive by young students from the "Aldo Galli" led Network Como School of fine arts all keeping in line with the "Made in Italy" banner.

Theme 3

The third theme in this book reviews cases of luxury "Made in Italy" start-ups and challenges toward the sustainable innovation giving rise to a wave of born and bred native sustainable "Made in Italy" luxury brands. The call for sustainable consumption is innovating the "Made in Italy" in the luxury sector and their brands' identity and characteristics, impacting their manufacturing operations and social engagement.

The premise of the brand Rifò hinges on the unconventional idea of recovering 100% of the raw materials from used clothing and knitwear and limiting the use of new fibers. The successful collaborative circular economy project "Rethink your jeans" involved consumers in the act of returning old jeans garments that can be used for a regeneration process, which gave birth to the first "Made in Italy" Rifò sweater. The methods of procurement of fibers are not without their challenges. As discussed in the chapter, wool and cashmere are fibers that fall into the post-consumer category derived from used or discarded clothing. Cotton is a pre-consumer category fiber and is more difficult to recover from used garments as they are also mixed with man-made synthetic fibers in a mixed composition that is mainly synthetic. But the common goal of partnerships with Recooper and Pinori Filati clearly embraced the concept of the circular economy, which led to its success of the start-up of the born and bred native sustainable brand.

Another born and bred native luxury sustainable brand, La Milanesa clearly illustrates how environmental and social sustainability can interact and integrate with brand authenticity built on perceived brand heritage and the perceived product quality. La Milanesa focuses on brand consistency of an ethically authentic brand through sustainability efforts by embedding manufacturing traditions (crocheting) through social sustainability actions, and local traditions (natural resources) through cultural sustainability actions. Moreover, La Milanesa reflects in all its collections, the use of natural or recycled materials, and its manufacturing projects are aimed at socially reintegrating women living in marginalized conditions. The case study clearly illustrates how tradition and innovation can come together to generate a nostalgic appeal. Further, all these activities are based on a shared collective ideology building a brand that shows its connection to preserving natural resources through the preservation of a cultural heritage.

The final case study on born and bred native luxury sustainable brands looks at how ACBC challenges itself to produce quality non-leather "Made in Italy" footwear. This architectural innovation sparks subsequent modular innovations in which the thinking about and production of the components became as important as the overall strategy of the footwear industry's value chain. The chapter presents in-depth how the business model of ACBC, revolutionizes the concept of thinking of shoes in modular terms further reinvent its supply chain to allow for micro-disposability while advancing the design of its shoes embracing the circular economy. It challenges and offers new thinking of the way we produce, consume, and dispose of goods. In an interview with ACBC, this modular initiative of the patent has the potential of ingredient branding, perhaps a label of "ACBC Inside" in other luxury branded shoes in the very near future. In short, ACBC has successfully integrated Italian leather craftsmanship and excellence with 100% animal-free approach to leather production "Made in Italy" without compromising on genuine leather's aesthetics, quality, and comfort.

Concluding comments

The key premise of this book is the enduring question if, "Made in Italy" luxury brands are able to integrate sustainability into the product features and attributes that are relevant to their customers. More importantly, is this a sincere and real engagement or purely providing lip service to keep with this trend? For one, "Made in Italy" continues to be a distinctive asset in the face of luxury transformation and a distinctive ever of sustainability in the luxury industry. Through the different case studies that span across different industries, it is clear that the variety of initiatives and directives on making sustainability a priority is overwhelming. The rise of born and bred, native, sustainable "Made in Italy" luxury brands has certainly grown in recent years paving the way to this initiative.

Through the rich perspectives of the sustainability landscape in luxury across the different themes described in this book, it is probably not enough to be "Made in Italy" but also imperative to implement sustainability into the existing label. There is enough evidence that "Made in Italy", sustainability, and luxury can co-exist. It is also clear that Italian brands can benefit from the "Made in Italy" concept, as a megabrand, to position Italian products as intrinsically sustainable together with attributes of excellent quality and craftsmanship through production, natural materials or ingredients, and innate authenticity. Some have also suggested that we should embrace the "Made green in Italy" as the new Italian policy initiative aimed to support and promote environmentally sustainable products on the national level. An interview with the born and bred native sustainable luxury, ACBC, also coined with the idea of focusing on "Made how in Italy" rather than just "Made in Italy". Certainly, this will spark new debate on the relevance of the more than half a decade of "country-of-origin" studies. But should we also pursue other offshoots from this debate? A stream of research could emerge from the appeal of this concept. For instance, there is certainly room to investigate the emotion of pride from purchasing a label of Diesel Second Hand. Is it pride evoked from the durability and prestige of "Made in Italy" Diesel Second Hand? Or is it simply the shared pride embraced by Diesel Second Hand of its sustainability stance?

Index

Note: Page references in *italics* denote figures and in **bold** tables.